Jon E. Lewis is a writer and historian. His many previous books include the best-selling *The Mammoth Book of the Edge*, *The Mammoth Book of How It Happened: Everest* and *The Mammoth Book of Wild Journeys*.

D0291205

The Mammoth Book of

COVER-UPS

An Encyclopedia of Conspiracy Theories

JON E. LEWIS

With Emma Daffern

ROBINSON RUNNING PRESS
PHILADELPHIA · LONDON

Constable & Robinson Ltd
3 The Lanchesters
162 Fulham Palace Road
London W6 9ER
www.constablerobinson.com

First edition published in the UK by Robinson,
an imprint of Constable & Robinson Ltd, 2007

A copy of the British Library Cataloguing in Publication Data is
available from the British Library

UK ISBN 978-1-84529-608-7

9 10 8

First published in the United States in 2007
by Running Press Book Publishers

US Library of Congress number: 2007939692

US ISBN 978-0-7867-1968-6

Running Press Book Publishers
2300 Chestnut Street
Philadelphia, PA 19103-4371

Visit us on the web!
www.runningpress.com

Printed and bound in the EU

CONTENTS

CONTENTS

INTRODUCTION

This is the boom time of conspiracy theory. 9/11, the War on Terror, the death of Diana, Opus Dei (as featured in Dan Brown's bestselling conspiracy novel *The Da Vinci Code*): the list of conspiracies seemingly perpetrated by "them" against "us" goes on endlessly. More and more people subscribe to alternative histories of events, such as Michael Moore's celebrated documentary *Fahrenheit 9/11*, and less and less do people accept the word of the establishment – of government, business, the Church – at face value.

The conspiracy theory "boom" has been rolling towards us and gathering pace since 22 November 1963, when President John F. Kennedy was assassinated. That the most famous man in the world could be murdered in broad Texan sunlight by a "lone gunman" beggared belief. A sense of innocence was lost that day. It was beaten into oblivion by the succession of American figures who were also, supposedly, assassinated by "lone gunmen": Robert F. Kennedy, Martin Luther King, and Malcolm X. The proof that there was something rotten in the state of Western politics came in the next decade. Watergate.

Of course, there were conspiracies and assumed conspiracies before 1963: some considered the Bolsheviks a product of conspiracy, others the Jews, yet others the Freemasons and yet more the bankers of Wall Street. Hitler's Nazis indisputably conspired to burn the Reichstag, put the blame on the Communists, and so engineer a *coup d'état*. But in 1963 paranoia began to eat away at the soul of society. Conspiracy theories spread from the fringe into the centre of the body politic.

The word "conspiracy" comes from the Latin *conspirare*, meaning "to breathe together". But everybody understands its time-amended meaning of two or more individuals secretly plotting and perpetrating an action that would be widely considered negative or harmful to specific individuals, or to society as a whole. Nobody conspires to do something good, like feed the poor. Conspiracy theory is the how and the why of the plot, and the mechanics of the cover-up. Almost without exception the alternative conspiracy theory of history proposes that any large-scale or far-reaching event was not the result of chance or of accident, or of the widely accepted view of its cause, but of some secret plan by someone, somewhere.

Or the event didn't happen. Period. Thus Hitler still lives. As does Elvis (whose name is a natty anagram of LIVES).

It has been said that conspiracy theory is the new religion. With the decline of a widespread belief in God, people seek the guilty hand of man (or alien invaders) in unfathomable events. The new power is a secret cabal. This cabal goes under numerous names (and its composition depends on the political eye of the beholder) and paradoxically the smaller a cabal is suspected of being, the more powerful its hold is thought to be. The Illuminati, the Bilderberg Group, the Trilateral Commission are just three of the tiny elites believed to pull the strings of the entire world.

If conspiracy theory is the new religion, the new medium for spreading its word is the internet. Once upon a printed-piece-of-paper time, counter beliefs would spread oh so slowly, via *samizdat* magazines and word of mouth. Nowadays a variant thought, conjecture, a piece of evidence from anybody with access to a PC and a telephone line is transmitted around the globe in seconds. Dissemination of material over the internet mainly sidesteps the censorship of states and companies. It's a space where the truth can emerge into the light.

The internet is also a democracy of fools, where everybody's opinion is aired as though of equal merit: a cyberspace where the lunatic and the malicious weigh in at the same weight as the rational, concerned citizen. Just as some people believe just about every conspiracy theory punted their way, the madness of some internet-borne conspiracy theories produces an opposite reaction: numerous rational citizens disbelieve *every* conspiracy theory they encounter. It's the fear of association. After all, who wants to be connected even remotely with David Icke's shape-shifting lizards or the Aryan supremacists who reckon that Adolf Hitler is currently shacked up in an ice-cave in Antarctica?

Hostility to conspiracy theory is as useless in understanding the world as an indiscriminate acceptance of it. The task, surely, is to disentangle the mad and bad conspiracies from those that illuminate the darkened, secret corners of power. To this end *The Mammoth Book of Cover-Ups* takes a considered, objective scalpel to one hundred of the most compelling conspiracy theories of modern times. The theories are arranged alphabetically, assessed and interrogated. Where appropriate, the relevant documents are reproduced, and details of where to look to find out more are listed. Each conspiracy theory is assigned an "Alert Level" rating indicating its likely veracity.

But this is only an indication: the reader must make up his or her own mind.

It's only "them" who tell you what you *must* believe.

Jon E. Lewis
2008

ALIEN ABDUCTION

They're not out there. They're here . . .

Early morning, 19 September 1961. Betty and Barney Hill are driving home from vacation in Niagara Falls. On Route 3 south of Lancaster, New Hampshire, the Hills notice a bright light in the sky which seems to be following them. Perplexed, Barney halts the car and gets out and recognizes the white light as a UFO; inside the alien craft Barney Hill can clearly see beings looking out at him. When Barney approaches within 75 feet (23m) of the flying saucer a door in the craft opens and Barney, fearing he is going to be captured, runs back to the car and drives off. A little while later the Hills hear a strange bleeping sound and the car is enveloped in white haze. Suddenly the Hills realize they are miles from where they should be. Later, after the Hills reach home, they discover the journey has taken two hours more than it ought.

The next day Betty Hill contacted the local Air Force base; their experience was in due course recorded in **Project Blue Book**, albeit only in the "insufficient data" section. But more data was forthcoming when the Hills, suffering nightmares and insomnia, sought out a psychiatrist. Dr Benjamin Simon gave Betty and Barney separate courses of hypnotic therapy, during which they both recalled being kidnapped by small grey humanoids and taken aboard the UFO. The mystery of the missing two hours was now explained: the Hills had been abducted by aliens, who communicated with them by telepathy.

A sort of pregnancy test was conducted by the aliens on Betty Hill, who was also shown an astral chart; the aliens pointed to a star which Betty deduced was the home sun of the space travellers. After their examination, the Hills were replaced in their car and sent on their way.

There had been one previous reported case of alien kidnap (in 1957 by the Brazilian Antonio Villas-Boas, who claimed that his female alien captor had sex with him), but it was the Hills' case which truly began the alien abduction phenomenon. Written up with the help of author John G. Fuller, the Hills' account of their close encounter, *The Interrupted Journey*, was a bestseller. The episode contained all the core elements of later abductions: missing time; it happens at night; paralysis; examination by the aliens, with resultant inexplicable marks left on victim's skin; telepathic communication with the aliens; post-abduction sleep disorders . . .

After the release of *The Interrupted Journey* in 1966, a parade of alien abductions followed, including:

- In November 1975 six woodcutters claimed that their colleague, Travis Walton, had vanished after encountering a UFO. When Walton reappeared he claimed that he, like the Hills, had been abducted by the aliens known throughout the UFO fraternity as "Greys".
- In 1987 the horror novelist Whitley Strieber claimed in his book *Communion* (later filmed starring Christopher Walken) to have been abducted and anally probed by aliens.
- In 1991 Linda Cortile alleged that she was beamed out of her New York apartment into a UFO; the "case of the century" was researched by UFOlogist Budd Hopkins, who maintains he found two secret servicemen attached to the United Nations who witnessed Cortile's aerial passage into the UFO.

In the same year as Cortile's alleged abduction, the Roper polling organization found that 2 per cent of the US's 300 million population had been abducted by aliens. Most abductees reported multiple abductions over their lifetimes. On an average, humdrum day in the US, it follows, some 2,740 Americans are being taken aboard spaceships and examined, probed and raped.

Why is abduction on this scale not a major news event? There are claims that the media systematically covers up the abduction phenomenon because the media's masters in the **New World Order** gain from collusion with the aliens: the New World Order trades the citizens of America for futuristic technology. Anyone who dares to whistle-blow on this cosy arrangement is threatened with permanent silence by the **Men in Black**.

Another scenario suggests itself: alien abduction is hooey. In almost all cases of alien abduction the only evidence is the abductee's story, and 87 per cent of abductees are, according to one survey, fantasists. That is to say, most abductees make up, either consciously or unconsciously, their abduction experience. A telling point against alien abduction is that the abductees tend to repeat the Hill experience; yet, if aliens have the ability to travel a trillion miles, might they not have the ability to vary their experiments on humans a little? The church-going Hills themselves were likely victims of the psychological condition known as *folie à deux*, where two (or more) people subconsciously influence each other into sincerely believing a lie or delusion. Some would-be abductees have been found to be suffering from sleep terrors or temporal lobe epilepsy, both of which can cause vivid hallucinations.

Then there is the primary tool for obtaining evidence of abduction experiences: hypnosis. While abduction supporters such as John E. Mack, sometime professor of psychiatry at Harvard, argue that hypnosis is necessary to circumvent the mental blocks put on the abduction experience by the aliens, the reliability of memories recovered under hypnosis is extremely poor. There is growing evidence that recovered memories either play to what the patient believes the therapist wants or are "confabulations", amalgams of fact and fantasy.

No physical evidence of alien interference with a human, be it an operation or the placing of an implant, has ever stood up to investigation. One "alien implant" was found to be a mercury dental filling!

Humans are abducted by aliens with the collusion of the Earth's establishment: ALERT LEVEL 3

Further Reading
Eric Elfman, *Almanac of Alien Encounters*, 2001
John Fuller, *The Interrupted Journey*, 1966
Budd Hopkins, *Intruders*, 1987
John E. Mack, *Abduction: Human Encounters with Aliens*, 1994

AMERICAN MIA IN VIETNAM

In *Rambo: First Blood Part II*, Sylvester Stallone's gun-toting hero lands in Vietnam to rescue American POWs left behind after the conclusion of the war in 1973.

But were there any such POWs in real life? No, said successive US governments, starting with Richard Nixon's Republicans in 1973. Sociology professors agreed, labelling the "MIA myth" as mass conservative hysteria, a psychological unwillingness to let go of Vietnam as a hopeless cause.

Yes, said an awful lot of US soldiers and intelligence agents, starting with US Marine Bobby Garfield. Garfield was captured by the Viet Cong in 1965 and released in 1979 – that is, five years after the US government had assured the nation that all MIAs and POWs had been accounted for. Families of MIAs/POWs then asked the Pentagon for declassified documents about their loved ones – only for the Pentagon to reclassify these documents. When the wife of one MIA wrote to President Reagan, he replied that his administration had planned a rescue raid for the MIA by Green Berets under the command of Colonel Bo Gritz in 1981.

Eh? The official line was that no US MIA remained alive in Indochina.

Some sense of the contradictions and denials of the White House was made by the authors Monika Jensen-Stevenson and William Stevenson in their 1990 book *Kiss the Boys Goodbye*. The Stevensons reported that Dr Henry Kissinger negotiated a secret clause in the Paris Peace Accord (which ended the war in

Nam) whereby the US would pay North Vietnam $4 billion in reparations in return for POWs held by Hanoi. The US then reneged on the reparations – and the POWs stayed in Vietnam. "We had thousands of Americans after the release of 1973," a Vietnamese secret police chief informed the Stevensons.

Confirmation of the Stevensons' case came in 1992 with the testimony of Richard Allen before Senator John Kerry's Senate Select Committee on the fate of the American MIA. Allen informed the Committee that in 1981 Vietnam had offered to free the POWs it still held – some dozens – if the US handed over the $4 billion it had originally promised. The offer was rebuffed by the Reagan government because it was not willing to pay ransom money for hostages (a piece of high-mindedness that apparently ended at the border of Iran; in 1987 Reagan confessed on TV that he had traded arms for American hostages and funnelled the funds to the Contras in Nicaragua – see **Iran–Contra Scandal**). Some observers, however, considered that the Reagan rebuff was simply because his administration wanted to close down the MIA/POW issue for fear of exposing the US's illegal operations in Laos, bordering Vietnam, where many POWs were believed held. According to whistle-blowing CIA agents, there were any number of embarrassing schemes operated by the agency in Laos, from drug-running to arms sales, waiting to be turned into headline news by the media. Better, then, to sacrifice the POWs and keep newshound noses out of Laos.

So John Rambo had it right: there *were* MIAs/POWs left behind in Vietnam.

Sadly, the chances of any POWs being left alive today, after 30 years of privation and imprisonment, are remote.

The US government deliberately failed to rescue MIAs and POWs left behind in Vietnam: ALERT LEVEL 8

Further Reading
Monika Jensen-Stevenson and William Stevenson, *Kiss the Boys Goodbye*, 1990

AREA 51

Also known as the Groom Lake Facility, Area 51 is a high-security military base in the Nevada desert, 90 miles (145 km) north of Las Vegas. The facility, which comprises thousands of acres, is surrounded by security fencing and intruder-detection systems, and is regularly patrolled. A no-fly zone operates above it.

So far, so military-base humdrum. Where Area 51 differs from other military installations is in the longstanding belief by conspiracists that it houses the UFO disc found at **Roswell**, as well as other crashed alien spaceships. At Area 51, the theory goes, the recovered UFOs are back-engineered so that their technology can be utilized by the US military. The latter are helped – either willingly or unwillingly – by captured alien pilots.

Few of the human government employees who work at Groom have ever talked about their work, but two who did were Leo Williams and Bob Lazar. Williams claimed to have worked in alien technology evaluation, the results of which informed the design of the B-2 stealth bomber. In 1989 Lazar announced on local TV that he too had been involved in "back engineering" at Groom's S-4 hangars complex, including assessment of the Roswell craft's propulsion system. He had even uncovered "Gravity B", a force arising from the manipulation of a new nuclear element, "ununpentium".

Neither Williams nor Lazar proved very convincing witnesses. Lazar had invented his purported MIT physics

qualification and before working in back-engineering had been
engaged in the rather less than cutting-edge employment of
managing a photo shop. A steady stream of sightings of strange
lights and craft at Groom, however, kept alive the notion of Area
51 as a top-secret UFO lab, perhaps the manufacturing plant of
Black Helicopters.

Certainly, Area 51 has been the testing centre for weird and
wonderful aircraft. The U-2 spy plane was flown there; so was
the SR-71 Blackbird, the B-2 stealth bomber and the F-117
stealth fighter. And these are only the planes the public has been
informed about. It's reasonable to suppose that other prototype
and avant-garde aircraft have taken to the air at Groom, less
reasonable to suppose that they have been developed from alien
technology.

Area 51 is the holding centre for crashed alien ships:
ALERT LEVEL 3

Further Reading

David Darlington, *Area 51: The Dreamland Chronicles,* 1998

Eric Elfman, *Almanac of Alien Encounters,* 2001

Phil Patton, *Dreamland: Travels Inside the Secret World of
Roswell and Area 51,* 1998

BABYLONIAN
BROTHERHOOD

Remember *V*, the science fiction TV series where reptilian humanoids took over the Earth?

David Icke does. According to the New Age guru and conspiracist, 12-foot (3.66m) lizards from the planet Draco have colonized Earth (above and below ground) and, organized into the Babylonian Brotherhood, rule it through such "Global Elites" as The **Illuminati** and The **Bilderberg Group**. The Babylonian Brotherhood are externally convincing as humans, but their reptilian-humanoid DNA courses through the veins of the world's rulers; indeed, it is precisely this hybrid genetic plus which gives them the necessary attributes for ruling:

> The Rothschilds, Rockefellers, the British royal family, and the ruling political and economic families of the US and the rest of the world come from these SAME bloodlines . . . the reptilian-mammalian DNA.

In such books as *The Biggest Secret* (1999) and *Children of the Matrix* (2001), Icke has assiduously tracked the doings of the Brotherhood and their human supporters as they seek to gain ever tighter control over the world. The Brotherhood's *modus operandi* is, according to Icke, the "problem-reaction-solution", whereby the Brotherhood perpetrates some outrage – such as **9/11** or the **Oklahoma City Bombings** – so that the public clamours for a policy change. Which, of course, is exactly what the Brotherhood wants.

Icke shares some of the same political bed as the armed American militias, who likewise identify the **New World Order** project as the source of all modern evil. On occasion Icke has addressed US patriot groups. Where Icke and the militias part company is on the "Jewish Question": the militias are virulently anti-Semitic, Icke is not. "This [the Brotherhood] is not a Jewish plot," Icke told the British journalist Jon Ronson in the latter's book *Them* (2001). Travelling with Icke and his entourage, Ronson, a Jew, found little evidence of race hatred.

The suggestion that humanoid-reptilians rule the Earth is not Icke's first visit to the furthest shores of the imagination. Born in Leicester, England, in 1952, Icke was originally a professional footballer, playing for Coventry and Hereford, before arthritis forced a change of career to sports reporting for the BBC. Outside the studio he became increasingly involved with politics, first with the Liberal Democrats and then with the Green Party. It was during a session of spiritual healing in 1990 for arthritis that messages from "master souls and Extra-Terrestrials" reached Icke, informing him that he was the Son of God. "I am a channel for the Christ Spirit. The truth was given me very recently by the Godhead," Icke said at the time. Dressed completely in turquoise, claiming to be the risen Christ, Icke became a figure of such national fun that he went and hid for years.

Re-emerging as the clarion sounder against the Brotherhood, Icke is a fluent, persuasive, telegenic communicator, a natural politician.

Which raises a dread possibility. If he is so gifted a leader, might Icke be a lizard disguised as a human himself?

The world is run by reptiles disguised as humans: ALERT LEVEL 1

Further Reading
David Icke, *The Biggest Secret*, 1999
David Icke, *Children of the Matrix*, 2001
Jon Ronson, *Them: Adventures Among Extremists*, 2001

BARCODES

For most people barcodes are the handy black and white stripes on products that facilitate quick payment at the store: instead of the assistant keying in the price, the item is swiped over red laser lights which read it off. For the shopkeeper, barcodes have the advantage that swiping the barcode allows instant stock control.

Oh, those poor deluded souls. They need to read the 1982 book *The New Money System: 666* by Mary Stewart Relfe. For Relfe has divined that barcodes have Satanic importance. The guard bars on the code indicate 666 – the mark of the Devil and his cashless economy. It says so in *Revelations* 13:16–18:

> And he causeth all, both small and great, rich and poor, free and bond, to receive a mark in their right hand, or in their foreheads: And that no man might buy or sell, save he that had the mark, or the name of the beast, or the number of his name. Here is wisdom. Let him that hath understanding count the number of the beast: for it is the number of a man; and his number is Six hundred threescore and six.

David Icke (he who, *inter alia*, tracks the doings of the **Babylonian Brotherhood**) is another to have a problem with barcodes, because they enable mass observation: everything you buy with a credit or debit card can be put against your name. Soon the government and the backroom cabal that runs it will know exactly what's in your home.

Icke may be a nut, but he might be right. The trend of the era is towards microscopic surveillance of citizens' consumer habits. In 2005 the BBC reported that the Tesco supermarket chain had trialled Radio Frequency Identification (RFID) chips, which allowed products to be tracked via radio waves. Privacy groups labelled these chips "spy chips" because the tags could be used to track the behaviour of customers.

There is clearly a need for citizens to watch out for what big business and governments are up to. The Devil, though, is not in the detail of the UPC and EAN barcodes used in America and Europe respectively.

> Barcodes are part of the prophecy of the Beast's takeover:
> ALERT LEVEL 3

Further Reading
Mary Stewart Relfe, *The New Money System: 666*, 1982

BCCI (Bank of Commerce and Credit International)

Whoever controls the volume of money in any country is absolute master of all industry and commerce.

President James Garfield

It used to be called usury. These days it's called "charging interest on loans" and is the *raison d'être* of those ubiquitous institutions, banks. Since the 17th century banks have loaned money to nations and companies as well as to individuals, and accordingly they have been charged with manipulation of national and international affairs. According to the *True Conspiracies* website the following, among other sins, can be laid at the reinforced doors of "the banks" (punctuation, spelling, capitalization, etc., *sic*):

- Boom and bust cycles along with the depressions, stock market crashes and wars are deliberately caused to make people lose money to the conspirators. They also weaken the people and tame governments into accepting the conspirators' solutions.
- The history books controlled by the conspiracy do not tell the full truth on why many events happen. For example the conspirators blame slavery for the American civil war but the real reason was to establish a central bank in the USA and to force a war to enable them to lend money at interest. [. . .]
- The conspirators bribed members of the government by paying them and having them work for the bank. Intense deceptive

media publicity convinced the public and politicians of the benefit of the Federal Reserve Act. It was done in ways such as by lying and saying that the banks will reduce boom and bust cycles. The Federal Reserve Act was passed near Christmas when few people were present to vote against it.

- Hitler was funded by the USA and Britain to create a bigger war. The U.S. government controlled by the bankers conspiracy, wanted Hitler to invade America but he declined due to the risk of the number of Americans with guns. The U.S. government also encouraged Japan to invade Pearl Harbor to get America into the war.
- The bankers funded Arab and Japanese companies to buy up property around the world so the bankers could gain more control of it.
- Manipulation of agriculture has and will be used to force the population to accept the conspirators' demands such as having to surrender guns to get food.
- The U.S. deliberately tried to lose the Korean and Vietnam wars so the communists would remain with territory. [. . .]
- Although involved with the conspiracy since his initial rise to power, President Kennedy was killed by an agent of the conspiracy for wanting to pull out of Vietnam and printing silver currency.
- Many countries now with conflicts had peace until the influence of International Bankers Conspiracy.
- The collapse of the Soviet Union was a hoax to fool the world into a false sense of security and also to slowly cause the world to accept communism. The bankers funded the Soviet Union to create an arms race, which cost time and money. Also it caused the nations to gladly surrender their arms in the name of peace so that the goal of a one-world army could be formed under the control of the United Nations.
- In World War 2 the US and British governments controlled by the bankers succeeded in getting the Soviet Union to control much of Eastern Europe.
- They can control the weather for Biological warfare. They are deliberately ruining the environment to gain more control.

Phew. And there's plenty more where that came from! In the fevered minds of some conspiracy theorists, the banks are run by a cabal of families – principally the Rothschilds, the Warburgs, Loebs and the Rockefellers – who hammer out their joint policy in the **Bilderberg Group** and implement said policy via various front organizations. The Bank of England, the Federal Reserve, the International Monetary Fund and the World Bank all hold a special chill place in the hearts of the conspiracy theorists as the business end of the international banking conspiracy. And the end goal of that conspiracy? A **New World Order**, naturally.

A distinct flaw in the international banking conspiracy theory is that the national banks continue to operate with patriotic bias. The Bank of England still promotes British interests above all others; the Bundesbank acts resolutely in favour of German strategy (which, according to some on the British left, is a conspiracy to run Europe from Berlin, a sort of soft-glove Third Reich), and so on and so forth. Then there's that nasty sheen of anti-Semitism over much of the banking conspiracy theory, just as it had in the 1930s when Adolf Hitler blamed "Jew financiers" for the world's woes, principally Bolshevism. Sixty years later it's still the Jews who "destroyed Christian old line companies . . . who want Islamic owned companies excluded from Dow Jones . . . [who] live on the labour of others" according to the internet site *Jew Watch*. It's not difficult to debunk the anti-Semitic fantasy: It takes just one name, the name of J.P. Morgan. The superbanker was a white Christian.

Take out the anti-Semitism and the puppet-and-string notion of politics, however, and the conspiracists raise legitimate concerns about the most powerful of financial institutions. Banks *are* one of the globalizing forces seeking to enervate the nation state, and banks *do* discuss mutual interests in elite forums such as Bilderberg, *Le Cercle* and the **Trilateral Commission**. The International Monetary Fund *does* operate in the worldwide capitalist interest (as numerous left-wing regimes have discovered when obliged to alter their internal economies in return for aid). Sometimes banks *are* immoral: the Vatican Bank allegedly laundered money for the Mafia (see Roberto **Calvi**), the Banco Nationale del Lavoro funded illegal arms purchases, Barclays underpinned the apartheid regime of South Africa before, with breathtaking hypocrisy, funding the black dictatorship of Mugabe in Zimbabwe . . .

For sheer criminality, however, the Bank of Commerce and Credit International (BCCI) remains unsurpassed. The sorry tale of the BCCI is also one which ties in some of the biggest names of late 20th-century history, among them George W. Bush, Henry Kissinger and Osama bin Laden.

The BCCI was founded in 1972 by the Pakistani banker Agha Hasan Abedi, with an initial chest of £2.5 million. In an astute piece of marketing it proclaimed itself the "Third World Bank", with a mission to promote prosperity in the corners of the globe that Western banks ignored. Within a decade it had a million depositors and was working its way to a paper value of $25 billion. Despite its "Third World Bank" tag, BCCI was keen to break into North America, where in 1977 it bought four banks, including the First American Bank.

BCCI's vigorous asset-buying hid the bank's true financial status: it was verging on insolvency. And much of whatever money BCCI *was* making was coming from illegal activities. By the mid-1980s the CIA, the Internal Revenue Service and the Drug Enforcement Agency were respectively informing the US State, Treasury and Justice departments that BCCI was laundering drugs money. These alarms were all ignored – possibly because some branches of the CIA itself were using BCCI for clandestine purposes – until 1987, when president Manuel Noriega of Panama was discovered to be among those using BCCI to launder drugs money. The lid could no longer be kept on. The US Senate Subcommittee on Terrorism, Narcotics and International Operations launched an investigation into BCCI under Senator John Kerry. When Kerry eventually delivered his report on "The BCCI Affair" to the Committee on Foreign Relations, US Senate, in December 1992, he recorded a catalogue of larceny by BCCI that ranged from narcotics trafficking to money-laundering.

Such a catalogue of criminality would, one might presume, have the US administration champing at the bit to close BCCI down. Not a bit of it. Which is where the allegation of "conspiracy" enters stage right. One of the companies which borrowed money from BCCI, Harken Energy, had on its board of directors one George W. Bush, the US president's scion. BCCI lobbyists and advisers included Henry Kissinger's consultancy, Kissinger Associates. The CIA, while denouncing BCCI on the one hand, was "float[ing] in and out of BCCI" (Kerry) on the other, was possibly using the bank to run funds to the Mujahadeen in Afghanistan, and was definitely working to some unspecified end through BCCI's affiliate, Capcom. Even smiling Jimmy Carter and rainbow coalition leader Jesse Jackson were receivers of BCCI's largesse. In other words, a vast number of US luminaries had a vested interest in halting Kerry's work – which is exactly what happened in 1989, when the Justice Department stalled his investigation. According to *Washington Monthly*, personal pressure from no less than Jacqueline Kennedy Onassis was put on Kerry to desist. To Kerry's credit he refused to give up completely, and approached New York District Attorney Robert Morgenthau with irrefutable evidence that BCCI was handling the accounts of the Colombian Medellin drugs cartel and diverting funds to the terrorist Abu Nidal. In 1990 the Bush administration gave BCCI a rap over the knuckles, but refused to close the bank down. That task fell eventually to the Bank of England in July 1991, although the publication of Kerry's report (now co-authored by Senator Hank Brown) in the following year administered the *coup de grâce*. BCCI was indicted for money-laundering, bribery and grand larceny.

Shutting the doors of BCCI did not prevent $13 billion going missing – not that any of the monies went to the bank's staff or small investors, the latter queueing fruitlessly to retrieve their deposits from BCCI branches. There are no answers as to where the missing monies went, although there are hints that some of the bank's bigger clients received larger than usual remunerations in the run-up to the collapse.

An investigation by the French intelligence service found that one Osama bin Laden was a BCCI customer. It is within the bounds of possibility that bin Laden was among those who benefited in the last days of the BCCI criminal empire.

US Senator John Kerry's investigation into BCCI was deliberately blocked by vested interests: ALERT LEVEL 9

Further Reading

J. Beaty and S. C. Gwyne, *The Outlaw Bank: A Wild Ride into the Secret Heart of BCCI*, 1993

Senator John Kerry and Senator Hank Brown, *The BCCI Affair: A Report to the Committee on Foreign Relations, United States Senate*, December 1992, 102nd Congress 2nd Session, Senate Print 102-140

Peter Truell and Larry Gurwin, *False Profits: The Inside Story of BCCI*, 1992

DOCUMENT: REPORT OF SENATOR JOHN KERRY ON "THE BCCI AFFAIR" TO THE COMMITTEE ON FOREIGN RELATIONS, UNITED STATES SENATE, IN DECEMBER 1992

BCCI's unique criminal structure – an elaborate corporate spider-web with BCCI's founder, Agha Hasan Abedi, and his assistant, Swaleh Naqvi, in the middle – was an essential component of its spectacular growth, and a guarantee of its eventual collapse. The structure was conceived by Abedi and managed by Naqvi for the specific purpose of evading regulation or control by governments. It functioned to frustrate the full understanding of BCCI's operations by anyone. Unlike any ordinary bank, BCCI was from its earliest days made up of multiplying layers of entities, related to one another through an impenetrable series of holding companies, affiliates, subsidiaries, banks-within-banks, insider dealings and nominee relationships. By fracturing corporate structure, record keeping, regulatory review, and audits, the complex BCCI family of entities created by Abedi was able to evade ordinary legal restrictions on the movement of capital and goods as a matter of daily practice and routine. In creating BCCI as a vehicle fundamentally free of government control, Abedi developed in BCCI an ideal mechanism for facilitating illicit activity by others, including such activity by officials of many of the governments whose laws BCCI was breaking.
[. . .]
Among BCCI's principal mechanisms for committing crimes were shell corporations, bank confidentiality and secrecy havens, layering of corporate structure, front-men and nominees, back-to-back financial documentation among BCCI controlled entities, kick-backs and bribes, intimidation of witnesses, and retention of well-placed insiders to discourage governmental action.
[. . .]

However daunting the task of explicating the full extent of BCCI's criminality, it is essential to recognize that at core, BCCI was not a bank which made an adequate return on investment through lending out depositors' funds like other banks, but a "Ponzi scheme," which used new depositors' funds to pay current expenses and to repay earlier depositors, creating a pyramid of mounting obligations that ultimately and inevitably would bring about BCCI's collapse.
[. . .]
From the beginning, BCCI President Abedi conceived of BCCI as a machine with two driving mechanisms – asset growth and faith. The latter was essential to prevent a day of reckoning when depositors and creditors alike would cause a run on the bank. The former was necessary to sustain the latter through bad times. Together, they worked to sustain the illusion that BCCI was solvent, when in fact, it is unlikely BCCI was ever solvent.

On 18 December 1991, in an agreement with the Justice Department and New York District Attorney, BCCI's liquidators pleaded guilty to having engaged in a criminal conspiracy through financial fraud, and thereby constituting a Racketeering Influenced and Corrupt Organization (RICO), whose entire assets, legitimate and illegitimate, were subject to confiscation by the government. Specific crimes admitted to by BCCI's liquidators in the agreement included:
• Seeking deposits of drug proceeds and laundering drug money
• Seeking deposits from persons attempt to evade US income taxes
• Using "straws" and nominees to acquire control of US financial institutions
• Lying to regulators and falsifying regulatory documents
• Creating false bank records and engaging in sham transactions to deceive regulators.
[. . .]

The New York District Attorney found that among the major actions taken by BCCI to carry out its fraud were:

- Employing the ruling families of a number of Middle Eastern states as nominees for BCCI, who pretended to be at risk in BCCI but who were in fact guaranteed to be held harmless by BCCI for any actual losses.
- Using bank secrecy havens including Luxembourg and the Cayman Islands to avoid regulation on a consolidated basis by any single regulator of BCCI, and thereby to permit BCCI to transfer assets and liabilities from bank to bank as needed to conceal BCCI's true economic status.
- Paying bribes and kickbacks to agents of other banking and financial institutions, thereby avoiding the scrutiny of regulators.

[. . .]

Money-Laundering

From the time of BCCI's indictment on drug money-laundering charges in Tampa, Florida in October, 1988, there was little doubt to anyone looking at the facts that BCCI had been used to launder drug money.

The Customs agents working on the "C-Chase" case against BCCI moved millions of dollars in US currency, representing the proceeds of cocaine sales, through BCCI Panama, BCCI Luxembourg, and LOANS Switzerland as a result of the knowing participation of several BCCI officials.

As Robert Mazur, the Customs agent in Tampa who selected BCCI as the target of the Customs money-laundering sting testified, BCCI bank executives volunteered methods to enhance and improve his techniques for money-laundering, and shortly before the sting ended the operation, offered to introduce Mazur to other potential "cash" customers for money-laundering services from Bogota, Colombia.

[. . .]

Given BCCI's size and dispersion, money-laundering at BCCI would have been inevitable under any circumstances.

Given BCCI's never ending quest for assets and its management's attitude towards laws, it was ubiquitous. As Akbar Bilgrami explained, Abedi was constantly telling BCCI employees that the only thing that mattered was the generation of assets. When Bilgrami was in Colombia in the mid-1980s [*sic*], a period when Colombia had already developed the reputation as the center for cocaine smuggling and drug money, Abedi told him that he needed to increase BCCI's activity in Colombia to $1 billion in local currency in deposits, and $1 billion in US denominated deposits – funds which obviously could only be generated, directly or indirectly, from the drug trade.

[. . .]

The degree of BCCI-US's reliance on money-laundering as a principal business was demonstrated by what happened when BCCI put into place a "compliance program" as part of its January 1990 plea agreement resolving the Tampa money-laundering case: business dropped noticeably, especially referrals from other BCCI locations, because neither BCCI nor its customers wanted to provide details about the customers' businesses.

BCCI's clients for money-laundering included Panamanian General Manuel Noriega, for whom it managed some $23 million of criminal proceeds out of its London branches; Pablo Escobar, of the Medellin cartel; Rodriguez Gacha, of the Medellin cartel; and several members of the Ochoa family.

Bribery

Bribery was a key component of BCCI's strategy for asset growth worldwide, from the earliest days of the bank. In some cases, the recipients of funding from BCCI may not have considered the payments to be "bribes," but simply a mechanism by which BCCI obtained what it wanted from an official, and in return the official helped BCCI, such as BCCI's payments to two of the Gulf emirs in return for the

use of their names as nominees for the purchase of First American. In other cases, the bribes were naked and direct *quid pro quos*, such as BCCI's payments to Central Bank officials in return for Central Bank deposits in countries like Peru. In other cases, BCCI made campaign contributions to politicians, such as it did with General Zia in Pakistan and Carlos Andres Perez in Venezuela. In still other cases, BCCI's payments came in the guise of charitable contributions, and provided BCCI with an entree to generate deposits from others, as in the case of President Jimmy Carter. Among the Americans who BCCI provided with financial assistance in addition to Carter were US Ambassador to the United Nations Andrew Young, Bert Lance, and Jesse Jackson. Abroad, important figures with extensive contact with BCCI included former British Prime Minister James Callaghan, then United Nations Secretary General Javier Perez de Cuellar, Jamaican prime minister Edward Seaga, Antiguan prime minister Lester Byrd; a large number of African heads of state; and many Third World central bank officials.
[. . .]

Support of Terrorism and Arms Trafficking
BCCI's support of terrorism and arms trafficking developed out of several factors. First, as a principal financial institution for a number of Gulf sheikhdoms, with branches all over the world, it was a logical choice for terrorist organizations, who received payment at BCCI-London and other branches directly from Gulf-state patrons, and then transferred those funds wherever they wished without apparent scrutiny. Secondly, BCCI's flexibility regarding the falsification of documentation was helpful for such activities. Finally, to the extent that pragmatic considerations were not sufficient of themselves to recommend BCCI, the bank's pan-third world and pro-Islam ideology would have recommended it to Arab terrorist groups.

Arms trafficking involving BCCI included the financing of Pakistan's procurement of nuclear weapons through BCCI Canada, as documented in the Parvez case, involving a Pakistani who attempted to procure nuclear-related materials financed by BCCI through the United States.

In a letter of 22 November 1991 to the Subcommittee, the CIA stated that "the Agency did have some reporting [as of 1987] on BCCI being used by third world regimes to acquire weapons and transfer technology," but was unwilling to elaborate on the nature of this activity in public.

In early August, 1991, the Committee was provided with documents from the Latin American and Caribbean Region Office (LACRO) of BCCI, describing the offer for sale by the Argentine air force of 22 Mirage aircraft for $110 million. The planned sale was to have been made to Iraq, as part of Saddam Hussein's massive military build up prior to the Gulf war. BCCI was acting as the broker for the transaction, which was to take place in August or September of 1989, but not completed as a result of a dispute within the Argentine military itself. Arms sales involving BCCI from Latin America to the Middle East remain, as of April 1992, under active investigation by US law enforcement.

Abu Nidal

In the United Kingdom, a key window on BCCI's support of terrorism was an informant named Ghassan Qassem, the former manager of the Sloan [*sic*] Street branch of BCCI in London. Qassem had been given the accounts of Palestinian terrorist Abu Nidal at BCCI, and then proceeded, while at BCCI, to provide detailed information on the accounts to British and American intelligence, apparently as a paid informant, according to press accounts based on interviews with Qassem.

As of 1986, the information obtained about Abu Nidal's use of BCCI was sufficiently detailed as to justify dissemination within the US intelligence community.

[. . .]

Other terrorist groups continued to make use of BCCI, including one "state sponsor of terrorism," and the Qassar brothers, Manzur and Ghassan, who have been associated with terrorism, arms trafficking, and narcotics trafficking in connection with the Government of Syria, and with the provision of East Bloc arms to the Nicaraguan contras in a transaction with the North/Secord enterprise paid for with funds from the secret US arms sales to Iran.
[. . .]

Prostitution
BCCI's involvement in prostitution arose out of its creation of its special protocol department in Pakistan to service the personal requirements of the Al-Nahyan family of Abu Dhabi, and on an as-needed basis, other BCCI VIPs, including the families of other Middle Eastern rulers. Several BCCI officers described the protocol department's handling of prostitution to Senate investigators in private, and two – Abdur Sakhia and Nazir Chinoy – confirmed their general knowledge of the practice in testimony. The prostitution handled by BCCI was carried over from practices originally instituted by Abedi at the United Bank, when, working with a woman, Begum Asghari Rahim, he cemented his relationship with the Al-Nahyan family through providing them with Pakistani prostitutes.

BILDERBERG GROUP

The problem with being rich, powerful and influential these days is that ordinary people just don't understand you; it's only other rich, powerful, influential people to whom you can really relate, spend quality time with. So along with the invitation to party on down at the **Bohemian Grove** comes membership of a very exclusive, no-holds-barred talking shop, the Bilderberg Group.

The Group's meetings take place once a year at a luxurious hotel somewhere nice, safe, civilized and very secret. The steering committee of around 20 members draws up a list of 100 people they think reflect the great and the good, one or two up-and-coming politicians or business people and even the odd NGO representative if it seems to make economic sense. Once gathered, the chosen ones are catered by hand-picked chefs, have the venue checked by the CIA and are guarded by mercenaries. Those, however, are all the details we have. As soon as the delegates sit down together, the media blackout begins. No one speaks about what has been discussed at the Group's meetings, no details are leaked, no paparazzi stalk the place with their long lenses. So the kind of privacy any royal or celebrity would kill for is accorded to an innocent group of concerned and informed individuals chatting about new directions in world politics and business.

Seems fishy? Plenty of people think so. The Group is distrusted by the ultra-right, who believe it's part of a Zionist plot to rule the world, while the far left deeply distrust its capitalist credentials. Hardline conspiracy theorists claim the Bilderberg Group has caused wars and recessions, ordered murders, ousted leaders such as **John F. Kennedy** and Margaret Thatcher, and dictated national policies. Unsurprisingly, the Group is also accused of having the achievement of the **New World Order** at the top of its secret agenda. The promotion of free trade and the elimination of protectionist policies are the first steps in its dastardly plan to undermine individual nationality, followed by a series of international conflicts which would destabilize national boundaries still further and reward its acolytes with bulging profits (lucrative Iraqi reconstruction contracts, anyone?).

The list of ready believers in this conspiracy, disturbingly, includes Osama bin Laden, Timothy McVeigh, the perpetrator of the **Oklahoma City Bombings**, and convicted London nail-bomber David Copeland – all apparently convinced that Bilderberg pulls governments' strings.

The guest list for meetings certainly includes names weighty enough to set any sensitive terrorist's paranoid antennae vibrating. George W. Bush and his neo-conservative cohorts Colin Powell, Richard Armitage, Richard Perle and Paul Wolfowitz (quondam president of the World Bank), Tony Blair, Bill Clinton, Lord Healey, Henry Kissinger and the conspiracy theorists' favourite, David Rockefeller, have all been invited. One-third of the invitees are drawn from North America and the rest from Europe, with well over half being from the business, media and education worlds, while the rest are politicians or even royalty: the Queen of the Netherlands and the Crown Prince of Belgium have both attended, as have more unlikely candidates such as Jonathon Porritt from Friends of the Earth. There's no suggestion that Prince Charles has joined the club yet.

Members of the Bilderberg Group stress that it's only an upmarket talking-shop, but it's hard to believe that members do not influence each other or that the guest list is not manipulated to put the right people together. Will Hutton, editor of the

Economist and ex-Bilderberger, came close to breaking the self-
imposed code of silence when he likened Bilderberg to the
World Economic Forum, where "the consensus established is
the backdrop against which policy is made worldwide".

If Hutton is correct, then the Group will have surpassed its
creators' intentions. The original aim was to bring America and
a united Europe closer together in the face of the emerging
threat from Stalin's Soviet Union and post-war anti-American
feeling. The first meeting was masterminded by one Joseph
Retinger, a Polish American with contacts in the top ranks of
governments and the military, who believed peace was too
important to be left to democratic means and was best brokered
by powerful multinational organizations. The chosen group met
in May 1954 at the Hotel de Bilderberg in Oosterbeck, near
Arnhem, and was hosted by former SS officer Prince Bernhard
of the Netherlands.

Since then it has met annually, and occasionally twice a year,
to encourage trans-Atlantic co-operation, always with the CIA
on hand to handle security (guaranteed to get any conspiracy
theorist's blood racing) and sheltered from prying eyes by a self-
imposed ban by the world's media; newspaper editors and
media moguls are also invited to attend. It is this need for
absolute privacy which seems to stick in the throats of Bilderberg's critics. Tony Gosling, a former journalist and organizer
of an anti-Bilderberg website, puts his fears succinctly: "My
main problem is the secrecy. When so many people with so
much power get together in one place I think we are owed an
explanation of what is going on . . . One of the first places I
heard about the determination of the US forces to attack Iraq
was from leaks that came out of the 2002 Bilderberg meeting."

According to conspiracy-theory students David Southwell
and Sean Twist, the way the secrecy is maintained also suggests
there is more than a polite discussion of current affairs going on
behind those closed doors. They cite the occasion of the 2003
Bilderberg meeting in Versailles, which almost coincided with
the beginning of a Group of Seven meeting of finance ministers
in nearby Paris. The proximity of the two events made local

French security police uneasy and they tried to have the Bilderberg meeting cancelled. Someone in the force even went so far as to leak an internal memo complaining of the huge numbers of mercenaries being used to protect members, and hinted they believed the event was merely a front for something "much more sinister".

On the other hand, defenders of the Group would say that, in the face of often biased reporting from the world's press, business leaders and politicians have much to gain from being able to voice opinions freely without the risk of their views being taken out of context, and it is this honesty which allows a greater understanding of political situations to be reached. *Financial Times* journalist Martin Wolf supports this view: "It's privacy, rather than secrecy, that is key to such a meeting. The idea that such meetings cannot be held in private is fundamentally totalitarian. It's not an executive body; no decisions are taken there."

Is the average citizen to assume, then, that all that happens at the Bilderberg's meetings is talk with no action? Some credit the Group with responsibility for the creation of the Treaty of Rome in 1957; only 18 months earlier, the Group's 1955 meeting had concluded there was a pressing need for a closely knit European market. Others say that the 1996 delegation, which included Valery Giscard d'Estaing, Helmut Kohl, Henry Kissinger and Margaret Thatcher, plotted the war in Kosovo that would ultimately bring down Serbia's Slobodan Milosevic, a view apparently broadcast by Serbian news agencies at the time.

On other occasions it would appear that a mere invitation is enough to set a train of events in motion. Bill Clinton was brought to the 1991 meeting in Germany when Governor of Arkansas; two years later he was US President. Tony Blair got his call to address the meeting in 1993. Good talent-spotting on the part of the Bilderberg committee, or a cynical boost to those politicians whose views are friendly to big business?

As the machinations of multinational boardrooms remain beyond the realm of "public interest", there is no way of telling what effect the Group's meetings have had on the business and financial worlds. Company directors are not democratically elected and are accountable only to their shareholders, but the same cannot be said of the politicians who count themselves as Bilderbergers. These people are the democratic leaders of the Western world, accountable to millions of people and supposedly upholders of free speech and open government. Why then would they need to discuss major issues "off the record"? The answer may lie in the very economic system which they claim is integral to democracy. As conspiracy-theory journalist Alasdair Spark says, "The idea that a shadowy clique is running the world is nothing new . . . Shouldn't we expect that the rich and powerful organize things in their own interests? It's called capitalism."

The Bilderberg Group secretly rule the world: ALERT LEVEL 4

Further Reading
Brian Crozer, *Free Agent,* 1993
Robert Eringer, *The Global Manipulators,* 1980
Dennis Healey, *The Time of Life,* 1990
Robin Ramsay, *Conspiracy Theories,* 2006
David Rockefeller, *Memoirs,* 2002
Jon Ronson, *Them: Adventures Among Extremists,* 2001
www.news.bbc.co.uk/1/hi/magazine/3773019.stm
www.news.bbc.co.uk/1/hi/world/americas/4290944.stm
www.bilderberggroup.net

DOCUMENT: DELEGATES & AGENDA, 47TH BILDERBERG MEETING, JUNE 3–6 1999

Introduction
The forty-seventh Bilderberg Meeting was held at the Caesar Park Hotel, Penha Longa, Sintra, Portugal, from June 3–6 1999. There were 111 participants from 24 countries. The participants represented government, diplomacy, politics, business, law, education, journalism and institutes specializing in national and international studies. All participants spoke in a personal capacity, not as representatives of their national governments or employers. As is usual at Bilderberg Meetings, in order to permit frank and open discussion, no public reporting of the conference took place.

This booklet is an account of the 1999 Bilderberg Meeting and is distributed only to participants of this and past conferences and to prospective participants of future conferences. It represents a summary of the panellists' opening remarks for each session, and of the comments and interventions in the subsequent discussion.

[Page 4]
Participants
HONORARY
CHAIRMAN
Belgium   **Etienne Davignon** Chairman, Societe
                             Generale de Belgique

HONORARY
SECRETARY
GENERAL
Netherlands   **Victor Halberstadt** Professor of
                             Economics, Leiden University

PARTICIPANTS
Italy   **Umberto Agnelli** Chairman, IFIL-
                             Finanziaraia di Partecipazioni
Spain   **Esperanza Aguirre y Gil de Biedma**
                             President of the Spanish Senate

United States of America	**Paul A. Allaire** Chairman, Xerox Corporation
Portugal	**Joaquim F. do Amaral** Member of Parliament
Sweden	**Anders Aslund** Senior Associate, Carnegie Endowment for International Peace
Portugal	**Francisco Pinto Balsemao** Professor of Communication Science, New University, Lisbon; Chairman, IMPRESA
Sweden	**Percy Barnevik** Chairman, Investor
United States of America	**Evan Bayh** Senator (Democrat, Indiana)
Italy	**Franco Bernabe** Managing Director and CEO, Telecom Italia
Sweden	**Carl Bildt** Member of Parliament
Canada	**Conrad M. Black** Chairman, Telegraph Group
United States of America	**Charles G. Boyd** Executive Director, National Security Study Group
Canada	**John A. D. de Chastelain** Chairman, Independent International Commission on Decommissioning
Great Britain	**Kenneth Clarke** Member of Parliament
Norway	**Kristin Clemet** Deputy Director General, Confederation of Business and Industry
France	**Bertrand Collomb** Chairman and CEO, Lafarge
United States of America	**Jon S. Corzine** Retired Senior Partner, Goldman Sachs & Co.
Portugal	**Joao Cardona G. Cravinho** Minister for Infrastructure, Planning and Territorial Administration
Greece	**George A. David** Chairman of the Board, Hellenic Bottling Company
United States of America	**Christopher J. Dodd** Senator (Democrat, Connecticut)

[Page 5]

United States of America	**Thomas E. Donilon** Attorney-at-Law, O'Melveney & Meyers
Turkey	**Gazi Ercel** Governor, Central Bank of Turkey
Turkey	**Sedat Ergin** Ankara Bureau Chief, *Hürriyet*

United States of America	**Martin S. Feldstein** President and CEO, National Bureau of Economic Research
International	**Stanley Fischer** First Deputy Managing Director, International Monetary Fund
Italy	**Paolo Fresco** Chairman, Fiat
Italy	**Francesco Giavazzi** Professor of Economics, Bocconi University, Milan
Canada	**Peter Godsoe** Chairman and CEO, Bank of Nova Scotia
United States of America	**Donald E. Graham** Publisher, *The Washington Post*
Netherlands	**Frank H. G. de Grave** Minister of Defence
Portugal	**Eduardo C. Marcal Grilo** Minister of Education
United States of America	**Chuck Hagel** Senator (Republican, Nebraska)
Sweden	**Tom C. Hedelius** Chairman, Svenska Handelsbanken
Norway	**Per Egil Hegge** Editor, *Aftenposten*
Canada	**Peter A. Herrndorf** Former Chairman and CEO, TVOntario; Senior Visiting Fellow, University of Toronto
United States of America	**Jim Hoagland** Associate Editor, *The Washington Post*
Norway	**Westye Hoegh** Chairman of the Board, Leif Hoegh & Co.; Former President, Norwegian Shipowners' Association
United States of America	**Richard C. Holbrooke** Ambassador to the UN designate
Belgium	**Jan Huyghebaert** Chairman, Almanij N.V.
International	**Otmar Issing** Member of the Executive Board, European Central Bank
United States of America	**Vernon E. Jordan Jr** Senior Partner, Akin, Gump, Strauss, Hauer & Feld, LLP (Attorneys-at-Law)
Bulgaria	**Nikolai Kamov** Member of Parliament
Turkey	**Suna Kirac** Vice-Chairman of the Board, Koc Holding
United States of America	**Henry A. Kissinger** Chairman, Kissinger Associates
Germany	**Hilmar Kopper** Chairman of the Supervisory Board, Deutsche Bank

[Page 6]

Greece	**Yannos Kranidiotis** Alternate Minister for Foreign Affairs
United States of America	**Marie-Josee Kravis** Senior Fellow, Hudson Institute
United States of America	**Jan Leschly** CEO, SmithKline Beecham
International	**Erkki Liikanen** Member of the European Commission
Canada	**Roy MacLaren** High Commissioner for Canada in Britain
Canada	**Margaret O. MacMillan** Editor, *International Journal*
Great Britain	**Peter Mandelson** Member of Parliament
United States of America	**Jessica T. Mathews** President, Carnegie Endowment for International Peace
United States of America	**William J. McDonough** President, Federal Reserve Bank of New York
United States of America	**Richard A. McGinn** Chairman and CEO, Lucent Technologies
Portugal	**Vasco de Mello** Vice Chairman and CEO, Grupo Jose de Mello
Ukraine	**Ihor Mityukov** Minister of Finance
France	**Dominique Moisi** Deputy Director, IFRI
International	**Mario Monti** Member of the European Commission
Portugal	**Francisco Murteira Nabo** President and CEO, Portugal Telecom
Germany	**Matthias Nass** Deputy Editor, *Die Zeit*
Netherlands	**Her Majesty the Queen of the Netherlands**
Iceland	**David Oddsson** Prime Minister
Poland	**Andrzej Olechowski** Chairman, Central Europe Trust
Finland	**Jorma Ollila** Chairman of the Board and CEO, Nokia Corporation
International	**Tommaso Padoa-Schioppa** Member of the Executive Board, European Central Bank
Germany	**Werner A. Perger** Political Correspondent, *Die Zeit*
Great Britain	**Jonathon Porritt** Programme Director, Forum for the Future

Italy	**Alessandro Profumo** CEO, Credito Italiano
Switzerland	**David de Pury** Chairman, de Pury Pictet Turrettini & Co.
Austria	**Gerhard Randa** CEO and Chairman, Bank Austria
United States of America	**Steven Rattner** Deputy Chief Executive, Lazard Freres & Co.
United States of America	**Bill Richardson** Secretary of Energy

[Page 7]

United States of America	**David Rockefeller** Chairman, Chase Manhattan Bank International Advisory Committee
Spain	**Matias Rodriguez Inciarte** Executive Vice Chairman, BSCH
Sweden	**Mauricio Rojas** Associate Professor of Economic History, Lund University; Director of Timbro's Centre for Welfare Reform
Great Britain	**Eric Roll** Senior Adviser, Warburg Dillon Read
Sweden	**Bjorn Rosengren** Minister for Industry, Employment and Communication
Portugal	**Ricardo E. S. Salgado** President and CEO, Grupo Espirito Santo
Portugal	**Jorge Sampaio** President of Portugal
Portugal	**Nicolau Santos** Editor-in-Chief, EXPRESSO
Netherlands	**Ad J. Scheepbouwer** Chairman and CEO, TNT Post Group
Austria	**Richard Schenz** CEO and Chairman of the Board, OMV
Austria	**Rudolf Scholten** Member of the Board of Executive Directors, Oesterreichische Kontrollbank
Germany	**Jurgen E. Schrempp** Chairman of the Board of Management, DaimlerChrysler
Denmark	**Tøger Seidenfaden** Editor-in-Chief, *Politiken*
United States of America	**Robert B. Shapiro** Chairman and CEO, Monsanto Company

Russia	**Lilia Shevtsova** Carnegie Moscow Center
Portugal	**Artur Santos Silva** President and CEO, BPI Group
Spain	**Pedro Solbes Mira** Member of Parliament, Socialist Party
Hungary	**Gyorgy Suranyi** President, National Bank of Hungary
Great Britain	**J. Martin Taylor** Former Chief Executive, Barclays
United States of America	**G. Richard Thoman** President and CEO, Xerox Corporation
United States of America	**John L. Thornton** President and CO-COO, Goldman Sachs Group
Russia	**Dmitri V. Trenin** Deputy Director, Carnegie Moscow Center
France	**Jean-Claude Trichet** Governor, Banque de France
United States of America	**Laura d'Andrea Tyson** Dean, Haas School of Business, University of California at Berkeley
Finland	**Matti Vanhala** Chairman of the Board, Bank of Finland
Finland	**Pentti Vartia** Managing Director, Research Institute of the Finnish Economy (ETLA)

[Page 8]

Switzerland	**Daniel L Vasella** Chairman and CEO, Novartis
Greece	**Thanos M. Veremis** Professor of Political History, University of Athens; President of Eliamep
Austria	**Franz Vranitzky** Former Federal Chancellor
Netherlands	**Lodewijk J. de Waal** Chairman, Dutch Confederation of Trade Unions (FNV)
Great Britain	**Martin Wolf** Associate Editor and Economics Commentator, *The Financial Times*
International/ United States of America	**James D. Wolfensohn** President, The World Bank
Germany	**Otto Wolff von Amerongen** Chairman and CEO of Otto Wolff GmbH

Turkey	**Erkut Yucaoglu** Chairman, Tusiad
Czechoslovakia	**Michael Zantovsk** Chairman of the Committee on Foreign Affairs, Defense and Security, Czech Senate
Austria	**Norbert Zimmermann** Chairman, Berndorf

RAPPORTEURS

Great Britain	**John Micklethwait** New York Bureau Chief, *The Economist*
Great Britain	**Adrian Wooldridge** Foreign Correspondent, *The Economist*

IN ATTENDANCE

Netherlands	**Maja Banck** Executive Secretary, Bilderberg Meetings
Portugal	**Joao A. Estarreja** Local Organizer 1999 Conference
United States of America	**Michael J. Farren** Adviser, American Friends of Bilderberg, Inc.
Austria	**Diemut Kastner** Local Organizer 2000 Conference

BLACK HELICOPTERS

Sinister silent black helicopters are used for the surveillance of patriotic groups opposed to the takeover of the US by the United Nations/**New World Order**/foreign powers.

So claimed the late Jim Keith in his celebrated books *Black Helicopters Over America: Strikeforce for the New World Order* and *Black Helicopters II: The End Game Strategy*. He was not alone in believing the US government uses military aircraft for surveillance of backwoods patriots: a militia in Montana tried to shoot down a National Guard AH-64 Apache as it flew over a member's ranch. Congresswoman Helen Chenoweth of Idaho publicly charged that federal agents in black helicopters were harassing Idaho ranchers, although in her version the helicopters were implementing the Endangered Species Act for the federal government. Ranches seem a popular visiting place for black helicopters: the first sightings, in the 1970s, were associated with cattle mutilations by aliens. Extraterrestrial technology from back-engineering at **Area 51** is believed by some ultra-patriots to be used in the making of the black choppers.

There is no doubt that the military and law-enforcement agencies of the US do use black helicopters, as the "Black Hawk Down" special forces fiasco in Somalia reminded the entire world. Indeed the stealthy UH-60 Black Hawk perfectly fits the "black helicopter" bill – except that it is not employed by the UN in a takeover bid of the Land of the Free. Used by the federal Drug Enforcement Agency for narcotics busting maybe, by the CIA in surveillance of the Midwest militias plausibly, but by the UN or New World Order, no.

Keith's claim that vast garrisons of UN troops, up to 20,000 strong, are already established in America, along with their matt-black choppers, might seem alarming were it not for the fact that no one save Keith and a handful of far-right paranoiacs has ever seen them. And even in the wide open spaces of the US, 20,000 commie-leaning blue-hatted UN troops are hard to conceal.

> Black helicopters are advance guard of UN takeover of US: ALERT LEVEL 2

Further Reading
Jim Keith, *Black Helicopters Over America: Strikeforce for the New World Order*, 1994
Jim Keith, *Black Helicopters II: The End Game Strategy*, 1998

BOHEMIAN GROVE

If you go down to the Californian Sequoia woods in July you're sure of a big surprise . . .

Occupying 2,712 acres (1,098ha) of ancient redwood forest near Monte Rio in Sonoma County, California, the Bohemian Grove is a private camping site for an annual two-week gathering of 2,000 or so of America's great and their guests. It is run by San Francisco's Bohemian Club, established in 1872 as a gentlemanly refuge from the crudities of frontier life. Initially the Club membership comprised journalists, writers and artists – hence the "Bohemian" nomenclature – among them being Mark Twain and the socialist writer Jack London. However, the Club was persuaded by member Ed Bosque that it needed monied types to pay for better facilities. Once let into the nest, the money-men took over. On a visit to the Bohemians, the Victorian dramatist Oscar Wilde quipped that, "I have never see so many well-dressed, well-fed businesslike bohemians in all my life."

Bored with city life at their elegant San Francisco clubhouse, the Bohemians determined to take to the woods in an annual summer camp at the Grove. For a hundred years or more, the "Bohos" have claimed that the camp is merely an occasion for letting elite hair down and doing some uninterrupted male-bonding (women are excluded). Or, as Grove regular President Herbert Hoover put it, the Grove "is the greatest men's party on Earth". Heavy drinking, frat-pack-style "jinks", lavish meals and musical and theatrical entertainments are certainly core to the Grove experience, in which the members and guests sleep in some 104 log-cabin "camps" scattered among the trees. As if in proof of the Bohos' hedonistic intentions, an effigy of "Dull Care" (representing the burdens of everyday life) is burned every 14 July at the foot of a 40-foot (12m) concrete owl in the Grove's mock-druidic "Cremation of Care Ceremony". The motto of the Grove is: "Weaving spiders, come not here."

But weaving spiders do go to the Grove, and some of them are tarantulas. And what a tangled web they spin! As the leading academic historian of the Grove, Peter Martin Phillips, observed: "A person would have to look very hard to find such a dense concentration and variety of American socio-economic elites in one place anywhere else in the United States." Additionally, one would be hard pushed outside of the KKK to find a whiter crowd of Americans: just 1 per cent of the Club's members are not Caucasian.

Every American Republican president since Calvin Coolidge has attended the Grove, including Richard Nixon, who complained that "it was the most faggy goddamned thing you could ever imagine". Current US politicians who attend the Grove include Henry Kissinger, Colin Powell (a rare non-white) and Newt Gingrich. Meanwhile, approximately one-third of the leading US companies have a representative at the Grove summer fest; by Phillips's estimate 11 per cent of Bohemian Club members together own US$30.476 billion of corporate stock. Alan Greenspan, once of the Federal Bank, and A. W. Clausen of the World Bank are both Grove habitues. It beggars belief that these elites do not "talk shop" together. Indeed, by the Grove's own admission, the Manhattan Project to build the US atomic bomb was conceived in Mandalay camp at the Grove. Dwight Eisenhower began his bid for the presidency after canvassing support at the Grove.

A feature of the Bohemian Grove is the daily "Lakeside Chat", a lecture by a worthy in his field. Ostensibly these "Chats" can be on any conceivable subject, but they tend to be skewed towards politics. Titles include "Defining the New World Order" and "America's Health Revolution: Who Lives, Who Dies, Who Pays?"

With its potent amalgamation of secrecy, money and power, the Bohemian Grove has been a target for investigative exposes. In *Trance Formation of America* (1995) Grove worker Cathy O'Brien recorded lurid tales of sex slaves, although no such torrid goings-on were found by British reporter Jon Ronson when he crashed the Grove for his book *Them*. Ronson similarly failed to find the **Babylonian Brotherhood** transforming themselves into giant lizards, as David Icke insisted he would, and nor did he find the **New World Order** there. "My lasting impression," wrote Ronson, "was of an all-pervading sense of immaturity: the Elvis impersonators, the cod-pagan spooky rituals, the heavy drinking . . . emotionally they [the Grovers] seemed trapped in their college years."

Many of the liberal-left political protests against the Grove are co-ordinated by the Bohemian Grove Action Network. According to BGAN:

> When powerful people work together, they become even more powerful. The Grove membership is wealthy, and becoming more so, while the middle class is steadily becoming poorer. This close-knit group determines whether prices rise or fall (by their control of the banking system, money supply, and markets), and they make money whichever way markets fluctuate. They determine what our rights are and which laws have effect, by appointing judges. They decide who our highest officials shall be by consensus among themselves, and then selling candidates to us via the media which they own. Important issues and facts are omitted from discussion in the press, or slanted to suit their goals, but they are discussed frankly at the Grove. Is there true democracy when so much power is concentrated in so few hands? Is there any real difference between the public and private sectors when cabinet members come from the boardrooms of large corporations? Is the spending of billions on weapons, which are

by consensus no longer needed, really the will of the people? Or is it the will of General Electric, General Dynamics, and the other weapons contractors represented at the Grove?

The BGAN overstates the case: the Grove is too unwieldy to rule America and thus the world. Aside from injecting an annual morale-boosting shot in the arm to the US Eurocentric male elite, the Grove is a good ole boys' networking opportunity. It is *the* place in America to win friends (and contracts, jobs . . .) and influence people in high places.

> Bohemian Grovers rule America as invisible dictators: ALERT LEVEL 4

Further Reading
Peter Martin Phillips, *A Relative Advantage: Sociology of the San Francisco Bohemian Club*, PhD thesis, University of California Davis, 1994
Jon Ronson, *Them: Adventures Among Extremists*, 2001

MARTIN BORMANN

Old Nazis never die. They go to Antarctica or, in the case of Adolf Hitler, to the **Nazi Moon Base**. Or, more plausibly, in the case of Martin Bormann they go to the Soviet Union.

In May 1941 Bormann was made Nazi Party Chancellor, a position he used to become the Third Reich's main bureaucrat. He was also Hitler's right-hand man, his personal secretary and his sounding board, and remained with the Fuhrer until the end. The last incontestable sighting of Bormann was in the early hours of 2 May 1945, on Invalidenstrasse Bridge in Berlin, as he sought to escape from encircling Russian troops. Post-war investigation by the Allies surmised that Bormann had committed suicide or been killed near the bridge, but in the absence of a body there could be no confirmation. For two decades rumours flew that Bormann was alive and well and living in (variously) Germany, South America and Spain. Then, in 1971, Reinhard Gehlen published his memoirs, *The Service*, which stated as fact that Bormann had survived the war and hidden from view in the unlikeliest place of all, the USSR, where he had only recently died.

Unlike other Bormann spotters, Gehlen had pedigree. He was the former head of Nazi intelligence on the Eastern Front and, with the help of the CIA and the **Sovereign Military Order of Malta**, had taken on the job of spy chief in the new Federal Republic of Germany. Gehlen asserted that there existed film of Bormann watching sports with Soviet bigwigs. And he made another sensational claim: Bormann was the Russian spy code-named Werther who had infiltrated Hitler's military planning sessions, and passed on the top-secret knowledge to Moscow that Russia needed to win Stalingrad, Kursk and other battles on the Eastern Front.

Gehlen's identification of Bormann as Werther received a boost in 2000 with the publication of *Hitler's Traitor: Martin Bormann and the Defeat of the Reich* by Louis Kilzer. So fast was intelligence passed from Hitler's ops room to Stalin's, Kilzer posited, that it must have come from someone right at Hitler's side: Bormann. If Bormann was Werther it makes it natural that Stalin would have given him sanctuary after the war – hence the sightings of him in the USSR.

There is, however, strong forensic evidence that Bormann died during the battle of Berlin in 1945. In 1972 construction workers at Lehrter Banhof dug up two bodies, one of which was identified as Bormann's by his wartime dentist Dr Hugo Blaschke. (The other body belonged to SS doctor Ludwig Stumpfegger.) The bodies were found just 40 feet (12m) from where Albert Krumnow, a postal worker, had previously claimed to have buried Bormann and Stumpfegger. In 1998 DNA tests on the skull of one of the Lehrter corpses confirmed it as Martin Bormann's. Traces of glass in the jaws suggested the two men had committed suicide by biting on cyanide capsules.

The positive identification of the Lehrter corpse as Bormann's holes the "Bormann was Werther" theory – because, if Bormann had been a Soviet spy, presumably events would indeed have followed the scenario Gehlen proposed. So who was Werther? Bernd Ruland, a teleprinter supervisor at Hitler's wartime radio centre at Zossen, suggested in a 1973 book that Werther was not one but two people: two female teleprinters at Zossen.

Almost inevitably, the forensic identification of Bormann's corpse has not killed off the conspiracy theories. In *Doppelgängers*, Hugh Thomas suggested there were forensic indicators that Bormann died later than 1945, notably that the condition of the teeth were those of a man older than 45 (Bormann's age in 1945) and that there appeared to be dental work in excess of the 1945 record. Moreover, the skull contained traces of a volcanic red clay not found in Berlin but common in Paraguay – where there had been several Bormann sightings. Since DNA testing proved the skull to be Bormann's, the necessary inference was that Bormann did survive the war and was reburied in Berlin by accomplices to give credence to the story that he fell in 1945.

Old Nazis *do* eventually die, but the conspiracy theories about them go on for ever.

Martin Bormann survived the Second World War: ALERT LEVEL 8

Further Reading
Reinhard Gehlen, *The Service*, 1971
Louis Kilzer, *Hitler's Traitor: Martin Bormann and the Defeat of the Reich*, 2000
Hugh Thomas, *Doppelgängers*, 1995

BRITISH ROYAL FAMILY

Send her victorious,
Happy and Glorious,
Long to reign over us,
God Save the Queen!
From *God Save the Queen,* the
British national anthem

Long to reign over us? Not a popular sentiment with followers of conspiracy theorist Lyndon LaRouche, who has the eighty-something Queen of Great Britain fingered as a drugs-runner and her husband Philip as the instigator of the Rwanda genocide, thanks to his private army the World Wildlife Fund (I know, *you* thought it was about saving pandas), and quite possibly the eliminator of Princess **Diana**.

According to sometime Marxist and perennial US presidential candidate LaRouche, the Royal Family heads a cabal of around 500 which operates through two agencies: one is a government department, the Overseas Development Office, and the other is a highly secret society called the Club of the Isles. Although the latter is not British-only, having Dutch and Swiss aristocrats and magnates aboard, its aim is a "one-world empire" – a British global empire, that is.

Since the Royal Family and their lickspittles are few in number, for them to rule the world in the feudal manner to which they wish to become reaccustomed, the globe's population has to be reduced by about 80 per cent. Enter Prince Philip and the World Wildlife Fund. According to a 1994 report in LaRouche's *Executive Intelligence Review*:

> The 1994 Rwanda genocide is but the latest instance of the WWF in action. How did it work? Since 1990, the WWF has been managing a "gorilla protection program" in Gorilla Park in Uganda right on the Rwanda–Zaire border, in the adjacent Volcans Park on the Rwandan side of the border, and in Zaire's Virunga Park. Along with the Akagera Park in Rwanda along the Kenya and Uganda border, all these parks served as training bases, staging areas, and arms depots for the invading "rebels" – who were in reality all soldiers and officers in the Ugandan Army of British puppet Yoweri Museveni. Museveni is run by Britain's Overseas Development Minister Lady Lynda Chalker. So the entire Rwandan genocide had nothing to do with tribal or civil warfare. It was a British-orchestrated assassination and invasion program.

The Rwandan is, apparently, far from the only recent population-reducing atrocity to have been stirred up by the WWF and its "military arm", the SAS. There are also the disasters in the Sudan, Kenya, Afghanistan, Sri Lanka and South Africa – in fact, through its "Afghanisi" terrorist puppets (aka Islamic extremists) the SAS is wreaking havoc just about everywhere on Earth. Comprising nearly 5,000 soldiers, the three SAS regiments are "directly beholden to the Sovereign", thus completely outside the control of the British government . . .

But the perfidious British crown has subtle weapons at its disposal in addition to these 5,000 SAS commandos. In *The New Dark Ages Conspiracy* by LaRouche follower Carol Schitzner White, the plot by British writer H. G. Wells to keep the world in ignorance (thus easier to manage) by restricting scientific knowledge to an elite priesthood was uncovered. To keep the masses really ignorant, the British also promoted the morality-sapping counterculture that led to the liberal society of the 1960s. In this scenario the Grateful Dead were "a British

intelligence operation", a weapon of mass distraction. Meanwhile, the British domination of the narcotics trade since the
Opium Wars has allowed the British to gather super-profits
from money laundering in offshore banking colonies *and* stu-
pefy the poor masses even more by chemically addling their
brains. "Of course," LaRouche once said of the Queen in an
interview, "she's pushing drugs . . . [she is] the head of a gang
pushing drugs."

You may wonder who, if Britain is the bad guy of the world, is
the good guy? Thankfully a 1977 *Executive Intelligence Review*
study entitled "Britain's 'Invisible' Empire Unleashes the Dogs
of War" provides "even more documentation of the ongoing
war which the British Empire is waging to seize the mineral
wealth of the planet, and to destroy that nation-state uniquely
capable of stopping the Empire's designs: the United States."

Yes, the US can save the world from the "Satan" who lives in
London. The US has survived the biggest threat to its existence,
the Civil War (orchestrated by the British in an attempt to turn
the North into an unthreatening agrarian economy), and *if only*
the American electorate will vote in Lyndon H. LaRouche Jr to
the White House all will be well. Trouble is, according to
LaRouche's own *Executive Intelligence Review*, the House of
Windsor and its agents in MI6 are seeking to assassinate him.
Debra Hanania-Freeman, national spokeswoman for LaRouche,
reported that the assassination order appeared covertly in a
British woman's magazine called *Take a Break* . . .

It's not only Yankee *über*-patriots like Lyndon LaRouche who
have the British Royal Family fingered for fascist hegemony. So
does New Age conspiracy guru David Icke, who identifies the
Windsors as "senior members of the SS". More than this, in
Icke's **Illuminati** DVD he ties the British Royal Family into an
Illuminati-**Babylonian Brotherhood** conspiracy which includes black magic, Zionistic Kabbalism and Satanism. Not
bad going for 12-foot (3.66m) shapeshifting lizards.

Did I mention the lizards?

Yes, the Windsors are alien lizards with a penchant for ritual
sacrifice. Just one human to be slaughtered on the altar of their

cold-blooded inhumanity was Princess Diana, who had to be killed after she discovered her in-laws' extraterrestrial nature (no, it's not a metaphor).

According to Icke's researches, the reptilian bloodline of the British Royal Family has a sub-branch that runs through the US, where the President is always the candidate with the greatest number of royal genes. Consequently, "United States Presidents are not chosen by ballot, they are chosen by blood." That means the Brits *already* have their hands on the US . . . Don't tell Lyndon LaRouche.

> British Royal Family are the imperial masters of the planet:
> ALERT LEVEL 2

Further Reading

David Goldman, Konstandinos Kalimtgis and Jeffrey Steinberg, *Dope, Inc.*, 1978

David Icke, *The Biggest Secret*, 1999

Lyndon LaRouche *et al.*, "The Coming Fall of the House of Windsor", *Executive Intelligence Review*, 28 October 1994, vol. 21, No. 43

Carol Schitzner White, *The New Dark Ages Conspiracy: Britain's Plot to Destroy Civilization*, 1980

BUSH–BIN LADEN CONNECTION

The Bushes and the bin Ladens. One family is a straight-arrow American political dynasty, the other a Saudi construction-industry clan whose scion is the most wanted terrorist on Earth, the head honcho of al-Qaeda. Never the twain shall meet, right?

Wrong. Ponder this. On the very morning of the **9/11** attacks, former president of the US George H. W. Bush was in a meeting at the Ritz Carlton Hotel with Shafiq bin Laden, Osama's brother. Yes, that's right: the incumbent US President's father was meeting with the 9/11 mastermind's brother.

And ponder this, too. In the days immediately after 9/11, commercial flights from the US were locked down. There was one exception. A 747 departed to Saudi Arabia with members of the bin Laden family aboard. They were, the FBI concurs, allowed out without questioning.

The Bushes and the bin Ladens go way back. They first became connected in Houston, Texas, in the 1970s when George H. W. Bush's Arbusto 78 oil company received a $1 million investment from Salem bin Laden, Osama's older brother. The investment came courtesy of the offices of Jim Bath, a Bush family friend who also happened to be the US representative of Salem bin Laden, the head of the vast bin Laden building, arms and car-dealing enterprise. (The bin Ladens, due to a cosy deal with the House of Saud, were the official builders in Saudi Arabia; so extensive was their wealth that they once loaned money to the Saudi Treasury.) Despite the bin Laden investment, Arbusto 78 was a failure, and by 1987 the company, and Bush's other oil ventures, had been taken over by Harken Energy. In that same year, Harken had $25 million underwritten by the Union des Banques Suisses and **BCCI.** Shortly afterwards, BCCI would be investigated for money-laundering for the CIA and for funding terrorism. Jim Bath also found himself under official scrutiny; the FBI believed he was directing Saudi funds into Texan companies in hopes of influencing American foreign policy. Once he became US President, George W. Bush initially claimed not to know Bath – despite evidence that they had been friends since serving in the Texas National Guard together. Bath had also bankrolled Bush Junior's Texas gubernatorial campaign.

While the BCCI scandal rumbled on, Bush Senior was out of the business loop, being first VP and then President of the US. (Some more paranoid, or maybe more clear-minded, conspiracy researchers consider that Bush Senior was every inch the tycoon whilst in the White House, being CEO of America Inc. and fighting the Gulf War to ensure that Iraq did not get a stranglehold on Kuwaiti oil supplies.) On leaving the White House, he resumed his financial wheeling and dealing. One company which welcomed him with open arms was the Carlyle Group, a private equity firm based in Washington DC. Founded in 1987, the Carlyle Group handled an arms, technology and security portfolio estimated at $25 million. On the group's behalf, George Bush Sr went at least twice to Saudi Arabia to meet – guess who? – the bin Laden family. Guess who invested heavily in the Carlyle Group? Bingo. Bush's old homeys, the bin Laden family.

It was a meeting of the Carlyle Group that Bush Senior and Shafiq bin Laden were attending on the fateful morning of 9/11. By some accounts Bush, bin Laden and former US Defense Secretary James Baker watched TV coverage of the attacks together.

What of Bush Jr, meanwhile? President George W. Bush was given a briefing by the CIA in August 2001 outlining al-Qaeda's intention to attack the US. The name Osama bin Laden is reported as having been explicitly mentioned. The Bush White House has consistently refused to release a copy of the briefing, even to the Congressional inquiry into 9/11.

Did Bush Jr turn a blind eye to the activities of Osama bin Laden because he was the son (even if the black sheep son) of the Bush family friends the bin Ladens? Did Bush make an error of judgment because the Bushes and the bin Ladens had a three-decade-long tie?

If he did, many Americans paid the highest price.

A footnote: George W. Bush appointed Thomas Kean to chair the 9/11 Investigation. Thomas Kean has had business ties with Khalid bin Mahfouz, Osama bin Laden's brother-in-law.

> George W. Bush made errors of judgment pre-9/11 because of his family's ties to the bin Ladens: ALERT LEVEL 8

Further Reading
Craig Unger, *House of Bush, House of Saud: The Secret Relationship Between the World's Two Most Powerful Dynasties*, 2004
www.fahrenheit911.com

ROBERTO CALVI

On 18 June 1982 the body of Roberto Calvi was found swinging on a length of orange nylon rope beneath Blackfriars Bridge, London. He had £10,000 worth of sterling, Italian lire and Swiss francs in his wallet and his trousers were stuffed with bricks and stones from a nearby building site.

The British coroner recorded a case of suicide.

Roberto Calvi certainly had reasons to kill himself. The 62-year-old Italian had chaired Banco Ambrosiano, Italy's second largest private bank, and seen it collapse with debts of £800 million. The day before Calvi's death, his former secretary had jumped out of a Milan fourth-floor window in despair at the bank's crash. And Calvi had other woes. He was linked to the alleged murder of **John Paul I**. He had been found guilty of the illegal export of billions of lire, and was free only pending an imminent appeal. During his sojourn in prison he had tried to take his own life.

Twenty years later, in September 2003, the initial British coroner's verdict would be overturned by an Italian court, which heard evidence that Calvi was murdered by strangulation and that his hands had never touched the bricks in his pockets. According to a Mafia supergrass, Francesco Mannino Mannoia, Calvi had been killed on the orders of the Mafia boss Giuseppe "The Cashier" Calo, because Calvi had embezzled Mafia money. The Mafia also, allegedly, wanted to ensure that Calvi did not reveal the Vatican's money-laundering activities on their behalf.

On 5 October 2005 Calo, along with four other defendants (Flavio Carboni, Manuela Kleinszig, Ernesto Diotallevi, and Calvi's former chauffeur/bodyguard Silvano Vittor), went on trial for the banker's murder. Calvi's son, Carlo, is adamant that his father was murdered to protect the money-launderers at the Vatican Bank and their allies in the Masonic lodge **P2**, whose members sometimes refer to themselves as *frati neri* or "black friars". Calvi himself had been a member of P2. This has led to the suggestion that his body was hung symbolically under Blackfriars Bridge as a masonic warning to others.

The City of London Police, forensic experts in Rome, Kroll Associates, a private detective agency hired by Carlo Calvi and forensic scientist Professor Bernd Brinkmann of Munster University all concur that Calvi was murdered. However, on 6 June 2007 the Italian court threw out the charges against the five accused. A new investigation is under way.

> God's Banker was murdered to conceal money-laundering by the Mafia: ALERT LEVEL 9

Further Reading
The Observer, "Who Killed Calvi?", 7 December 2003
Rupert Cornwell, *God's Banker: The Life and Death of Roberto Calvi*, 1984
Philip Willan, *The Last Supper: The Mafia, the Masons and the Killing of Roberto Calvi*, 2007

CANCER

> However, the Medical Mafia (with the help of the Elite) has
> suppressed all this non-pharma (Allopathic) cancer knowledge as
> well as the causes (and prevention), the main suspects being Death
> Towers, Chemtrails, Junk Food, chemicals and drugs such as
> Pesticides, and vaccines, along with sugar, root-canals and miasms,
> while they have **actively promoted** the widespread use of cancer
> agents, such as fluoridation, Aspartame & MSG . . . And the
> deaths resulting from this enforced, mostly deadly cancer medicine,
> can be **added** to the 783,936 yearly USA Allopathic deaths.
>
> The Cancer Conspiracy,
> http://www.whale.to/a/cancer-c.html

In 1932 the US Public Health Service experimented on black
syphilitic farmers in Tuskegee, Alabama, and later withheld
penicillin, which could have cured them. Bill Clinton apolo-
gized personally on behalf of the US government to the Tuskegee farmers in 1997.

In 2004 the New York Attorney General began a law suit
against GlaxoSmithKline asserting that the pharmaceutical
giant had deliberately buried information proving that some
users of fluoxetine hydrochloride (one of the brand names of
which is Prozac) developed suicidal tendencies. The company
settled out of court for $2.5 million.

Medical – and more specifically pharmaceutical – conspiracies do exist. Is there, though, one centred on cancer, whereby

the pharmaceutical industry and the medical profession have colluded to obscure the availability of a cure? A full 27 per cent of Americans think so, according to *Cancer* journal.

Since President Nixon declared his "War Against Cancer" in 1971, $20 billion have been spent on cancer research in the US alone, to little apparent avail. One in four people in the Western world currently dies from cancer, and this rate of incidence will increase, according to the WHO, to 50 per cent by 2020. What reason could there be for such an abject and expensive failure other than a cover-up by vested interests?

One of the first to condemn the "cancer conspiracy" was Dr Raymond Rife, an optics engineer in San Diego, who in the 1930s claimed to have discovered the bacteria that cause cancer and then invented the "Rife Ray Tube", a machine that cured cancerous growths by bombarding them with oscillating electromagnetic waves. Proof that the Rife Ray Tube worked came from the University of California, who – according to Rife's supporters – cured sixteen terminally ill patients with the device. Before the Tube could go into mass production, however, the American Medical Association ordered an outright ban on its use. All Rife's papers were destroyed by arson. Rife is alleged to have been murdered in 1971. (Violence against critics of "the cancer conspiracy" is, if internet sites are to be believed, routine. "One wintry night our house was burned to the ground," writes one critic Dr William Kelley. ". . . These lawless [Medical] Establishment devils went to work and Poisoned . . . me 3 times . . . Tried to shoot me once during this time.")

Rife's proposition that cancer has a bacterial cause subsequently found favour with, among others, Dr Wilhelm Reich, in *The Cancer Biopathy* (1948), Dr Virginia Livingston-Wheeler in *The Conquest of Cancer* (1984) and Dr Alan Cantwell in *The Cancer Microbe* (1990). In *The Cancer Cure That Worked* (1987) and *Healing of Cancer, the Cures, the Cover-ups and the Solution Now!* (1990) Barry Lynes proselytized on behalf of Rife's cure, and reconstructions of the Rife Ray Tube are currently for sale on the internet. There is no independent evidence that they work.

According to Cantwell, who is also a polemicist against "the AIDS conspiracy", "recognition of microscopic cancer bacteria" would be a massive embarrassment to the medical profession and would require the dumping not only of existing research programmes but also of the entire expensive array of radiation and chemotherapy equipment which fills oncology units. It is certainly the case that the "medical establishment" keeps its bifocals firmly fixed on chemotherapy and radiation as the only worthwhile treatments for cancer, as many believe is shown by the story of Harry Hoxsey's Tonic.

For three decades the American Medical Association, headed by Morris Fishbein, hounded the alternative practitioner Harry Hoxsey for selling "Hoxsey's Tonic" as a cure for cancer. In 1956 46,000 PUBLIC WARNING AGAINST HOXSEY CANCER TREATMENT posters were put up in US post offices; in one 16-month period Hoxsey was arrested over 100 times for practising medicine without a licence. Hoxsey was certainly without medical training (he was a coal miner), but generations of apologists have claimed that his tonic, which you might have expected to be snake-oil, in fact wasn't – indeed that the AMA belatedly admitted the stuff worked on skin cancer, at the very least. The tonic had supposedly been invented by Hoxsey's great-grandfather (or father; Hoxsey told several versions of the tale), who had noticed that one of his horses cured itself of cancer by eating selected herbs. And indeed subsequent research by *The Lancet*, say the apologists, confirmed that herbal ingredients contained in Hoxsey's Tonic, such as barberry and buckthorn, were effective agents against tumours. In fact, what the AMA discovered was that a primary constituent of Hoxsey's Tonic was arsenic. Arsenic has the property that it "burns" away cells, and of course isn't choosy about whether those cells are cancerous or healthy. So, yes, if you smeared Hoxsey's Tonic on a skin cancer you'd get rid of the cancerous cells . . . along with any other cells with which the stuff came in contact. You'd have no guarantee the cancer wouldn't return, of course, and more particularly you'd have done nothing about any metastasis that might already have taken place. In a sense, then, Hoxsey's Tonic was found to have some effect on skin cancer – the same effect you could have got by cauterization, or amputation . . .

Surely doctors, those most trusted of people, could not be participants in a mass conspiracy to deny cancer sufferers life-saving treatments? As the late cancer victim Michael Higgins wrote on the MyCancerFacts website: "I have been living with cancer for 3 years and during that time been treated by approximately half a dozen medical professionals . . . They are the people I am being asked to believe are conspiring to keep the truth hidden from me in order to keep their jobs." Higgins's point is telling: it is unlikely that tens of thousands of oncologists could be persuaded by pharmaceutical companies and powerful research institutes to knowingly deny the Hippocratic oath. (Error is possible, however: Thalidomide, Rotavirus vaccine and Vioxx are just three miracle cures that your doctor sincerely swore were safe – before they were withdrawn.)

On the balance of probability, the conspicuous failure to find a cure for cancer is to be explained by a mundane reason, not a sinister one. There isn't *a* cure. Cancers come in various different forms, and may have differing causes. It follows that different treatments may be necessary. Whether the medical profession can embrace divergent thinking is another question. The only thing that can safely be said in the cancer debate is that prevention is easier than cure. Most cancers seem possibly to be the result of the polluted, chemical-laden, fast-food, alcohol- and tobacco-fuelled 21st-century lifestyle. Change that for the better and cancer rates will dwindle to those of the days of yore.

Cancer cure is suppressed by pharmaceutical companies and medical establishment: ALERT LEVEL 6

Further Reading
Dr Alan C. Cantwell, *The Cancer Microbe*, 1990
Barry Lynes, *The Cancer Cure That Worked*, 1987
Barry Lynes, *Healing of Cancer, the Cures, the Cover-ups and the Solution Now!* , 1990

LE CERCLE (The Circle)

Like the **Bilderberg Group** and the **Bohemian Grove**, *Le Cercle* is a transnational cabal of statesmen, corporate titans, intelligence officers and military top brass. Unlike the other two, the ultra-secretive, conservative *Le Cercle* wars against its enemies more than it jaws about them.

Founded in the 1950s by the sometime French prime minister Antoine Pinay (hence the organization's original name of "The Pinay Circle") together with the French Nazi collaborator Jean Violet, *Le Cercle* sought the creation of a unified Europe. To this end it drew together the luminaries of the two most mutually antagonistic states, France and Germany, including German Chancellor Konrad Adenauer and French prime minister Robert Schuman. Jean Monnet, the architect of European integration in the shape of the EEC, was also an early member.

Le Cercle was funded by the CIA. (See diaries of attendee Alan Clark MP. Even without CIA finance, *Le Cercle* was unlikely to be short of money: members over the years have included the financiers Sir James Goldsmith, Carlo Il Pesenti and the ubiquitous David Rockefeller.) The attraction of *Le Cercle* for the CIA was not its pan-Europeanism but its other face: militant anti-leftism. *Le Cercle* chairman Brian Crozier used his private National Association of Freedom to support the MI5 "dirty tricks" campaign against Labour Prime Minister Harold **Wilson**, who eventually resigned from office in 1975. Across the Channel, *Le Cercle* members in the Service for

External Documentation and Espionage spread disinformation against Socialist presidential candidate Francois Mitterrand. (Mitterrand took his revenge post-election by closing SEDE down.) More controversially, critics claim *Le* **Cercle** arranged the assassination of Swedish prime minister Olof Palme by agents of the Swedish intelligence service, SAPO. *Le* **Cercle** **is even claimed to have been the instigator of the death of Princess Diana**, her "crime" being her anti-landmine campaign that would have deprived defence industrialists of millions.

Further past and present members/attendees of *Le* **Cercle** include: Jonathan Aitken MP, Julian Amery MP, Lord Norman Lamont, Dr Henry Kissinger, Zbigniew Brzezinski, William Colby, Otto von Hapsburg and Giulio Andreotti.

> *Le Cercle* is the one ring that controls global affairs: ALERT LEVEL 5

Further Reading
http://home.planet.nl-Project for the Exposure of Hidden Institutions-*Le* **Cercle**

CHAPPAQUIDDICK

Do we operate under a system of equal justice under law? Or is there one system for the average citizen and another for the high and mighty?

Senator Edward Kennedy, 1973

The Kennedy brothers have an arm-lock on the conspiracies of the 1960s. **John F. Kennedy** and **Robert F. Kennedy** were allegedly assassinated as a result of conspiracies. Edward Kennedy, as is the way of the baby of the family, decided to be altogether different: he decided to perpetrate a conspiracy. Allegedly.

On the evening of 18 July 1969, Senator Edward – "Teddy" to family and friends – Kennedy organized a house party on the tiny island of Chappaquiddick, off Martha's Vineyard. The party was to reward the "Boiler Room Girls", six secretaries and researchers who had worked in the office of Teddy Kennedy's recently assassinated brother, Robert. The Boiler Room Girls were Mary Jo Kopechne, Susan Tannenbaum, Rosemary Keough, Ann Lyons, Maryellen Lyons and Esther Newburgh. Also in attendance were six men, all married: Senator Kennedy himself, Joe Gargan (Kennedy's cousin), Charles Tretter, Raymond La Rosa, John Crimmins and Attorney General Paul Markham. Crimmins supplied the booze: two bottles of rum, three half-gallons of vodka, four fifths of whisky and two cases of beer.

According to his own account, Kennedy left the party to drive 28-year-old Kopechne to the ferry.

"On 18 July 1969, at approximately 11.15 p.m. in Chappaquiddick, Martha's Vinyard, Massachusetts, I was driving my car on Main Street on my way to get the ferry back to Edgartown. I was unfamiliar with the road and turned right onto Dike Road, instead of bearing hard left on Main Street. After proceeding for approximately one-half mile on Dike Road I descended a hill and came upon a narrow bridge. The car went off the side of the bridge. There was one passenger with me, one Miss Mary [Kennedy was not sure of the spelling of the dead girl's surname, and gave a phonetic approximation], a former secretary of my brother Sen. Robert Kennedy. The car turned over and sank into the water and landed with the roof resting on the bottom. I attempted to open the door and the window of the car but have no recollection of how I got out of the car. I came to the surface and then repeatedly dove down to the car in an attempt to see if the passenger was still in the car. I was unsuccessful in the attempt. I was exhausted and in a state of shock. I recall walking back to where my friends were eating. There was a car parked in front of the cottage and I climbed into the back seat. I then asked for someone to bring me back to Edgartown. I remember walking around for a period of time and then going back to my hotel room. When I fully realized what had happened this morning, I immediately contacted the police."

Kennedy's version was accepted by the police and courts. He was given a two-month suspended sentence for failing to remain at the scene of an accident and failing to report it (a crime that bore a mandatory jail sentence). But there are a number of anomalies and concerns in his account:

• Deputy Sheriff Christopher Look remembered seeing, at 12.30 p.m., a car on the island which he believed to be Kennedy's Oldsmobile. When he approached this car it reversed fast down the lane towards Dike Bridge, where Kopechne died. If the car was Kennedy's he cannot have been driving Kopechne to the ferry because the last boat had long since gone. Many suspect that Kennedy and Kopechne deliberately drove on to the unlit dirt track to have sex, either in the car or on the beach at the end of the track.

- Kennedy claimed in his statement that he was unfamiliar with the dirt Dike Road. At the inquest, however, Judge Boyle concluded that "Earlier on 18 July, he [Kennedy] had been driven over Chappaquiddick Road three times, and over Dike Road and Dike Bridge twice. Kopechne had been driven over Chappaquiddick Road five times and over Dike Road and Dike Bridge twice."

- According to Gargan's later testimony, when Kennedy returned to the cottage after the accident his main worry was to cover up the accident. He (Kennedy) proposed saying that Kopechne had been driving the car alone.

- According to Gargan and Markham, Kennedy only reported the accident the following morning at their insistence. Before going to the police he conferred with his family by telephone.

- Kennedy denied drinking at the alcohol-plentiful party, although this is disputed by others. By the time he presented himself to the police it was conveniently too late to test his word. While Kennedy reported to the police on the morning of 19 July, Gargan organized a clean-up of the cottage so that no traces of revelry remained.

- For someone shocked and confused, Kennedy was remarkably able to navigate his way to the ferry, swim a 500-foot (150m) channel and find his hotel.

- If Kennedy really wanted to save Kopechne's life why did he not call for help from the cottages near the bridge, instead of going all the way back to the party? It is difficult not to believe that Senator Kennedy put his career before Kopechne's life.

The conspiracy kicks in thereafter:

- There are speculations that the Kennedy clan put subtle pressure on the police to avoid scrutinizing the Kopechne accident too closely.

- On 19 July, when Registry Inspector George Kennedy (no relation) requested a copy of Edward M. Kennedy's driving licence from the Boston Registry, it was confirmed that it had expired; the next day it had been miraculously fixed and updated.
- Kennedy possessed a litany of driving offences, but the court did not learn about them because his driving record miraculously disappeared from the system.
- No autopsy was performed on Kopechne. This caused a public outcry, leading to a motion to have her body exhumed. The request was successfully challenged by the Kopechnes' lawyer Joseph Flanagan. Flanagan was hired and paid for by Teddy Kennedy.

If an autopsy had been carried out it might have come to a chilling conclusion. Diver John Farrar, on entering the sunken car, found Kopechne's corpse in a posture that suggested she'd been trapped in an air pocket – she'd died, therefore, not of drowning but of suffocation. It has been estimated the air in the pocket could have supported her for over two hours – plenty of time, then, for her to have been rescued had Teddy Kennedy acted more expeditiously.

> The Kennedy family protected Teddy Kennedy from proper criminal proceedings following death of Mary Jo Kopechne at Chappaquiddick: ALERT LEVEL 9

Further Reading
Jack Olsen, *The Bridge at Chappaquiddick*, 1970
http://www.ytedk.com

CHECHEN BOMBINGS

The bombings started on 4 September 1999, when an explosion destroyed a block of military flats in the southern Russian city of Buinaksk, killing 62 people. Two civilian apartment blocks in Moscow were blown up on 9 and 13 September that same year, with 212 fatalities. Then, on 16 September, 17 people died in a truck-bomb blast in Volgodonsk.

The Russian secret service, the Federalnaya Sluzhba Bezopasnosti (FSB), quickly identified one of the perpetrators as Achimez Gochiyaev, a foot soldier for the Chechen warlord Shamil Basayev. Since 1994 the Chechens, led by Basayev, had been fighting fanatically for independence from Russia. Case closed: the bombings were committed by Chechen militants as part of their terrorist campaign for a free Chechnya. In response, the acting prime minister of Russia, Vladimir Putin, ordered a mass counter-terrorism campaign in Chechnya, a piece of hardman politicking that so endeared him to a fearful Russian electorate that they voted the former FSB director their President in 2000.

Conspiracy theorists pounced. And not just conspiracy theorists, but respected politicians like British Conservative MP Julian Lewis, and respected journalists, like the *Financial Times*'s Moscow correspondent David Satter. What sense did it make for the Chechens to commit outrages likely to cause an invasion of Chechnya? Not much. What tangible evidence did the Russian authorities offer to prove Chechen involvement in the bombings?

None. Strangest of all was the bomb that failed to explode in the city of Ryazan, where an apartment resident noted two men acting suspiciously and reported the matter to the city police. On investigating the apartment block's basement the police found sacks of hexogen (also known as RDX, the explosive ingredient used in the four bombings) and timers. Swiftly the FSB confiscated the sacks, before announcing that they contained sugar and had been used as a prop in a counter-terrorist exercise.

Evidence that the bombings were a "false flag" operation undertaken by the FSB to provide a *casus belli* for a Russian incursion into Chechnya mounted. In December 1999 Lieutenant Alexei Galkin, a Russian spy captured by the Chechens in the siege of Grozny, testified to Western journalists that the Russian secret services had planted at least some of the "Chechen" bombs. The transcript of his interview included:

Journalist/Interpreter: Can you introduce yourself please.
Galkin: Assistant head of sector senior lieutenant Alexei Viktorovich Galkin, employee of the Central Intelligence Office [GRU] of the Russian Federation.
[. . .]
Journalist: Did you take part in the bombing of buildings in Moscow and Dagestan?
Galkin: I personally did not take part in the bombing of the buildings in Moscow and Dagestan, but I know who blew them up, who is behind the bombing of buildings in Moscow and who blew up the buildings in Buinaksk.
Journalist: Can you tell us who?
Galkin: Russian special forces, the FSB together with GRU [Central Intelligence Office] are responsible for blowing up the buildings in Moscow and in Volgodonsk. The bombing of the buildings in Buinaksk was the work of some members of our group, which at the time was on a mission in Dagestan.
Journalist: And as far as I know, here you have been recorded on tape, you confessed to all this, apparently you were filmed with a video camera. And when . . . when you,

during the filming were you acting on your own wishes?

Voice off camera of the head of the Chechen Security Service Abu Movsaev: That . . . Don't answer that question.

Journalist: How have you been treated here?

Galkin: I've been treated well here. As a prisoner of war I have not been beaten here, they have fed me three times a day and when necessary given me medical assistance.

Journalist: Here is the statement given by you. Do you confirm that you made it voluntarily without any pressure on the part of anyone?

Galkin: This statement is printed from my words. I wrote this statement by hand [holds the piece of paper in front of his face], with my personal signature.

Journalist: Now, at this moment, as you are speaking with us, are you afraid of anything?

Galkin: No, it is simply that this is the first time I have faced journalists . . . journalists from western television companies, so I am a bit nervous.

Abu Movsaev's voice off camera: The special forces are not allowed to appear on . . .

Galkin: It is quite simply that due to the nature of our work we have to . . . we are not supposed to show ourselves in front of television cameras. [Smiles tensely.]

[. . .]

Journalist: Do you personally and does your unit have anything to do with the explosions in Moscow?

Galkin: Personally our unit has nothing to do with the explosions in Moscow, since at that time we were in Dagestan. The members of our unit, the members of our unit of twelve men, who were in Dagestan at that time, carried out the bombing of the house in Buinaksk.

After Galkin, it was the turn of former FSB officer Alexander **Litvinenko** to accuse his ex-colleagues of orchestrating the apartment block bombings in his book *Blowing Up Russia*, which was underwritten by the exiled tycoon Boris Berezovsky.

More than 5,000 copies of the book were confiscated by Russian authorities in 2003. Boris Berezovsky also financed a documentary film, *FSB Blows Up Russia*, which again accused Russian special services of organizing the explosions in Volgodonsk and Moscow. Meanwhile, sometime KGB colonel Konstantin Preobrazhensky asserted that the Chechen rebels lacked the materiel to organize the bombings "without the help of high-ranking Moscow officials" and the *Los Angeles Times* claimed to have identified FSB operative Vladimir Romanovich as the person who rented the basement where one of the bombs was detonated.

The FSB denied everything. Meanwhile, Berezovsky was compromised by his overt hostility to the Russian regime, which had accused him of financial wrongdoings. Yet suspicions that the FSB had something to hide over the apartment bombings refused to go away. Indeed, they were only increased by the strange circumstances which surrounded other "Chechen" terrorist acts in Russia, notably the October 2004 siege of Moscow's Dubrovka theatre which ended when security forces pumped in a mysterious gas to overcome the hostage-takers. Why, if the hostage-takers were incapacitated, were they summarily executed with bullets? Then there was the atrocity at Beslan elementary school, where "Chechen" terrorists held a thousand parents and children hostage before the siege ended in an inferno of explosions and gunfire, killing over 300. The Chechen authorities blamed pro-Putin forces in Russia as the instigators of the siege, a claim that was given credence by the Russian defence department's forced admission that none of the hostage-takers at Beslan were actually Chechens. Beslan residents themselves organized protests against Russian complicity in the siege.

The truth of the apartment bombings may never properly emerge from the murky war between Russian neo-imperialists and Chechen separatists. Matters have not been aided by a pro-Kremlin bloc in the Russian Duma (parliament), which stymied an investigation into the attempted Ryazan bombing, or by the inconvenient fate that met two members of an independent public investigation, Sergei Yushenkov and Yuri Shchekochi-kin. They died in circumstances which suggested assassination. And then, of course, there was the **Litvinenko** case . . .

The Russian apartment bombings were a false-flag FSB operation intended to justify the Russian invasion which started the second Chechnya war: ALERT LEVEL 7

Further Reading
Alexander Litvinenko and Yuri Felshtinsky, *Blowing Up Russia: The Secret Plot to Bring Back KGB Terror*, 2004
David Satter, *Darkness at Dawn: The Rise of the Russian Criminal State*, 2003

CHEMTRAILS

The last decade has seen a dramatic rise in the number of planes in our skies. No-frills airlines, cheap seats and the lure of ever more exotic destinations have put more jumbos over our cities and countryside. To some people, though, there's something a lot more sinister behind the streams of white cloud subdividing our aerial space than the obvious concerns about increased global warming and the widening of carbon footprints.

"Contrail" is the name given to the white plume of cloud which can be seen following a jet plane through the sky. For a contrail to form, the plane must be flying above 33,000 feet (10,000m), at which altitude the hot engine exhaust condenses into ice crystals to form a pencil-thin vapour trail that (relatively) quickly vanishes. Chemtrails, observers claim, are very evidently different. These appear much thicker and extend across the sky, often in criss-cross patterns, grids or parallel lines. The trails do not dissipate quickly but persist, expanding slowly into feathers and mares' tails until they form wispy white veils or "fake cirrus-type" clouds that last for hours.

Reports of chemtrails have come from many, mostly highly developed countries, including France, Britain, Canada, Germany and New Zealand, but the most activity appears to be centred on the United States. One video produced by seasoned chemtrail campaigner Clifford Carnicom warns people to make the most of blue skies now – blue skies, he believes, will become a thing of the past once chemtrails have become so prevalent they obscure the sun permanently from view.

The real question, though, is: what's in those chemtrails that makes them behave so differently from the innocent contrail? The answer is that no one really knows for sure. Concerned activists say they cannot raise enough funds to hire a plane at short notice to fly up to high altitudes and capture some of the chemtrail vapour to conduct a proper analysis, nor do they believe they would be given flight clearance to do so. Some claim to have collected solid matter fallen from a chemtrail-filled sky which reputedly contains high bacterial numbers, but other samples have been mysteriously mislaid, or their existence has been denied following their arrival at official government laboratories.

One amazed Californian says he noted no more than the usual amount of chemtrails over his property one morning but this was followed several hours later by skeins of white, waxy material falling on to trees, pavements and so on, where it slowly dissolved. He collected some of the strange material and placed it in a sealed jar, but within 24 hours over half of it had disappeared. He sealed the jar more closely, but when he opened it some days later he was, he said, overwhelmed by a noxious gas that stung his throat and burned his lips. Somehow he managed to preserve some of the material. Under the microscope it appeared fibrous and sticky, but it has remained unidentified. The US Environmental Protection Agency (EPA) reportedly no longer accepts any such samples for testing even though its stated remit is to protect the American people from possible sources of contamination.

Just what the purpose is behind chemtrails and (according to the theorists) other covert tinkering with the atmosphere is unclear, but the US government, backed up by its "shadowy" masters, seems top of the list of perpetrators. In typical conspiracy mode, leading chemtrail researcher Clifford Carnicom maintains that the subject "is a managed and controlled topic of discussion in the United States. It must be assumed now in this country that communication on this topic is monitored."

The most probable constituent of the chemtrails would seem to be aluminium. Documented aerial tests have been carried out to test a theory perpetrated by Dr Edward Teller (one of the creators of the hydrogen bomb) that aluminium particles seeded into the atmosphere would reflect sunlight back out into space and reduce the effects of global warming. There is no indication how much aluminium it would actually take to affect global warming rates and what proportion of the world's atmosphere would have to be treated. Naturally human health and the natural environment could be threatened by the dispersion of large quantities of aluminium (Alzheimer's, here we come!), making it a rather heavy-handed solution, but the US government has recently publicly stated its intention to research physical methods of reducing warming rather than relying wholly on the reduction of carbon emissions to halt a rise in worldwide temperatures.

If clouds of aluminium were not bad enough there are yet more terrifying alternatives. Conspiracy theorists claim that biological weapons are being used by supporters of the **New World Order** to reduce the global population. The American authors of the http://educate-yourself.org website claim the US government is under the control of the **Illuminati** (architects of the New World Order). This group's goal to reduce the world population from 6 billion to 4 billion by 2050 is openly stated, the authors say, in the Global 2000 report assembled by the Carter administration in the late 1970s.

Obviously, genocide on this scale would require some exceptionally devious means, not just to reach enough of the population but to be carried out without anyone noticing. This method might also have to be more subtle than just poisoning whole populations. To which end, what better than to spray us all with a biohazardous pathogen which will slowly attack the immune systems of vulnerable groups such as the elderly, the young and the sick, particularly those already suffering such auto-immune disorders as AIDS, allowing them to succumb fatally to a barrage of influenza-type illnesses, which, as everybody knows, are notoriously difficult to contain or treat, there being so many different strains? Telltale symptoms to look out for next time there's a jumbo jet in your area are: hacking coughs, upper respiratory and intestinal distress, pneumonia, extreme fatigue, lethargy, dizziness, disorientation, headaches, aching joints and muscles, depression, loss of bladder control, nervous tics.

Barium salt mixtures have been identified as carriers for a whole host of pathogens or chemicals which could contaminate the people living beneath the chemtrails, breaking down their immune systems and poisoning them slowly and undetectably. To support their argument, chemtrail researchers point to recent rises in the incidence of "flu-type" epidemics across the Western world, along with an increase in mystery illnesses, allergies and respiratory disorders.

Other theorists, by contrast, suggest that chemtrails are being used not to kill people but to inoculate them secretly against the biological weapons that might be unleashed by enemy states, and that it is the reaction to this inoculation process which causes the flu-like symptoms.

The fact that its supporters appear to be singing from different hymn sheets rather dents the credibility of the chemtrail theory. While one camp maintains chemtrails are intended to reduce world population by 85 per cent, China is apparently exempt because it is viewed as such a perfect example of the New World Order in action that it is being groomed to replace the US as the next superpower. Other camps state, however, that bird flu is one of the organisms that has been spread by chemtrail; if so, that would seem to scupper the Chinese-immunity theory, as bird flu was first identified there – not to mention the fact that, as holder of 20 per cent of the global population, China would have to bear a stupendous death rate in order for the world's population as a whole to achieve that 85 per cent reduction. Might there be only the Chinese left? Not much fun being a superpower with no one left to lord it over, is it?

But this particular conspiracy theory is undermined by a much simpler flaw. It is a question not so much of what might be in the chemtrails but of how they are delivered in the first place. If as theorists claim these trails are dispensed by special units attached or hidden in the fuselage of both military and commercial jets, that would imply that every airline pilot and every maintenance-crew member was party to the conspiracy, and that not one of all these people has let the secret slip out. Even claims that rogue chemicals are being added directly to jet fuel seem highly implausible: what pathogen could survive ignition in a jumbo jet engine?

Official sources in the American military and scientific community remain adamant that what people are noticing are not chemtrails but ordinary contrails. Astronauts aboard the International Space Station observed the absence of contrails on the days following 9/11. "I'll tell you one thing that's really strange. Normally when we go over the US, the sky is like a spider web of contrails," outpost commander Frank Culbertson told flight controllers at NASA's Mission Control Centre in Houston. "There are no contrails in the sky. It's very, very weird."

A prominent meteorologist quoted on the wonderfully named New Mexicans for Science and Reason website (www.nmsr.org) cites atmospheric differences as the cause of persistent contrails, saying that, if relative humidity is high, especially at the subzero temperatures of the upper atmosphere, the addition of even a tiny amount of water vapour acts as a catalyst, causing the thin cirrus-type clouds to form.

However reasoned and scientific the debunkers of the chemtrails theory may be, they will always have an uphill battle to convince the theorists themselves, because the theorists' worst nightmare has already come true. The US government has already been guilty of secretly exposing its citizens to artificial pathogens and chemicals. The US Army's biological defence programme sprayed "simulant" agents over hundreds of populated areas around the country in the 20 years from 1949 to 1969. According to a Dr Cole who testified before the Committee on Veteran Affairs on 6 May 1994, citizens reported illnesses in those areas but their health was never monitored because the army assumed the bacteria and chemicals they were spraying were harmless. These simulants included

Aspergillis fumigatus, a bacterium which gives rise to a potentially fatal disease known as aspergillosis, and zinc cadmium sulphide, which is known to cause cancer. Even in safe old Blighty it has also recently become public that the flood disaster in August 1952 at Lynmouth, north Devon, was precipitated by cloud-seeding experiments carried out by the American military over Exmoor.

In spite of these "little accidents", it's still pretty hard to swallow the chemtrail story. We would have to believe national governments are masterminding attempts to poison large numbers of their own people, not to mention contaminate the global atmosphere. Perhaps this theory is one is for those of a particularly pessimistic frame of mind. Or you might choose to believe that the combination of particular atmospheric conditions, humidity levels and weather can combine to produce an obtrusive pattern of contrails along major flight paths. Unsightly, yes; deadly, no.

The degradation of our natural environment by the increasing presence of airplane contrails and the threat airplane emissions present are surely cause for action on the part of concerned citizens, with no conspiracies required.

Clouds of chemical and biological warfare agents are raining death and disease: ALERT LEVEL 3.5

Further Reading
Will Thomas, "Chemtrails: Covert Climate Control?", *Nexus*, Vol. 8, No. 6, October–November 2001
www.chemtrailcentral.com
http://educate-yourself.org
www.stopchemtrailsuk.bravehost.com
www.rense.com/politics6/chemdatapage.html
www.carnicom.com/contrails.htm
www.nmsr.org/chemtrls.htm

CLUB OF ROME

In conspiriology the Club of Rome (est. 1966) is an umbrella organization of Anglo-American financiers and the old Black Nobility of Europe which is charged with bringing into being the **New World Order**. Since the Earth is running low on natural resources and high on population, the New World Order requires the mass cull of "useless mouths" – a strategy the Club of Rome has pursued with abandon. The Rwanda genocide and AIDS, among other disasters, are the dark work of the Club, according to its detractors.

The Club's reputation for virulent population control began with its publication in 1972 of the wildly successful *Limits to Growth* by professors Donella H. Meadows, Dennis L. Meadows, Jørgen Randers, and William W. Behrens III. The book was translated into over 30 languages and sold over 12 million copies, making it the bestselling environmental tome in history. The essential conclusions of *Limits to Growth* were:

• If the present growth trends in world population, pollution, industrialization, food production and depletion of natural resources continue unabated, the limits to growth on this planet will be reached some time within the next 100 years. Some raw materials, such as copper and oil, would run out in the 1990s. In all likelihood, there will be a sudden and uncontrollable decline in both population and industrial capacity.

- Societal collapse can be avoided only by an immediate limit on population and pollution, as well as a cessation of economic growth.

In the furore the book created, "Neo-Malthusianism" was the least of the abuse directed at it, "Nazism" the frequent worst. The truth is that *Limits to Growth* was just plain wrong. The "systems dynamics" on which it computer-modelled the future was new and unreliable, and the proof was in our eating of the very resources *Limits to Growth* said would run out. Neither oil nor copper came to extinction in the 1990s.

Undeterred by its conspicuous failure, the Club has continued to prognosticate on all manner of human affairs. Recent titles issued by the Club include:

- *My Expectations for World Energy Dialogue*
- *Synergies between the Millennium Goals, the Global Marshall Plan, The EU Sustainable Development Strategy and The Lisbon Strategy*
- *The Role of Religion in Peacemaking*
- *The Sustainability Axiom in the Light of the World Culture*s

The founders of the Club of Rome were the Italian industrialist/ scholar Aurelio Peccei and the Scottish scientist Alexander King, who between them helmed the organization until 1990 when King retired (Peccei had died in 1984). King, a chemist with the Organization for Economic Cooperation and Development, has a footnote in science history for coining the name "DDT" for the chlorine compound used as an insecticide; he died in 2007, aged 98. The current president of the Club is HRH Prince El Hassan bin Talal of Amman (the author of all the zappily titled works above), and the other 100 members are a mix of C-list politicians and industrialists and, especially, academics. The second, associate tier of membership is no more inspiring.

Overseer of the New World Order? Suggestions that the Club of Rome holds such an exalted position in global affairs fall down on the significant fact that, in nearly 40 years, the Club has failed to achieve its alleged goal of removing "useless mouths" from the Earth. World population is increasing, not decreasing. Even *if* the Club were the shadowy cabal that controls human destiny, it is demonstrably useless at doing so. We can sleep easy in our beds.

The verdict? The worthies of the Club of Rome, like all members of elite think-tanks, have a self-regarding do-goodery, and seek back-door influence on institutions and nations. In a word, they're lobbyists.

> The Club of Rome seeks and oversees depopulation of the world: ALERT LEVEL 1

Further Reading
Anonymous, "Obituary: Alexander King", *The Daily Telegraph*, 26 March 2007
Alexander King, *Let the Cat Turn Round*, 2006

DOCUMENT: THE CLUB OF ROME'S DECLARATION OF INTENT

We, the members of the Club of Rome, are convinced that the future of humankind is not determined once and for all, and that it is possible to avoid present and foreseeable catastrophes – when they are the result of human selfishness or of mistakes made in managing world affairs. It is important to emphasize the signs of hope and the progress accomplished. We must also combat the threats to humankind, and be aware that these issues of survival are becoming ever more urgent.

The virtue of optimism that becomes rooted in the human spirit would appear to be an essential requirement of our times. We believe that, in order to counter the current trends towards either arrogant triumphalism or pessimism or resignation, we must adopt an attitude of confidence based on personal commitment and optimism, willingness and perseverance by all responsible citizens.

We believe that every human being can choose to take charge of his or her own future rather than be a victim of events. Imagination and creativity of every individual, combined with a greater sense of social responsibility, can contribute to changing our attitudes and making our societies better suited to cope with the multifaceted crises that trouble the world. We believe that the information society that is evolving, although it involves clear risks and constraints, offers considerable opportunities for building this better future.

The world is undergoing a period of unprecedented upheavals and fluctuations in its evolution into a global society for which people are not mentally prepared. As a result, their reaction is often negative, inspired by fear of the unknown and by unawareness of the global dimension of problems which seem no longer on a human scale. These fears, if not tackled, risk driving people to dangerous extremism, sterile nationalism and major social confrontations.

We do not know what this society will be like or how it will work. We must from now on learn to manage this period of fundamental transition, which may last several decades or become a permanent process, and prepare for a future in which humanity can develop in well-being and prosperity.

The times in which we live demand both individual and collective efforts to build systems and societies in which the human being, respect for others and compassion are key values; "competition" should be directed not to dominate and consume, but to stimulate and participate.

We must move towards a society that honours those who do the most to promote human happiness and well-being, not those who wield the greatest destructive power or indulge in the most profligate forms of consumption. Towards this end, education geared to the whole person, and to developing each individual's unique potential and abilities for the greater good of the community, acquires an ever more crucial role.

We believe in the need to stimulate general debates on the major issues that have global implications for all aspects of the human condition, taking a holistic approach that covers their moral, material, cultural, social and scientific aspects. To this end, we publish works that will encourage governments, international agencies, business leaders and non-governmental organizations, youth movements and the positive forces in societies throughout the world, to adopt policies and take strategic decisions that are appropriate to constantly changing circumstances. It is clear that public opinion must play an increasingly critical role in this growth of awareness.

We, the members of the Club of Rome, are one hundred individuals, at present drawn from 52 countries and five continents. We represent different educations, philosophies, religions and cultures; we have different professional backgrounds and expertises. Naturally we often have different visions of the future. Yet we are united by a common concern – the future of humankind – and we therefore study the major issues affecting the world which we all share.

For as long as each member of the Club of Rome is able to fulfil his or her responsibilities, each of us undertakes to devote a significant proportion of his or her time and talents to working on behalf of humankind, and in particular helping to build societies that are more humane, more sustainable, more equitable and more peaceful.

With a view to serving humanity, the Club of Rome wishes to strengthen its role as a catalyst of change and as a centre of innovation and initiative; it can do this thanks to its wealth of ideas and energies, to the diversity of its membership and the ability of its members to act acquired as a result of their past or present positions and experience.

We trust in the ultimate capacity of men and women to express and to live in accordance with their ethical and spiritual values, while respecting the diversity of humankind.

We call upon men and women of good will, especially the young people of today, to share with us this work of reflection and action.

COUNCIL ON FOREIGN RELATIONS

The Council on Foreign Relations is a secretive – its members would say "private" – think-tank of the masters of America. In the worst-case conspiracy scenario, the CFR is directly linked to the **Bilderberg Group**, the CIA and the UK's **Royal Institute of International Affairs** in a plot to instal the **New World Order**.

Founded in 1921, the remit of the Council is to debate and develop "American internationalism based on American interests". Although its proceedings are held *in camera*, its journal, *Foreign Affairs*, is publicly available, and has been contributed to by political figures as diverse as Russian premier Nikita Khrushchev and US national security adviser Henry Kissinger.

The Council on Foreign Relations does not deny that it seeks to influence the US elite, or that it embodies a good proportion of said elite. FBI boss John Foster Dulles was an early member, and the Andrew Carnegie Foundation its sometime banker. What *is* surprising about the Council is its agenda. Far from promoting the usual monetarist, hawkish fare typical of elite institutes, the Council's politics are decidedly liberal. The Council early denounced Adolf Hitler and was among the first influential think-tanks to allow black members.

> Cabal of capitalist one-worlders masquerades as US think-tank: ALERT LEVEL 3

Further Reading
James Perloff, *The Shadows of Power: The Council on Foreign Relations and American Decline*, 1985
Robin Ramsay, *Conspiracy Theories*, 2006
R. D. Schulzinger, *The Wise Men of Foreign Affairs*, 1984

CROP CIRCLES

A crop "circle" is a geometric pattern, often intricate, appearing in a field, usually a wheat field and usually in Britain. Evidence of crop circles is said to exist in the ancient folklore of Northern Europe, and a 1678 woodcut shows a "Mowing Devil" making a circle in a field of oats. The phenomenon, however, first came to widespread attention in the 1970s.

Conspiracy theorists believe the designs are messages from aliens, attempting to communicate with Earthlings via symbols; or maybe the patterns are made inadvertently by UFOs as they touch down. In either case, the government does not want you to know about it. You might panic. You might wonder what the aliens are doing here (see **Alien Abduction**).

Almost all crop circles are known to have been caused by pranksters. In 1991 UFOlogists and artists Doug Bower and David Chorley admitted to faking 250 circles in England, including the first to appear in the 1970s. To make the circles, they used their feet, string and a board. There remain a small number of puzzling circles in which the biological structure of the flattened plants has changed. Sometimes in these circles the local magnetic field appears to have been affected, resulting in electrical equipment failure, even in airplanes flying overhead.

Cerealogists (after Ceres, the Roman goddess of agriculture) speculate on a number of origins for these non-prankster circles. The favoured theories are that they are caused by eddies in the Earth's magnetic field or by "plasma vortices", mini-tornadoes

of electrically charged gas. The plasma vortices theory, propounded by meteorologist Dr Terence Meaden, would account
for the apparent heat burst in a crop circle which causes nodes
on affected plants to burst. Meaden also hypothesized that a
plasma vortex would create a whining sound. When, in 1991, a
couple claimed they'd been standing in the middle of a crop
circle as it formed, a whining sound is exactly what they said
they'd heard.

Crop circles are caused by aliens: ALERT LEVEL 4

Further Reading
Pat Delgado and Colin Andrews, *Circular Evidence*, 1989
Jim Schnabel, *Round in Circles: Physicists, Poltergeists, Prank-
sters and the Secret History of the Cropwatchers*, 1994

DEAD SEA SCROLLS

In early 1947, near Qumran on the north-west shore of the Dead Sea, a Bedouin herder named Mohammed Ahmed el-Hamed (or el-Dhib, "the Wolf") tossed a stone into a cave in an attempt to flush out a missing goat. To his surprise there came back not the bleat of a goat but the sound of pottery breaking. Entering the cave, he found an ancient jar containing scrolls wrapped in linen. Later, through the offices of a local cobbler and antiquities dealer, Khalil Eskander Shahin ("Kando"), el-Dhib managed to sell some of the scrolls he'd discovered, and word slowly spread about the discoveries in the desert. The first archaeological excavations took place in February 1949. In 1952, another series of caves was found, and eventually over 800 scrolls were recovered from 11 caves around Wadi Qumran. The scrolls – many of which exist only as fragments – include versions of all but one book of the Old Testament, along with Biblical commentaries, non-Biblical texts on religious conduct, and oddities such as the Copper Scroll, which lists the hiding places for treasure in Israel. Mostly written in Hebrew, the Dead Sea Scrolls have been carbon-dated to as early as 200 BC. The scrolls thus include the earliest edition of the Bible; before Mohammed el-Dhib tossed his stone into that cave, the oldest known Bible was the Ben Asher text, written in AD 1008.

Most of the discovered scrolls were published promptly, the notable exception being the scrolls and fragments found in Cave 4, which represented nearly 40 per cent of the total Qumran material. The publication of the Cave 4 documents was entrusted to an "International Team" led by Father Roland de Vaux, a Domincan scholar from Jerusalem, and all others were barred from even viewing the material by the so-called "secrecy rule". Even after de Vaux's death in 1971, his successors repeatedly refused to allow publication even of photographs of the Cave 4 finds. Speculation began that the "International Team", predominantly Catholic, had found something in the Cave 4 that it sought to hide. Fanning the fires of surmise were the academics Andre Dupont-Sommer and John Allegro, who noted that the "Teacher of Righteousness" described in some of the Qumran documents strangely paralleled Jesus the Messiah. Then Professor Robert Eisenman, another Scrolls scholar, pumped pure oxygen into the blazing speculations: he mooted that the "Teacher of Righteousness" was actually James, Jesus's brother, and that *James* was the true founder of Christianity. Paul (Saul), in Eisenman's theory, was a Roman fink seeking to bring James's true Word into disrepute.

All the Dead Sea Scrolls controversy needed in order to flare up into a full-scale conspiracy theory was a couple of savvy writers on the look-out for a religious story to follow their hit book *Holy Blood, Holy Grail*. In *The Dead Sea Scrolls Deception* (1991) journalists Michael Baigent and Richard Leigh energetically purpled up the musings of Dupont-Sommer, Allegro and Eisenman into the theory that de Vaux was a Vatican fixer who sought to bury (literally) texts found in Cave 4 which proved that Jesus's life was mythicized by Paul, a Roman agent who faked his "conversion" in order to undermine anti-Roman messianic cults. *The Dead Sea Scrolls Deception*, in other words, suggested that the Vatican, Paul's church, was illegitimate – and that Christianity pre-dated Christ. Small wonder, if this were true, that de Vaux worked overtime in Cave 4 burying the evidence. Baigent and Leigh's book became a bestseller.

Among Old Testament scholars there was no consensus on the Qumran documents. Some believed them to have been produced on site by a Jewish apocalyptic cult, the Essenes, while Karl Rengstorf of the University of Munster asserted that the Qumran scrolls had been taken from the Jewish temple in Jerusalem for safekeeping during the siege of AD 67–70, a view supported by Professor Norman Golb of Chicago. In a sense the strength of Baigent and Leigh's case was the weakness and uncertainty of the alternatives.

Even on its publication, however, *The Dead Sea Scrolls Deception* looked a shaky proposition, and time has tumbled it to ruin. Far from being a Vatican hit-squad, the "International Team" comprised scholars of several Christian denominations, one of whom, Millar Burrows, wrote:

> It is quite true that as a liberal Protestant I do not share all the beliefs of my more conservative brethren. It is my considered conclusion, however, that if one will go through any of the historic statements of Christian faith he will find nothing that has been or can be disproved by the Dead Sea Scrolls. This is as true of things that I myself do not believe as it is of my most firm and cherished convictions. If I were so rash as to undertake a theological debate with a professor from either the Moody Bible Institute or Fordham University [a Catholic University] – which God forbid – I fear I should find no ammunition in the Dead Sea Scrolls to use against them.

Repeated carbon testing of the scrolls dates them to the last two centuries BC, a dating which agrees with archaeological and palaeographic evidence. Unless all the carbon-testing machines used have faulty meters, or the test results were faked, the scrolls pre-date Christ and have no bearing on the foundation of Christianity at all.

In the same year that *The Dead Sea Deception* hit the shelves, so began the publishing of *all* the scrolls so far found – and the claim that the Vatican was suppressing controversial scrolls was dealt a sledgehammer blow. The delay in publishing the contents of Cave 4 was largely due to innocent factors. As Florentino Garcia Martinez and Julio Trebolle Barrera write in *The People of the Dead Sea Scrolls, Their Writings, Beliefs and Practices*:

The real explanations for the delay in the publication of the texts are many and varied. The war, a tangled political situation and the premature death of the first two directors of the editorial project (Roland de Vaux and Pierre Benoit); also, several of the editors (Patrick Skehan, Yigael Yadin and Jean Starky) died before finishing their work. These are some of the factors which have influenced the present situation. However, the most important factor is the actual condition of the still unpublished texts, hundreds of minute fragments, with pathetic remains of incomplete works.

When the texts in question have been preserved in relatively large fragments, the task of reading, translation and interpretation is not extremely complicated. Even texts previously unknown can be published with relative speed. However, even in such cases, the speed of publication can have disastrous results, as the publication of the first set of texts from Cave 4 proves. Their publication in the official series, under John Allegro, appeared with great speed in 1968. However, this hasty edition (of only 90 pages of text) is so flawed that it cannot be used without the corrections (of over 100 pages) published in 1971 by the later director of the international team for the edition of the texts, John Strugnell, of the University of Harvard.

Martinez and Barrera might have added that academic jealousies also played their role in delay. At one juncture a dispute over which academic team had the right to publish went to court.

Debate over whether the Essenes authored the Dead Sea Scrolls still continues, warmed by archaeological evidence found in 2004, but few outside Baigent and Leigh's publishing house continue to seriously suggest that the Vatican has hidden scrolls damaging to its faith. The Dead Sea Scrolls is one alleged cover-up that can have the last rites read over it.

The Vatican suppressed Dead Sea Scrolls which rocked the
foundations of the Catholic faith: ALERT LEVEL 1

Further Reading

John Allegro, "The Untold Story of the Dead Sea Scrolls",
Harper's, August 1966

Michael Baigent and Richard Leigh, *The Dead Sea Scrolls
Deception: Why a Handful of Religious Scholars Conspired
to Suppress the Revolutionary Contents of the Dead Sea Scrolls*,
1991

Robert Eisenman and Michael Wise, *The Dead Sea Scrolls
Uncovered: The First Complete Translation and Interpretation
of 50 Key Documents Withheld for over 35 Years*, 1992

Florentino Garcia Martinez and Julio Trebolle Barrera, *The
People of the Dead Sea Scrolls, Their Writings, Beliefs and
Practices*, tr Wilfred G. E. Watson, 1995

DIANA, PRINCESS OF WALES

It was news that shocked the world. In the early hours (GMT) of Sunday 31 August 1997, reports started coming from Paris that Diana, Princess of Wales, had been injured in a car accident. Then came updates reporting she was dead. Also killed in the car crash in the tunnel beneath Pont de l'Alma were Diana's lover, Dodi Al-Fayed, and the driver, Henri Paul. Dodi's bodyguard, Trevor Rees-Jones, was seriously injured.

The cause of the crash seemed clear. Chased by paparazzi on motorcycles, Paul had driven too fast – 75 mph (120kph) according to one French police estimate – into the tunnel, clipped a white Fiat Uno and, in overcorrecting, had swerved the Mercedes S280 into the thirteenth pillar. There were also reports that he had been drinking. None of the occupants had been wearing seatbelts.

Autumn seemed to come early to Britain that year, as a stunned nation shed tears for "the Queen of Hearts". As the sorrow subsided, people began to wonder how the female icon of the latter half of the 20th century, the most famous and photographed woman on the planet, could have died in something so mundane as a car crash.

Perhaps, people began to say, it wasn't an accident. The loudest voice of suspicion belonged to Dodi's father, Mohamed Al-Fayed, the owner of the Harrods department store. According to Al-Fayed, Diana and his son were assassinated. Al-Fayed even named the guilty party: Prince Philip of the **British Royal**

Family. Naturally, Philip didn't dirty his hands personally – he ordered the security service MI6 to carry out the hit on his 36-year-old daughter-in-law. There are legion other Diana conspiracies (it was the IRA whatdunnit, it was *Le Cercle* who sponsored her death because of her opposition to wealth-generating landmines, she was a ritual sacrifice by Satanists, she faked her death to live a paparazzi-free life . . .) but Al-Fayed's retains the pole position.

In his view, the British Royal Family needed Diana eliminated because she had become pregnant by Dodi and intended to marry him. Their child would be a Muslim half-brother to the second and third in line to throne, an impossible embarrassment to the white, Anglican Windsors. Al-Fayed claims that Diana told him personally that her life had been threatened. "The person who is spearheading these threats," she said, "is Prince Philip." Diana also told a number of other people that she feared for her life. In his account of life as Diana's butler, *A Royal Duty* (2003), Paul Burrell recorded that ten months before her death she wrote to him claiming that "XXXX is planning an 'accident' in my car, brake failure and serious head injury in order to make the path clear for Charles to marry." She also told her voice coach Peter Settelen that she thought that her former lover, bodyguard Barry Mannakee, had been murdered in a faked motorcycle crash. Evidently, Diana had concerns over safety. And the Windsors had a motive of sorts.

Suddenly, it wasn't only Al-Fayed raising questions about the crash in the tunnel under Pont de l'Alma. Why had the lights and security cameras in the tunnel been turned off just before the crash? Why did the ambulance take 43 minutes to get Diana to Pitie-Salpetriere hospital? Why had her body been embalmed before a proper autopsy could be undertaken? Why had the crash site been cleansed and disinfected before a forensic examination could be carried out? And where was the driver of the white Fiat Uno? Wasn't it too convenient that Rees-Jones had "no memory" of the crash?

Then a former MI6 agent, Richard Tomlinson, revealed that MI6 had been planning an assassination at the time of Diana's death. In a sworn affidavit Tomlinson stated that MI6's Balkans operations officer had shown him the service's plan to assassinate Slobodan Milosevic, the Serbian president, in a car crash . . . in a tunnel. Tomlinson stated that MI6's planned assassination of Milosevic showed "remarkable similarities to the circumstances and witness accounts of the crash that killed the Princess of Wales, Dodi Al-Fayed, and Henri Paul". How had MI6 caused the car to crash? Possibly, suggested Tomlinson, with a disorientating strobe light held by an operative in the tunnel, or by another car forcing the Mercedes into the pillar. There were rumours that Henri Paul was a CIA/DGSE/MI6 agent and had deliberately taken the roundabout Pont de l'Alma route to the Al-Fayeds' Paris flat to get Diana into the killing zone. (If Paul was a spook this might explain, people said, the series of 40,000-franc deposits in his bank account.) A more far-fetched suggestion was that Rees-Jones, a former paratrooper, wrenched the wheel from Paul's grasp. Suspicions of a cover-up mushroomed when the body of James Andanson was found in a burnt-out car in 2000. Andanson, a paparazzo, had owned a white Fiat Uno three years before and had been investigated by the French police. There was a final oddity: just after Andanson's death his office was burgled. Meanwhile, an investigation by French forensic specialists found no significant mechanical faults in the Mercedes S280, ruling out the possibility that the crash had been caused by some internal failure.

So far, so bad for the Windsors. Yet Al-Fayed's case has a number of weaknesses:

- The only source for the story that Dodi and Diana were to be married, and that an engagement ring had been bought from Repossi in Paris, is Al-Fayed himself.
- Despite a multi-million-pound personal investigation, Al-Fayed has been unable to establish any link between Prince Philip and MI6.
- Although Diana reportedly told Frederic Mailliez, the off-duty doctor who first attended her in the Pont de l'Alma tunnel, that she was pregnant, the only other evidence of pregnancy came

from an anonymous French policeman who said he had the papers to prove this but to date has not made these public. By contrast, scientific tests carried out on Diana's pre-transfusion blood have shown no evidence of pregnancy. Myriah Daniels, a holistic healer who travelled with Dodi and Diana on their cruise aboard the *Jonikal* yacht at the end of August 1997, stated:

> I can say with one hundred per cent certainty that she was not pregnant. I will explain how I can be so sure of this fact. Firstly, she told me herself that she was not pregnant. Secondly . . . It is incomprehensible to me that Diana would have allowed me to carry out such an invasive treatment [massage] on her stomach and intestines if she thought she was pregnant.

- The Operation Paget Inquiry (see below) was given access to MI6 to investigate Tomlinson's claims. The inquiry tracked down the assassination plan he referred to and found the target to be not Slobodan Milosevic but another Serbian figure. Since it is against British government policy to carry out assassinations, the memo's author was disciplined. Tomlinson admitted this memo was the one he was referring to in his claim.
- Given the long-standing antipathy between France and Britain, why would the French police/security services collude in the conspiracy to kill Diana?
- In December 2006 the *Independent* newspaper stated there were at least 14 CCTV cameras in the Pont de l'Alma tunnel, yet none recorded footage of the fatal collision. Mohamed Al-Fayed has also raised the absence of CCTV images of the Mercedes' journey on the fateful night as evidence of conspiracy. A Brigade Criminelle investigation, however, found only 10 CCTV cameras along the route, and it was for a quite simple reason that none had relevant images: they were security cameras on buildings and were pointed at those buildings' exits and entrances. Inside the Alma underpass there was one camera, which was under the control of the Compagnie de Circulation Urbaines de Paris (Paris Urban Traffic Unit). The CCUP closed down at 11 p.m. and made no recordings after that time.

* The lengthy "43-minute" ambulance journey of Diana from the Pont de l'Alma tunnel to hospital was no such thing, taking from 1.41 to 2.06. The SAMU ambulance did admittedly stop en route for 10 minutes, but that was because the accompanying doctor needed the ambulance to be stationary while he gave Diana blood-pressure treatment. The ambulance did not go to the Hotel Dieu, the nearest hospital to the crash scene, because Pitie-Salpetriere was the main centre for multiple trauma cases.

* Fayed challenged the French investigators' conclusion that Henri Paul was drunk (with an alcohol level three times the legal limit) on the evening of the tragedy; his bearing, as captured on the Ritz hotel CCTV that evening, showed a man apparently sober. There were also suggestions that the blood samples tested belonged not to Henri but to another subject. There certainly seem to have been irregularities in the report of French forensic pathologist Dominique Lecomte, but in December 2006 DNA testing confirmed that the blood samples showing a level of alcohol in excess of legal limits did indeed belong to Paul.

Al-Fayed nonetheless maintained that his son and Diana died as the result of a vast conspiracy by the Royal Family and MI6. In response, the coroner of the royal household requested Lord Stevens, a former chief of the Metropolitan Police, to head an investigation into the deaths. The subsequent "Operation Paget" agreed that some questions asked by Al-Fayed were "right to be raised" and confirmed that Paul had been a low-level informer for the French domestic secret service, DST. The Operation Paget report also pointed out that hotel security staff the world over act as low-grade informers for their national spy organizations.

Essentially, the Operation Paget report came to the same conclusion as had the French inquiry into the tragedy. Mme Coujard, the prosecutor heading the French inquiry, determined: "The direct cause of the accident is the presence, at the wheel of the Mercedes S280, of a driver who had consumed a considerable amount of alcohol, combined with . . . medication, driving at a speed . . . faster than the maximum speed-limit in built-up areas."

In 2007 Mohamed Al-Fayed forced an inquest into the deaths of Dodi and Diana. At the time of going to press the inquest is ongoing, but its conclusion is unlikely to differ from those of previous investigations. It too will almost certainly be accused by Al-Fayed of being part of the cover-up.

There may be an innocuous reason for the serially identical conclusions: they are correct and the goddess-like Diana suffered the fate of many poor mortals. She was killed by a drunk driver.

> Prince Philip and MI6 assassinated Diana, Princess of Wales: ALERT LEVEL 4

Further Reading
Noel Botham, *The Assassination of Princess Diana*, 2004
Peter Hounam and Derek McAdam, *Who Killed Diana?*, 1998
Trevor Rees-Jones and Moira Johnston, *The Bodyguard's Story: Diana, the Crash, and the Sole Survivor*, 2000

DOCUMENT: OPERATION PAGET REPORT OVERVIEW, DECEMBER 2006

In January 2004, as Commissioner for the Metropolitan Police Service, I was asked by the Coroner of the Queen's Household and the County of Surrey, Mr Michael Burgess, to investigate a number of matters surrounding the car crash in Paris on 31 August 1997 in which Diana, Princess of Wales, Mr Dodi Al-Fayed and Mr Henri Paul died and Mr Trevor Rees-Jones was seriously injured. The Operation Paget report of that investigation, which has been wide-ranging and thorough, will, I hope, assist the present Coroner in charge of the case, Lady Elizabeth Butler-Sloss, to decide the scope of her inquests. This overview addresses the key issues that have emerged from what has been a most complex and challenging investigation.

The nature of this investigation has been unprecedented. I decided that only a thorough, methodical and detailed investigation would answer these extremely serious allegations. A dedicated team of New Scotland Yard Detectives from the Metropolitan Police Specialist Crime Directorate has worked on the case from the moment I took charge of the investigation. I want to thank them all for their dedication, especially the Senior Investigating Officer and his deputy.

Scope of the investigation
Together, we have examined and taken account of the French investigation but it has not been our role to pass judgment on French procedures and processes. I do, however, recognize that there are differences in the two systems. I must also make it clear that it is not our role to prejudge those matters that will be heard in the Coroner's court. It is for Lady Butler-Sloss to decide the questions of who the deceased were, and where, when and how they died.

The primary purpose of the investigation has been to

assess whether there is any credible evidence to support an allegation of conspiracy to murder.

Much has been written about the circumstances leading up to the crash and the effectiveness of the French investigation that followed. We have been acutely aware of the responsibility placed upon us to approach this investigation with an open mind and to ensure that the outcome was not predetermined.

This inquiry has largely concentrated on a number of separate claims made by Mr Mohamed Al-Fayed and his legal team in documents and public appearances over the nine years since the crash. At the heart of Mr Al-Fayed's allegation is his belief that the crash was not an accident but murder. Furthermore, that this murder was the result of a conspiracy by the "Establishment" and, in particular, by HRH Prince Philip and the Security and Intelligence Services because of the relationship between Mr Dodi Al-Fayed and the Princess of Wales. Mr Al-Fayed and his legal team have also expressed concern that the investigation, by the French authorities, was carried out in such a way as to prevent the truth from emerging.

I have personally ensured that every reasonable line of enquiry has been undertaken in order to evaluate fully any evidence that might support this extremely serious allegation.

We have had excellent cooperation from the French authorities throughout. They have shared the dossier containing the findings of their enquiries to date, carried out enquiries on our behalf, given us exhibits and provided much other practical support to my team. Our understanding of the French enquiry has led us to draw two principal conclusions. First, the differences in procedures between the French and English legal systems in themselves provide answers to some of Mr Al-Fayed's questions. Second, Mr Al-Fayed has brought to our attention his concerns about the French investigation and some of these have received wide publicity. They do not alter our conclusions in any way.

Representatives from Government, including the Secret Intelligence Service and the Security Service, have all given me their full cooperation and assistance, whether or not allegations were specifically made against their organizations. Some of these allegations of conspiracy to murder have been made against named individuals in the full glare of publicity. Myself and the two senior members of the team have personally examined MI5 and MI6 records. We have had unprecedented access to everything we wished to examine. We have contacted the American intelligence services and they have assured us that they have no relevant information that will in any way affect my conclusions. I am satisfied that no attempt has been made to hold back information. We are confident that the allegations made are unfounded. The relevant issues are detailed in the report.

I have been in communication with HRH Prince Philip, HRH Prince Charles, and HRH Prince William. I have spoken with Prince Charles and I have corresponded with Prince Philip and Prince William. I have always said that the direction of the investigation would be governed by the evidence. I have seen nothing that would justify further enquiries with any member of the Royal Family.

I know that this report will be the subject of closer scrutiny than anything I have done before and people may continue to raise issues – it is inevitable. However, that has not stopped the Metropolitan Police from taking the exceptional step of publishing this report. Not only do we believe that it is the right thing to do, but we also believe that the public should have the opportunity to view the investigation in its entirety. This will allow for properly informed debate about the evidence rather than discussions based on theory and speculation.

Scale and nature of the investigation

The team has interviewed over 300 witnesses, some for the first time. They have carried out over 500 actions and collected more than 600 exhibits. They have gone wherever necessary in order to pursue their enquiries. More than twenty International Letters of Request have been submitted to the French authorities. These enquiries, however, have not been carried out in order to re-investigate the French enquiry. The team has scrutinized all the statements taken from eyewitnesses at the time in order to assess if there was any possible evidence that might inform the investigation. They have not re-interviewed these witnesses. They did, however, manage to locate and interview two new eyewitnesses and full accounts have been taken from them. The evidence they provide has further informed our assessment.

Eyewitness accounts taken in France were done in accordance with the French legislation and procedures. The French authorities considered that after this length of time and so much media coverage, the proper place for these accounts to be heard was at the inquests. Many of these witnesses have agreed to attend. Both Coroners, Michael Burgess and Lady Elizabeth Butler-Sloss, have agreed that this is the correct and most appropriate course of action. I agree.

The recollections of eyewitnesses, so many years after such a fleeting and traumatic event, have to be dealt with very carefully. We have included in our report extracts from a very informative analysis by a respected psychologist. He explains these issues in detail. His full report will be made available to the inquests.

The team has drawn, during the course of the investigation, on some of the finest independent experts. We would like, in particular, to thank two of them who have been with us throughout the investigation:

- Professor Robert FORREST, is a Consultant in Clinical Chemistry and Toxicology. He has provided expert opinion concerning the analysis of Henri Paul's post-mortem samples.
- Dr Richard SHEPHERD, is a Consultant Forensic Pathologist and Home Office Pathologist. He has given me his expert opinion on the medical condition and injuries of the Princess of Wales, Dodi Al-Fayed and Henri Paul following the collision.

The team has taken advantage of the latest forensic and technical developments in the years since the crash. In February 2005 we, together with the French Judiciary and Police, carried out what I believe is the largest and most comprehensive survey and reconstruction of the scene of an incident ever. We used the specialist skills of surveyors, photographers and computer modellers to collect data from 186 million points and reproduce the scene of the crash and surrounding area to within an accuracy of one centimetre. This three-dimensional model and a validated model of the Mercedes were used by the world-renowned Transport Research Laboratory to simulate and recreate the crash.

This groundbreaking work has been of crucial importance in reaching our conclusions. It will be available for the Coroner to consider at the inquests and will be, I hope, of lasting benefit to many other future investigations, whether in the United Kingdom or overseas.

Since 1997 Mr Mohamed Al-Fayed has also employed a number of experts. They too are eminent in their respective fields. I am most grateful to him for the many questions he and they have raised and for the information they have provided to the investigation. Mr Al-Fayed has kindly made many of their reports available to the team and we have included a great deal of their content in the report. My team and the experts we have employed have met Mr Al-Fayed's experts and I have encouraged constant dialogue between them at all times.

The findings of the investigation

Our investigation into the overall allegation of conspiracy to murder has examined the following key areas: the motive for the alleged murder, and the opportunity and capability to carry it out.

Our conclusion is that, on all the evidence available at this time, there was no conspiracy to murder any of the occupants of the car. This was a tragic accident.

Motive

I and the team have spoken to people about sensitive matters, some of a deeply personal nature. We have spoken to close relatives, friends and the doctor of the Princess of Wales. All were very willing to help me in any way they could. I am most grateful for their cooperation and assistance.

We are not prepared to go into detail as much of what we have been told was on the understanding that it would be accorded proper sensitivity. However, we are certain that the Princess of Wales was not pregnant at the time of her death. Our conclusions were strengthened by forensic tests carried out on blood recovered from the Mercedes car.

From the evidence of her close friends and associates, she was not engaged and she was not about to get engaged.

Opportunity and capability

To stage an accident in order to murder the occupants of the car would in my opinion require careful, meticulous and coordinated planning. The team carried out a detailed and thorough investigation of the events leading up to the collision; from the very first beginnings of the relationship between the Princess of Wales and Mr Dodi Al-Fayed in St Tropez in July 1997, to the particular sequence of events which took place a few weeks later in Paris on the evening of 30 August 1997. The paparazzi were intent on following their every move from the moment they knew of the relationship and were aware of their plans to travel to Paris on Saturday

30 August 1997. Having been informed by contacts, they were waiting for them at the airport and followed them to the Ritz Hotel.

At 7 p.m. that evening Dodi Al-Fayed and the Princess of Wales left the Ritz Hotel to go to Dodi Al-Fayed's apartment in rue Arsene Houssaye. They had no intention of returning to the Ritz Hotel that night. We are also certain that Henri Paul had no intention of returning to the Ritz Hotel after he went off duty shortly after their departure. For a number of reasons the plans of all three individuals changed. The Princess of Wales and Dodi Al-Fayed had planned to dine at a well-known Paris restaurant and at about 9.40 p.m. they were being driven there. It was because of the attention of the paparazzi during this journey that Dodi Al-Fayed instructed his chauffeur to drive instead to the Ritz Hotel. They arrived there at 9.50 p.m. This was unexpected and consequently the night duty security officer called Henri Paul's mobile telephone and told him of their arrival. Henri Paul apparently expressed surprise but immediately returned to the hotel. All of the evidence we have examined indicates that this was entirely in keeping with Henri Paul's conscientious approach to his work.

Much has been made of Henri Paul's "missing three hours" between leaving the Ritz Hotel and returning on that Saturday evening. No one can be sure exactly where he was during those three hours, but it is clear that, until he was telephoned at 10 p.m. by the Ritz Hotel night duty security officer, he cannot have known that he would be returning to the Ritz Hotel and nor did anyone else.

Once back at the Ritz Hotel, Dodi Al-Fayed had a conversation with his father. Mohamed Al-Fayed recalls that Dodi informed him of his wish to return to the apartment in rue Arsene Houssaye in order to present the Princess of Wales with an engagement ring. Dodi Al-Fayed had purchased a ring for her that afternoon from Repossi Jewellers. The Princess of Wales was not with him at that time and we believe she never saw that ring. I do not know whether Dodi was going to ask her to marry him that night. I cannot say what the Princess of Wales' response would have been. However, we have spoken to many of her family and closest friends and none of them has indicated to us that she was either about to or wished to get engaged. Her last conversations with friends and confidantes were to the contrary. Prince William has confirmed to me that his mother had not given him the slightest indication about such plans for the future.

At around 10.20 p.m. Dodi Al-Fayed passed a message to Henri Paul through the night duty manager. Another car would now be required to take the couple back to his apartment in rue Arsene Houssaye. This car was to depart from the rear of the Ritz Hotel.

The car, the driver and the point of departure all therefore changed within a very short space of time. This left no opportunity, in my opinion, for anyone to put into action any plan, particularly one that would have required so much preparation and so many people to effect it.

At around 12.20 a.m. on Sunday 31 August 1997 the Princess of Wales, Dodi Al-Fayed and Trevor Rees-Jones left the Ritz Hotel in a Mercedes driven by Henri Paul. As we now know, Dodi's chauffeur-driven car and backup vehicle were to depart from the front of the hotel shortly afterwards.

The French investigation traced and identified many eyewitnesses, including drivers and their vehicles. There may be other eyewitnesses who have not come forward but I am confident that, on the evidence we have, a full and comprehensive picture of events can be constructed.

We know that the car travelled at excessive speed during the final part of the journey while again being followed by the paparazzi. We know the route it took. We can say with certainty that the car hit the kerb just before the thirteenth pillar of the central reservation in the Alma underpass, at a speed of 61 to 63 miles per hour. This is about twice the speed limit on that section of road. What exactly happened at the end of that journey is a matter for the inquests to decide. However, we conclude that nothing in the very rapid sequence of events we have reconstructed supports the allegation of conspiracy to murder. In particular, following the work done by police collision investigators and other experts, we are confident that any theories concerning flashing lights inside the Alma underpass can be discounted as the cause of this crash.

The Fiat Uno
We believe there was a glancing contact between the Mercedes, driven by Henri Paul, and a white Fiat Uno just before the Alma underpass. Much has been made of a French photojournalist, Mr James Andanson. It has been alleged that he was the driver of the Fiat Uno and an agent of the security services.

We are completely satisfied that this Fiat Uno did not belong to James Andanson, nor was it driven by him that night. James Andanson committed suicide in May 2000 and shortly afterwards the photographic offices he shared in Paris were burgled. The French conducted a full investigation into his death and we agree with their conclusion that James Andanson took his own life. Despite claims to the contrary, the burglary was fully investigated and known professional criminals arrested. There is no evidence that James Andanson was an agent of any security service.

In August 1997, James Andanson did own a white Fiat Uno, a popular make and model of car at that time. However, it was nine years old, in a state of disrepair, had been driven over 360,000 kms and was registered in his own name. He openly part-exchanged the car for a Fiat Punto at a local garage later that year. James Andanson's widow has given the team her full cooperation and assistance, for which I am grateful. We are satisfied James Andanson was at home with his wife on the night of Saturday 30 August 1997, before flying to Corsica on a photographic assignment the following morning.

Who was driving the white Fiat Uno and why they did not come forward are questions we have considered. The French investigation carried out a major search for the Fiat Uno but could not locate the car. After this length of time it is very unlikely that we shall do so. Failing to render assistance to a person in danger is an imprisonable offence in French law. This may have deterred witnesses from coming forward and giving their account.

After the accident
We are convinced that the French authorities took all reasonable steps to save the lives of those involved in the accident. We have seen the surgeons and medical staff who worked so hard that night to try to save the lives of those involved in the crash. I believe they did everything humanly possible to do that. Much has been said about the embalming of the body of the Princess of Wales and that this formed some part of the conspiracy. We have found the explanation for this and understand why it was done. Again the details are in the report.

It is clear that the Mercedes was travelling at excessive speed as it approached the Alma underpass. Henri Paul had consumed alcohol that evening. After returning to the Ritz Hotel he drank two Ricards in the Bar Vendome. This alone would have given him an alcohol level near to the French drink/driving limit, which is lower than the limit in this country. When Henri Paul returned, he could not have known he would be driving the Princess of Wales and Dodi Al-Fayed later that night. On the CCTV he does appear to be walking round the hotel normally but the tests on the forensic samples taken at both his post-mortem examinations show him to have had an alcohol level of around 1.74 grams per litre at the time of the crash – this is around twice the British drink/drive limit. We are satisfied from the DNA testing carried out on samples in France and by experts in the United Kingdom that those blood samples tested belonged to Henri Paul. Henri Paul had been drinking, but how much he had consumed is questionable. There has also been speculation surrounding the abnormal levels of carboxyhaemoglobin in Henri Paul's blood. The team, after meticulous research, has identified an explanation for this high reading. This information was shared with Mohamed Al-Fayed's team. It concerns how and from where the sample was taken and we have worked together to find an answer.

Conclusion
I have no doubt that speculation as to what happened that night will continue and that there are some matters, as in many other investigations, about which we may never find a definitive answer. However, I do not believe that any evidence currently exists that can substantiate the allegation of conspiracy to murder that has been made. Various legal cases are currently being pursued by Mr Al-Fayed through the French courts. They are unlikely, in my opinion, to have any bearing on my conclusion that there was no conspiracy or cover-up.

Three people tragically lost their lives in the accident and one was seriously injured. Many more have suffered from the intense scrutiny, speculation and misinformed judgments in the years that have followed. I very much hope that all the work we have done and the publication of this report will help to bring some closure to all who continue to mourn the deaths of Diana, Princess of Wales, Dodi Al-Fayed and Henri Paul.

FACE ON MARS

Humans are gregarious creatures, so it's no wonder we're uncomfortable with the idea of being all alone in the universe. Science has yet to conclusively prove that we are other than an insignificant anomaly in the grand scheme of things, so we can't be blamed for getting a little bit excited when what seems to be proof of the existence of neighbourhood aliens comes along.

On 25 July 1976 the craft *Viking Orbiter 1* was busy acquiring images of the Cydonia region of Mars in search of potential landing sites for *Viking Lander 2*. Its pictures of the Martian landscape revealed exciting geological formations, a mixture of plains and mesas and buttes (large rocky outcrops familiar in the American Southwest), but what the NASA scientists could not have expected to see was a giant face staring back at them from the planet's surface.

The photograph was not released immediately as the scientists believed it was nothing but an amusing coincidence. It was not until the image was "rediscovered" by Vincent DiPietro and Gregory Molenaar, two engineers at the Goddard Spaceflight Center, that the rest of the world had the opportunity to view this remarkable phenomenon.

The grainy images appeared to show a humanoid face with a deep-set eye socket, a narrow nose and half of a thin, unsmiling mouth. Deep shadows obscured the other half of the face but to the viewer the features appeared to be perfectly symmetrical. The structure itself was over 1.5 miles long by 1 mile wide by

1,500 feet high (2.5km x 1.6km x 0.45km), far larger than anything built on earth. Nevertheless, once the photograph was broadcast, people quickly identified a resemblance between the Martian face and those of ancient Egyptian pharaohs or of the Sphinx at Giza. NASA, however, stolidly maintained that it was by mere chance this particular hill resembled a face, and attempted to downplay the whole matter.

Those who believed the hill was artificial began to look for other clues to support their hypothesis. One was Richard C. Hoagland, a regular science correspondent on a radio talk show in Florida, who became convinced that the Face was part of a complex of other structures visible in the *Viking* pictures, including a "fortress", an artificial "cliff", a five-sided "pyramid" and a collection of rocky forms dubbed "The City Square". He went on to write a book about the subject and began a campaign to force NASA to admit that it was covering up the true nature of the discoveries. Debate began to rage about who could have built the monuments. Given the resemblances to Egyptian architecture, had a race of long-dead Martians visited the earth and constructed similar monuments? – a view that seemed to jibe nicely for those who had always maintained aliens had a hand in the building of the Pyramids. And, if the aliens had achieved that, what else could they have been responsible for? Where had human civilization – or, more dramatic still, human life – really begun? The implications for human history seemed enormous, and yet the scientific community continued to refuse to take the issue seriously. It seemed the scientists had a vested interest in keeping the Martian-civilization theory under wraps.

The suspicion of a cover-up appeared to be confirmed when NASA announced the launch of a second reconnaissance mission to Mars, this time with a camera aboard capable of taking high-resolution photographs that could pick out objects the size of a small airplane clearly on the planet's surface . . . but that the Face would not be one of them. NASA argued it had more pressing scientific priorities elsewhere and time on the camera was limited. It was soon forced by public outcry to reconsider its plans. The Face had been capturing people's imagination for over 20 years, and they wanted to know once and for all whether it was artificial. NASA backed down, and on 5 April 1998 the Mars Orbiter Camera re-photographed the Face.

Anti-climactically, the new pictures confirmed what scientists had been saying all along: the Face was just a lumpy, rather uninteresting hill. In the new photos there was no sign of any facial features at all. "All of its dimensions, in fact, are similar to other mesas. It's not exotic in any way," commented Jim Garvin, a NASA Mars scientist.

The believers in sentient life on Mars did not give up their dream so easily, however. The camera had taken the pictures during the Martian winter, they said; wispy cloud was obscuring the detail and making the image appear unnaturally flat. Not only that, NASA had doctored the photos to cover up the presence of an alien civilization on Mars. Once again NASA bowed to public pressure and a second pass was made over the Cydonia region in April 2001, this time during the Martian summer. These photographs appear startlingly clear, considering the distance from which they are taken, and once again show an ordinary mesa formation, complete with fissures and cracks, and no symmetrical features at all. This conclusion was backed up by evidence from the Mars Global Surveyor's onboard laser altimetry equipment, capable of measuring planetary features to within a foot (30cm), which delineated a rocky outcrop and not an alien-made structure. The same was true of other features such as the "cliff" and the "pyramid", and the whole mystery dissolved.

It's very hard to release an idea that's consumed you for a quarter of a century, and the Martian conspiracy theorists carry on regardless. Some are claiming the Face can still be clearly seen if only it is subjected to enough image processing. Others say NASA has released fake pictures in order to keep the uncomfortable knowledge of Martian life a secret. The rest of the world has quietly forgotten the Face.

Face on Mars: Has NASA covered up proof of life on the red planet? ALERT LEVEL 2

Further Reading

Richard C. Hoagland, *The Monuments of Mars: A City on the Edge of Forever*, 1987 (and various subsequent expansions)

http://www.nasa.gov – The Face on Mars

www.msss.com/education/facepage/face.html

http://metasearch.org/solar%20system/cydonia/proof_files/proof.asp

www.badastronomy.com/bad/misc/hoagland/face.html

http://paranormal.about.com/library/weekly/aa052900a.html

http://archives.cnn.com/2001/TECH/space/05/25/mars.faces/index.html

FLUORIDATION

Do you realize that fluoridation is the most monstrously conceived and dangerous Communist plot we have ever had to face?
General Jack D. Ripper, *Dr Strangelove or:*
How I Learned to Stop Worrying and Love the Bomb

Fluoride is a chemical added to the drinking-water supplies of many cities and municipalities of the world. The stated purpose of fluoridation is to prevent tooth decay, especially in children.

Since the widespread introduction of fluoridation in the 1950s, debate has raged about its pros and cons. Even medical professionals are divided on the issue: the American Dental Association and American Medical Association both endorse fluoridation, while the US National Research Council has stated that 80 per cent of children may have dental fluorosis (that is, their teeth have been weakened by fluoridation). In the UK, a leading supplier of drinking water, Welsh Water, calls fluoride "a toxic and potent chemical".

There are claims, too, that fluoridation is a plot by the candy industry to allow kids to eat all the confectionery they want without adverse dental consequences. Some even charge that fluoridation is a Nazi/CIA ploy.

There *is* evidence that sodium fluoride was used in Nazi mind-control experiments during the Second World War. At the end of the conflict, US scientist Charles Perkins visited the German IG Farben chemical works and later concluded from his researches of the work done there: "Repeated doses of infinitesimal amounts of fluoride will in time reduce an individual's power to resist domination, by slowly poisoning and narcotizing a certain area of the brain, thus making him submissive to the will of those who wish to govern him." According to the Nazi-plot story, IG Farben chemists and Nazi experimenters were shipped to the US at the end of the war to show the CIA **MK-ULTRA** boys how submission by fluoridation could be achieved.

The list of alleged fluoridation conspirators does not end with the Nazis and the CIA. The Commies, as General Jack D. Ripper famously noted, are also in the frame, since they too would benefit from a mindless America. More substantially, some identify the aluminium industry, specifically the American Aluminium Company (Alcoa), as the conspirator in chief.

Fluoride is a by-product of aluminium/uranium/steel production. Fluoridation, then, is simply these industries dumping their toxic waste under a false flag and making a nice profit. It is certainly cause for thought that Oscar Ewing, the public service official who fluoridated nearly 90 American cities, was also Alcoa's attorney.

Conspiracy or no, the pro-fluoridation lobby struggles to sail against the wind of public scepticism. Only 10 per cent of Britons are supplied with fluoridated water. In America, 60 per cent of the population have fluoride in their water.

> Domestic water supplies deliberately contaminated with industrial waste marketed as health giver: ALERT LEVEL 7

Further Reading
http://www.fluoridealert.org – Fluoride:Commie Plot or Capitalist Ploy

VINCENT FOSTER

It was meant to be another Arthurian age, with political knights in shining armour sallying forth from Camelot in Washington DC to slay the ugly dragons of America – poverty, inequality, and every *ism* that could be poked from under a stone. From the outset, instead, the reign of William Jefferson Clinton in the White House was sunk in waves of scandal.

One of the first controversies to lap at the door of the Oval Office was the death of Vincent Walker Foster Jr, a deputy White House legal counsel. A childhood friend of Bill Clinton and a partner in the Rose Law Firm of Arkansas with Hillary Clinton, Foster was found dead in Fort Marcy Park, Virginia, on 20 July 1993, with a gunshot wound to the head. The alleged weapon was still in his hand, the latter stained by gunpowder residue.

Foster was known to have been depressed, and only the day previously had contacted his physician and been prescribed a mild sedative/anti-depressant, Trazodone. In his briefcase was found a suicide note: "I was not meant for the job or the spotlight of public life in Washington. Here ruining people is considered sport."

Vincent Foster had run foul of the city's media for his role in "Travelgate", in which White House travel office workers had been sacked on corruption charges and replaced with operatives from Clinton's power base in Arkansas. The incident looked and smelled bad, and a *Washington Post* editorial specifically charged that Foster's internal investigation into Travelgate was a whitewash.

His death seemed an open and shut case of suicide, and investigations by the United States Park Police, the United States Congress and Independent Counsels Robert B. Fiske and Kenneth Starr all ruled that Foster took his own life.

"Fostergate", though, refused to die, largely because conservative opponents of Clinton saw in it a chance to bring him down. Leading the anti-Clinton charge was the right-wing multi-millionaire Richard Mellon Scaife, owner of the *Pittsburgh Tribune-Review*, who bankrolled an investigation into "Fostergate" by journalist Christopher W. Ruddy which would be published as *The Strange Death of Vincent Foster*. Close behind Scaife were Citizens for Honest Government, whose video *The Clinton Chronicles* not only fingered Foster's death as dubious but stated that some fifty other people associated with Bill and Hill had died in suspicious circumstances.

According to *The Clinton Chronicles*, Foster was plain murdered and the gun placed in his hand (the wrong hand) to make it look like a self-inflicted death. Why was he murdered? Probably because he knew too much about "Whitewatergate", yet another scandal pounding at the Clintons' doors – this time concerning land and banking deals from the time of Bill Clinton's gubernatorial stint in Arkansas. Or, maybe, because Foster was having an affair with Hillary Clinton, which needed to be terminated in the most effective way possible to save the president the humiliation of a public cuckolding.

Not all conspiracists believed that Foster was murdered. An alternative scenario had Foster committing suicide but doing so in a place likely to cause the Clintons a maximum bad news day; to obviate this, the Clintons had the body removed to far-off Fort Marcy. Since the body was transferred from the place of demise, this explained the surprising lack of blood said to be on and around Foster's corpse at Fort Marcy. Meanwhile, on the furthest shores of the Foster-suicide theory, journalists J. Orlin Grabbe and James R. Norman "discovered" that Foster committed suicide because he was about to be unmasked as a Mossad agent.

The conspiracists of "Fostergate" wished to get Clinton in the crosshairs but unerringly drew a bead on their own feet. One key "witness" in *The Clinton Chronicles* turned out to be the video's producer; two more – Arkansas state troopers Roger Perry and Larry Patteson – proved to have been paid for their "evidence".

Aside from the conspiracists there was, in the eyes of the public at least, one more party out to crucify Clinton. This was special prosecutor Kenneth Starr.

Son of a Texan minister and sometime member of Ronald Reagan's legal staff, Starr spent four years producing the *Starr Report*, which appeared in September 1998. This recommended the impeachment of the President. All the dirt that Starr could dredge up, after using $40 million of American taxpayers' money, was that the President had enjoyed fellatio from an intern and then lied about it. Blameworthy behaviour certainly, but hardly Nixon-ite immorality. Naturally, Starr in his zealousness examined the death of Vince Foster – and found it to be a suicide. Surely, if Kenneth Starr is content that Foster died by his own hand, the remainder of the American right could be?

For the record, here is the conclusion of Starr's report on the death of Vincent W. Foster, Jr:

> To sum up, the OIC [Office of the Independent Counsel] has investigated the cause and manner of Mr Foster's death. To ensure that all relevant issues were fully considered, carefully analyzed, and properly assessed, the OIC retained a number of experienced experts and criminal investigators. The experts included Dr Brian D. Blackbourne, Dr Henry C. Lee, and Dr Alan Berman. The investigators included an FBI agent detailed from the FBI-MPD Cold Case Homicide Squad in Washington, D.C.; an investigator who also had extensive homicide experience as a detective with the Metropolitan Police Department in Washington D.C., for over 20 years; and two other OIC investigators who had experience as FBI agents investigating the murders of federal

official and other homicides. The OIC legal staff in Washington, DC, and Little Rock, Arkansas, participated in assessing the evidence, examining the analyses and conclusions of the OIC experts and investigators, and preparing this report.

The autopsy report and the reports of the pathologists retained by the OIC and Mr Fiske's office demonstrate that the cause of death was a gunshot wound through the back of Mr Foster's mouth and out the back of his head. The autopsy photographs depict the wound in the back of the head, and the photographs show the trajectory rod through the wound. The evidence, including the photographic evidence, reveals no other trauma or wounds on Mr Foster's body.

The available evidence points clearly to suicide as the manner of death. That conclusion is based on the evidence gathered and the analyses performed during previous investigations, and the additional evidence gathered and analyses performed during the OIC investigation, including the evaluations of Dr Lee, Dr Blackbourne, Dr Berman, and the various OIC investigators.

When police and rescue personnel arrived at the scene, they found Mr Foster dead with a gun in his right hand. That gun, the evidence tends to show, belonged to Mr Foster. Gunshot residue-like material was observed on Mr Foster's right hand in a manner consistent with test firings of the gun and with the gun's cylinder gap. Gunshot residue was found in his mouth. DNA consistent with that of Mr Foster was found on the gun. Blood was detected on the paper initially used to package the gun. Blood spatters were detected on the lifts from the gun. In addition, lead residue was found on the clothes worn by Mr Foster when found at the scene. This evidence, taken together, leads to the conclusion that Mr Foster fired this gun into his mouth. This evidence also leads to the conclusion that this shot was fired while he was wearing the clothes in which he was found. Mr Foster's thumb was trapped in the trigger guard, and the trigger caused a noticeable indentation on the thumb, demonstrating that the gun remained in his hand after firing. The police detected no signs of a struggle at the scene, and examination of Mr Foster's clothes by Dr Lee revealed no evidence of a struggle or of dragging. Nor does the evidence reveal that Mr Foster was intoxicated or drugged.

Dr Lee found gunshot residue in a sample of the soil from the place where Mr Foster was found. He also found a bone chip containing DNA consistent with that of Mr Foster in debris from the clothing. Dr Lee observed blood-like spatter on vegetation in the photographs of the scene. Investigators found a quantity of blood under Mr Foster's back and head when the body was turned, and Dr Beyer, who performed the autopsy, found a large amount of blood in the body bag. In addition, the blood spatters on Mr Foster's face had not been altered or smudged, contrary to what would likely have occurred had the body been moved and the head wrapped or cleaned. Fort Marcy Park is publicly accessible and travelled; Mr Foster was discovered in that park in broad daylight; no one saw Mr Foster being carried into the park. All of this evidence, taken together, leads to the conclusion that the shot was fired by Mr Foster where he was found in Fort Marcy Park.

The evidence with respect to state of mind points as well to suicide. Mr Foster told his sister four days before his death that he was depressed; he cried at dinner with his wife four days before his death; he told his mother a day or two before his death that he was unhappy because work was a "grind"; he was consulting attorneys for legal advice the week before his death; he told several people he was considering resignation; he wrote a note that he "was not meant for the job of the spotlight of public life in Washington. Here ruining people is considered sport." The day before his death, he contacted a physician and indicated that he was under stress. He was prescribed antidepressant medication and took one tablet that evening.

Dr Berman concluded that Mr Foster's "last 96 hours show clear signs of crisis and uncharacteristic vulnerability." Dr

Berman stated, furthermore, that "[t]here is little doubt that Foster was clinically depressed . . . in early 1993, and, perhaps, sub-clinically even before this." Dr Berman concluded that "[i]n my opinion and to a 100 per cent degree of medical certainty, the death of Vincent Foster was a suicide. No plausible evidence has been presented to support any other conclusion."

In sum, based on all of the available evidence, which is considerable, the OIC agrees with the conclusion reached by every official entity that has examined the issue: Mr Foster committed suicide by gunshot in Fort Marcy Park on July 20, 1993.

> Bill Clinton aide killed to prevent him blabbing about president's illegal land deal: ALERT LEVEL 3

Further Reading
Christopher W. Ruddy, *The Strange Death of Vincent Foster*, 1997
Kenneth Starr, *Report on the Death of Vincent W. Foster, Jnr, by the Office of the Independent Counsel*, 1998

FREEMASONS

The whipping boys of conspiracy, the Freemasons have been blamed for every "evil" from the French Revolution to the Jack the Ripper murders, from Bolshevism to the death of Princess **Diana**. Their least, but most extensive, alleged crime is furtherance of their own interests against those of the "cowans" (non-Masons). Persecuted by Hitler and condemned by the Papacy in no fewer than seven bulls and encyclicals, the world's five million Freemasons not only deny any malevolent wrongdoings but claim to be charitable workers whose only desire is, as the Scottish Rite puts it, "the guarantee of equal rights to all people everywhere". Far from being a secret society, the Freemasons are, they say, merely a society with secrets.

Eccentric bunch of patriarchal do-gooders or sinister agents of satanic forces? If the history of Freemasonry is examined, there is no doubt that the Freemasons are closer to the truth than their detractors.

According to Freemasonry's own mythology, its origins lie in Biblical times, with the building of the Temple of Solomon by the master architect Hiram Abiff. After Abiff's murder, Solomon ordered that his coffin be opened so that the secrets of the building genius might be known. The first thing that was found was Hiram's hand. Thereafter a handshake became the secret sign by which Freemasons recognized themselves.

The Masonic authors Christopher Knight and Robert Lomas pursued the history of Freemasonry even further back in time, to Pharaonic Egypt, where Hebrew slaves learned the secrets of pyramid construction and Egyptian symbolism, later using this wisdom to build the wondrous Temple of Solomon. In Knight and Lomas's bestselling *The Hiram Key*, Jesus himself was apprised of the Masonic secrets of Hiram, which were passed to the modern age by the **Knights Templar** when they stumbled upon the Temple during the Crusades.

Knight and Lomas are far from alone in identifying the Templars as the "missing link" between the masons of antiquity and modern Freemasonry. Chevalier Andrew Ramsay had done so in an oration to the Grand Lodge of Paris in 1737, further suggesting that the prevalence of Freemasonry in Scotland was attributable to Templar refugees who washed up there.

Freemasons and conspiracists alike have a vested interest in claiming a long pedigree for the Brotherhood. For Freemasons a foundation in ancient times suggests esotericism, for conspiracists the longevity of the Brotherhood is proof of its malignant power. Disappointingly for the Brotherhood and the anti-Masons alike, there is no proof that Freemasonry was founded in Ancient Egypt, even in Biblical times. In fact, there is not even evidence of a link between the medieval guilds of "free masons" (that is, stone masons who worked with "free" stone, the sort used in windows and facades of cathedrals and other grand buildings) and "speculative" Freemasonry. The first records of Freemasonry appear in the 17th century; on 20 March 1641 Sir Robert Moray was initiated into an Edinburgh Masonic lodge; five years later the antiquarian Elias Ashmole, founder of the Ashmolean Museum in Oxford, and the soldier Colonel Henry Mainwaring were initiated as Freemasons in the Warrington Lodge.

Moray, Ashmole and Mainwaring were entirely typical recruits to Freemasonry: they were gentlemen. Freemasonry became a fad amongst the 17th- and 18th-century squirearchy, who found the craft an enticing mix of conviviality, in-crowd elitism, daring occultism – and Enlightenment philosophy: Masons were asked to believe in a "Grand Architect of the Universe", a concept which suggested Rationalism.

In 1717 four London lodges outed themselves as the Premier Grand Lodge of England, which caused a split in the ranks of English Freemasonry, some Masons electing to follow the older York lodge. Despite the schism (which was healed in 1813 when the London and York lodges were brought together as the United Grand Lodge of Ancient Free and Accepted Masons of England), all the lodges of Britain adopted three main degrees of Freemasonry – Apprentice, Fellow-Craft and Master Mason. On reaching the latter level the Mason received all the privileges and rights of the Lodge.

By 1720 Freemasonry had been exported to France, in 1730 it reached the US, and a decade later it arrived in Russia and Germany. Thereafter there were few corners of the world without a Masonic lodge, although the powerbase of the Brotherhood has continued to be Britain and its American ex-colony, where no fewer than 12 presidents have been Freemasons; the first incumbent, George Washington, laid the foundation stone of the Capitol wearing his Masonic apron. (US conspiracy websites allege that Masonic themes and symbols also pervade Washington's namesake city, including a pentagram in the street plan and, of course, the Pentagon itself.) To counter the spreading allure of Free-masonry, the Roman Catholic Church not only damned it repeatedly but set up a direct, religiously sound rival, the Knights of St Columbus. Despite Pope Clement XII's out-right ban on Catholic participation in Freemasonry in 1738, some Catholics joined the Brotherhood nonetheless, most notoriously as members of **P2**.

Religious condemnation of Freemasonry has not been restricted to the Catholic Church. Among the most vociferous contemporary critics of the craft are US conservative evange-lical groups, which declare Freemasonry to be at the very least atheistic, at worst a Satanic conspiracy to rule the world. These groups, which are conspiracy theorists *par excellence*, cite, as proof of Freemasonry's alliance with the Devil, Albert Pike's infamous *Morals and Dogma of the Ancient and Accepted Scottish Rite of Freemasonry* (1871), which hailed "Lucifer the Light Bearer!" (Pike, a former Confederate brigadier general, made the Scottish Rite the main form of Freemasonry in the South.) More ammunition for anti-Masons lies in *Memoirs of an Ex-Palladist by Miss Diana Vaughan* (1895), which describes Satanic rituals undertaken by Pike's Palladium network. Alas, the thrilling *Memoirs* were a fiction created by the 19th-century French anti-Masonic campaigner Leo Taxil. Then there is the dollar bill, which since 1935 has carried the Masonic motto *Novus Ordo Seclorum*, widely rendered as **"New World Order"** – although a more accurate translation is "New Order of the Ages" and, far from being a nod to a Satanic would-be hegemony, the quote is a learned nod to Ovid.

In Britain, opposition to Freemasonry has centred on allegations of political interference rather than religious deviation. At the top of the pyramid, the Royal Family is heavily tied into Freemasonry through Prince Philip, a senior figure of the Brotherhood. Philip is alleged by Mohammed Al-Fayed and some anti-Masons to have ordered the murder of Princess **Diana** and Dodi Al-Fayed. For these conspiracists there is significance in the place of Diana's death – the Pont de l'Alma Tunnel, Paris, which used to be a meeting place of the Knights Templar – and that she was wearing jewellery in the design of a pentagram.

The Duke of Edinburgh is not the only royal Freemason to be implicated in murder. In *Jack the Ripper: The Final Solution* (1976), Stephen Knight charged that Freemason Prime Minister Lord Salisbury ordered the Whitechapel killings to cover up the marriage of Victoria's grandson, Prince Eddy, to a commoner. The actual slaughtering was done by the royal surgeon and Freemason Sir William Gull, who carved Masonic symbols on the prostitute victims.

Knight continued his investigations into Freemasonry with *The Brotherhood* (1984), which less sensationally accused Freemasons of corruption and favouritism, especially in the police and judiciary. Shortly afterwards Knight died of a brain hae-morrhage (predictably there were claims that he had been murdered by Masons) but Masonic scandal-digging continued with Martin Short's *Inside the Brotherhood: Further Secrets of the Freemasons* (1989). This told tale after tale of anonymous High Court judges giving preferential treatment to fellow Masons.

For all the efforts of Knight and Short, they failed to land a knockout blow on the body Freemasonic. That some smalltown burghers, that some coppers, that some bewigged judges give special deals to those who proffer the secret handshake was distinctly underwhelming: much the same charge, if to a lesser degree, could be levelled against golf club members everywhere. Both authors failed conspicuously to punch Freemasonry's weakest spots: its racism and sexism. Although Lodges do not explicitly bar black and Asian members, Masons from ethnic minorities in Britain are rare, while in the US the Freemasons of the South are still tied into the KKK. No women are allowed to become Freemasons and, according to historian Jasper Ridley, Freemasons "also refuse to have any dealings with any other society that accepts women".

Anti-Masons might have less to fear from the Masons than they realize. Demographics are not on the Masons' side. White, male and getting older, the Masons may simply die out.

International society of middle-aged men in sinister plot to take over society: ALERT LEVEL 3

Further Reading
Walton Hannah, *Darkness Visible*, 1952
Walton Hannah, *Christians by Degrees*, 1954
Christopher Knight and Robert Lomas, *The Hiram Key: Pharaohs, Freemasons and the Discovery of the Secret Scrolls of Christ*, 1996
Stephen Knight, *Jack the Ripper: The Final Solution*, 1976

Stephen Knight, *The Brotherhood: The Secret World of the Freemasons*, 1984
Jasper Ridley, *The Freemasons*, 1999
Martin Short, *Inside the Brotherhood: Further Secrets of the Freemasons*, 1989

GEMSTONE FILE

The Gemstone File is the granddaddy of the meta-conspiracy, redefining 20th-century history as a vast plot to take over America. Along the way its tentacles pull in everybody from JFK to Howard Hughes to Aristotle Onassis, the villain of the piece. The Gemstone File's impact on popular culture can be seen in movies and TV shows from Oliver Stone's *JFK* to Chris Carter's *The X-Files*.

The Gemstone File first surfaced in the Bay Area of San Francisco in 1969, when Bruce Roberts claimed to have had his method of synthesizing rubies ("gemstones") stolen by the Howard Hughes Corporation. When Roberts investigated the "theft" he stumbled upon a mega-conspiracy – and wrote up his investigation in the form of letters, which he sent to various parties. One recipient was Californian conspiracy researcher Mae Brussell, who had made a minor name for herself for researching the Kennedy assassination. Although Brussell dismissed Roberts as a crank, she let freelance journalist Stephanie Caruana use the "gemstone file" for articles in *Playgirl* and other publications in 1974. Caruana, much impressed by the "gemstone file" and Roberts himself, determined to summarize Roberts's investigation. She called the precis *A Skeleton Key to the Gemstone File* (or *Files*; versions vary) and issued 24 photocopies of it, which were passed around the campuses of California. On the last page the *Key* implored:

At present the only way to spread this information here in America is hand to hand. Your help is needed. Please make 1, 5, 10, 100 copies or whatever you can, and give them to friends or politicians, groups, media. This game is nearly up. Either the Mafia goes or America goes.

With its urgent tone and its alternative "underground" style of dissemination, the *Skeleton Key* became a phenomenon, not only in counter-cultural California but across the world. Its content, though, was somewhat less than its form.

According to the *Skeleton Key*, a "Mafia" (not to be confused with those *other* gangsters from Sicily or Russia) headed by Greek shipping magnate Aristotle Onassis kidnapped rival billionaire Howard Hughes, killed him, and replaced him with a double. The *doppelgänger* was used to control the Las Vegas gaming industry. While Onassis was not counting his illicit money, he was engineering the coup by which **John F. Kennedy** and **Robert Kennedy** were removed from the American political scene. After JFK's assassination, Onassis took Jackie Kennedy to be his trophy wife.

Intriguingly Roberts/Caruana proposed that Lee Harvey Oswald was the "patsy" in the JFK shooting, and that the real killers were Jimmy Fratianno, Johnny Roselli and Eugene Brading, all of whom had links with the Mafia. As for the assassination of Robert Kennedy, the *Key* proposed that Sirhan Sirhan's shots went wild and the actual executioner was Thane Cesar, who was "loaned" for the occasion by Onassis to act, supposedly, as Robert Kennedy's guard. Cesar was right behind Kennedy when the latter died.

A Skeleton Key to the Gemstone File contains whispers of the truth. Onassis *was* linked to the Kennedys, and Nixon's family *was* in financial debt to Howard Hughes. However, the *Key* is too riven with inaccuracies to be convincing. Howard Hughes was not buried off Skorpios, Onassis's private island, and his handwriting could not have been faked in 1957 by a computer. President Hoover could not have been murdered by administration of "sodium morphate".

The suppressed history of the Gemstone File is fiction. But for sheer chutzpah and cultural impact, only the **Protocols of the Learned Elders of Zion** matches *A Skeleton Key to the Gemstone Files* in the annals of conspiracy theory.

Greek tycoon Onassis heads Mafia-like gang which assassinated JFK and RFK: ALERT LEVEL 1

Further Reading
Stephanie Caruana, *A Skeleton Key to the Gemstone File*, 1974
Kenn Thomas and David Hatcher Childress, *Inside the Gemstone File*, 1999

DOCUMENT: A SKELETON KEY TO THE GEMSTONE FILE, BY STEPHANIE CARUANA

The gemstone file was written in many segments over a period of years by an American man named Bruce Roberts. Parts of the file were released to certain Americans beginning in 1969. The number of handwritten pages is well over a thousand, of which I have read about four hundred. I do not have the time or the research facilities to verify the entire story. Perhaps others can help.

Since the scope of the work is so large, and the events described so complex and interlocking, it may be more easily understood with this skeleton outline of the gemstone thesis. Individual papers can then be read with greater comprehension.

1932: Onassis, a Greek drug pusher and ship owner who made his first million selling "Turkish tobacco" (Opium) in Argentina, worked out a profitable deal with Joseph Kennedy, Eugene Meyer, and Meyer Lansky. Onassis was to ship booze directly into Boston for Joseph Kennedy. Also involved was a heroin deal with Franklin and Elliott Roosevelt.

1934: Onassis, Rockefeller and the Seven Sisters (major oil companies) signed an agreement, outlined an oil cartel memo: Beat the Arabs out of their oil, ship it on Onassis's ships; Rockefeller and the Seven Sisters to get rich. All this was done.

Roberts, studying journalism and physics at the University of Wisconsin, learned these things via personal contacts. His special interest was in crystallography – and the creation of synthetic rubies, the original Gemstone experiment.

1936–40: Eugene Meyer buys the *Washington Post*, to get our news Media; other Mafia buy other papers, broadcasting, T.V., etc. News censorship of all major news goes into effect.

1941–45: World War II; very profitable for Onassis, Rockefeller, Kennedys, Roosevelts, I.G. Farben, etc. Onassis selling oil, arms and dope to both sides went through the war without losing a single ship or man.

1949: Onassis buys US surplus "Liberty Ships" in questionable (illegal) purchase. Lawyer Burke Marshall helps him.

1956: Howard Hughes, Texas millionaire, is meanwhile buying his way toward his own personal gain. He buys senators, governors, etc. He finally buys his last politician: newly elected V.P. Nixon, via a quarter-million-dollar non-repayable loan to Nixon's brother Donald.

Early 1957: V.P. Nixon repays the favor by having IRS Treasury grant tax-free status (refused twice before) to "Hughes Medical Foundation", sole owner of Hughes Aircraft, creating a tax-free, non-accountable money funnel or laundry, for whatever Hughes wanted to do. US Government also shelved anti-trust suits against Hughes' TWA, etc.

March 1957: Onassis carried out a carefully planned event: he has Hughes kidnapped from his bungalow at the Beverly Hills Hotel, using Hughes' own men (Chester Davis, born Cesare in Sicily, et al). Hughes' men either quit, get fired, or stay on in the new Onassis organization. A few days later, Mayor Cannon of Nevada (now Senator Cannon) arranges a fake "marriage" to Jean Peters, to explain Hughes' sudden loss of interest in chasing movie stars. Hughes, battered and brain damaged in the scuffle, is taken to the Emerald Isle Hotel in the Bahamas, where the entire top floor has been rented for thirty days, and is later dragged off to a cell on Onassis' island, Skorpios. Onassis now has a much larger power base in the US (the Hughes empire), as well as control over V.P. Nixon and other Hughes-purchased politicians.

L. Wayne Rector, Hughes' double since 1955, becomes "Hughes".

September, 1957: Onassis calls the Appalachian meeting to announce to US Mafia head his grab of Hughes and his adoption of Hughes' game plan for acquiring power: buying US senators, congressmen, governors, judges to take control legally of the US government. Onassis's radio message to Appalachia from a remote Pennsylvania farmhouse intercepted (reluctantly) by FBI's J. Edgar Hoover, on the basis of a tipoff from some Army Intelligence guys who weren't in on the plan.

Also in 1957: Joseph Kennedy takes John F. and Jackie to see Onassis on his yacht, introduces John and reminds Onassis of an old Mafia promise: the presidency for a Kennedy. Onassis agrees.

1958: Hordes of Mafia-selected, purchased and supported "grass roots" candidates sweep into office.

1959: Castro takes over Cuba from dictator Battista, thereby destroying cozy and lucrative Mafia gambling empire run for Onassis by Meyer Lansky. Castro scoops up $6 million in Mafia casino receipts. Onassis is furious, V.P. Nixon becomes operations chief for CIA-planned Bay of Pigs invasion, using CIA Hunt, McCord, etc., and Cuban ex-Battista strong-arm cops (Cuban freedom-fighters) Martinez, Consalez, etc., as well as winners like Frank Sturgis (Fiorini).

1959: Stirring election battle between Kennedy and Nixon. Either way Onassis wins, since he has control over both candidates.

1960: JFK elected. American people happy. Rose Kennedy happy. Onassis happy. Mafia ecstatic.

Roberts brings his synthetic rubies – the original gem-stones – to Hughes' aircraft in Los Angeles. They steal his rubies – the basis for laser beam research, laser bombs, etc., because of the optical quality of the rubies. One of the eleven possible sources for one of the ingredients involved in the Gemstone experiment was the Golden Triangle area. Roberts was married to the daughter of the former French consul in Indochina. In that area, Onassis's involvements in the Golden Triangle dope trade was no secret. Roberts investigation revealed the Onassis–Hughes connection, kid-nap and switch. "Gemstones" – synthetic rubies and sap-phires with accomplished "histories" – gemstone papers – were sold or given away to consular offices – in return for information. A world-wide information network was gradu-ally developed – a trade of the intelligence activities of many countries. This intelligence network is the source for much of the information in the Gemstone File.

January 1961: Joseph Kennedy has a stroke, ending his control over John and Bobby. The boys decide to rebel against Onassis's control. Why? Inter-Mafia struggle? Per-haps a dim hope of restoring this country to its mythical integrity? They began committing Mafia no-nos: arrested Wally Bird, owner of Air Thailand, who had been shipping Onassis's heroin out of the Golden Triangle (Laos, Cambo-dia, Vietnam), under contract with the CIA (Air Opium); arrested teamster Mafia Jimmy Hoffa, and put him in jail. Declared the 73$ million in forged "Hughes" land liens, deposited with San Francisco Bank of America, as "security" for the TWA judgment against Hughes, to be what they are: forgeries.

April 1961: CIA Bay of Pigs fiasco. Hunt, McCord, CIA, Battista's Cubans and Mafia angry about JFK's lack of enthusiasm. Mafia Onassis has his right-hand man "Hughes' Top aide" former FBI and CIA Robert Maheu (nicknamed

"IBM" for Iron Bob Maheu), hire and train a Mafia assassination team to get Castro. The team of a dozen or so includes John Roselli and Jimmy (The Weasel) Prattiano, expert Mafia hitmen, assisted by CIA Hunt and McCord and others. This was reported recently by Jack Anderson, who gets a lot of his "tips" from his friend, Frank (Fiorini) Sturgis – also on the Castro assassination team. The team tries five times to kill Castro with everything from long-range rifles to apple pie with sodium morphate in it.

Castro survives.

1963: Members of the Castro assassination team arrested at Lake Pontchartrain, La. by Bobby Kennedy's justice boys. Angered, Onassis stops trying to kill Castro. He changes target and goes for the head: JFK, who, according to Onassis, "welched" on a Mafia deal. JFK sets up "Group of 40" to fight Onassis.

August 1963: Two murders had to occur before the murder of JFK, of people who would understand the situation and might squawk:

Senator Estes Kefauver, whose crimes commission investigations had uncovered the 1932 deal between Onassis, Kennedy, Eugene Meyer, Lansky, Roosevelt, et al. Kefauver planned a speech on the Senate floor denouncing Mafia operations; instead, he ate a piece of apple pie laced with sodium morphate (used in rat poison), and had a sodium-morphate-induced "heart attack" on the Senate floor.

Phillip Graham: Editor of *The Washington Post*, Phillip had married Katherine Meyer, Eugene Meyer's daughter, who had inherited the *Washington Post* and allied media empire. Graham put together the Kennedy–Johnson ticket and was Kennedy's friend in the struggle with Onassis. According to Gemstone, Katherine Meyer Graham bribed some psychiatrists to certify that Phil was insane. He was allowed out of the nuthouse for the weekend and died of a shotgun wound in the head in the Graham home in Washington; death ruled "suicide".

1 November 1963: The hit on JFK was supposed to take place in true Mafia style: a triple execution, together with Diem and Nhu in Vietnam. Diem and Nhu got theirs, as scheduled. Onassis had invited Jackie for a cruise on the *Christina*, where she was when JFK got tipped off that big "O" planned to wipe him out. JFK called Jackie on the yacht, from the White House, hysterical: "Get off that yacht if you have to swim" and cancelled his appearance at a football stadium in Chicago, where this CIA–Mafia assassination team was poised for the kill. Jackie stayed on board, descended the gangplank a few days later on Onassis's arm, in Turkey, to impress the Bey, Mustapha. Madame Nhu in the US bitterly remarked, "Whatever has happened in Vietnam?"

One of the assassination teams was picked up in Chicago with a rifle and quickly released by the police. Three weeks later the Mafia's alternate and carefully arranged execution plan went into effect: JFK was assassinated in Dallas. A witness who recognized pictures of some of the people arrested in Dealey Plaza as having been in Chicago three weeks earlier told Black Panthers Hampton and Clark.

The JFK murder: Onassis–Hughes' man Robert Maheu reassigned the Mafia–CIA Castro assassination team to the murder of JFK, adding Eugene Brading, a third Mafia hit-man from the Denver Mafia Amaldones "family". Two months earlier Brading, on parole after a series of crimes, applied for a new driver's license, explaining to the California DMV that he had decided to change his name to Jim Brading. Brading got his California parole the first time to look things over and the second time when JFK was scheduled for his Dallas trip.

Lee Harvey Oswald, CIA, with carefully planned links to both the ultra right and to the Communists, was designated as the patsy. He was supposed to shoot Governor Connally and he did.

Each of the four shooters – Oswald, Brading, Frattiano and Roselli – had a timer and a back-up man. Back-up men were supposed to pick up the spent shells and get rid of the guns. Timers would give the signal to shoot. Hunt and McCord were there to help. Sturgis was in Miami.

Frattiano shot from a second story window in the Dal-Tex building across the street from the Texas School Book Depository. He apparently used a handgun – he is an excellent shot with a pistol. Frattiano and his back-up man were "arrested", driven away from the Dal-Tex building in a police car and released (without being booked). The Dallas police office is in the Dal-Tex building.

Roselli shot Kennedy once, hitting the right side of his head and blowing his brains out with a rifle from behind a fence in the grassy knoll area. Roselli and his timer went down a manhole behind the fence and followed the sewer line away from Dealey Plaza.

The third point of the triangulated ambush was supplied by Eugene Brading shooting from a small pagoda at Dealey Plaza across the street from the grassy knoll. (Brading missed because Roselli's and Frattiano's shots had just hit Kennedy in the head from the right and the rear nearly simultaneously). Brading's shot hit the curb and ricocheted off. Brading was photographed on the scene stuffing his gun under his coat. He wore a big leather hat, its hatband marked with large conspicuous X's. (Police had been instructed to let anyone with an X-marked hatband through the police lines. Some may have been told they were Secret Service.) After his shot, Brading ditched his gun with his back-up man and walked up the street toward the Dal-Tex building. Sheriff rushed up to Brading, assuming he was "Secret Service", and told him he had just seen a man come out of the Book Depository and jump into a station wagon. Brading was uninterested. Brading walked into the Dal-Tex building to "make a phone call". There he was arrested by another deputy sheriff, showed his "Jim Braden" driver's license and was released without being booked.

Oswald shot Connally twice from the Texas School Book Depository. He split from the front door. His back-up man was supposed to take the rifle out of the building (or so Oswald thought); instead he "hid" it behind some boxes, where it would be found later.

Three men dressed as tramps picked up the spent shells from Dealey Plaza. One was Howard Hunt. Then they drifted over to an empty boxcar sitting on the railway spur behind the grassy knoll area, and waited. A Dallas police officer ordered two Dallas cops to "go over to the boxcar and pick up the tramps". The three "tramps" paraded around Dealey Plaza to the Police Department in the Dal-Tex Building. They were held there until the alarm went out to pick up Oswald; then they were released, without being booked. In all, ten men were arrested immediately after the shooting; all were released soon after; none were booked; not a word about their existence is mentioned in the Warren Report.

Regarding Lee Harvey Oswald: Officer Tippett [sic; this was Officer J. D. Tippit] was dispatched in his police radio car to the Oak Cliff Section, where Oswald had rented a room. Tippett may have met Oswald on the street. He may have been supposed to kill Oswald, but something went wrong. Tippett was shot by two men using revolvers. The "witness", Domingo Benavides, who used Tippett's police car radio to report "we've had a shooting here", may have been one of the men who shot him. (A "Domingo Benavides" appears in connection with the Martin Luther King shooting also.)

Oswald went to the movies. A "shoe store manager" told the theatre cashier that a suspicious looking man had sneaked in without paying. Fifteen assorted cops and FBI charged out to the movie theatre to look for the guy who had sneaked in.

Oswald had a pistol that wouldn't fire. It may have been anticipated that the police would shoot the "cop-killer" for "resisting arrest". But since that didn't happen, the Dallas police brought Oswald out for small-time Mafia Jack Ruby to kill two days later.

Brading stayed at the Teamster-Mafia-Hoffa-financed "Cuban Hotel" in Dallas. Ruby had gone to the Cabana the night before the murder, says the Warren Report. The rest, as they say, is history. Onassis was so confident of his control over police, media, FBI, CIA, Secret Service and the US Judicial System that he had JFK murdered before the eyes of the entire nation; then systematically bought off, killed off, or frightened off all witnesses and had the evidence destroyed; then put a 75-year seal of secrecy over the entire matter. Cover-up participants included among many: Gerald Ford on the Warren Commission (a Nixon recommendation): CIA attorney Leon Jaworski, of the CIA front Anderson Foundation, representing

Texas before the Commission to see that the fair name of Texas was not besmirched by the investigation; CIA-Dallas Chief John McCone, his assistant; Richard Helms; and a passle of police, FBI, news media, etc.

[. . .]

After JFK's death, Onassis quickly established control over Lyndon Johnson through fear. On the trip back to Washington, Johnson was warned by radio relayed from an air force base: "There was no conspiracy, Oswald was a lone nut assassin. Get it, Lyndon? Otherwise, Air Force One might have unfortunate accident on flight back to Washington."

Onassis filled all important government posts with his own men. All government agencies became means to accomplish an end: rifle the American Treasury, steal as much as possible, keep the people confused and disorganized and leaderless; persuade world domination. JFK's original "Group of 40" was turned over to Rockefeller and his man, Kissinger, so that they could more effectively take over South America. (Onassis was one of the first to console Jackie when she got back from Dallas with JFK's body.)

[. . .]

1967: Onassis has always enjoyed the vast piles of money to be made through gambling (in Monaco in the 50s and in Cuba under Battista). Onassis took over Las Vegas in 1967, via the "Hughes" cover. US Government officials explained that it was all right because "at least Hughes isn't the Mafia."

Mafia Joe Alioto had Presidential ambitions, shored up by his participation in the Dallas pay-off. Everyone who helped kill JFK got a piece of the US pie. But J. Edgar Hoover, FBI head, blew his cover by releasing some of the raw FBI files on Alioto at the Democratic National Convention. Joe was out of the running for V.P. and Humphrey had to settle for Muskie. Humphrey planned to come to S.F. for a final pre-election rally, sparked by Joe Alioto. Roberts threatened to blow the hit-run story plus its Mafia ramifications open if Humphrey came to S.F. Humphrey didn't come; Humphrey lost in San Francisco, California and the election.

October 1968: Jackie Kennedy was now "free" to marry Onassis. An old Mafia rule: if someone welches on a deal, kill him and take his gun and his girl: in this case, Jackie and the Pentagon.

July, 1969: Mary Jo Kopechne, devoted JFK girl, and later one of Bobby's trusted aides, was in charge of packing up his files after his assassination in L.A. She read too much, learned about the Kennedy Mafia involvement and other things. She said to friends: "This isn't Camelot, this is murder." She was an idealistic American Catholic. She didn't like murdering hypocrites. She died trying to get off Chappaquiddick Island, where she had overheard (along with everyone else in the cottage) Teddy Kennedy's end of [. . .] telephone calls from John Tunney and to Joe Alioto,

and Democrat bigwigs Swig, Shorenstein, Schumann and Bechtel. [. . .] Mary Jo, up to there with Mafia, ran screaming out of the cottage on her way to Nader. Drunken Teddy offered to drive her to the ferry. Trying to get away from the curious Sheriff, Teddy sped off toward the Bridge, busted Mary Jo's nose when she tried to grab his arm from the back seat, and bailed out of the car as it went off the bridge. Mary Jo, with a busted nose, breathed in an air bubble in the car for more than two hours waiting for help, while Teddy, assuming she was dead, went to set up an alibi. Mary Jo finally suffocated in the air bubble, diluted with carbon dioxide. It took her 2 hours and 37 minutes to suffocate while Teddy called Jackie and Onassis on the *Christina*. Teddy also called Katherine Meyer Graham, lawyers, etc. Jackie called the Pope on Teddy's behalf, who assigned Cardinal Cushing to help. The next morning, the first person Teddy tried to call after deciding he'd have to take the rap himself was a lawyer, Burke Marshall, Onassis's friend in the US Liberty Ships deal back in the forties and also the designated custodian for JFK's brains after Dallas (the brains have since disappeared).
[. . .]
In the panic of trying to cover up Teddy's guilt at Chappaquiddick, many things came unglued. The JFK murder threatened to creep out of the woodwork again [. . .]

September 1969: "Gemstones", with histories, had been released around the globe for several years. In 1969, Roberts gave a Gemstone with history to Mack, head of California CREEP, for Nixon, with the proposition: the Presidency in return for wiping out the Mafia. The "history" included Teddy's phone calls to and from the Lawrence Cottage on Chappaquiddick billed to Teddy's home phone in Hyannisport. Nixon, being Mafia himself, wasn't interested; but kept the information to use on Teddy whenever it seemed advantageous.

4 May 1970: Charlotte Ford Niarchos called her ex-husband Stavros, worried about the Ford Foundation's involvement in the Chappaquiddick cover-up. Eugenie Livanos Niarchos, in bed with her husband, overheard the conversation. Stavros was forced to beat her to death; he ruptured her spleen and broke the cartilage in her throat. Cause of death was listed as "overdose of barbiturates", though autopsy showed these injuries.

NOTE: L. Wayne Rector was hired around 1955 by the Carl Byoir PR Agency (Hughes' L.A. PR firm) to act as Hughes double. In 1957 when Onassis grabbed Hughes, Rector continued to act as his stand-in. Rector was the Hughes surrogate in Las Vegas; Robert Maheu actually ran the show; Maheu got his orders from Onassis; the six "nursemaids", called the "Mormon Mafia", kept Rector sealed off from prying eyes.

17 June 1969: Bobby Kennedy knew who killed his brother; he wrote about it in his unpublished book, *The Enemy Within*. When he foolishly tried to run for President, Onassis had him offed, using a sophisticated new technique. Hypnotized, Sirhan Sirhan shot at him from the front, "security guard" (from Lockheed Aircraft) Thane Cesar shot from two or three inches away from Bobby's head from the rear. Sirhan's shots all missed. Evelle Younger, then the L.A. District Attorney, covered it all up including the squawks of the L.A. Coroner Thomas Noguchi. Younger was rewarded with the post of California Attorney General later. His son, Eric Younger, got a second generation Mafia reward; a judgeship at age 30. (See Ted Charach, L.A. author and director, *The Second Gun*, a documentary film on the RFK murder, bought and suppressed by Warner Brothers for more details.) After Bobby's death, Teddy knew who did it. He ran to Onassis, afraid for his life, and swore eternal obedience. In return, Onassis granted him his life and said he

could be President, too, just like his big brother, if he would behave himself and follow orders.

[. . .]

End of 1970: Howard Hughes' presence on earth no longer required. His handwriting could be duplicated by a computer. His biography, all the known facts about his life, had been compiled and a computerized biography issued to top Hughes executives. His double – Rector – had been doing "Hughes" for years. And Hughes was ill. Clifford Irving, author of *Hoax*, about an art forger, became interested in "Hughes". Living on Ibiza, he heard the Mediterranean gossip that "Hughes" was a hoax, too. He went to "Hughes" so-called "Mormon Mafia", the six nursemaids, for information. One of them – Merryman perhaps, tired of the game – gave Irving the computerized Hughes biography and from it Irving wrote his "autobiography". Hughes' death was expected shortly. Preparations were being made so that it would not interfere with the orderly continuation of his empire. Irving wrote his book and the publishers announced it. Onassis knew someone had given Irving the information. He thought it was Maheu and fired him in November 1970. On Thanksgiving Eve 1970, in the middle of the night "Hughes" (Rector) made a well-publicized "secret departure" from Las Vegas to the Bahamas.

December 1970: Onassis discovered his mistake and had Merryman killed. Robert Maheu, accidentally deprived of his half-million dollars annual salary, sued "Hughes" for millions, mentioning "Hughes" game plan for the purchase of Presidents, governors, Senators, judges, etc. Onassis paid him off, cheap at the price, to maintain his custodianship of "American democracy" and the "free world" and keep from hanging for multiple murders. The "Hughes" Mormon Mafia party, plus Rector, fled around the world from the Bahamas where they murdered an uncooperative Governor and Police Chief, to Nicaragua, where they shot the US

Ambassador between the eyes for noticing that there wasn't really any Hughes; and then to Canada, where Mormon Mafia nursemaid Sckersley looted a goodly sum in a swindle of the Canadian Stock Exchange; and on to London to Rothschild's Inn on the Park.

April 18, 1971: Howard Hughes, a human vegetable as the result of serious brain damage during his 1957 hustle, plus fourteen years of heroin, grew sicker and sicker. A final overdose of heroin did him in. His coffin was lowered into the sea from a rocky headland off the coast of Skorpios. Present at the funeral were: Jackie Kennedy Onassis, Teddy Kennedy, Francis L. Dale, Director of CREEP, and a South Vietnamese cardinal named Thue. Onassis allowed some pictures to be taken from a distance; he himself did not appear. The pictures were published in *Midnight*, a Canadian tabloid. Albanian frogmen, tipped off, were waiting under the water. They seized the coffin and took the corpse off to Yugoslavia, then to China, Russia and then perhaps to Boston in a foot locker. The corpse's dental work was compared to Hughes' very own dental records and they matched. News of Hughes' death, the US take-over by Onassis and the facts surrounding the murders of JFK, RFK, Martin Luther King, Mary Jo Kopechne, and many more and the subsequent cover-ups (involving still more murders) had been circulating around the globe for several years. Any country with this information can blackmail the US/Mafia government, which has no choice but to pay up. The alternative is to be exposed as a bunch of treasonous murderers. This is why China-hating, red-hating Nixon was forced to recognize China (which he now claims as his greatest accomplishment). And this is also why the USSR walks off with such good deals in US loans, grains and whatever else it wants. All they have to do is mention those magic words – "Hughes, JFK, RFK, MLK, Mary Jo" – and the US Mafia government crawls into a hole. Information once leaked can't be unleaked. The only way to end the dilemma is through a nuclear war and that wouldn't be one-sided. The other way would be to throw the Mafia out of the United States. Starting at the top with Ford, Rockefeller and Kissinger. Super-patriots please note: no one, not all of the radicals and subversives hounded by the US domestic intelligence put together, has done one fraction of the damage done to US economy, morality, power and prestige as by the thieves at the top.

[. . .]

May 1971: "Folk Hero" Daniel Ellsberg, a well-known hawk from the Rand Corporation, who had designed the missile ring around the "Iron Curtain" countries (how many missiles to aim at which cities) was told to release the faked-up "Pentagon Papers" to help distract people from Hughes, JFK, RFK, MLK etc. The papers were carefully designed by Ellsberg and his boss, Rand Chief and new World Bank Chief Bob (Body Count) McNamara, to make the Vietnamese War look like "just one of those incredibly dumb mistakes". This helped to cover up the real purpose of the war: continued control, for Onassis and his friends of the Golden Triangle dope trade: Vietnam, Laos and Cambodia; and for Onassis and the oil people of Eastern oil sources, to say nothing of control over huge Federal sums, which could be siphoned off in profitable arms contracts, or conveniently "disappear" in the war effort.

McNamara's "World Bank" handing-out of American money to "starving nations" actually set up huge private bank accounts for various dictators in the Onassis-controlled Swiss bank. The money could be used as needed to support and extend Mafia operations. Example: $8 billion in World Bank funds for "starving Ethiopians" wound up in Emperor Haile Selassie's personal accounts in the Swiss bank. This would make him the richest individual in the world, but other dictators have Swiss bank accounts too. Perhaps they are even larger. The money drained from America and other

captive Mafia nations feeds a greed that can never be satisfied.
[. . .]
June 1971: *New York Times* began publishing the Pentagon Papers, Rand Corp's prepared cover-up of the real reasons for the Vietnamese war. Nixon had gotten a copy of the first Gemstone Papers, circulated in the US back in 1969. He was now wondering how much information Democratic Chairman Larry O'Brien had about Hughes, Onassis, JFK, RFK, etc. and more specifically how much of the dirt the Democrats planned to use. Nixon set up the "plumbers unit" to stop security leaks, investigate other security matters. Erlichman, Krogh, Liddy, Hunt, Young, etc. Hunt as "White House consultant" supposedly worked for the Mullen Corp. a CIA cover. Mullen's head client was "Howard Hughes"; Robert Bennett was the head of the Mullen Corp.

June 28, 1971: Ellsberg indicted for leaking the Pentagon Papers.

September 3, 1971: The Watergate team broke into Ellsberg's doctor's (Fielding's) office to get Ellsberg's psychiatric records. Team members CIA Hunt and Liddy, Cuban "Freedom fighters" De Denio, Martinez, Bernard Barker. All except Liddy had worked together back at the Bay of Pigs.
[. . .]
27 January 1972: Liddy and Dean met in Mitchell's office, with Liddy's charts for his $1 million "plan" for spying, kidnapping, etc. The plans included breaking into Hank Greenspun's Las Vegas office safe, in hopes of recovering Greenspun's file on the Hughes kidnapping and Onassis's Vegas operations, which Greenspun had successfully used to blackmail Onassis out of $4 million or so. A "Hughes" getaway plane would stand by to take the White House burglars to Mexico.

February, 1972: [. . .] Liddy, Hunt and other Watergaters dropped by for a beer at the Drift Inn, where they were photographed on bar stools for Katherine Graham. These photos were later used in the *Washington Post*, when Liddy, Hunt and others were arrested at Watergate because CIA men like Liddy and Hunt aren't usually photographed. [. . .]

February 1972: Francis L. Dale, head of CREEP and ITT Board of Directors member, pushed Magruder to push Liddy into Watergate. In a Mafia-style effort to shut Roberts up, his father was murdered by "plumbers" team members Liz Dale (Francis L. Dale's ex-wife), Martinez, Gonzales, Barker; in Hahnemann's hospital, S.F., where Mr Roberts had been taken after swallowing a sodium morphate "pill" slipped into his medicine bottle at home by Watergate locksmith [. . .] Gonzales. The pill didn't kill him. He had a weak digestion and vomited enough of the sodium morphate up (it burned his lips and tongue on the way out) but he had emphysema and went to the hospital. In the hospital, "nurse" Liz Dale and "doctor" Martinez assisted him to sniff a quadruple-strength can of aerosol medicine enough to kill him the next day.

The day before, Tisseront, head of the College of Cardinals at the Vatican, was pushed out of a Vatican window. Tisseront had followed the career of the present Pope, Montini (whose mother was Jewish). Montini sodium-morphate murdered Pope Pius XI; was banished from Rome for it by Pius XII; became Pope in 1963. Tisseront wrote it all down; called the Pope "The Deputy of Christ at Auschwitz", and the fulfillment of the Fatima 3 Prophecy that "The anti-Christ shall rise to become the head of the Church." Tisseront also wrote about all the suppressed secrets of the Roman Catholic Church: i.e., that Jesus Christ was an Arab, born 16 April 6 BC at the rare conjunction of Saturn and Jupiter. Arab (Persian) astronomers (the Magi) came to Bethlehem to look for their king, an Arab baby, and found him in a stable, because the Jews wouldn't let Arabs Joseph and Mary into their nice clean inns, even then. When Jesus overturned the tables of the money lenders at the Temple, the Jews had the Romans nail him to a cross. He died on the cross when the Roman soldiers stuck a spear in his side, pulled out his liver, and ate it. Tacitus, the Roman historian, described it all in a chunk of history deleted by the Church. Nero burned Rome but that didn't stop the spreading of Moses' teachings by the early Christians (Arabs). So the Romans decided to adopt the religion, clean it up, make Christ a Jew and Mary a virgin, and work out a church/state deal to fool the people in the name of God and country that has been operating ever since. Around AD 311 at the Council of Nicosia the Christian Orthodoxy was established; a dissenting bishop had his hands chopped off; another bishop was assigned to round up all the old copies of the Bible and destroy them in favor of the "revised" de-Arabized version. Cleaned up Matthew, Mark, Luke, and John were declared "it", the other Gospels were declared Apocryphal and heretical. Roman Emperor Constantine became the first "Christian" emperor.

[. . .]

May 1972: J. Edgar Hoover had the Gemstone File: threatened to expose Dallas–JFK in an "anonymous" book, *The Texas Mafia*. Instead, someone put sodium morphate in his apple pie. The corpse was carted away from his home in the back seat of a VW and his files were "burned", but some of them got away.

28 May 1972: First break-in at Watergate: McCord, Barker, Martinez, Garcia, Gonzales, Sturgis, DeDiego and Pico stood guard outside. Hunt and Liddy directed the operation from a (safe?) distance – across the street. The object was to check on Onassis's two men at Democratic Party HQ: Larry O'Brien and Spencer Oliver. (O'Brien's chief PR client had been "Hughes"; Oliver's father worked for Onassis.)

McCord wire-tapped their phones. But!!!! little did McCord know that the plumbers were being observed by Hal Lipset, Katherine Graham's S.F. detective who had followed two of the plumbers from Liz Dale's side in S.F. to Watergate. Lipset "watched in amazement" as the plumbers broke in and bugged the phones: then reported back to his boss Katherine Graham. Lipset and Graham set the trap for the Watergaters when they returned to remove their bugs and equipment.

[. . .]

February 1974: Mafia Hearst's daughter Patty "kidnapped" by Lipset's SLA in a fake terrorist action.

Martin Luther King's mother was murdered by a black student, a self-declared "Israelite" – "acting alone", who was escorted to the church by somebody – and who had a list of other mothers as targets. Next day the target Shirley Chisholm got the message and rushed to sign off the DNC suit against CREEP naming Francis L. Dale; she had been the last to hold out.

[. . .]

6 August 1974: Nixon and Ford signed a paper at the White House. It was an agreement: Ford could be President. Nixon got to burn his tapes and files and murder anyone he needed to cover it all up.

7 August 1974: [. . .] Rockefeller sent Kissinger to the White House with Nixon's marching orders: "Resign right now." Nixon and Julie cried. But there was still some hope, if Nixon resigned immediately, of drawing the line somewhere – before it got to the King of the Mountain himself – Onassis. Nixon, on trial, would blurt out those names to save himself: Onassis, Dale, "Hughes", even JFK.

8 August 1974: Nixon stepped down, and Ford stepped up: to keep the cover-up going.

[. . .]

30 August 1974: Ford hires Mafia lawyer Becker to work out a pardon deal for Nixon, who might otherwise name Onassis, Graham, and Pope Martini to save himself.
[. . .]
8 September 1974: Ford pardons Nixon for "all crimes committed" from 20 June 1969 (make that January) through August 1974.
[. . .]
October 1974: Ford drops "extradition" of Hughes from the Bahamas. Explanation: "We dropped it because we knew he wouldn't come." THAT'S FOR SURE.

"Four documents; four bodies twisting slowly in the breeze."

Lyndon Johnson: Sodium morphate "heart attack" at his ranch on the Pedernales River. Among his last words: "You know, fellows, it really was a conspiracy . . ."

Alexander Onassis's plane crash at the "1000 foot Walter Reuther Level", via a fixed altimeter, at Athens Airport.

Eugene Wyman: California Democratic Party Chairman and JFK assassination pay-off bagman: Heart attack.

L. Wayne Rector, Hughes' double: Killed at Rothchild's Inn of the Park, London.
[. . .]
Losing his son Alexander took all the fun out of killing for Onassis. Who was there left to inherit the world empire he had dreamed of handing over to his son?

December 1974: Brezhnev had scheduled a meeting with Sadat. The outcome wouldn't help the US, no matter how many trips Henry made to the mid-East with clean socks and blank checks. A new US "secret weapon" was apparently used, a tiny speck of metal, introduced somehow into Brezhnev's lymph system. It lodged in the cluster of lymph nodes over his heart, and there it was coated with layers of phlegm, much as an oyster creates a pearl around an irritating grain of sand. Brezhnev's lymph system clogged up: he got the flu and the meeting with Sadat was cancelled. Russian doctors X-rayed him and found a huge lump in his chest. Then they put him before a Kirlian camera and checked his aura for cancer. No cancer.

Note: Kirlian photography is the latest Russian diagnostic tool. It reveals the presence of disease, physical or moral (it also detects lies).

Brezhnev's lump had to be treated with radiation therapy: hence the rumors he had cancer. It took six weeks to clear up.

March 1975: Onassis died. The Mafia Organization regrouped itself. Prince Faisal watched his uncle, King Faisal, silently watch the shift of Mafia Power and couldn't stand it any more. He shot his uncle, the spiritual leader of 60,000,000 Moslems, who had played ball with Onassis all along.

South Vietnam's Thieu, dubious about which way the Mafia cookie would crumble, now that Onassis was dead, decided the time was right for him to split. He abandoned the war effort, cursed the US, and split for Taiwan, his plane so overloaded with gold bullion that he had to dump some of it overboard.

15 March 1975: Roberts got the "Brezhnev Flu" and spent 2 weeks at UC Hospital. Doctors there, without the Kirlian photography diagnostic technique, assumed the softball-sized lump over his heart was cancer. It wasn't.

April 1975: The Cambodian domino was no fun at all – it fell right over. Premier Lon Nol fled to exile in a Hawaiian suburb.
[. . .]
Which brings us almost to the present time. Ford, Kissinger and Rockefeller squat like toads on the corpse of America. By the time of the Bicentennial the stink may be unbearable.

Ford now plans a propaganda mode version of his book, *Portrait of an Assassin*, which will reiterate the exploded cock and bull notion that Oswald was JFK's lone assassin. With singular inept misunderstanding of the times, he seems to think Americans will take his word for it and be reassured in the face of those crackpot conspiracy theories. He doesn't seem to realize that he will be reminding or informing Americans of his role on the infamous Warren Commission.

I hope this outline will make individual Gemstone papers easier to understand.

If You Found This Outline Interesting
You won't be reading it in the papers for quite some time. At present the only way to spread this information here in America is hand to hand.

Your help is needed. Please make 1, 5, 10, 100 copies or whatever you can, and give them to friends or politicians, groups, media. This game is nearly up. Either the Mafia goes or AMERICA goes.

GUNPOWDER PLOT

It seems odd that the most famous political conspiracy in English history should have made an obscure soldier with a fondness for explosives quite so famous. You have to wonder why it's Guy Fawkes's effigy that's burned on 5 November and not that of Robert Catesby, the ringleader, or even Robert Cecil, the king's spymaster and, so some have suggested, the real conspirator.

The details of the plot itself are well known. At dispute is not the story of Guy Fawkes caught red-handed in a cellar under the House of Lords with 36 barrels of gunpowder and an awful lot of brushwood – rather the train of events which led him there. Plot organizer Robert Catesby came from a family of devout and active Catholics and was said to possess great personal magnetism, which he used to recruit others to his cause of Catholic rebellion. His coterie of conspirators included minor members of disaffected Catholic gentry, a fair few of Catesby's relations and even one of his own servants, and a few big hitters who had the funds and horses to lead the uprising which was planned to follow the assassination of king and Parliament.

Guy Fawkes had been recruited in Flanders, where he was working for the Spanish military, and returned to join the conspiracy. However, on a return trip to Flanders to drum up support for their plot, Fawkes was spotted by one of Robert Cecil's spies. Cecil had succeeded his father, Lord Burghley, as right-hand man to first Elizabeth I and then James I, and had inherited the vast network of spies and informants set up by his father and Walsingham during Elizabeth's reign. Cecil soon made the connection between Fawkes and Catesby, though he seems to have taken little action to pursue the matter further at that time – around six months before the plot was uncovered.

By 26 October 1605, everything was ready. The gunpowder had been brought in and installed in a cellar the plotters had leased, which was placed handily under the main House of Lords chamber. On this night, however, Lord Monteagle, a Catholic MP, who had not been known to be "at home" during any previous evening during 1605, just happened to be around to receive an anonymous letter warning him to avoid the opening of Parliament on 5 November. He took the letter straight to Robert Cecil. Six days elapsed before the Monteagle letter was shown to the king and the search of Westminster was not ordered until the night of 4 November, nine days later. On Fawkes's capture, he was tortured to make him reveal the names of his co-conspirators. Days later, a confession was finally extracted, though Fawkes's signature on the document bore little resemblance to his usual one (presumably in consequence of the torture). Fawkes's statement read:

I confese, that a practise in generall was first broken unto me, against his Majestir for reliefe of the Catholic cause, and not invented or propounded by my selfe. And this was first propounded unto mee about Easter Last was twelve moneth beyond the seas, in the Lowe Countries of the *Archdukes* obeisance, by *Thomas Winter*, who came thereupon with mee into England, and there imparted our purpose to three other Gentleman more, namely *Robert Catesby*, *Thomas Percy*, and *Iohn Wright*, who all five consulting together of the means how to execute the same, and taking a vow among ourselves for secrecie, *Catesby* propounded to have it performed by Gunpowder, and by making a Myne under the upper House of Parliament: which place wee made a choice of the rather because Religion having been unjustly suppressed there, it was fittest that Justice and punishment should be executed there.

This being resolved amongst us, *Thomas Percy* hired an House at Westminster for that purpose, neere adioyning to the Parliament House, and there we begun to make our Myne about the II of December 1604.

The five that first enterd into the worke were *Thomas Percy*, *Thomas Cateby*, *Thomas Winter*, *Iohn Wright* and myself: and soon after wee tooke another unto us, *Christopher Wright* having Sworne him also, and taken the Sacrament for secrecie.

When we came to the very foundation of the Wall of the House, which was about three yards thicke, and found it a matter of great difficultie, wee tooke unto us another Gentleman *Robert Winter*, in like manner with oath and sacrament as afore said.

It was about Christmas when we brought our myne unto the Wall, and about Candlemas we had wrought the wall halfe through: and whilst they were working, I stood as Sentinell to descrie any man that came neere, whereof I gave them warning, and so they ceased until I gave notice again to proceede.

All we seven lay in the House, and had Shot and Powder, being resolved to die in that place before we should yield or be taken. As they were working upon the wall they heard a rushing in the Cellar of removing of Coales, whereupon we feared we had been discovered: and they sent me to go to the Cellar, who finding that the Coales were a-selling and the Cellar was to bee let, viewing the commoditie thereof for our purpose, *Percy* went and hired the same for yeerely rent.

We had before this provided and brought into the House twentie Barrels of Powder, which we removed into the Cellar, and covered the same with Billets and Faggots, which were provided for that purpose.

About Easter, the Parliament being prorogued till October next, we dispersed ourselves and I retired into the Low countreys by advice and direction of the rest, as well to aquaint *Owen* with the particulars of the Plot, as also lest by my longer stay I might have growen suspicious, and so have come into question.

In the meantime *Percy* having the key of the Cellar, laide in more Powder and wood into it. I returned about the beginning of September next, and then receiving the key again of Percy, we brought in more Powder and Billets to cover the same again, and so I went for a time into the Countrey till the 30 of October.

It was a further resolve amongst us that the same day that this act should have been performed, some other of our Confederates should have surprised the person of Lady Elizabeth the King's eldest daughter, who was kept in Warwickshire at Lo.[rd] *Harrington*'s house, and presently have her proclaimed as Queen, having a project of a Proclamation ready for that purpose, wherein we made no mention of altering of Religion, nor would have avowed the deede to be ours, until we should have had powder enough to make our partie good and then we would have avowed both.

Concerning Duke Charles, the King's second sonne, wee had sundry consultations how to seise on his Person. But because we found no means how to compasse it (the Duke being kept neere London, where we had not Forces y-nough) we resolved to serve our turn with Lady Elizabeth.

THE NAMES OF OTHER PRINCIPALL
Persons, that were made privy
Afterwards to this horrible
Conspiracie

Catesby and his followers were tracked to Holbeche House, Staffordshire, where he and several others died in the ensuing gun battle. The rest were captured and committed for trial.

Except, that is, for one Francis Tresham. He alone out of all the plotters was spared the horror of being hung, drawn and quartered, which seems odd considering that anyone else who had anything remotely to do with the plot was summarily executed. Perhaps his immunity from that horrible fate can be explained by his association with Cecil. It was assumed that

Tresham was the author of that anonymous letter to his friend Monteagle, though some claim it was Cecil himself. In any event, Monteagle's loyalty to the crown had already been bought by the king's previous leniency.

In 1601 the Earl of Essex, Robert Devereux, had marched on the city of London to highlight abuses he felt had been perpetrated by the Privy Council in general and Robert Cecil in particular. Devereux was arrested along with his supporters Robert Catesby, Lord Monteagle and Francis Tresham.

Those who believe Cecil was behind the whole Gunpowder Plot claim that, at this point, Tresham and even Catesby himself became double-agents for Cecil in return for being spared execution. Certainly, having one or more men on the inside of the conspiracy would have explained why Cecil had been in no rush to uncover the plot. It would also explain how he could have masterminded events to further his own ends, giving the green light to further persecution of Catholics – whom he despised for their allegiance to another ruler (i.e. the Pope) – and to the lucrative confiscation of monastic lands.

In the end, it is Cecil's own character as a ruthlessly ambitious and efficient man which scuppers this theory of a conspiracy within a conspiracy. The benefits do not seem radical enough by half to have been worth his effort. In the end, a handful of political bit players were executed, the Jesuits were expelled from England and had their lands taken, and the general Catholic populace was forced to keep its head down for the next two hundred years. However, prominent Catholic aristocrats remained influential members of the king's inner circle and England soon signed a lasting peace treaty with Catholic Spain. Perhaps, in the end, Cecil appreciated how far the boat could be rocked but knew not to push it any further.

Guy Fawkes was a patsy in plot by Elizabethan secret service to justify religious cleansing of Catholics in England: ALERT LEVEL 2

Further Reading
Francis Edwards, *Guy Fawkes and the Real Story of the Gunpowder Plot*, 1969
Antonia Fraser, *The Gunpowder Plot*, 2000
Martin Stephens, *The Desperate Remedy: Henry Gresham and the Gunpowder Plot*, 2001 [a novel]

HAARP

Near Gakona, Alaska, is the 33-acre (12ha) site which houses America's High Frequency Active Auroral Research Program, or HAARP. Here scientists transmit a 3.6MW signal into the ionosphere so that other colleagues in white overalls can "understand . . . and control ionospheric processes that might alter the performance of communication and surveillance systems". Put another way: if the nature of the ionosphere, that layer of sky which commences 30 miles (50km) above the planet's surface, is properly understood we can all have better satellite TV and telephone signals.

A worthy aim. But maybe improved communications is not HAARP's true purpose. HAARP is funded by the Office of Naval Research and administered by the US Navy together with the United States Air Force and the University of Alaska. Of course the military, more than most, have a vested interest in communications and navigation, but the prevalent suspicion about HAARP is that it is a weapon capable of delivering several types of mass destruction.

Suggestions that HAARP could be used for "geophysical warfare" first appeared in *Angels Don't Play This HAARP* (1995) by Nick Begich and Jeanne Mannings, with the investigation continued by Jerry E. Smith in *HAARP: The Ultimate Weapon of the Conspiracy* (1998). HAARP's transmitter works by heating the ionosphere above the site, leading some to claim that it is designed to alter the world's weather systems to the advantage of the US. Even the Indian Ocean tsunami of 2004 is said to have been caused by a HAARP firing, the proof offered being one of *cui bono* ("who benefits?"): the tsunami devastated the economies of America's Asian competitors; *ergo*, the US was responsible. Smith also asserts that HAARP uses extremely-low-frequency (ELF) waves which can be used for remote mind control.

More plausible is the notion that HAARP's Ionospheric Research Instrument (IRI) transmitter can be used as a "death beam". HAARP is much like the patented weapon system designed by Dr Bernard Eastlund to destroy missiles and aircraft systems by transmitting pulses of electromagnetic radiation. (Eastlund's patent, as the Texan physicist himself acknowledges, owes much to the work on "weapons of doom" undertaken by the eccentric Croat genius Nikola Tesla, many of whose inventions are supposedly still kept under strict wraps by the US authorities even though Tesla died over 50 years ago.)

All such nefarious purposes for HAARP are denied by US officialdom, who point out that the HAARP site holds open days every summer. Since HAARP is situated in an inaccessible corner of Alaska, this offer may not be so generous as it seems. Critics also wonder why HAARP is managed by an official from the Defense Advanced Research Project Agency (DARPA) rather than a boffin from a university science department.

HAARP is not the US's only "ionospheric heater"; there are others at Fairbanks, Alaska, and at the Arecibo observatory in Puerto Rico. Russia has one (Sura), near Nizhniy Novgorodlol, and the EC one at Tromsø, Norway.

Even if HAARP and the other ionospheric heating projects are as innocent as they claim, is tampering with the ionosphere good for the earth? A scientist at the University of Alaska Fairbanks Geophysical Institute once compared HAARP to "an immersion heater in the Yukon". Meteorologists have been less benign, pointing out that the "effects of HAARP on the climate are completely unknown". Global warming, anybody?

HAARP is a covert weapon of doom: ALERT LEVEL 5

Further Reading
Nick Begich and Jeanne Mannings, *Angels Don't Play This HAARP*, 1995
Jerry E. Smith, *HAARP: The Ultimate Weapon of the Conspiracy*, 1998.

RUDOLF HESS

Scotland, the late morning of 10 May 1941. Out of the spring sky to the east a lone Me110 German fighter appears over Glasgow and circles unhurriedly as though searching for something, before its pilot bales out over the village of Eaglesham, to the south of the city. On his apprehension on the ground by local soldiers, the Luftwaffe pilot announces in English that he is Captain Alfred Horn and adds: "I wish to see the Duke of Hamilton. Will you take me to him?"

A few days later, "Captain Horn" is revealed by the British authorities to be none other than Rudolf Hess, the Deputy Fuhrer of Germany. Hitler, from Berlin, denounces Hess as a madman who stole an aircraft to go on a private peace mission. The British confine Hess until immediately after the war, when they too claim Hess is mad – but not *too* mad, sane enough to stand trial at Nuremberg for war crimes. There, despite his "sanity", Hess is unable to recognize fellow Nazi bigwigs and betrays little recognition of events in his own life. Nevertheless he is sentenced to life imprisonment in Spandau and dies, apparently by his own hand, in 1987, aged 93. British documents relating to the case are put under lock and key for 65 years.

Even in the briefest recounting, the story of Rudolf Hess overflows with questions and contradictions. How could the Deputy Fuhrer "steal", from the very public surroundings of Augsburg Messerschmitt works, an Me110 which just happened to have been specially adapted (at his own instigation) with long-range fuel tanks? Why was Hess's Me110 not accorded the usual Glasgow greeting given to the Luftwaffe – sirens, flak and interception by Fighter Command? Why did Hess want to meet the Duke of Hamilton? Why is there such a long time-lock on the Hess documents? And (the question of questions): was it actually Hess or a double who stood in the dock in Nuremberg?

Rudolf Hess is invariably viewed through the lens of his 1941 mission, which provides a portrait of a sincere if somewhat neurotic loner who, cast out from the inner sanctum of Nazism, wished peace in a time of total war. Hess was the Good Nazi, a status underlined by his lenient sentence at Nuremberg: the other main leaders of Nazi Germany were condemned to death or, like Goring, committed suicide. Hess was condemned to prison. In truth, Hess was an ardent anti-Semite and, along with Hitler, the founder of the National Socialist German Workers Party (NSDAP) in 1920. So close and loyal to Hitler was Hess thereafter that fellow Nazis dubbed Hess "the Fraulein" – Hitler's wife. Foreign journalists also noted the strength of the men's relationship: Pierre van Passen of the Canadian *Evening World* thought Hess to be Hitler's "alter ego". Time did little to diminish the closeness. There was no fall from grace for Hess; he disliked some aspects of the bloody purge of the SA, and Hitler was no fan of Hess's "biodynamic" eating habits, modelled on the alternative philosophy of Rudolf Steiner, but otherwise the men were in complete accord. If they hadn't been, Hitler would not have maintained Hess as his right-hand man.

So, when he flew to Scotland in 1941, Hess did not do so as a lone, powerless, out-of-favour maverick. He can only have gone as Hitler's personal peace emissary. Hitler's later rants against "madman" Hess were merely attempts to lay down a smokescreen over a diplomatic debacle. (Tellingly, Hitler took little or no action after 1941 against Hess's family, as was his wont with traitors; on the contrary, he ensured that Hess's wife remained in her villa and received a state pension.) Hitler desperately wanted peace with Britain in mid-1941 because he sought above all to turn his entire military attention to the real enemy:

Bolshevik Russia. War with Britain had never been Hitler's intention; indeed, in *Mein Kampf* he had saluted Britain as Germany's "most valuable ally in the world". His fatal miscalculation had been to presume that Britain would endlessly turn a blind eye to the Nazi appropriation of central Europe.

Hitler's hope for reconciliation with Britain was not an unreasonable one. Although it is generally swept under the national carpet, there existed in wartime Britain a distinct vein of sentiment which, for reasons of pro-Nazism or pro-pacifism, did not want the conflict to continue. One peace proponent was Douglas Douglas-Hamilton, the Duke of Hamilton, RAF wing commander and privy councillor, and a member of the Anglo-German Club. Something of Hamilton's sentiments regarding the war can be gauged by his letter to *The Times* of 6 October 1939, when the war was a month old:

Sir,

Many, like yourself, have had the opportunity of hearing a great deal of what the men and women of my generation are thinking. There is no doubt in any quarter, irrespective of any party, that this country had no choice but to accept the challenge of Hitler's aggression against one country in Europe after another. If Hitler is right when he claims that the whole of the German nation is with him in his cruelties and treacheries, both within Germany and without, then this war must be fought to the bitter end. It may well last for many years, but the people of the British Empire will not falter in their determination to see it through.

But I believe that the moment the menace of aggression and bad faith has been removed, war against Germany becomes wrong and meaningless. This generation is conscious that injustices were done to the German people in the era after the last war. There must be no repetition of that. To seek anything but a just and comprehensive peace to lay to rest the fears and discords in Europe would be a betrayal of our fallen.

I look forward to the day when a trusted Germany will again come into her own and believe that there is such a

Germany, which would be loath to inflict wrong on other nations such as she would not like to suffer herself. That day may be far off, but when it comes, then hostilities could and should cease, and all efforts be concentrated on righting the wrongs in Europe by free negotiations between the disputing parties, all parties binding themselves to submit their disputes to an impartial equity tribunal in case they cannot reach agreement.

We do not begrudge Germany Lebensraum, provided that Lebensraum is not made the grave of other nations. We should be ready to search for and find a colonial settlement, just to all peoples concerned, as soon as there exist effective guarantees that no race will be exposed to being treated as Hitler treated the Jews on 9 November last year [Kristallnacht]. We shall, I trust, live to see the day when such a healing peace is negotiated between honourable men and the bitter memories of twenty-five years of unhappy tension between Germany and the Western democracies are wiped away in their responsible co-operation for building a better Europe.

Hamilton's letter, which may have been covertly backed by Neville Chamberlain, was not just for British consumption: it was evidently designed to alert Nazi Germany to the fact that there were Britons who would deal with them. Overtures from Nazi Germany duly arrived, via the floating Nazi emissary Albrecht Haushofer – the son of Hess's friend and mentor Professor Karl Haushofer. The younger Haushofer not only knew Hess but was a friend of Hamilton, hence the familiar tone he uses in his letter to Hamilton of 23 September 1940:

My dear Douglo

. . . If you remember some of my last communications in July 1939 you and your friends in high places may find some significance in the fact that I am able to ask you whether you could find time to have a talk with me somewhere on the outskirts of Europe, perhaps in Portugal . . .

On receiving Haushofer's letter, Hamilton apparently showed it to the Air Minister, Sir Archibald Sinclair, and the Foreign Secretary, Lord Halifax, both of whom were well known to be lukewarm for war. The letter was deliberately kept from Churchill the bulldog. According to *Double Standards* (2001), the account of the Hess mission by Picknett, Prince and Prior, there then followed months of arrangements for Hess's secret flight to Britain – made with Hitler's connivance – to deal with an elite pro-peace lobby which had sufficient control of a sector of the RAF to ensure no one shot down Hess's Me110 as it neared Scotland. Two Czech pilots with the RAF, Vaclav "Felix" Bauman and Leopold Srom, later recounted that they intercepted Hess's Me110 but, as they moved in for the kill, Bauman was told by his radio controller, "Sorry, Felix, old boy. It is not possible. You must return. Now."

Although Hamilton would later profess total amazement that Hess was seeking him out, it is more likely that he was expecting the Deputy Fuhrer. According to eyewitnesses, Hamilton was shocked and agitated when he found that "Horn" had been captured by the Home Guard – Hess had bungled the operation by failing to land at Hamilton's house, Dungavel. After the plane had crashed noisily and "Horn" been publicly captured, any chance of a secret meeting between Hess and the pro-peace group had gone.

The Hess affair massively increased Churchill's power vis-a-vis the peace wing of the British establishment (which included the Duke of Kent and ex-Prime Minister Lloyd George). Not only had the peacemongers committed an embarrassing *faux pas*, they had given Churchill a pawn in a disinformation campaign. As Pierre van Passen noted in *That Day Alone* (1941), Churchill publicly pretended to take Hess's peace proposal seriously – in return Hitler de-intensified the Blitz and diverted his focus towards the Soviet Union. When the Wehrmacht's tanks rolled into Russia in July 1941, Britain was no longer alone in the fight against Nazism. Henceforth it was unlikely to lose a war that only weeks before Hess's flight had seemed unwinnable.

There was, though, the problem of what to do with Hess. Initially, the ex-Deputy Fuhrer was imprisoned in the Tower of London, then at Mytchett Place, Surrey, then at Maindiff Court near Abergavenny in Wales. Confusingly, intelligence reports by Nazi Abwehr spies in Britain placed Hess in Scotland, in the western Highlands, at the same time he was in Wales. How could Hess be in two places at once? Either the Abwehr was mistaken – or, fantastically, there were two Rudolf Hesses.

The Hess "*doppelgänger*" theory was given credence in 1979 in *The Murder of Rudolf Hess* by Dr Hugh Thomas, a military surgeon who had examined Hess in Spandau prison six years before. To Thomas's befuddlement, his examination of Prisoner Number Seven failed to detect the First World War bullet wound that Hess was known to have received. Thomas's book prompted other researches, many of which ostensibly confirmed the *doppelgänger* thesis. Under influence of the truth drug sodium pentothal in 1944 at Maindiff Court, "Hess" apparently refused to recognize the names of intimates, including Karl Haushofer and Willy Messerschmitt. Then there was his bizarre inability at Nuremberg to remember former colleagues. Amnesia might account for these mental lapses; less easy to explain is the fact that the dental records of the Hess held in 1941 seem to belong to someone other than the person held at Maindiff in 1943. And why did Hess the prisoner at Spandau refuse to see his wife and son for 26 years?

Thomas hypothesizes that the real Hess was shot down (on Goring's instructions) and that it was the *doppelgänger* Hess who arrived in Scotland in 1941. Aviation records, including testimony by Hess's aircrew, refute this: Hess's Me110 bore the identification code VJ OQ and the Messerschmitt which crashed in Scotland bore this marking. (A section of fuselage is on display in the Imperial War Museum, London.) A more plausible explanation is suggested by Peter Allen in *The Crown and the Swastika* (1983): the *doppelgänger* was substituted while Hess was in British custody. Allen cites in evidence the recollections of Charles Fraser-Smith, the intelligence service gadget-maker who was the inspiration for Q in the Bond movies. In the immediate aftermath of Hess's arrest, Fraser-Smith was asked to make an identical copy of Hess's uniform. Fraser-Smith could think of no reason for the request unless the uniform was to be worn by a double. According to him, MI6 held a top-level meeting in 1975 to discuss the identity of "Hess".

If the Hess incarcerated in Spandau was the *doppelgänger*, where was the real one? Intriguingly, Picknett, Prince and Prior suggest that the fate of the real Hess was tied into the mysterious plane crash which killed George, Duke of Kent, on 25 August 1942. On that day the Duke's RAF Sunderland flying boat crashed into Eagle's Rock, Caithness, Scotland, an event an MOD inquiry found to be caused by: "A/C [AIRCRAFT] BEING ON WRONG TRACK AT TO [SIC] LOW ALTITUDE TO CLEAR RISING GROUND . . . CAPT OF A/C CHANGED FLIGHT-PLAN FOR REASONS UNKNOWN & DESCENDED THROUGH CLOUD WITHOUT MAKING SURE HE WAS OVER WATER."

The Duke's flying boat was piloted by some of the RAF's most experienced crew. By operational rules it should not have been flown over land. Immediately after the crash, the MOD announced that all 15 crew had been killed and their bodies recovered. A day later a survivor, Andy Jack, wandered dazed into a crofter's cottage. That made *16* men aboard the doomed Sunderland, one more than the take-off complement. The extra man was, Picknett, Prince and Prior suggest, Hess himself, who had been picked up from a nearby loch by Kent, the king's brother and a known softliner on Germany, with the intention of taking the Deputy Fuhrer to neutral Sweden. Kent's Sunderland, it later transpired, had been painted white – the colour for flights to neutral countries. Numerous records relating to the Duke's crash are missing from the Public Record Office.

A frequent objection to the *doppelgänger* theory is that the false Hess would never have admitted to war crimes at Nuremberg and accepted life in prison. He would have shouted his innocence to the court ceiling. Unless, that is, the false Hess had been brainwashed. This seems fanciful . . . until the success of the Russians in the 1930s Show Trials and the CIA with its **MK-ULTRA** programme is recalled.

Almost fittingly, the death of "Hess" in Spandau on 17 August 1987 was as much a mystery as his life had been. During a walk in the prison garden, Hess's guard was called away to take a telephone call. When he returned he found Hess lying in the garden hut with electrical cable wound around his neck. Two days later a post-mortem by the British army concluded that that the cause of death was suspension (hanging).

Matters might have rested there, except that Hess's family secretly arranged an independent autopsy when they received the corpse for burial. The conclusion of the independent post-mortem, carried out by a Dr Spann, was that Hess's death was due not to suspension but to strangulation. The pattern made on the neck of Prisoner Number Seven by the electrical cord was horizontal; this is impossible in hanging, where the pattern is a V rising towards the point of suspension. Moreover, the 93-year-old Hess was nearly crippled by arthritis and the effects of strokes. According to his nurse, Abdallah Melaouhi, it would have been impossible for him to have raised his arms or found the dexterity to tie the cord to the window latch to hang himself. Prisoner Number Seven could not even tie his shoelaces any more.

Under pressure from the Hess family and a BBC 'Newsnight' programme featuring Abdallah Melaouhi, in 1989 the British government ordered a review of Hess's death. After receiving a report from Scotland Yard, the Director of Public Prosecutions decided there was no convincing evidence to show Hess had been murdered. When the Labour MP Rhodri Morgan asked to see the Scotland Yard report, his request was denied. Further attempts to view the Yard's investigation have been refused under "Public Interest Immunity", the legal clause used by the government when disclosure of information might not be in the national interest.

Wolf Hess, the Deputy Fuhrer's son, is certain his father was murdered, and he believes he knows who did it and why. For

Wolf Hess the prisoner in Spandau was, to his satisfaction, his father, and he dismisses the *doppelgänger* theory outright. (To him the inconsistent and missing records are merely evidence of the British tendency towards inefficiency and cock-up.) Under pressure from the Soviet Union and a worldwide humanitarian campaign, Hess was about to be released in late summer 1987. This the British could not allow, because the released Hess would have revealed the full details of the peace proposals with which he flew to Britain in 1941. So Hess was murdered by two soldiers (from the SAS, according to several sources) infiltrated into Spandau.

Of course, if Prisoner Number Seven was the Hess *doppelgänger*, he still would have required "termination" – precisely because his identity as the false Hess could not be allowed to be discovered. Dead *doppelgängers* tell no tales.

Was Hess murdered to prevent his disclosing that his 1941 mission was official business with a peace wing of the British establishment? ALERT LEVEL 9

Was Prisoner Number Seven a *doppelgänger* of Hess? ALERT LEVEL 5

Further Reading
Peter Allen, *The Crown and the Swastika: Hitler, Hess and the Duke of Windsor*, 1983
James Douglas-Hamilton, *The Truth About Rudolf Hess*, 1993
Richard Griffiths, *Fellow Travellers of the Right: British Enthusiasts for Germany 1933-39*, 1980
Wolf Rudiger Hess, *My Father, Rudolf Hess*, 1984
Peter Padfield, *Hess: Flight for the Fuhrer*, 1991
Lynn Picknett, Clive Prince and Stephen Prior, *Double Standards: The Rudolf Hess Cover-Up*, 2001
Hugh Thomas, *The Murder of Rudolf Hess*, 1979

HIV/AIDS

Acquired Immuno-Deficiency Syndrome (AIDS) is the ultimate stage of infection for people who contract Human
Immunodeficiency Virus (HIV). HIV annihilates the human
immune system to the point where it ceases to function. AIDS
victims do not die of HIV; they die of, commonly, pneumonia,
cancers such as Kaposi's sarcoma, or some other secondary or
tertiary infection.

The first recorded AIDS victims were four young Los
Angeles homosexuals in 1981, though it gradually became
apparent that the epicentre of the AIDS holocaust was not
the gay scene in LA or NY but Africa below the Sahara. By
2004, 25 million Africans had died from "Slim".

Africa, according to the leading HIV virologist Professor
Robert Gallo, was also the source of HIV, which had crossed
species from the green monkey to humans via a monkey bite or
consumption of infected monkey "bush meat". This "little
green monkey" theory failed to convince everyone, even sections of the medical establishment. How, cynics asked, could 80
million people become infected via sexual intercourse/intrave-
nous drug use/blood transfusions from a single source in the
space of three decades? The numbers did not stack up.

Enter Doctor Robert B. Strecker, MD PhD. In 1983 Strecker
was conducting research for the Security Pacific Bank in the US
into the risks of providing health cover for people who were
HIV positive. During this research Strecker and his attorney

brother Ted allegedly discovered thousands of documents which proved that AIDS was a manmade disease. When they sent their proof to politicians and government, they were ignored, so they made the video *The Strecker Memorandum*. According to the Streckers' own advertising:

> It [*The Strecker Memorandum*] is 96 minutes of the most startling, controversial, and information-packed video you will ever see. It disputes virtually everything the American public is being told by the government, the so-called AIDS experts and the media. In fact, after seeing it YOU will know more about AIDS than 99 percent of all doctors in America.

The controversial truth revealed to those who paid $30.95 (at 2007 prices) for *The Strecker Memorandum* was that HIV was a virus artificially created by the US military which had then been distributed by the World Health Organization under the auspices of its smallpox vaccination programme. Strecker claimed also that the HIV virus was so minute it could pass through the molecular structure of condoms (thus rendering the "safe sex" campaign useless), and indeed that HIV could be transmitted human-to-human without exchange of body fluids.

In 1988 Ted Strecker was found dead at his home in Springfield, Missouri. Officially the verdict was suicide. The Strecker Group claimed that Ted Strecker left "No note, no message, no goodbyes to anyone. Very untypical of him."

Strecker was by no means the only AIDS conspiracy theorist to identify the Chemical Biological Warfare department at Fort Detrick, Maryland, as the lab where HIV was manufactured. So did Jakob Segal of the Humboldt University in East Berlin. In 1986 Segal and his wife Lilli announced that HIV was an artificial "splice" between visna virus (which affects sheep) and HTLV-1 (a retrovirus which affects humans), and that it had been created at Fort Detrick in 1977 and tested on nearby prisoners, who had then gone into the general community and spread the virus. The Segals' "discovery" was later disclosed by KGB defector Vasili Mitrokhin to be a Soviet disinformation campaign.

If the Segals posited HIV as the dirty work of the US government, William Campbell Douglass MD was equally convinced that HIV was a plot by the USSR. In "WHO Murdered Africa" in *Health Freedom News*, September 1987, Douglass asserted that the USSR, via its covert control of the WHO, was responsible for the AIDS holocaust on the continent. Despite being a white member of the reactionary John Birch Society, Douglass became, bizarrely, a major influence on Black American militants of the Nation of Islam, who claim AIDS is a genocidal attack on their ethnic kind.

After all, the evidence seems to fit the "black holocaust" scenario. The black/white ratio for new AIDS cases in the US is 5/1 male and 15/1 female. AIDS is the leading killer of black Americans aged 25–44. Approximately 60 per cent of all AIDS cases worldwide have occurred in black Africa. There is also the indisputable proof that the US government has experimented on black citizens. Starting in 1932, the Tuskegee Syphilis Study deliberately infected hundreds of black Alabama men with the sexually transmitted disease to monitor the effects of nontreatment. The experiment was not wound up until 1972 when a worker "blew the whistle".

The black-genocide thesis was given added fuel by Dr Leonard Horowitz's 1996 *Emerging Viruses: AIDS and Ebola: Nature, Accident or Intentional?* According to Horowitz, AIDS was invented at Fort Detrick (of course) and the Rockefeller Institute for Medical Research by proteges of the Nazi eugenics scientists brought to the US after the Second World War. The purpose of AIDS, Horowitz claimed, was to reduce the numbers of blacks, gays, Hispanics and Jews in the world in line with a 1974 memo by Dr Henry Kissinger, then US National Security Adviser: "Depopulation should be the highest priority of US foreign policy towards the Third World . . . Reduction of the rate of population in these States is a matter of vital US national security. The US economy will require large and increasing amounts of minerals from abroad, especially less developed countries."

The verdict? Just as there is no visible end to the AIDS epidemic, there is no sight of an unambiguous understanding of its origins or its course. At least one leading molecular biologist, Professor Peter Duesberg of the University of California, even denies any connection between HIV and AIDS, while *The Times* of London published in 1987 a four-page report with strong evidence that AIDS in Africa did shadow the WHO smallpox vaccination programme, probably because the vaccination activated a dormant HIV virus in the recipient. Or, in other words, the mad Dr Strecker may have been partially right. Where science failed to authoritatively fill the vacuum, it is hardly surprising that conspiracy theories should have rushed in and flourished. At least 50 per cent of black Americans, according to a 2005 study by a University of Oregon academic, believe that AIDS is an artificial construct, and 10 per cent hold that the CIA developed the HIV virus.

Unfortunately, many of the AIDS conspiracy theories are as deadly as the disease itself: they deny the validity of safe-sex and clean-needle programmes. After all, why bother using condoms if AIDS is a bio-weapon that can be caught by "casual contact"? Nor is there any real evidence that the "alternative" cures promoted by Strecker ("Raman spectroscopy"), Boyd Graves ("colloidal silver") and others have any effect in treating AIDS.

> AIDS is an engineered virus designed to reduce black population of the globe: ALERT LEVEL 2

Further Reading
Douglass, William Campbell, "WHO Murdered Africa", *Health Freedom News*, September 1987
Horowitz, Leonard G., *Emerging Viruses: AIDS and Ebola: Nature, Accident or Intentional?*, 1996

JIMMY HOFFA

There is a scene in the comedy movie *Bruce Almighty* (2003) where Jim Carrey's character, Bruce, an investigative journalist who literally becomes God, discovers the body of missing ex-Teamster boss Jimmy Hoffa. The joke is that one would need to be God to discover Hoffa's body – because no mere mortal has done so, despite three decades of searches.

On 30 July 1975, James Hoffa, president of the powerful US Teamsters (truckers) Union 1957–67, walked out of the Machus Red Fox restaurant in Detroit and into American myth. He was never seen again. James Riddle Hoffa had fought his way into the leadership of the International Brotherhood of Teamsters during the 1930s, when labour and capital were engaged in struggles that bordered on the class warfare dreamed of by Marxists. Hoffa's own brother was shot. For protection, the Teamsters turned to the Mafia, who also helped the Teamsters extort money from employers. Hoffa used the overflowing union pension fund as his own private bank, and as a slush fund to buy favour with politicians at all levels, from city districts to the US Senate.

When **Robert F. Kennedy** became chief counsel to the Senate Select Committee on Improper Activities in the Labor or Management Field, he targeted Hoffa for special attention. When **John F. Kennedy** became US president, Bobby was appointed Attorney General and the pressure to convict Hoffa was stepped up. Hoffa, according to an FBI informant, swore he would get Robert Kennedy, and put out a contract on him. In the book *Double Cross* (1992), Chuck Giancana, brother of Mob boss Sam Giancana, also fingered Hoffa as one of the killers of **Marilyn Monroe**.

In 1962, Hoffa went on trial for extortion and managed to get a hung jury. How he achieved this remarkable result was soon revealed. He was subsequently tried and found guilty of jury-tampering, a crime for which he received a 15-year sentence. In 1964 he was convicted of defrauding the union pension fund of almost two million dollars. When in 1967 his legal team ran out of appeals, Hoffa began serving his sentences in the federal penitentiary at Lewisburg, Pennsylvania.

To run the union in his place, Hoffa engineered the election as its president of his protege Frank Fitzsimmons. Fitzsimmons, to Hoffa's chagrin, refused to be a puppet whose strings could be pulled by Hoffa from the Lewisburg pen. Hoffa swore he would regain the leadership of the union.

Four years after he'd entered prison, Hoffa's sentences were commuted, by Republican President Richard Nixon, to time served – on condition that Hoffa agreed to stay out of union affairs for 10 years. Hoffa was planning to mount a legal challenge to that restriction in order to reassert his power over the Teamsters when he disappeared, at 2.30 p.m on 30 July 1975, from the parking lot of the Machus Red Fox Restaurant. He had been due to meet two Mafia leaders, Anthony "Tony Jack" Giacalone from Detroit and Anthony "Tony Pro" Provenzano from New York.

In the standard homicide investigation, the principal question is: whodunnit? In the case of Jimmy Hoffa it was more a question of: who *didn't* do it? At least three Mafia hitmen – Donald Frankos, Louie Milito and Richard "The Iceman" Kurlinski – have claimed to have offed the Hoff. Motives likewise abound. Hoffa was stealing from the Mob, elements loyal to Fitzsimmons (like Hoffa, a Mafia associate) sought to prevent Hoffa's return to the union leadership, Hoffa carried too many secrets about the Mob's role in the assassination of RFK and Marilyn Monroe . . .

In the three decades since Hoffa's disappearance, there have been many unsuccessful searches for his remains. All manner of rumours have surfaced about the body being under the Giants' Stadium, or in a swamp, compacted by a car-crusher, or processed through a meat rendering plant.

Frank "The Irishman" Sheerhan was a Teamster official, a close associate of Hoffa, and a Mafia hitman. Near the end of his life, as he lay dying of cancer, he confessed to his lawyer Charles Brandt that it was *he* who had gunned down Hoffa at his house in Detroit.

Brandt: How many shots were fired at Jimmy?
Sheerhan: Two.
Brandt: You were the shooter?
Sheerhan: That's right.

Brandt wrote a book based on Sheerhan's confession, *I Heard You Paint Houses*, that has convinced many Sheerhan was telling the truth. DNA evidence taken from the car and from the house support Sheerhan's version. In the FBI's original "Hoffex" memo, Sheerhan was listed as a prime suspect but, despite FBI pressure, he refused to talk until his deathbed confession. According to Sheerhan, Hoffa's body was cremated in a Mafia-run funeral parlour.

Sheerhan identified two brothers, Tom and Steve Andretta, as the "cleaners" who tidied up the house after the killing. Both men are listed among the FBI's original suspects.

While no one was ever convicted for the Hoffa murder, the Department of Justice prosecuted more than 30 Mafia figures for other crimes uncovered during the Hoffa investigation. In a twist of divine justice, everyone likely to have participated in the Hoffa murder ended up doing time anyway.

> Teamster boss Jimmy Hoffa was murdered by the Mob:
> ALERT LEVEL 9

Further Reading

Charles Brandt, *I Heard You Paint Houses: Frank "The Irish-man" Sheerhan and the Inside Story of the Mafia, the Team-sters, and the Last Ride of Jimmy Hoffa*, 2004

Sam and Chuck Giancana, *Double Cross: The Story of the Man Who Controlled America*, 1992

Dan E. Moldea, *The Hoffa Wars*, 1978

HOLLOW EARTH

You didn't think Jules Verne's *Journey to the Centre of the Earth* (1863) was fiction, did you?

Believers in Hollow Earth theory hold that the earth is a shell with openings at the poles. Inside lives an advanced civilization, the Agartha, who sometimes emerge into our world in UFOs.

Hollow Earth theories date back to Ancient Greece, whose people believed that the dead lived in an underworld called Hades. Modern Hollow Earth theory can be traced at least to the 17th-century British astronomer Edmond Halley, who proposed that our world consists of four concentric spheres and that its interior is lit by a luminous atmosphere. The *aurora borealis* is caused by the escape of this luminous gas through the thin crust at the poles.

The idea of the Hollow Earth was especially promoted by 1812 War veteran John Cleves Symmes; after his death in 1829 a stone monument was erected in Hamilton, Ohio – it showed, naturally, a Hollow Earth. According to Symmes, the main entrance to the inner world was located at the North Pole. Cyrus Teed, an alchemist from Utica, N.Y., was so obsessed with the idea that we humans live in the *inner* world that he founded a religion based on the idea, Koreshanity, in 1888. In 1913, Marshall B. Gardner published *Journey to the Earth's Interior*, in which he rejected Halley's notion of concentric spheres but maintained that inside the Earth was a sun 600 miles (1,000km) in diameter. And Hollow Earth theory really hotted up in the

1940s with a series of articles by Richard Shaver in *Amazing Stories* magazine, in which he recounted his meetings with aliens living inside the earth.

Many adherents to Hollow Earth ideas volunteer the long history of legends and stories about the inner world (the Devil, you may care to remember, lives down *there*) as evidence of their claim. Diaries of Admiral Byrd, who flew over both the North and South Poles, purportedly claim that he also flew into the holes there. The fact that satellite images do not show the entrance holes to inner Earth is easily explained: the images are doctored by governments who wish to keep the matter secret, because they gain technological knowhow from the aliens of the inner world. Among the politicos in on the secret were the Nazis. In the late 1930s the Nazis organized expeditions to Antarctica, where they seized the territory formerly claimed by Norway and named it Neuschwabenland (New Swabia). There they encountered inner-world aliens who helped them develop flying saucers. After Hitler escaped to Neuschwabenland in 1945, Nazi flying saucers beat off an American invasion, code-named Operation High Jump, led by Admiral Byrd (yes, him again).

Or you could choose to believe that Hitler died in the bunker in Berlin in 1945, Admiral Byrd's 1946–47 Antarctic expedition was defeated by extreme weather, and that the earth is *not* hollow and full of "innerterrestrials"!

> Earth is hollow and inhabited by aliens with UFOs: ALERT LEVEL 1

Further Reading
Dr R. W. Bernard, *The Hollow Earth,* 1964
Jan Lamprecht, *Hollow Planets,* 1998

HOLOCAUST DENIAL

The Holocaust is the name given to the extermination of some six million Jews and other "undesirables" by the Third Reich of Germany between 1933 and 1945. To industrialize the genocide process, the Nazis purpose-built a number of death camps such as Auschwitz, which gassed the Jews in batches; most victims, however, simply died of malnourishment in concentration camps. In occupied Eastern Europe, from where more than five million Jews were taken, special SS killing squads, *Einsatz-gruppen*, sometimes shot Jews *in situ*.

A wide spread of sources confirms the nature and extent of the Holocaust: the thousandfold testimonies of camp survivors; film and photographs taken by Allied reporters as the camps were liberated in 1945; the confession by Auschwitz SS camp commandant Rudolf Hoss; the prosecution of Adolf Eichmann in 1960–62 and his sentencing to death for "crimes against humanity". But all of this is disputed by a number of historians and politicians, who speculate that the Holocaust, if it happened at all, was on at most a minor scale.

One early Holocaust "denier" was the American David Hoggan, who in 1968 published *The Myth of the Six Million*, in which he asserted that the Jews had falsely accused the Germans of mass murder in order to gain reparations. Hoggan's book set a common pattern in Holocaust denial: that the Holocaust was a Jewish fabrication for gain, this being either money or international sympathy, the latter leading the United

Nations to look more kindly on the creation of a Jewish homeland in Israel. From the 1970s, neo-Nazi Willis Carto's
Institute for Historical Review has been the most prominent
voicepiece for Holocaust denial in the US. Publications from
the IHR and other Holocaust deniers in the US speculate that
the chambers at Auschwitz had an innocent purpose: fumiga-
tion to rid inmates of lice. A variant in Holocaust denial is that
there was limited extermination of Jews under the Third Reich
but that this was never official Nazi policy. According to the
British historian David Irving, Hitler was too busy fighting
the war to become entangled with the "Final Solution" for the
Jews, of which he was unaware.

Irving's version of Hitler and the Holocaust was challenged
by author Deborah Lipstadt in her 1993 book *Denying the
Holocaust*, which accused Irving of "distorting evidence" and
anti-Semitism. Irving sued Lipstadt and her British publisher,
Penguin, for libel. Lipstadt and Penguin hired Cambridge
historian Richard J. Evans, who read Irving's works and found
that Irving had knowingly used suspect documentation, including the infamous Leuchter Report. (A builder of execution
equipment, Fred Leuchter found no significant deposits of
cyanide at Auschwitz; however, this was in 1988, nearly 40
years after the camp was used, and Leuchter had no forensic
training.) Irving's books contained such phrases as: "Jews are
among the scum of humanity." The judge found that Irving "is
an active Holocaust denier; that he is anti-semite and racist, and
that he associates with right-wing extremists who promote neo-
Nazism".

As far as the participation of Hitler in the Final Solution is
concerned, the Fuhrer may have been preoccupied by his
disastrous generalship yet he clearly knew the scope of the
Final Solution if not the particulars of every train of victims
sent to Sobibor. Hitler set the agenda for the Holocaust. One
excerpt from one speech in 1939 will serve: "If international
Jewish financiers inside and outside Europe again succeed in
plunging the nations into a world war, the result will be . . . the
annihilation of the Jewish race in Europe." Other senior Third

Reich figures are incriminated by the 1942 Wannsee Protocol, which minutes a meeting held outside Berlin by 15 Nazi officials on how to best expedite the Final Solution.

The Holocaust happened. Most reputable historians put the lower limit of Jews, gypsies, Romanies, homosexuals, Jehovah's Witnesses, the disabled and the mentally ill exterminated by the Nazis at five million. The upper limit is as high as 11 million.

In 1979 the Institute for Historical Review offered a $50,000 reward to anybody who "could prove that the Nazis operated gas chambers to terminate Jews". Mel Mermelstein, an Auschwitz survivor, forwarded to the IHR affidavits concerning the fate of his family in Auschwitz plus other documentation, and duly claimed his money. When the IHR failed to give him the $50,000 he sued. The court awarded him the $50,000 plus an extra $40,000 for distress. In other words, the leading outfit for Holocaust denial, giving it its best shot, could not convince a neutral jury of its case.

The Holocaust was a hoax invented by Jews to gain money and justify the creation of Israel: ALERT LEVEL 0

Further Reading

Arthur R. Butz, *The Hoax of the Twentieth Century: The Case Against the Presumed Extermination of European Jewry*, 1992

Deborah Lipstadt, *Denying the Holocaust: The Growing Assault on Truth and Memory*, 1993

Michael Shermer, Alex Grobman and Arthur Hertzberg, *Denying History: Who Says the Holocaust Never Happened and Why Do They Say It?*, 2002

http://www.ihr.org/main/about.shtml

ILLUMINATI

A diabolical and Satanic . . . scheme has been designed and is being prepared for global implementation by anti-Christ agents of an organization called "The Illuminati".

An "Alert" on the Christian Science University website, 2000

In the pyramid of covert power, few rank higher than the Illuminati. Through infiltrated organizations such as the **Freemasons**, the **Bohemian Grove**, the **Skull & Bones**, the **Bilderberg Group** and the **Trilateral Commission**, to name but a handful, the Illuminati are poised to usher in the **New World Order**.

They've come a long way since their foundation in 1776 as a philosophical society in a hick Bavarian town by one Professor Adam Weishaupt. Like many similar groups that sprang up during the 18th-century Enlightenment, the Illuminati, or "Order of Perfectabilists", flirted with counter-establishment ideas, including atheism and anti-monarchism. Again, it was not atypical that they adopted esoteric rituals and signs, partly for reasons of security, partly for the glamour of exclusivity. And they shared the same fate as many compatriot groups: they attracted the attention of the autocratic ruler of Bavaria, the Elector Prince Karl-Theodor, who in 1784 banned all secret societies in an attempt to halt the growing tide of Jacobinism (republicanism). In the following year the Illuminati were disbanded and Weishaupt quit Bavaria in a hurry.

Rumours that the Illuminati lived on were rife, however, and were boosted by the arrest of the occultist "Count" Cagliostro in Rome in 1789. Under interrogation by the Inquisition, Cagliostro loquaciously confessed the secrets of the Masons and the **Knights Templar** and, warming to his theme, declared that the Illuminati were plotting to oust both the Holy See and the Bourbons. At overthrowing the *ancien régime* of France the Illuminati were, according to the *Memoirs Illustrating the History of Jacobinism* (1797) by Abbe Augustin Barruel, 1797, successful; the French Revolution was an experiment in "Illuminism". Within a decade, the Illumanti had become premier bogeymen in the fetid, fevered minds of conservative Europe: Professor John Robison fingered them in his *Proofs of a Conspiracy Against All the Religions and Governments of Europe, Carried on in the Secret Meetings of Free-Masons, Illuminati and Reading Societies* (1798), while Johann August Starck, in his *Triumph der Philosophie in Achtzenten Jahrhundert* (1803), considered the Illuminati the poisonous bloom of a conspiracy that could trace its roots to the Ancient Greeks.

That there was no evidence for the continued existence of the Illuminati bothered none of these writers, just as it failed to trouble the British writer Nesta H. Webster, whose *Secret Societies and Subversive Movements* (1924) detected the hands of the Illuminati in the recent Russian Revolution. Webster's book enjoyed some influence in her home country, but was really taken to be conspiracy gospel by the US far right. Today, the Illuminati are Public Enemy Number One for the John Birch Society, the militias and the Christian fundamentalists, who claim to have detected the Illuminati's real goal: a single, authoritarian, Satanic global government – the **New World Order**.

There is a secret sign of America's special role for the Illuminati: the motto *Novus Ordo Seclorum* (to be translated as "New World Order") on the US dollar bill. Alas, a better translation is "New Order of the Ages" or even just "fresh new start". This is typical of the evidence posited for the Illuminati's existence beyond the 18th century by Robison, Starck, Webster and modern epigones such as William Cooper, which is without exception either specious or self-referential.

There is, then, only a difference of degree between "exposes" of the Illuminati and pure fictional potboilers such as Dan Brown's *Angels and Demons* and the Robert Shea/Robert Anton Wilson *Illuminatus!* Trilogy. In both genres, the Illuminati are useful stock bad guys.

> Secret society the Illuminati is intent on global control: ALERT LEVEL 2

Further Reading
William Cooper, *Behold a Pale Horse*, 1991
Arkon Daraul, *A History of Secret Societies*, 1961
John Robison, *Proofs of a Conspiracy Against All the Religions and Governments of Europe*, 1798
http://www.conspiracyarchive.com

DOCUMENT: THE FOUNDATION OF THE ILLUMINATI, FROM CHAPTER 2 OF JOHN ROBISON'S *PROOF OF A CONSPIRACY AGAINST ALL THE RELIGIONS AND GOVERNMENTS OF EUROPE*

[. . .] Of the zealous members of the Lodge Theodore [in Munich, Bavaria] the most conspicuous was Dr Adam Weishaupt, Professor of Canon Law in the university of Ingolstadt. This person had been educated among the Jesuits; but the abolition of their order made him change his views, and from being their pupil, he became their most bitter enemy. He had acquired a high reputation in his profession, and was attended not only by those intended for the practice in the law-courts, but also by the young gentlemen at large, in their course of general education; and he brought numbers from the neighbouring states to this university, and gave a *ton* to the studies of the place. He embraced with great keenness this opportunity of spreading the favorite doctrines of the Lodge, and his auditory became the seminary of Cosmopolitism. The engaging picture of the possible felicity of a society where every office is held by a man of talents and virtue, and where every talent is set in a place fitted for its exertion, forcibly catches the generous and unsuspecting minds of youth, and in a Roman Catholic state, far advanced in the habits of gross superstition (a character given to Bavaria by its neighbours) and abounding in monks and idle dignitaries, the opportunities must be frequent for observing the inconsiderate dominion of the clergy, and the abject and indolent submission of the laity. Accordingly Professor Weishaupt says, in his Apology for Illuminatism, that Deism, Infidelity, and Atheism are more prevalent in Bavaria than in any country he was acquainted with. Discourses, therefore, in which the absurdity and horrors of superstition and spiritual tyranny were strongly painted, could not fail of making a deep impression. And during this state of the minds of the auditory the transition to general infidelity and irreligion is so easy, and so inviting to sanguine youth, prompted perhaps by a latent wish that the restraints which religion imposes on the expectants of a future state might be found, on enquiry, to be nothing but groundless terrors, that I imagine it requires the most anxious care of the public teacher to keep the minds of his audience impressed with the reality and importance of the great truths of religion, while he frees them from the shackles of blind and absurd superstition. I fear that this celebrated instructor had none of this anxiety, but was satisfied with his great success in the last part of this task, the emancipation of his young hearers from the terrors of superstition. I suppose also that this was the more agreeable to him, as it procured him the triumph over the Jesuits, with whom he had long struggled for the direction of the university.

This was in 1777. Weishaupt had long been scheming the establishment of an Association or Order which, in time, should govern the world. In his first fervour and high expectations, he hinted to several ex-Jesuits the probability of their recovering, under a new name, the influence which they formerly possessed, and of being again of great service to society, by directing the education of youth of distinction, now emancipated from all civil and religious prejudices. He prevailed on some to join him, but they all retracted but two. After this disappointment Weishaupt became the implacable enemy of the Jesuits; and his sanguine temper made him frequently lay himself open to their piercing eye, and drew on him their keenest resentment, and at last made him the victim of their enmity.

The Lodge Theodore was the place where the above-mentioned doctrines were most zealously propagated. [. . . It] became remarkable for the very bold sentiments in politics and religion which were frequently uttered in their harangues; and its members were noted for their zeal in making proselytes. Many bitter pasquinades, satires, and other offensive pamphlets were in secret circulation, and even larger works of very dangerous tendency, and several of them were traced to that Lodge. The Elector often expressed his disapprobation of such proceedings, and sent them kind messages, desiring them to be careful not to disturb the peace of the country, and particularly to recollect the solemn declaration made to every entrant into the Fraternity of Free Masons, "That no subject of religion or politics shall ever be touched on in the Lodge"; a declaration which alone could have procured his permission of any secret assembly whatever, and on the sincerity and honour of which he had reckoned when he gave his sanction to their establishment. But repeated accounts of the same kind increased the alarm, and the Elector ordered a judicial enquiry into the proceedings of the Lodge Theodore.

It was then discovered that this and several associated Lodges were the nursery or preparation-school for another Order of Masons, who called themselves the ILLUMINATED, and that the express aim of this Order was to abolish Christianity, and overturn all civil government. But the result of the enquiry was very imperfect and unsatisfactory. No Illuminati were to be found. They were unknown in the Lodge. Some of the members occasionally heard of certain candidates for illumination called MINERVALS, who were sometimes seen among them. But whether these had been admitted, or who received them, was known only to themselves. Some of these were examined in private by the Elector himself. They said that they were bound by honour to secrecy: But they assured the Elector, on their honour, that the aim of the Order was in the highest degree praiseworthy, and useful both to church and state: But this could not allay the anxiety of the profane public; and it was repeatedly stated to the Elector, that members of the Lodge Theodore had unguardedly spoken of this Order as one that in time must rule the world. He therefore issued an order forbidding, during his pleasure, all secret assemblies, and shutting up the Mason Lodges. It was not meant to be rigorously enforced, but was intended as a trial of the deference of these Associations for civil authority. The Lodge Theodore distinguished itself by pointed opposition, continuing its meetings; and the members, out of doors, openly reprobated the prohibition as an absurd and unjustifiable tyranny.

In the beginning of 1783, four professors of the Marianen Academy, founded by the widow of the late Elector, viz. Utschneider, Cossandey, Renner, and Grunberger, with two others, were summoned before the Court of Enquiry, and questioned, on their allegiance, respecting the Order of the Illuminati. They acknowledged that they belonged to it, and when more closely examined, they related several circumstances of its constitution and principles. Their declarations were immediately published, and were very unfavourable. The Order was said to abjure Christianity, and to refuse admission into the higher degrees to all who adhered to any of the three confessions. Sensual pleasures were restored to the rank they held in the Epicurean philosophy. Self-murder was justified on Stoical principles. In the Lodges death was declared an eternal sleep; patriotism and loyalty were called narrow-minded prejudices, and incompatible with universal benevolence; continual declamations were made on liberty and equality as the unalienable rights of man. The baneful influence of accumulated property was declared an insurmountable obstacle to the happiness of any nation whose chief laws were framed for its protection and increase. Nothing was so frequently discoursed of as the propriety of employing, for a good purpose, the means which the wicked employed for evil purposes; and it was taught, that the preponderancy of good in the ultimate result consecrated every means employed; and that wisdom and virtue consisted in properly determining this balance. [. . .] They concluded by saying that the method of education made them all spies on each other and on all around them. But all this was denied by the Illuminati. Some of them were said to be absolutely false; and the rest were said to be mistakes. The apostate professors had acknowledged their ignorance of many things. Two of them were only Minervals, another was an Illuminatus of the lowest class, and the fourth was but one step farther advanced. Pamphlets appeared on both sides, with very little effect. The Elector called before him one of the superiors, a young nobleman, who denied these injurious charges, and said that they were ready to lay before his Highness their whole archives and all constitutional papers.

Notwithstanding all this, the government had received such an impression of the dangerous tendency of the Order, that the Elector issued another edict, forbidding all hidden assemblies; and a third, expressly abolishing the Order of Illuminati. It was followed by a search after their papers. The Lodge Theodore was immediately searched, but none were to be found. They said now that they had burnt them all, as of no use, since that Order was at an end.

It was now discovered, that Weishaupt was the head and founder of the Order. He was deprived of his Professor's chair, and banished from the Bavarian States; but with a pension of 800 florins, which he refused. He went to Regensburg, on the confines of Switzerland. Two Italians, the Marquis Constanza and Marquis Savioli, were also banished, with equal pensions (about L. 40) which they accepted. One Zwack, a counsellor, holding some law-office, was also banished. Others were imprisoned for some time. Weishaupt went afterwards into the service of the D. of Saxe Gotha, a person of a romantic turn of mind, and whom we shall again meet with. Zwack went into the service of the Pr. de Salms, who soon after had so great a hand in the disturbances in Holland.

By destroying the papers, all opportunity was lost for authenticating the innocence and usefulness of the Order. After much altercation and paper war, Weishaupt, now safe in Regensburg, published an account of the Order, namely, the account which was given to every *Novice* in a discourse read at his reception. To this were added, the statutes and the rules proceeding, as far as the degree of *Illuminatus Minor*, inclusive. This account he affirmed to be conformant to the real practice of the Order. But this publication did by no means satisfy the public mind. It differed exceedingly from the accounts given by the four professors. It made no mention of the higher degrees, which had been most blamed by them. Besides, it was alleged, that it was all a fiction, written in order to lull the suspicions which had been raised (and this was found to be the case, except in respect of the very lowest degree). The real constitution was brought to light by degrees, and shall be laid before the reader, in the order in which it was gradually discovered, that we may be the better judge of things not fully known by the conduct of the leaders during the detection. The first account given by Weishaupt is correct, as far as I shall make use of it, and shows clearly the methods that were taken to recommend the Order to strangers.

The Order of ILLUMINATI appears as an accessory to Free Masonry. It is in the Lodges of Free Masons that the Minervals are found, and there they are prepared for Illumination. They must have previously obtained the three English degrees. The founder says more. He says that his doctrines are the only true Free Masonry. He was the chief promoter of the *Eclectic System*. This he urged as the best method for getting information of all the explanations which have been given of the Masonic Mysteries. He was also a *Strict Observant*, and an adept Rosycrucian. The result of all his knowledge is worthy of particular remark, and shall therefore be given at large.

"I declare," says he, "and I challenge all mankind to contradict my declaration, that no man can give any account of the Order of Free Masonry, of its origin, of its history, of its object, nor any explanation of its mysteries and symbols, which does not leave the mind in total uncertainty on all these points. Every man is entitled, therefore, to give any explanation of the symbols, and any system of the doctrines, that he can render palatable. Hence have sprung up that variety of systems which for twenty years have divided the Order. The simple tale of the English, and the fifty degrees of the French, and the Knights of Baron Hunde, are equally authentic, and have equally had the support of intelligent and zealous Brethren. These systems are in fact but one. They have all sprung from the Blue Lodge of Three degrees, take these for their standard, and found on these all the improvements by which each system is afterwards suited to the particular object which it keeps in view. There is no man, nor system, in the world, which can show by undoubted succession that it should stand at the head of the Order. Our ignorance in this particular frets me. Do but consider our short history of 120 years. – Who will show me the Mother Lodge? Those of London we have discovered to be self-erected in 1716. Ask for their archives. They tell you they were burnt. They have nothing but the wretched sophistications of the Englishman Anderson, and the Frenchman Desaguilliers. Where is the Lodge of York, which pretends to the priority, with their King Bouden, and the archives that he brought from the East? These too are all burnt. What is the Chapter of Old Aberdeen, and its Holy Clericate? Did we not find it unknown, and the Mason Lodges there the most ignorant of all the ignorant, gaping for instruction from our deputies? Did we not find the same thing at London? And have not their missionaries been among us, prying into our mysteries, and eager to learn from us what is true Free Masonry? It is in vain, therefore, to appeal to judges; they are no where to be found; all claim for themselves the sceptre of the Order; all indeed are on an equal footing. They obtained followers, not from their authenticity, but from their conduciveness to the end which they proposed, and from the importance of that end. It is by this scale that we must measure the mad and wicked explanations of the Rosycrucians, the Exorcists, and Cabalists. These are rejected by all good Masons, because incompatible with social happiness. Only such systems as promote this are retained. But alas, they are all sadly deficient, because they leave us under the dominion of political and religious prejudice; and they are as inefficient as the sleepy dose of an ordinary sermon.

"But I have contrived an explanation which has every advantage; is inviting to Christians of every communion; gradually frees them from all religious prejudices; cultivates the social virtues; and animates them by a great, a feasible, and *speedy* prospect of universal happiness, in a state of liberty and moral equality, freed from the obstacles which subordination, rank, and riches, continually throw in our way. My explanation is accurate, and complete, my means are effectual, and irresistible. Our secret Association works in a way that nothing can withstand, *and man shall soon be free and happy*.

"This is the great object held out by this Association: and the means of attaining it is Illumination, enlightening the understanding by the sun of reason, which will dispel the clouds of superstition and of prejudice. The proficients in this Order are therefore justly named the Illuminated. And of all Illumination which human reason can give, none is comparable to the discovery of what we are, our nature, our obligations, what happiness we are capable of, and what are the means of attaining it. In comparison with this, the most brilliant sciences are but amusements for the idle and luxurious. To fit man by Illumination for active virtue, to engage him to it by the strongest motives, to render the attainment of it easy and certain, by finding employment for every talent, and by placing every talent in its proper sphere of action, so that all, without feeling any extraordinary effort, and in conjunction with and completion of ordinary business, shall urge forward, with united powers, the general task. This indeed will be an employment suited to noble natures, grand in its views, and delightful in its exercise.

"And what is this general object? THE HAPPINESS OF THE HUMAN RACE. Is it not distressing to a generous mind, after contemplating what human nature is capable of, to see how little we enjoy? When we look at this goodly world, and see that every man *may* be happy, but that the happiness of one depends on the conduct of another; when we see the wicked so powerful, and the good so weak; and that it is in vain to strive, singly and alone, against the general current of vice and oppression; the wish naturally arises in the mind, that it were possible to form a durable combination of the most worthy persons, who should work together in removing the obstacles to human happiness, become terrible to the wicked, and give their aid to all the good without distinction, and should by the most powerful means, first fetter, and by fettering, lessen vice; means which at the same time should promote virtue, by rendering the inclination to rectitude, hitherto too feeble, more powerful and engaging. Would not such an association be a blessing to the world? [. . .]"

Such is the aim, and such are the hopes of the Order of the Illuminated [. . .]

IRAN–CONTRA SCANDAL

Like Watergate, the Iran–Contra scandal – "Irangate" – was unambiguously true. A president didn't fall, but he wobbled alarmingly. Worse for succeeding administrations, the lid on the can of worms that is US foreign policy *in extremis* was opened . . . and it was an unforgettable sight.

The beginnings of Irangate lie in the 1979 Islamic revolution, which overthrew the pro-Western Shah of Iran. Supporters of Ayatollah Khomeini's regime invaded the US Embassy in Tehran and held staff hostage for a year. The inability of US President Jimmy Carter to secure the hostages' release cost him a second term. (By the "October Surprise" conspiracy theory, candidate Ronald Reagan did a deal with Tehran that they would delay the hostages' freedom until the presidential election campaign was done so he could win.) The anti-American militancy of the Khomeini regime, together with its sponsorship of Islamic terrorist outfits like Hezbollah, led Washington DC to implement Operation Staunch: an arms embargo against Iran.

Once in power, the new Republican administration of Ronald Reagan found it had its own personal hostage crisis. In Lebanon, CIA station chief William Buckley was seized by Hezbollah. A moderate wing of Khomeini's regime suggested to Israel that, if the US sent Iran a shipment of arms, it would secure Buckley's release. On 18 July 1985 Reagan, his chief of staff Donald Regan and National

Security Adviser Robert McFarlane discussed the Iran deal, and two weeks later, over the opposition of some government advisers, it was agreed to send Iran a shipment of BGM-71 100 TOW (Tube launched, Optically tracked, Wire guided) missiles.

No hostages were released. The Iranian moderates asked for 400 more TOW missiles, at which Hezbollah released not Buckley but another hostage, Reverend Benjamin Weir. A further 3,500 missiles were sent to Iran. McFarlane and a National Security Council staff officer, Lieutenant-Colonel Oliver D. North, went to Iran secretly to press the US case – in clear contravention of the Reagan mantra that "America will never make concessions to terrorists" – but Hezbollah still failed to release Buckley. At this point the Lebanese newspaper *Ash-Shiraa* published a report on the arms deals between the US and Iran, which Iran confirmed. The Iranian side of the Iran–Contra scandal was well and truly public. In a damage-limitation exercise, Reagan set up a commission of inquiry under John Tower on 26 November 1986. A Republican, Tower was criticized for going softly, softly on the scandal (which was arguably the intention in appointing him), but his commission did find incriminating Iran-deal emails on Oliver D. North's computer. The investigators also found evidence of another covert US operation with North at its nexus: the Contra part of the scandal.

In 1979, the same year that Khomeini ejected the Shah of Iran, halfway across the world in Nicaragua left-wing Sandinistas overthrew the military dictatorship of Anastasio Somoza. Later, the Sandinistas (more properly known as Frente Sandinista de Liberacion Nacional) won free and fair democratic elections. Somoza supporters, meanwhile, kept up a contra-revolution (hence "Contras") against the Sandinista regime. In 1982 Reagan authorized the CIA to create a 500-strong army of Nicaraguan exiles to fight alongside the Contras. Queried by a Congressional intelligence committee over this "action team", CIA director William Casey misleadingly stated that its activity was restricted to intercepting arms sent by the Sandinistas to El Salvadoran Marxist revolutionaries. The disingenuity of Casey's reply was exposed, and Congress passed the Boland Amendment which banned the spending of federal money on the Contras. Ignoring the Boland Amendment, Reagan tasked the CIA with mining Nicaragua's harbours. Congress responded in June 1984 with a second Boland Amendment, which explicitly forbade all CIA operations in Nicaragua.

Fast forward two years. On 5 October 1986 a plane piloted by one Eugene Hasenfus was shot down over Nicaragua while carrying arms to the Contras. Hasenfus appeared on TV, where he publicly announced that his co-workers were CIA operatives. This story coincided almost exactly with *Ash-Shiraa*'s investigation into US–Iranian arms deals. A political A-bomb detonated. On 25 November Reagan's Attorney General Edwin Meese admitted that the Contra scandal was connected to the recent Iranian arms scandal. Oliver North had directly channelled profits from the Iran arms deals to the Contras, thereby neatly but illegally bypassing Congress, the United Nations and everyone else who might disapprove. Reagan, meanwhile, tried to keep it all at arm's length by, on 26 November, setting up the Tower Commission.

Oliver North and his immediate superior, Admiral John Poindexter, the National Security Advisor who had replaced McFarlane, were convicted on multiple accounts of lying and obstruction of justice, but their convictions were overturned on appeal because their testimonies had been used against them despite a grant of immunity. A final 1987 report into the affair by Congress failed to answer the key question: how much Reagan knew. Some researchers consider that North's five memos sent to the president on the Contras' illegal funding might give a clue. Then there is the entry in Reagan's own diary from January 1986: "I agreed to sell TOWs to Iran."

William Buckley was killed after torture by captors in Iran.

Reagan approved illegal arms deals to Iran which enabled
illegal funding of Contras in Nicaragua: ALERT LEVEL 10

Further Reading
Lawrence Walsh, Independent Counsel for Iran/Contra Mat-
ters, *Final Report of the Independent Counsel for Iran/Contra
Matters,* 1993

DOCUMENT: FROM *THE FINAL REPORT OF THE INDEPENDENT COUNSEL FOR IRAN/CONTRA MATTERS* (THE WALSH REPORT)

Part III
The Operational Conspiracy: A Legal Analysis
The central and perhaps the most important criminal charge developed by Independent Counsel was the conspiracy charge against Oliver L. North, John M. Poindexter, Richard V. Secord and Albert Hakim. According to that charge – set forth as Count One of the indictment returned on 16 March 1988 – these four men conspired to defraud the United States by deceitfully (1) supporting a war in Nicaragua in defiance of congressional controls; (2) using the Iran arms sales to raise funds to be spent at the direction of North and Poindexter, rather than the United States Government; and (3) endangering the effort to rescue Americans held hostage in Lebanon by pursuing ends that were both unauthorized and inconsistent with the goal of releasing the hostages.
[. . .]
The Reagan Administration was unambiguously hostile to this count. In a move that Judge Gerhard A. Gesell described as "unprecedented", the Justice Department in November 1988 filed an amicus brief supporting North's claim that the count was legally insufficient and should be dismissed. Subsequently, having been informed by Independent Counsel that the conspiracy count could be tried only if a small amount of classified information were declassified, the Administration refused to release that information. Because there was no way to appeal such a refusal to declassify, Independent Counsel was forced in January 1989 to drop Count One in North and a related charge that the diversion of

profits from the Iran arms sales was a theft of Government funds.

Although Count One was not tried, it was established as a matter of law that if North, Poindexter, and the others had done what they were charged with doing, they had committed criminal acts. In rejecting the challenges of the Department of Justice and North, Judge Gesell ruled that the count "allege[d] [a] well-established offens[e]" and that the activity set forth in the count was criminal. He stated: "The indictment clearly alleges a conspiracy which involved concealing the very existence of the profits of the enterprise from the start and hiding from Congress information relating to the conspirators' assistance for the Contras." In addition to holding that the indictment set forth a crime, Judge Gesell also found that his review of the evidence presented to the Grand Jury indicated there was probable cause that that crime had in fact been committed.

At the heart of the Iran/Contra affair, then, were criminal acts of Reagan Administration officials that the Reagan Administration, by withholding non-secret classified information, ensured would never be tried. Yet Judge Gesell's decision marked an important, if incomplete, accomplishment of Independent Counsel. Judge Gesell's decision unambiguously established that high national security officials who engage in a conspiracy to subvert the laws of this country have engaged in criminal acts, even when the laws themselves provide no criminal sanctions.

A successful prosecution would have allowed Independent Counsel to present comprehensively the results of his investigation into the operational conspiracy. Much of the evidence of the conspiracy was presented at the trials of the dismembered individual charges of obstruction and false statements but the questions of intent were different, the diversion of funds from Iran to the contras was peripheral rather than central, and the absence of the conspiracy charge

deprived the North case of its cohesiveness and complete-
ness.

The following discussion is an attempt to present in an
abbreviated fashion what would have been Independent
Counsel's case at a conspiracy trial of North, Secord, Poindexter and Hakim, and an explanation of the criminal nature
of their actions.

[. . .]

First Object of the Conspiracy: The Secret War Activities
The crux of the first charged object of the conspiracy was an
agreement to provide military assistance to the Nicaraguan
Contras and to deceive Congress about the fact that support
was being provided. Poindexter, North, and their co-
conspirators carried out their "secret war" in a way calculated to defeat legal restrictions governing the conduct of
military and covert operations and congressional control of
appropriations, and they concealed their activities from legitimate congressional oversight.

Had the case been tried as indicted, the Government's
proof of US secret war activities would have fallen into three
broad categories: (1) the organization and direction of a
resupply operation to provide the Contras with logistical
and other support; (2) funding of the resupply operation,
including exploitation of the Iran initiative; and (3) attempts
to conceal from Congress the conspirators' involvement in
these activities.

The Evidence
Organization and Direction of the Resupply Network
During the last half of 1984 and the first half of 1985, North
had developed a loose structure for Contra support. Secord,
responding to Contra requests through North, was selling
arms. Thomas G. Clines, a Secord associate, arranged for
their purchase; Hakim, assisted by Swiss money manager
Willard I. Zucker, set up the structure to finance the

activities with funds provided to the Contras through North and raised primarily by President Reagan and National Security Advisor Robert C. McFarlane.

The creation of the conspirators' more tightly organized secret resupply network dated from a meeting in Miami, Florida on 28 June 1985. This meeting was attended by, among others, North, Adolfo Calero (political leader of one Contra faction known as the FDN), Enrique Bermudez (commander of the FDN's military forces), Secord, Clines and Rafael Quintero, an associate of Secord. At the Miami meeting, North informed Calero and Bermudez that the Contras would no longer be left to decide what arms they would purchase or from whom they would buy them. In the future, North would provide the Contras with materiel, and Secord would deliver it to the Contras in the field. In addition, North directed that actions be taken to develop and resupply a "southern front" along the border of Costa Rica and Nicaragua.

Following the Miami meeting, North assumed a central role in the Contra war effort. Using Robert W. Owen as a courier, North provided the Contras with significant military advice and guidance. At the same time, with the assistance of Secord, North in the following fashion secretly brought into being the resupply operation that he had described on 28 June.

First, North directed Owen and William Haskell, another North courier, to travel to Costa Rica and help activate a southern military front. Owen and Haskell, aided by CIA Costa Rican Station Chief Joseph F. Fernandez, undertook to build a clandestine airstrip to be used to resupply it. Haskell eventually negotiated the acquisition of property for the strip, which was funded using Swiss accounts controlled directly by Secord and Hakim, and indirectly by North. Within the United States, North attended planning sessions and personally commissioned private individuals to do preliminary site work and engineering tasks necessary for the construction of a usable airstrip.

North arranged for Haskell and Owen to be introduced to Fernandez. Fernandez minimized and concealed from his superiors at the CIA the true nature of his contacts with North and North's private representatives. Fernandez and North eventually developed a secret communications network using National Security Agency (NSA)-supplied KL-43 encryption devices, outside normal CIA communications channels. [. . .] Under the direction of North, Fernandez and US Ambassador to Costa Rica Lewis A. Tambs used their influence as representatives of the United States to obtain the support of senior Costa Rican officials for the airstrip project.

Second, North directed Secord to purchase aircraft capable of resupplying Contra forces. From January to August 1986, private parties working on behalf of North and Secord purchased four military aircraft costing approximately $1.8 million, as well as additional equipment for operation of these aircraft. The funds for these purchases came from Hakim and Secord's secret Swiss bank accounts.

North took an active part in the purchase of the aircraft. He reviewed and approved a technical proposal for the resupply organization solicited by Secord from Richard B. Gadd, a Secord associate. North and Secord then directed Gadd in November 1985 to approach the Government of Venezuela in an unsuccessful attempt to purchase military aircraft. North used his influence as a Government official to vouch for Gadd's bona fides with the government of Venezuela. Similarly, North exercised final approval on major expenditures for equipment. In January 1986, North personally directed Secord to provide Gadd with over $100,000 for anticipated costs. Later in 1986, North directed Secord to purchase a package of spare parts required by the resupply operation that cost in excess of $200,000. North personally approved the purchase of a fourth military aircraft in August

1986 at a cost of $250,000. When there was a dispute between Gadd and Secord as to the ownership of the aircraft, North resolved it in favor of Secord's Enterprise.

Third, North secretly undertook to obtain the use of Ilopango air base in El Salvador for his resupply operation. In a letter dated September 20, 1985, North requested that Felix Rodriguez, an American citizen with close ties to the commander of the Salvadoran Air Force, solicit permission to use the base for his resupply operation. [. . .]

Fourth, at North's instruction, Secord through Clines purchased in Europe and delivered to Central America thousands of pounds of arms from December 1985 to September 1986. The cost of purchase and transport of these arms was paid from the secret Swiss accounts.

Fifth, North, with the assistance of Secord, secretly directed the actual administration of the resupply project during 1986. Secord hired first Gadd and then Robert Dutton as project managers. Gadd and Dutton, through the corporation Amalgamated Commercial Enterprises (ACE), in turn hired numerous other employees. By the summer of 1986, the resupply operation had over 20 full-time employees whose combined salaries totalled over $60,000 per month. The cost of equipment and salaries for the operation was paid from the Enterprise's secret Swiss accounts.

The activities at the Ilopango air base were supervised by Quintero for Secord. Rodriguez served as liaison with the base commander, General Juan Rafael Bustillo. Additional assistance and supervision was provided by the military group detailed to the US Embassy in El Salvador.

Gadd and Dutton reported directly to Secord. At the same time, they had frequent – often daily – contact with North, from whom they accepted guidance and direction. North frequently gave them orders regarding specific operations, usually in order to accelerate resupply drops to the Contras. [. . .]

Under North's and Secord's direction, the resupply operation in 1986 improved and ultimately delivered to the Contras in the field in Nicaragua thousands of pounds of arms previously purchased by Secord. North generally received detailed inventories of the lethal supplies provided [to] Contra forces. The resupply operation also delivered substantial quantities of nonlethal aid and engaged in projects such as training Contra forces in the use of explosives. These operational activities of the Enterprise ended in early October 1986 when an Enterprise aircraft was shot down over Nicaragua, killing three crew members and leading to the capture of Eugene Hasenfus, an American who told his Nicaraguan captors that he was working for the CIA.

Funding of the Resupply Operation
Funds for the secret war came primarily from three sources: (a) the National Endowment for the Preservation of Liberty (NEPL); (b) the Iran arms sales; and (c) foreign governments. As set forth in the "Flow of Funds" chapter of this Report, the total amount of funds deposited in Enterprise accounts in Switzerland was $47.6 million. By the time the Iran/Contra affair became public, the Enterprise had given to the Contras or had spent on efforts related to the Contras approximately $17.6 million of these funds.

Foreign Donations
From December 1984 through July 1985, the Contras paid into Enterprise accounts approximately $11.3 million for a variety of services and goods. Most of these funds came from the Saudis, who contributed $32 million in 1984 and 1985. The Saudi funds were nearly exhausted by mid-1985.

After North held his June meeting in Miami, the Contras were no longer the direct recipient of such funds. Thereafter, the conspirators directed to Enterprise bank accounts all funds from third countries that had been solicited by US officials on behalf of the Contras, even though some of them had been restricted for only humanitarian purposes.

In August 1985, North asked Gaston Sigur, an NSC staff officer, to arrange a meeting between North and an official of the Taiwanese government for the purpose of soliciting funds for the Contras. Following this meeting, North had Sigur confirm the decision by Taiwan to provide the Contras with $1 million. North then directed Robert Owen to deliver an envelope containing the number of an Enterprise account to the Taiwanese official. On 20 September 1985, $1 million was received by the Enterprise. In late 1985, North renewed his request, via Sigur, that Taiwan provide additional funds to the Contras. In February 1986, a second transfer of $1 million was received in an Enterprise account.

Similarly, in June 1986, when the State Department planned to raise $10 million for the Contras from the Sultan of Brunei, North undertook to divert the funds to the Enterprise by giving one of its Swiss account numbers to Assistant Secretary of State Elliott Abrams. Fawn Hall, North's secretary, apparently made a transcription error in the account number so the funds were misdirected and never received.

On November 20, 1985, the Enterprise received $1 million from the government of Israel to pay the Enterprise for transporting a number of shipments of weapons from Israel to Iran. That weapons transfer was abandoned after the first shipment. The Enterprise's expenses for that shipment were less than $200,000, but the Enterprise kept the balance.

[. . .]

Exploitation of the Iran Arms Sales
The Iran arms sales were the major source of the Enterprise's funds for the secret war activities. In all, the Enterprise

received slightly more than $30 million for the sale of Government arms and returned only $12.2 million to the United States. At least $3.6 million was to fund the Enterprise's resupply operation in support of the Contras.

Concealment

Soon after the June 1985 meeting in Miami, a series of congressional inquiries sought to determine exactly what the US Government, and North in particular, were doing on behalf of the Contras. McFarlane, Poindexter and North responded by actively deceiving committees of Congress with a series of false statements and by other efforts to ensure that Congress would never find out about the secret Contra military support.

The first false statements came in McFarlane's 5 September 1985 letter to the House Permanent Select Committee on Intelligence, a letter on which McFarlane, Poindexter, and North all worked. The letter contained false denials of North's fund-raising activities and his provision of tactical advice to the Contras, as well as a false assurance that no one on the NSC staff had "violate[d] the letter or spirit" of the Boland prohibition on military aid. 12 September 1985 and 7 October 1985 letters under McFarlane's signature, both jointly drafted by North and McFarlane, contained similar false statements.

McFarlane's replacement by Poindexter as National Security Advisor on 4 December 1985 did not alter the pattern of deceit. North continued to work to prevent dissemination of information about his activities. On 16 June 1986, North sent Fernandez a KL-43 message that stated in part:

I do not think we ought to contemplate these operations without [Quintero] being on scene. Too many things go wrong that then directly involve you and me in what should be deniable for both of us.

On 15 May 1986, Poindexter sent this computer message to North:

> I am afraid you are letting your operational role become too public. From now on I don't want you to talk to anybody else, including Casey, except me about any of your operational roles. In fact you need to generate a cover story that I have insisted that you stop.

North responded to Poindexter on the same day with a computer note that said "Done." North subsequently had Robert Dutton inform Enterprise employees in El Salvador that the resupply operation had been taken over by a new entity known as "B.C. Washington."

Nevertheless, on 10 June 1986 Poindexter reminded North via computer: "I still want you to reduce your visibility." [. . .]

In the summer of 1986, Congress renewed its inquiries. On 21 July 1986, responding to a House resolution of inquiry, Poindexter sent letters to two committee chairmen, stating that McFarlane's 1985 letters to Congress accurately described the activities of the NSC staff. When members of the House Intelligence Committee questioned North in person, he falsely denied his Contra-support activities.

The deception continued after one of the resupply organization's planes carrying Hasenfus was shot down in October 1986. Congress was about to authorize resumption of Contra support by the CIA, with an appropriation of $100 million. Administration officials denied any connection with the aircraft. In October and November 1986, North altered, destroyed, and removed documents and official records relating to the resupply operation. On November 23, 1986, he lied to the Attorney General to conceal Secord's operation and his own responsibility in directing the secret resupply activities and the control of the funds used to finance them.

Between 22 and 29 November 1986, Poindexter unsuccessfully tried to delete from the White House computer system all of his communications with North. Finally, on December 8, 1986, McFarlane told the House Foreign Affairs Committee that he was unaware that the government or citizens of Saudi Arabia had been involved in financing the Contras. [. . .]

POPE JOHN PAUL I

Even in Italy, land of the conspiracy, no plot comes more entangled than the death of Pope John Paul I.

When white smoke puffed above the Vatican on 26 August 1978 to signal the election of Albino Luciani to the papacy no one was more surprised than Luciani himself. A Vatican low-profiler, Luciani was a deeply modest man, who refused the papal tiara at his coronation and endeared himself to many, not just Catholics, by his smiling kindness.

Just 33 days later, he was dead. According to the Vatican, John Paul I's death was natural. But then they would say that, wouldn't they?

Suggestions that the new pontiff's demise was anything but natural circulated immediately, fuelled by the easily disprovable lies and oddities emanating from Vatican itself:

- At first it was announced that John Paul had been found dead in his bed, with a copy of Thomas a Kempis's *Imitation of Christ* propped before him, by his secretaries Magee and Lorenzi; in fact, the body was discovered by a nun, Sister Vincenza.
- The Vatican blamed John Paul's untimely death – he was 66 – on his heavy smoking. But he didn't smoke.
- A false time of death was issued.
- Most controversially of all, a post mortem was not conducted because, insisted the Vatican, post mortems on pontiffs are

prohibited by Vatican law. Yet a post mortem had been conducted on the remains of Pope Pius VIII in 1830.
* Within 24 hours of his death John Paul I was embalmed.

John Paul I had enemies as well as friends. David Yallop, in *In God's Name* (1984), identifies Vatican reactionaries, Freemasons, and Mafiosi as an unholy alliance which loathed the new Pope – loathed him enough to murder him by the administration of digitalis to initiate a heart attack. According to Yallop, the liberal John Paul I was intending to soften the Catholic position on contraception, thus raising the ire of Vatican conservatives. The **Freemasons** of Propaganda Due (**P2**), meanwhile, feared a papal expose of their secret caucus inside the Vatican. More worried still were the Mafiosi, who believed that the new pontiff was intending to clean up the Vatican Bank.

Something had long been rotten in the state of the Vatican's banking system. In the aftermath of the Second World War, Vatican bank officials had laundered money filched by the Nazis, as well as setting up "rat lines" for Nazi war criminals to escape to South America. When the **Nazi Gold** dried up, the Vatican banks, especially the Istituto per le Opere Religiose (IOR), became money-launderers for the Mafia. The key figures in the IOR's money-laundering for the Mob were Roberto "God's Banker" **Calvi**, director of the IOR's Milan-based outlet Banco Ambrosiano, and, allegedly, Archbishop Paul Marcinkus. Michele "The Shark" Sindona, a Sicilian financier, was, in Yallop's scenario, the linkman between the bank and the Mafia.

If the Vatican Bank's corrupt officials were dismissed, the Mafia would lose a favoured means of disposing of its ill-gotten gains. The Pope had to go.

In Yallop's scenario, the murder of John Paul I worked out nearly perfectly, since he was replaced by John Paul II, who was socially conservative (thus opposed to contraception) and who, far from cleaning up the Vatican Bank, gave Archbishop Marcinkus immunity from prosecution.

Yallop's case, though strong, is circumstantial. The Vatican Bank *was* corrupt to the core, and one of the major players,

Roberto Calvi, met a retirement not usually associated with the banking profession. But did John Paul I himself meet an unnatural death? A persuasive counter-blast to Yallop's book came in 1989 with *A Thief in the Night* by John Cornwell, an English journalist who, after conducting his own investigation, concluded that John Paul I died of a pulmonary embolism. Indeed, John Paul I had manifested the classic symptom of the condition: swollen feet.

Of course, it might be objected that John Cornwell would say that, wouldn't he? He was asked to write *A Thief in the Night* by . . . the Vatican.

Pope John Paul I was victim of homicidal reactionary and criminal element in Vatican: ALERT LEVEL 6

Further Reading
John Cornwell, *A Thief in the Night*, 1989
David Yallop, *In God's Name*, 1984

JONESTOWN

Rumours of brainwashing, torture and murder had long
attended the People's Temple, an American hippie cult living
in Guyana, when Democratic US Congressman Leo Ryan
decided to investigate first-hand. Arriving on 17 November
1978 at "Jonestown", the cult's jungle encampment, Ryan was
accompanied by Richard Dwyer (a US embassy official in
Guyana), media representatives and members of "Concerned
Relatives of People's Temple Members". After touring around,
making notes and gathering together a small group of People's
Temple members who wished to return to the US, Ryan and his
entourage made for the airstrip at nearby Port Kaituma. There
the Ryan group was ambushed by People's Temple loyalists of
the "Red Brigade". Ryan, among others, was shot dead.

Back in Jonestown, the cult's messianic leader and founder,
the "Reverend" Jim Jones, called for a "white night", one of
the practice mass suicides the cult periodically held. This time,
however, it was for real: mixed in to the Kool Aid they drank
was potassium cyanide and valium. Nearly 920 of Jones's
followers, including 276 children, ingested the poison and
died. Photographs taken afterwards show close, orderly rows
of bodies, neatly dressed, often with their arms around each
other.

A year later, the House Foreign Affairs Committee of the US
Congress issued a 782-page report in which it concluded that
the Jonestown massacre was a mass suicide brought on by

Jones's "extreme paranoia". Many disagreed. Initial reports by such heavyweight newspapers as the *New York Times* suggested that 400 People's Temple followers had committed suicide, but more had escaped into the jungle; a week later the death toll had risen to 900. So how did the extra 500 die? A Guyanese pathologist, Dr Lesie Mootoo, discounted cyanide as the sole cause of death; many of the Jonestown corpses were free of the eerie rictus that is the hallmark of the agonizing death that comes with cyanide poisoning. Some corpses had strange needle marks on them, and some of the People's Temple dead had been shot. In fact, Mootoo thought that all but three of the People's Temple dead had been murdered. Guyanese newpapers reported that Guyanese troops, US green berets and UK Black Watch troops were on exercises near Jonestown at the time of the massacre. Why did they not intervene? Or were they responsible for the deaths of the 500?

Speculation that the CIA might be involved in the Jonestown massacre started up in 1980 when reporter Jack Anderson published a syndicated article called "CIA Involved in Jonestown Massacre". According to Anderson, Jim Jones himself was tied to the CIA, and certainly there were oddities in his political background; Jones's father was a Klansman and Jones Jr had been a virulent anti-Communist before his damascene conversion to utopianism in the mid-1960s. Was the conversion fake and Jones a CIA mole in the counterculture? Anderson also suggested that Richard Dwyer, who accompanied Ryan to Jonestown, was a CIA operative. On the audio tape made by Jones of the Ryan visit, the cult leader can be clearly heard during a fractious moment saying, "Get Dwyer out of here before something happens to him!"

By one conspiracy theory, the CIA used the Ryan visit to Jamestown to assassinate Leo Ryan, who was a vocal critic of the CIA, having co-authored the Hughes–Ryan amendment bill which, if passed, would have required the CIA to disclose its planned covert missions to Congress for approval. The Jonestown congregation was murdered, in this scenario, in an attempt to cover up Leo Ryan's assassination. Another CIA-guilty scenario is advanced by John Judge in "The Black Hole of Guyana" (in *Secret and Suppressed*, 1993). Here it is suggested that the People's Temple, from its very origin, was a CIA exercise in mind control. Judge points out that many of the drugs found at Jonestown matched those used in the CIA's **MK-ULTRA** programme and that Larry Layton, Jones's right-hand man, was the son of the chief of the US Army's Chemical–Biological Warfare Division. Surviving People's Temple official Joyce Shaw speculated that Jonestown was "some kind of horrible government experiment . . . a plan like that of the Germans to exterminate blacks". (The majority of the People's Temple congregation were black women.) Since Jones was showing signs of mental instability, so the story goes, the CIA decided to kill – literally – the People's Temple project rather than risk its exposure.

In *Was Jonestown a CIA Medical Experiment?* (1989) Michael Meiers posits that Congressman Ryan was about to make such an exposure, hence his assassination. Meiers adds another twist, suggesting that Jonestown was the site of the CIA's **HIV/AIDS** experiments. Then there is the suggestion by S. F. Alinin, B. G. Antonov and A. N. Itskov that the CIA massacred the People's Temple because it was a socialist, not a religious, organization, and was about to embarrass the US by defecting *en masse* to the USSR. It's a matter of record that Jones had meetings with Soviet and Cuban officials, and almost his last order was that luggage containing money and documents was to be taken to Guyana's Soviet embassy.

Possible CIA involvement in the Jonestown massacre was investigated by the House Select Committee on Intelligence, which concluded in 1980 that the agency had no links with Jones or any part in the massacre. A lawsuit by Ryan's children alleging that the CIA ran Jonestown as part of MK-ULTRA was thrown out.

Amid the flurry of Jonestown theories, the obvious explanation still holds up: it was the work of a messianic guru who exercised an almost hypnotic hold over his psychologically needy followers. Jones was, if you like, a little Hitler.

Affidavits by People's Temple survivors detail all too clearly Jones's long-held plans for a mass suicide should his little Reich be jeopardized. The People's Temple former financial director, Deborah Layton Blakey, who escaped the cult, issued a public affidavit six months before the massacre warning that Jones was intent on a mass suicide. Most convincing of all is the audio-tape retrieved from Jonestown, widely believed to be genuine, in which Jones can be heard discussing the deteriorating situation:

Jones: It's all over. The congressman has been murdered. *(Music and singing.)* Well, it's all over, all over. What a legacy, what a legacy. What the Red Brigade doin' that once ever made any sense anyway? They invaded our privacy. They came into our home. They followed us six thousand miles away. Red Brigade showed them justice. The congressman's dead. *(Music only.)*

Please get us some medication. It's simple. It's simple. There's no convulsions with it. It's just simple. Just, please get it. Before it's too late. The GDF [Guyanese Defense Force] will be here, I tell you. Get movin', get movin', get movin'.

Woman 6: Now. Do it now!

Jones: Don't be afraid to die. You'll see, there'll be a few people land out here. They'll torture some of our children here. They'll torture our people. They'll torture our seniors. We cannot have this. Are you going to separate yourself from whoever shot the congressman? I don't know who shot him.

Voices: No. No. No.

Jones: Please, can we hasten? Can we hasten with that medication? You don't know what you've done. I tried. *(Applause, music, singing.)* They saw it happen and ran into the bush and dropped the machine guns. I never in my life. But not any more. But we've got to move. Are you gonna get that medication here? You've got to move. Marceline, about forty minutes.

[. . .]

Jones: Please. For God's sake, let's get on with it. We've lived
– we've lived as no other people lived and loved. We've had as
much of this world as you're gonna get. Let's just be done
with it. Let's be done with the agony of it. *(Applause.)* It's
far, far harder to have to walk through every day, die slowly –
and from the time you're a child 'til the time you get grey,
you're dying. Dishonest, and I'm sure that they'll – they'll
pay for it. They'll pay for it. This is a revolutionary suicide.
This is not a self-destructive suicide. So they'll pay for this.
They brought this upon us. And they'll pay for that. I leave
that destiny to them. *(Voices.)* Who wants to go with their
child has a right to go with their child. I think it's humane. I
want to go – I want to see you go, though. They can take me
and do what they want – whatever they want to do. I want to
see you go. I don't want to see you go through this hell no
more. No more. No more. No more. We're trying. If everybody will relax. The best thing you do to relax, and you will
have no problem. You'll have no problem with this thing if
you just relax.

[. . .]

Jones: Where's the vat, the vat, the vat? Where's the vat with
the Green C on it? The vat with the Green C in. Bring it so
the adults can begin.

Jonestown: a mass suicide called by a delusional, mind-games-
playing tyrant. So why, then, do 5,000 pages of the House
Committee on Foreign Affairs (HCFA) 1979 hearing remain
classified?

The Jonestown massacre was carried out by CIA to disguise
mind-control experiments: ALERT LEVEL 5

Further Reading
John Judge, "The Black Hole of Guyana", *Secret and Suppressed*, ed. Jim Keith, 1993

Deborah Layton, *Seductive Poison: A Survivor of Jonestown Shares Her Story*, 1999

Michael Meiers, *Was Jonestown a CIA Medical Experiment?: A Review of the Evidence*, 1989

KAL007

On 1 September 1983 a Korean Air Lines 747 set off from Alaska for Seoul. Instead of following the prescribed route, the civilian flight went 365 miles (590km) off-course and into Soviet airspace. There it was engaged by Soviet fighters, which launched two air-to-air missiles at the airliner, sending KAL007 down into the Sea of Japan with the loss of 269 passengers and crew aboard.

These were the bad old days of the Cold War. Ronald Reagan was in the White House, Yuri Andropov in the Kremlin. On the face of it, the shooting down of KAL007 was cold-blooded, unprovoked murder by the Soviets and was condemned as such by the White House. But was it? According to R. W. Johnson in *Shootdown* (1986), KAL007 was on a CIA/US military mission to fly into Soviet airspace and thereby trigger the Reds' defence systems – which could then be monitored by NATO and Japanese surveillance systems. One of the monitoring stations, Johnson hypothesizes, was the space-shuttle *Challenger*, which flew over the Sea of Japan four times during KAL007's flight. To lend weight to his argument he details a history of "mistaken" Korean Air Lines infringements of Soviet airspace, including the 1978 gunning-down of a strayed Korean airliner. According to lawyer Melvin Belli, who represented some of the passengers' families, the KAL007 pilot said to his wife before departure: "This is the last trip. It's too dangerous."

KAL had an incentive to tag along with a CIA spying scheme. The company was in a poor financial state and required US government dispensations to survive.

Johnson concluded that the US government bet the Soviets wouldn't open fire on a civilian airliner, but got it disastrously wrong. His case has to be weighed against the investigations of the International Civil Aviation Organization, which determined that the 747 went off-course because the inattentive pilot failed to engage the Inertial Navigation System, relying instead on the magnetic compass to guide the plane. He would have to have been very drowsy indeed, and likewise the remainder of the flight crew. The plane's ground mapping radar would have informed them that they were flying over land and not sea as indicated on the flight plan.

No one, incidentally, could call R. W. Johnson the usual conspiracy theory suspect. He's an Oxford professor and heavyweight political historian.

> Civilian flight KAL007 was undertaking a clandestine US mission over Russia when it was shot down: ALERT LEVEL 8

Further Reading
R. W. Johnson, *Shootdown*, 1986

DR DAVID KELLY

Those implicated in the 2003 demise of Dr David Kelly include the Iraqi secret service, the French secret service, and not least, Kelly himself. Whatever the truth about his death, he was as much a victim of the war in Iraq as any soldier or civilian killed on the battlefield.

The confusion, briefings and counter-briefings that surrounded the days running up to the invasion of Iraq in 2002 and early 2003 created a nervousness and state of tension which caused all parties involved to act in unpredictable ways. During this time the UK government released two dossiers which set out evidence for its belief that Saddam Hussein's regime posed a real threat to world security: the September 2002 document which stated that Iraq possessed weapons of mass destruction (WMDs) and that, crucially, these weapons could be deployed within 45 minutes; and a second, in February 2003, which detailed secret arms networks. A month later the UK had deployed troops in Iraq to secure Hussein's downfall in spite of vocal protests from the government's own MPs and many other groups.

On 20 May 2003, BBC Radio's flagship current affairs programme *Today* featured a report from its defence correspondent, Andrew Gilligan, in which he revealed that a senior source at the Ministry of Defence accused a member of the Downing Street press office (later identified as Alastair Campbell) of having "sexed up" the September dossier by inserting the information about the 45-minute deployment. The BBC's *Newsnight* correspondent Susan Watts also reported that a "senior official" believed the intelligence services came under heavy political pressure to include the 45-minute claim in its dossier.

The government, enraged by the leak, demanded that Gilligan reveal his source, and weeks of accusation and counter-accusation began, with the BBC defending Gilligan and the anonymity of his source and the government's press machine attempting to discredit the story. Richard Sambrook, the BBC's director of news, described the attacks as "an unprecedented level of pressure from Downing Street". Both Gilligan and Campbell were asked to appear before the Foreign Affairs Select Committee (FAC) to explain their actions.

The media frenzy must have worried Dr Kelly, who wrote to his line manager at the ministry admitting he had met Gilligan on May 22 and could have been one of the sources for his story. After another ten days of increasing pressure to reveal the identity of the source, the MoD then identified Kelly indirectly by pointedly refusing to deny he was involved when a list of possible sources was read out at a press conference, although Kelly himself was not informed his name was being released to the press.

On 15 and 16 July Dr Kelly sat in front of the FAC facing allegations that it was he who had been the source of the Gilligan story. He appeared deeply uncomfortable at being the centre of so much public attention, and spoke so softly that air-conditioning fans had to be turned off so the committee members could hear what he was saying. Despite much probing, Kelly maintained that, although he had spoken to Gilligan, he had not been his primary source. Kelly said the controversial point about the 45-minute deployment claim being added by Alastair Campbell could not have come from him as he had no part in the actual compilation of the dossier, but had merely presented information for possible inclusion, and thus had not been not party to the decisions by the Joint Intelligence Committee, who had produced the document.

At the end of the two days the FAC had concluded that Kelly was "most unlikely" to be the source of the "sexed-up" claim. Kelly, too, had relaxed, and was laughing and joking with the committee members.

The following day, 17 July, he left his home at 3 p.m., telling his wife he was going for his usual afternoon walk. He did not return. At 11.45 p.m. his family contacted the police and reported him missing. He was found at 9.20 the next morning by two search volunteers in woods on Harrowdown Hill, about a mile and a half (2.5km) from his home. The police did not confirm the body as his until 19 July, and then stated that they believed he had committed suicide by taking the powerful painkiller co-proxamol and then cutting his left wrist. A day later, after talking to his family, the BBC issued a statement naming Dr Kelly as the source of both Gilligan's and Watts's reports.

In the light of the previous train of events and unusual vigour with which the government had pursued Andrew Gilligan and his source, it seems understandable that an independent inquiry into the whole affair was announced as the best way of uncovering the truth surrounding Kelly's death and the lingering accusation that Downing Street had tampered with intelligence reports. Lord Hutton was appointed to head the inquiry, and his inquiry heard several months' worth of evidence from experts, Kelly's friends and family, and members of the Cabinet, including Tony Blair. Five months later, after much hype and speculation, Hutton concluded that the government had behaved properly, that the BBC should be heavily criticized for its actions, and that Kelly's death had been by his own hand.

There, it was presumably hoped, is where the whole unfortunate episode would end, but there were some who pointed to inconsistencies in the official version of events. Many people who had been close to Kelly, professionally and personally, did not believe the suicide story, and others believed his death bore all the hallmarks of a planned assassination.

The first to speak publicly of their misgivings were the two paramedics who had attended the scene of Dr Kelly's death,

Paul Bartlett and Vanessa Hunt. Interviewed by Anthony Barnett in the *Observer* in December 2004, they said they found little or no evidence of the major bleeding that would have taken place if the severed wrist artery had been the cause of death, as stated by the pathologist. "When somebody cuts an artery, whether accidentally or intentionally, the blood pumps everywhere. I just think it is incredibly unlikely that he died from the wrist wound we saw," said Hunt.

The paramedics' views were soon supported by a group of doctors who wrote to the *Guardian* newspaper, saying they too were deeply unhappy with the official cause of death. The severed ulnar artery, they argued, was too thin to have allowed a major haemorrhage, especially as, out in the open, the blood vessel would have been closed off by surrounding muscle long before Kelly bled to death. David Halpin, a trauma surgeon and one of the authors of the letter, maintains that even the deepest cut in the region of the ulnar artery would not have caused death: ". . . a completely transacted artery retracts immediately and thus stops bleeding, even at a relatively high blood pressure". The artery itself lies deep in the wrist on the little finger side of the hand, under other nerves and tendons, and cannot be accidentally slashed like the more superficial radial artery. Following the suicide theory would mean believing Kelly had managed to cut down deep into his own wrist to locate and cut the ulnar artery . . . with a blunt pruning knife.

The physicians also questioned the toxicology results, pointing out that the concentration of the drug co-proxamol in Kelly's blood was not high enough to have killed him, being only a third of a fatal dose. Kelly's stomach was virtually empty on examination, containing the equivalent of a fifth of one tablet, suggesting that, if he did swallow the cited 29 tablets, he had regurgitated most of them before the drug could be absorbed.

As suicides go, this was a pretty amateur affair, considering Kelly must have had an intimate knowledge of human biology in his work as a microbiologist and authority on biological weapons. He was the only person to die using these methods in the whole of 2003. Co-proxamol is often used in suicide attempts but most commonly in conjunction with alcohol. Severing the ulnar artery does not automatically lead to a fatal loss of blood. Kelly is known to have had an aversion to swallowing tablets. If his suicide was premeditated, why bring a small blunt concave-edged knife to do a tricky slicing job, along with the tablets? And if it was a spontaneous act, why did he bring 30 painkilling tablets with him on his daily constitutional?

As if there were not enough mystery surrounding the suicide, it became apparent during the Hutton Inquiry that there were other major discrepancies. The volunteers who found Dr Kelly's body said he was sitting or slumped against a tree when they discovered him, but in his evidence DC Coe of the Thames Valley Police stated Kelly was flat on his back and away from the tree. The volunteers swore that the knife, an opened bottle of Evian and a watch were not present when they were there, but these items had appeared next to the body by the time DC Coe left the scene.

As any viewer of TV crime will know, most solved cases are so because of the work of the forensics people, but in this case there was surprisingly little forensic evidence forthcoming. For instance, whose fingerprints were on the knife? Was any foreign DNA detected in the blood samples? Was the watch found beside Dr Kelly broken or intact, and, if broken, what time did it show? What were the last calls made to him on his mobile phone? None of these questions was asked during the inquiry, and no answers were volunteered.

In March 2005, Lib Dem MP Norman Baker resigned his front bench job expressly to investigate the circumstances surrounding Kelly's death. A year later he published his findings on his own website and contributed to a BBC TV programme, *Conspiracy Files*, which focused on Kelly. Baker voiced his serious doubts over the conclusion of the inquiry, not only on the basis of the medical evidence and the suicide verdict but also concerning the "irregularities in the actions of the coroner", the choice of pathologist, the actions of the police at the beginning of the investigation, and why Lord Hutton, in particular, was picked to head the inquiry.

Baker questions why the Lord Chancellor, Lord Falconer, decided the inquiry should not be held under the usual rules, so that witnesses could not be subpoenaed, nor did they have to give evidence under oath, making the whole procedure less rigorous than a standard coroner inquest. Even more bizarrely, the Oxfordshire coroner, Nicholas Gardiner, pre-empted the findings of the inquiry by issuing a full death certificate on 18 August, while Hutton's investigation was still in its early stages, in spite of rules stating that at most only an interim certificate should be issued while an inquest is in adjournment. Baker doesn't think much of the appointed pathologist either, describing the medical evidence presented by him to the inquiry as "incomplete, inconsistent and inadequate".

As for the conduct of the police force, the most puzzling fact that has come to light has been that Operation Mason, as it was named, began at 2.30 p.m. on 17 July, about nine hours before Dr Kelly's family reported him missing and half an hour before he left his home to go for his walk. Quite how the police knew what was going to happen, they are not willing to divulge. Nor are they willing to say why they felt it necessary to erect a 45-foot-high (15.7m) antenna in the Kellys' garden, or turn Mrs Kelly out of her home in the middle of the night for some considerable time while a search dog was put through the house. According to Baker, one of the most senior police officers in the country, on being consulted, was at a loss as to why either action would have been required.

Norman Baker reserves particular scepticism for the choice of Lord Hutton to head the inquiry and the part Tony Blair played in the decision. In spite of being on a jet somewhere between Washington and Tokyo when formally advised of Dr Kelly's death, Blair decided on an inquiry and appointed Lord Brian Hutton as its head even before the journey was over. Parliament, perhaps rather conveniently, had adjourned for the summer, and the appointment was made on the advice of Lord Falconer and, Baker suspects, Peter Mandelson. The man they chose had no experience of chairing any other public inquiry but, during his distinguished career, plenty of history of upholding the views of the government of the day.

It was highly unlikely, therefore, that the Hutton Inquiry was going to answer such sticky questions as why a highly respected scientist chose to take his life in quite such an unconventional way, days after being embroiled in a political scandal that was potentially deeply damaging to the government. Kelly had been deeply upset by being thrust into the media spotlight and, no doubt, bewildered by the the MoD's decision to leak his name to the press. However, he was also cheerful and joky with members of the Foreign Affairs Select Committee the day before his death, and had made plans to fly to Iraq the following week; one of his daughters was looking forward to her impending wedding day. Most importantly, perhaps, he was a practising member of the Baha'i faith, which forbids the act of suicide.

An email to a New York journalist, Judith Miller, on the morning of 17 July suggests that Dr Kelly realized that there was something worrying going on behind the soundbites and political posturing:

David, I heard from another member of your fan club that things went well for you today. Hope it's true.

(Original message sent by Judith Miller, 16 July 00.30)

I will wait until the end of the week before judging – many dark actors playing games. Thanks for your support. I appreciate your friendship at this time.

(Dr Kelly's reply, sent 17 July 11.18)

Conspiracy theorists believe Kelly had been labelled a loose cannon and as such a threat to the stability of the government. If Britain lost Blair, Europe lost an important ally in its struggle for greater political and economic union. Michael Shrimpton, a barrister and intelligence services expert who also acted for the Kelly Investigation Group, claimed he was told Kelly had been assassinated. Speaking in an interview with Canadian broadcaster Alex Jones in 2004 he said: "Within 48 hours of the murder I was contacted by a British Intelligence officer who told me [Kelly had] been murdered . . . now that source told me he'd done some digging and discovered that, he didn't name names, but he discovered that it had been known in Whitehall prior to 17 July that David Kelly was going to be taken down."

Shrimpton went on to explain that clever governments get the secret services of their allies to do their dirty work for them, and that Kelly's death bore all the hallmarks of a job by the DGSE (Direction Generale de la Securite Exterieure), the French equivalent of MI6. The tablets found in Kelly's pocket would have been a cover; he would actually have been killed by a lethal injection of dextropropoxythene, the active ingredient of co-proxamol, and the muscle relaxant succinylcholine, "a favourite method" of murder by intelligence services, with his wrist clumsily cut to disguise the needle's puncture mark. Shrimpton said the assassination team would most likely have been recruited from Iraqis living in Damascus, to disguise French involvement, and then its members killed after the event to ensure absolute secrecy.

There are others, such as UN weapons inspector Richard Spertzel, who claim it was the Iraqis themselves who killed Dr Kelly in revenge for all the trouble he'd brought upon Saddam Hussein's regime through his work. This seems far-fetched. Although Kelly had said he supported the invasion of Iraq, he had not been the author of the 45-minute claim which had precipitated military action. And he had only recently inspected trailers, claimed to be bio-weapons laboratories, and declared them to be no such thing. More hard-line conspiracy theorists maintain Dr Kelly's death was yet another in a suspicious pattern of untimely deaths among the world's leading micro-biologists, who are being systematically bumped off for reasons that remain unclear.

However weird the theories, Kelly's death was not properly investigated. The glaring omissions and conflicts of evidence; the choice of an inquiry, headed by a judge rather than a coroner, with terms drawn up at the outset by the government;

the continuing unease of expert doctors and political figures, willing to risk their own reputations to publicize their misgivings – all this suggests there is far more to this event than the government is willing to be open about. Given that the present government would still have much to lose should it be revealed that Kelly's death was unlawful, it is likely to be a long time before all the factors surrounding this case reach the light of day.

> WMD whistle-blower Dr David Kelly was murdered: ALERT LEVEL 9

Further Reading
www.thehutton-inquiry.org.uk/content/evidence.htm
www.news.bbc.co.uk/1/hi/uk_politics/3076869.stm
http://politics.guardian.co.uk/kelly/story/0,,1021802.00.html
http://politics.guardian.co.uk/kelly/story/0,,1779197,00.html
www.prisonplanet.com/021204medicalevidence.html
www.prisonplanet.com/022504shrimptontranscript.html
www.globalresearch.ca/index.php?context = viewArticle&co-
     de + CH020070226&articleId + 4944
www.normanbaker.org.uk/concerns/kellymail.htm
www.guardian.co.uk/hutton/story/0,13822,1372077,00.html

JOHN F. KENNEDY

More than 40 years on, the images still loop:

Kennedy in the back of the open-top Lincoln, next to Jackie, all smiles and waves in the sun . . .

Kennedy, his head slumped sideways . . .

Jackie leaning over to her husband . . .

Jackie trying to climb up the back of the car . . .

A blur of speeding cars and motorbike outriders . . .

Lyndon B. Johnson inside Air Force One taking the oath of presidency, Jackie statue-like by his side . . .

Elected to the White House in 1960 aged 46, Democrat John F. Kennedy was supposedly the bringer of a fresh new dawn. Handsome, charismatic and liberal, JFK promised hope for an entire generation. That hope was snuffed out at 12.30 p.m. on 22 November 1963 in Dealey Plaza, Dallas.

Kennedy had chosen to visit Dallas to boost the Democratic cause in Texas, a marginal state, and to generate funds for the upcoming November 1964 presidential election. Both Kennedy and his staff had expressed concerns about security because, only a month earlier, US Ambassador to the UN Adlai Stevenson had been jostled and spat upon during a visit to Dallas. Nevertheless, the route the president's motorcade would take through Dallas was published in Dallas newspapers on the eve of the visit, 21 November 1963. The next day, a little before 12.30 p.m. CST, his Lincoln limousine entered Dealey Plaza and slowly approached the Texas School Book Depository. It then turned 120 degrees left, directly in front of the Depository, just 65 feet (20m) away.

As the presidential Lincoln passed the Depository and continued down Elm Street, shots were fired at Kennedy, who was waving to the crowds on his right. One shot entered his upper back, penetrated his neck, and exited his throat. He raised his clenched fists up to his neck and leaned to his left as Jacqueline Kennedy put her arms around him. Texas Governor John Connally, sitting with his wife in front of the Kennedys in the limousine, was hit in the back and yelled out, "Oh, no, no, no . . . My God, they're going to kill us all!"

The final shot occurred as the presidential limo passed in front of the John Neely Bryan pergola. As the shot sounded, President Kennedy's head exploded, covering the interior of the Lincoln with blood and tissue.

Secret Service agent Clint Hill was riding on the running board of the car behind the limousine. After the first shot struck the president, Hill jumped off and ran to overtake it. By then the president had been hit in the head and Mrs Kennedy was climbing on to the boot of the car. Hill jumped on the back of the limousine, pushed Mrs Kennedy back into her seat, and clung to the car as it sped to Parkland Memorial Hospital. At 1.00 p.m. President John F. Kennedy was pronounced dead by hospital staff, although he was certainly dead before he reached the hospital.

Meanwhile, back in Dealey Plaza, the first witnesses were talking to police. Howard Brennan, across from the Texas School Book Depository, distinctly heard gunshots from that building. So did Harold Norman, James Jarman Jr and Bonnic Ray Williams, employees of the Depository who had watched the motorcade from a window at the south-east corner of the fifth floor; they heard three shots from directly over their heads. (Of the eye and ear witnesses who would eventually give testimony as to the direction from which the fatal shots came, 56 [53.8 per cent] believed they came from the direction of the Depository, 35 [33.7 per cent] thought they came from a "grassy knoll" on the north side of the Plaza, and 8 [7.7 per cent] thought the shots came from other locations. Only 5 [4.8 per cent] thought they heard shots from two separate locations.) A police search of the Book Depository revealed that one employee, Lee Harvey Oswald, was missing, having left the building immediately after the shooting. After 80 minutes of frantic manhunt Oswald was spotted on a sidewalk by Dallas police officer J. D. Tippit, who on approaching Oswald was shot dead. One hour later Oswald was cornered in a movie house and arrested. The next day he was charged with the murders of Kennedy and Tippit. He denied shooting anyone and claimed he'd been set up as a "patsy".

On 24 November at 11.21 a.m., as Oswald was being transferred from Dallas Police Headquarters to the county jail, a local strip-club owner, Jack Ruby, stepped out of the crowd and fatally gunned him down. Ruby was convicted of Oswald's murder in 1964, but the conviction was overturned. Ruby died in jail awaiting retrial.

A week after Kennedy's assassination, President Lyndon Baines Johnson ("LBJ") set up a commission under Chief Justice Earl Warren to investigate the killing. The Warren Commission published its findings in September 1964. According to the Commission, Lee Harvey Oswald had shot Kennedy from the sixth floor of the Texas Book Depository, where an Italian Mannlicher–Carcano M91/38 bolt-action rifle had been found with his fingerprints on it. A bullet on Governor Connally's stretcher matched this rifle. Oswald, a misfit with Marxist leanings, had been instrumental in setting up the New Orleans branch of the pro-Castro Fair Play for Cuba Committee. He had, concluded the Commission, "an overriding hostility to his environment . . . [a] hatred for American society" and had sought "a place in history". The Commission "could not find any persuasive evidence of a domestic or foreign conspiracy involving any other person(s), group(s), or country(ies), and [believed] that Lee Harvey Oswald acted alone".

In a US still traumatized by the event, the Warren Commission report was initially met with a sense of relief and acceptance. The mood, however, gradually passed to unease and then outright distrust, as it became clear that LBJ had embargoed huge swathes of the report for 30 years. Moreover, the bits and pieces of the report that had been released contained as many questions as they did answers. Why hadn't the Commission interviewed Ruby, especially as he had informed them he would "come clean"? Then there was the matter of the murder weapon: could a bolt-action relic of the Second World War really deliver three accurate shots, at this range, in 6–7 seconds?

With the manifest inadequacy of the official investigation into Kennedy's death, numerous independent investigations tried to get at the truth. Among the keenest-eyed readers of the Warren Report's selected extracts was New Orleans District Attorney Jim Garrison, who spotted a passing reference to one Clay Bertrand, whom Garrison identified as homosexual New Orleans businessman Clay Shaw. In 1969 Garrison prosecuted Shaw for conspiring to murder the president; unfortunately for Garrison, two of his key witnesses, David Ferrie and Guy Bannister, died in suspicious circumstances before they could testify. (Aside from Oswald, Ruby, Ferrie and Bannister, anything up to 40 witnesses in the JFK case have mysteriously died or been murdered.) Shaw was acquitted after less than an hour of deliberation by the jury, yet Garrison's quest was not in vain; Ferrie would later be identified as a possible co-conspirator by the 1976 House of Representatives Select Committee on Assassinations (HSCA). Also, Garrison forced the first public showing of the 486-frame, 8mm movie shot by Abraham Zapruder of Kennedy's killing, which shows a backwards blast of brains and blood from Kennedy's head. On the Zapruder film, it looks as though the president has been shot from in front; Oswald was high up, to the President's right, at the time of the shooting. If the fatal bullet came from the front, there must have been another gunman. In its 1979 report, the HSCA concluded that there was "a high probability that two gunmen" fired at Kennedy, and that he was "probably assassinated as a result of a conspiracy". In evidence, the HSCA heard a Dictabelt recording from a Dallas police motorcyclist's radio, on which four gunshots could be heard, one more than Oswald supposedly fired. Among the other evidence supporting the two-gunmen theory was the testimony of Dr McClelland, a physician in the Portland emergency room, that the back right-hand part of President Kennedy's head had been blown out. Top rifle experts of the FBI could not make the Mannlicher rifle used by Oswald fire two shots in the 2.3-second timeframe that Oswald allegedly fired off his first two rounds. Neither could Gunnery Sergeant Carlos Hathcock, the senior instructor for the US Marine Corps Sniper Instructor School at Quantico, Virginia. "We reconstructed the whole thing," said Hathcock, "the angle, the range, the moving target, the time limit, the obstacles, everything. I don't know how many times we tried it, but we couldn't duplicate what the Warren Commission said Oswald did. Now if I can't do it, how in the world could a guy who was a non-qual on the rifle range and later only qualified 'marksman' do it?"

Disregarding the truly lunatic theories that John F. Kennedy was murdered by **Martin Bormann** (who, like **Elvis Presley**, never dies) or time-travelling aliens, the finger of suspicion points at four main potential culprits:

The Communists

Early JFK conspiracy theories centred on the USSR and its stooges. Kennedy had, of course, gone toe-to-toe with the USSR during the Cuban Missile Crisis. In *Plot and Counterplot* Edward J. Epstein suggested that Dallas was payback time by a smarting Moscow. Oswald, who had once defected to the USSR but returned to the US, was according to this hypothesis a KGB agent. A variant is that the Communist leader of Cuba, Fidel Castro, organized the assassination. As LBJ neatly put it: "Kennedy was trying to kill Castro. Castro got him first." The strongest evidence in support of the Castro theory is that Oswald contacted the Cuban embassy in Mexico City in

September 1963; but whether this was on his own initiative or at the instigation of the Cuban Intelligence Service, G-2, is unknown.

Against the Communist and/or Castro hypothesis is that both Cuba and the USSR were in rapprochement with Kennedy at the time of his assassination. During its investigation, HSCA visited Cuba and interviewed Castro about Cuban complicity in Kennedy's assassination. He replied:

> That [the Cuban Government might have been involved in Kennedy's death] was insane. From the ideological point of view it was insane. And from the political point of view, it was a tremendous insanity. I am going to tell you here that nobody, nobody ever had the idea of such things. What would it do? We just tried to defend our folks here, within our territory. Anyone who subscribed to that idea would have been judged insane . . . absolutely sick. Never, in 20 years of revolution, I never heard anyone suggest nor even speculate about a measure of that sort, because who could think of the idea of organizing the death of the President of the United States? That would have been the most perfect pretext for the United States to invade our country, which is what I have tried to prevent for all these years, in every possible sense. Since the United States is much more powerful than we are, what could we gain from a war with the United States? The United States would lose nothing. The destruction would have been here.

Obviously Castro might have been lying to HSCA, but his point is good: why give the US a 22-carat pretext to invade Cuba by assassinating its leader?

Castro/the USSR assassinated JFK: ALERT LEVEL 3

LBJ

In 2003 Barr McClellan published *Blood, Money and Power: How LBJ Killed JFK,* which argued that Kennedy's successor Lyndon B. Johnson, together with an accomplice, Edward Clark, planned and covered up the assassination in Dallas. LBJ certainly had a motive: aside from the intrinsic attraction of succeeding to the most important job in the world, Johnson was the subject of four major criminal investigations involving government contract violations, misappropriation of funds, money-laundering and bribery at the time of Kennedy's murder. All these investigations were terminated upon LBJ's assumption of the Presidency. Worse, LBJ knew Malcolm "Mac" Wallace, a convicted murderer who was the sometime boyfriend of LBJ's sister Josefa; in 1998 JFK assassination researcher Walt Brown announced that he had identified a fingerprint in the "sniper's nest" in the Book Depository as belonging to Wallace. Former CIA officer and Watergate agent E. Howard Hunt also implicated LBJ in a deathbed confession, along with CIA agents Bill Harvey, Cord Meyer, Bill Harvey and David Sanchez Morales; in Hunt's confession the shooter was named Lucien Sarti and shot Kennedy from the grassy knoll. Hunt, according to his own account, was one of the "three hoboes" seen on the grassy knoll on the afternoon of 22 November 1963.

LBJ apparently had no shortage of willing helpers. Mark North's *Act of Treason* (1991) posits that LBJ was helped by J. Edgar Hoover, head of the FBI, who was known to loathe JFK and his brother Bobby, the Attorney General.

LBJ conspired to kill his predecessor: ALERT LEVEL 6

CIA and Anti-Castro Cuban Exile Conspiracy

Something very bad is going on within the CIA and I want to know what it is. I want to shred the CIA into a thousand pieces and scatter them to the four winds.

President John F. Kennedy

Kennedy despised the CIA for bungling the Bay of Pigs invasion of Cuba in April 1961, and afterwards accepted the resignation of the CIA chief Allen Dulles. The Agency reciprocated Kennedy's feeling because, aside from his stinging criticism, he was intending to withdraw from Vietnam and seek detente with the Communists. According to *Crime and Cover-Up* (1977) by Peter Dale Scott, Kennedy's initiatives would have caused the scaling down of the CIA empire, as well as the curbing of its lucrative narcotics-trafficking business. The Military-Industrial Complex financed the hit, since it had a vested interest in continuing the war in 'Nam, from which it was making billions. Assassination was the CIA's stock-in-trade. It had participated in the successful murders of two (at least) heads of state, Ngo Dinh Diem of Vietnam and Rafael Trujillo of the Dominican Republic. Why not murder its own head of state? It had the expertise, after all.

HSCA reviewed these theories and concluded that, although Oswald assassinated Kennedy in a conspiracy with others, the conspiracy did not include any US Intelligence agencies. HSCA did believe, however, that anti-Castro Cuban exiles might have participated in Kennedy's murder. These exiles had worked closely with CIA operatives in covert operations against Castro's Cuba.

The CIA assassinated JFK: ALERT LEVEL 2.5

Anti-Castro Cuban exiles assassinated JFK: ALERT LEVEL 7

The Mob

The HSCA investigation also identified the Mafia as possible conspirators in the plot to assassinate Kennedy. The Mob, so the theory runs, murdered JFK in retaliation for the heat put upon them by Attorney General Robert Kennedy (who had increased by 12 times the number of prosecutions under President Eisenhower). What HSCA was too discreet to mention was that the Kennedys had long been in bed with the Mob (literally in the case of JFK, who had an affair with Sam Giancana's girlfriend Judith Campbell Exner) and had used Mafia money in the campaign to secure the White House. The Mob didn't like the campaign against them, and even less did it like the Kennedys' hypocrisy. Mafia bosses Carlos Marcello, Sam Giancana and Santo Trafficante Jr top the list of HSCA gangster suspects. For good measure, HSCA also found ties, admittedly tenuous, between Oswald, Jack Ruby and the Marcello mob of New Orleans. Ruby, a sometime foot soldier for Capone in Chicago, was tasked with "offing" Oswald before he could squeal. An argument against Mafia culpability is that the JFK assassination did not bear the hallmark of Mafia hits, which tend to be up close and personal; if the Mob did kill Kennedy then it must have hired a trained military marksman, possibly someone in or on the dissident fringes of the CIA, with whom the Mob had co-operated in attempted assassinations of Castro.

An added twist to the Mob theory is given by Mark North in *Act of Treason*, in which he claims that Marcello tipped off J. Edgar Hoover of the FBI in 1962 that the assassination was being planned. Hoover, who despised Kennedy's civil rights agenda, intentionally sat on the information and let JFK die.

The Mob killed Kennedy: ALERT LEVEL 6

There is no shortage of other possible culprits. The **Freemasons** (antipathetic to JFK's Catholicism), Jackie Kennedy (embarrassed and shamed by her husband's affairs), Richard Nixon (desiring revenge for his defeat in the 1960 presidential election) and the Israelis (in anger at JFK's use of Nazi scientists in his nuclear programme and his opposition to theirs) have all had their 15 minutes of infamy as the suspected sponsors of the hit. A remarkable number – more than 30 – hoodlums, policemen and government agents have all stepped into the limelight to claim that *they* pulled the trigger on 22 November 1963, and for a while the diary entry of Dallas policeman Roscoe White, in which he detailed the murder, had many convinced – until it was proven to be a forgery. Around 2,000 books have been published on the JFK assassination and, just when everyone thought it was safe to say JFK was murdered by a conspiracy, there has been a recent tendency to support the Warren Commission's "lone gunman" theory, headed by Gerald Posner's *Case Closed* (1994) and Mark Furhman's *A Simple Act of Murder* (2006). Oswald, an ex-Marine, was a good shot, the cavalcade was moving slowly, and a single bullet might have hit both JFK and Governor Connally, meaning that Oswald had to fire only two shots in the timeframe, not three.

The arguments of the "anti-conspirators" fall on stony ground. An ABC News poll in 2003 found that 70 per cent of American respondents "suspect a plot" in the assassination of President Kennedy. Jack Leon Ruby is the weak link in the anti-conspiracy case. Why did Ruby step out of the crowd and gun down Oswald? Because he was so morally or politically outraged by Oswald's murder of JFK that he had to take revenge? Ruby was a hood of no fixed moral views, so: no. For the fame of it? Possibly, but the HSCA found no evidence that 56-year-old Ruby was psychologically flawed to the degree that he wished to make his mark in history as a shootist. And, when Ruby informed the Warren Commission that he would "come clean", what was he about to divulge? On balance, it must be assumed that Ruby stepped forward with his gun because he was either paid or pressurized by others to silence Oswald permanently. If someone needed to silence Lee Harvey Oswald, then there was a conspiracy.

The whos and whys of the conspiracy may never be known. In all likelihood, the conspiracy was small-scale, not institutional, and was created in the murky backrooms of the anti-Castro exiles in New Orleans, which maverick CIA agents and the Mob also frequented. This is the thrust of the 1991 Oliver Stone movie *JFK* – based on Jim Garrison's investigation – and of the HSCA report.

> JFK was killed by a conspiracy, not a "lone gunman": ALERT LEVEL 7

Further Reading
Mark Fuhrman, *A Simple Act of Murder*, 2006
Barr McClellan, *Blood, Money and Power: How LBJ Killed JFK*, 2003
Jim Marrs, *Crossfire: The Plot that Killed Kennedy*, 1989
Mark North, *Act of Treason*, 1991
Gerald Posner, *Case Closed*, 1994
Robin Ramsay, *Who Shot JFK?*, 2000
Peter Dale Scott, *Crime and Cover-Up: The CIA, the Mafia, and the Dallas–Watergate Connection*, 1977

DOCUMENT: EXTRACTS FROM THE REPORT OF THE SELECT COMMITTEE ON ASSASSINATIONS OF THE US HOUSE OF REPRESENTATIVES

C. The Committee believes, on the basis of the evidence available to it, that President John F. Kennedy was probably assassinated as a result of a conspiracy. The Committee is unable to identify the other gunman or the extent of the conspiracy.

- The committee believes, on the basis of the evidence available to it, that the Soviet Government was not involved in the assassination of President Kennedy.
- The committee believes, on the basis of the evidence available to it, that the Cuban Government was not involved in the assassination of President Kennedy.
- The committee believes, on the basis of the evidence available to it, that anti-Castro Cuban groups, as groups, were not involved in the assassination of President Kennedy, but that the available evidence does not preclude the possibility that individual members may have been involved.
- The committee believes, on the basis of the evidence available to it, that the national syndicate of organized crime, as a group, was not involved in the assassination of President Kennedy, but that the available evidence does not preclude the possibility that individual members may have been involved.
- The Secret Service, Federal Bureau of Investigation, and Central Intelligence Agency were not involved in the assassination of President Kennedy.

[. . .]

Based on the evidence available to it, the committee could not preclude the possibility that individual members of anti-Castro Cuban groups or the national syndicate of organized crime were involved in the assassination. There was insufficient evidence, however, to support a finding that any individual members were involved. The ramifications of a conspiracy involving such individuals would be significant, although of perhaps less import than would be the case if a group itself – the national syndicate, for example – had been involved.

The committee recognized that a finding that two gunmen fired simultaneously at the President did not, by itself, establish that there was a conspiracy to assassinate the President. It is theoretically possible that the gunmen were acting independently, each totally unaware of the other. It was the committee's opinion, however, that such a theoretical possibility is extremely remote. The more logical and probable inference to be drawn from two gunmen firing at the same person at the same time and in the same place is that they were acting in concert, that is, as a result of a conspiracy.

The committee found that, to be precise and loyal to the facts it established, it was compelled to find that President Kennedy was probably killed as a result of a conspiracy. The committee's finding that President Kennedy was probably assassinated as a result of a conspiracy was premised on four factors:

1) Since the Warren Commission's and FBI's investigation into the possibility of a conspiracy was seriously flawed, their failure to develop evidence of a conspiracy could not be given independent weight.

2) The Warren Commission was, in fact, incorrect in concluding that Oswald and Ruby had no significant associations, and therefore its finding of no conspiracy was not reliable.

3) While it cannot be inferred from the significant associations of Oswald and Ruby that any of the major groups examined by the committee were involved in the assassination, a more limited conspiracy could not be ruled out.

4) There was a high probability that a second gunman fired at the President. At the same time, the committee candidly stated, in expressing its finding of conspiracy in the Kennedy

assassination, that it was "unable to identify the other gunman or the extent of the conspiracy."

The photographic and other scientific evidence available to
the committee was insufficient to permit the committee to
answer these questions. In addition, the committee's other
investigative efforts did not develop evidence from which
Oswald's conspirator or conspirators could be firmly identified. It is possible, of course, that the extent of the conspiracy
was so limited that it involved only Oswald and the second
gunman. The committee was not able to reach such a conclusion, for it would have been based on speculation, not
evidence. Aspects of the investigation did suggest that the
conspiracy may have been relatively limited, but to state with
precision exactly how small was not possible. Other aspects
of the committee's investigation did suggest, however, that
while the conspiracy may not have involved a major group, it
may not have been limited to only two people. [. . .]

If the conspiracy to assassinate President Kennedy was
limited to Oswald and a second gunman, its main societal
significance may be in the realization that agencies of the
US Government inadequately investigated the possibility of
such a conspiracy. In terms of its implications for government and society, an assassination as a consequence of a
conspiracy composed solely of Oswald and a small number
of persons, possibly only one, and possibly a person akin to
Oswald in temperament and ideology, would not have been
fundamentally different from an assassination by Oswald
alone. [. . .]

*3. THE COMMITTEE BELIEVES, ON THE BASIS OF
THE EVIDENCE AVAILABLE TO IT, THAT ANTI-
CASTRO CUBAN GROUPS, AS GROUPS, WERE
NOT INVOLVED IN THE ASSASSINATION OF
PRESIDENT KENNEDY, BUT THAT THE AVAIL-
ABLE EVIDENCE DOES NOT PRECLUDE THE*

POSSIBILITY THAT INDIVIDUAL MEMBERS MAY HAVE BEEN INVOLVED.

[. . .]

The committee investigated possible involvement in the assassination by a number of anti-Castro Cuban groups and individual activists for two primary reasons:

First, they had the motive, based on what they considered President Kennedy's betrayal of their cause, the liberation of Cuba from the Castro regime; the means, since they were trained and practiced in violent acts, the result of the guerrilla warfare they were waging against Castro; and the opportunity, whenever the President, as he did from time to time, appeared at public gatherings, as in Dallas on 22 November 1963.

Second, the committee's investigation revealed that certain associations of Lee Harvey Oswald were or may have been with anti-Castro activists.

The committee, therefore, paid close attention to the activities of anti-Castro Cubans – in Miami, where most of them were concentrated and their organizations were headquartered, and in New Orleans and Dallas, where Oswald, while living in these cities in the months preceding the assassination, reportedly was in contact with anti-Castro activists.

[. . .]

(2) Attitude of anti-Castro Cubans toward Kennedy.–President Kennedy's popularity among the Cuban exiles had plunged deeply by 1963. Their bitterness is illustrated in a tape recording of a meeting of anti-Castro Cubans and right-wing Americans in the Dallas suburb of Farmer's Branch on 1 October 1963. In it, a Cuban identified as Nestor Castellanos vehemently criticized the United States and blamed President Kennedy for the US Government's policy of

"non-interference" with respect to the Cuban issue. Holding a copy of the September 26 edition of the *Dallas Morning News*, featuring a front-page account of the President's planned trip to Texas in November, Castellanos vented his hostility without restraint:

Castellanos: . . . we're waiting for Kennedy the 22nd, buddy. We're going to see him in one way or the other. We're going to give him the works when he gets in Dallas. Mr good ol' Kennedy. I wouldn't even call him President Kennedy. He stinks.

Questioner: Are you insinuating that since this downfall came through the leader there [Castro in Cuba], that this might come to us . . . ?

Castellanos: Yes ma'am, your present leader. He's the one who is doing everything right now to help the United States to become Communist.

(b) The committee investigation

The committee initiated its investigation by identifying the most violent and frustrated anti-Castro groups and their leaders from among the more than 100 Cuban exile organizations in existence in November 1963. These groups included Alpha 66, the Cuban Revolutionary Junta (JURE), Commandos L, the Directorio Revolutionary Estudiantil (DRE), the Cuban Revolutionary Council (CRC) which included the Frente Revolucionario Democratico (FRD), the Junta del Gobierno de Cuba en el Exilio (JGCE), the 30th of November, the International Penetration Forces (InterPen), the Revolutionary Recovery Movement (MRR), and the Ejercito Invasor Cubano (EIC). Their election evolved both from the committee's independent field investigation and the examination of the files and records maintained by the Federal and local agencies [that were] then monitoring Cuban exile activity. These agencies included local police departments, the FBI, the CIA, the Bureau of Narcotics and Dangerous

Drugs (now the Drug Enforcement Administration, or DEA), the Customs Service, the Immigration and Naturalization Service and the Department of Defense.

The groups that received the committee's attention were "action groups" – those most involved in military actions and propaganda campaigns. Unlike most others, they did not merely talk about anti-Castro operations, they actually carried out infiltrations into Cuba, planned, and sometimes attempted, Castro's assassination, and shipped arms into Cuba. These were also the groups whose leaders felt most betrayed by US policy toward Cuba and by the President; they were also those whose operations were frustrated by American law enforcement efforts after the missile crisis.

(1) Homer S. Echevarria.–For the most part the committee found that the anti-Castro Cuban leaders were more vociferous than potentially violent in their tirades against the President. Nevertheless, it was unable to conclude with certainty that all of the threats were benign. For example, one that the committee found particularly disturbing – especially so, since it was not thoroughly looked into in the 1963–4 investigation – came to the attention of the Secret Service within days of the President's death, prompting the Acting Special Agent-in-Charge of the Chicago field office to write an urgent memorandum indicating he had received reliable information of "a group in the Chicago area who [sic] may have a connection with the J.F.K. assassination." The memorandum was based on a tip from an informant who reported a conversation on 21 November 1963 with a Cuban activist named Homer S. Echevarria. They were discussing an illegal arms sale, and Echevarria was quoted as saying his group now had "plenty of money" and that his backers would proceed "as soon as we take care of Kennedy."

Following the initial memorandum, the Secret Service instructed its informant to continue his association with Echevarria and notified the Chicago FBI field office. It learned that Echevarria might have been a member of the 30th of November anti-Castro organization, that he was associated with Juan Francisco Blanco-Fernandez, military director of the DRE, and that the arms deal was being financed through one Paulino Sierra Martinez by hoodlum elements in Chicago and elsewhere.

Although the Secret Service recommended further investigation, the FBI initially took the position that the Echevarria case "was primarily a protection matter and that the continued investigation would be left to the US Secret Service," and that the Cuban group in question was probably not involved in illegal activities. The Secret Service initially was reluctant to accept this position, since it had developed evidence that illegal acts were, in fact, involved. Then, on 29 November 1963, President Johnson created the Warren Commission and gave the FBI primary investigative responsibility in the assassination. Based on its initial understanding that the President's order meant primary, not exclusive, investigative responsibility, the Secret Service continued its efforts; but when the FBI made clear that it wanted the Secret Service to terminate its investigation, it did so, turning over its files to the FBI. The FBI, in turn, did not pursue the Echevarria case.

While it was unable to substantiate the content of the informant's alleged conversations with Echevarria or any connection to the events in Dallas, the committee did establish that the original judgment of the Secret Service was correct, that the Echevarria case did warrant a thorough investigation. It found, for example, that the 30th of November group was backed financially by the Junta del Gobierno de Cuba en el Exilio (JGCE), a Chicago-based organization run by Paulino Sierra Martinez. JGCE was a coalition of many of the more active anti-Castro groups that had been founded in April 1963; it was dissolved soon after the assassination. Its purpose was to back the activities of the more militant groups, including Alpha 66 and the Student

Directorate, or DRE, both of which had reportedly been in contact with Lee Harvey Oswald. Much of JGCE's financial support, moreover, allegedly came from individuals connected to organized crime.

As it surveyed the various anti-Castro organizations, the committee focused its interest on reported contacts with Oswald. Unless an association with the President's assassin could be established, it is doubtful that it could be shown that the anti-Castro groups were involved in the assassination. The Warren Commission, discounting the recommendations of Slawson and Coleman, had either regarded these contacts as insignificant or as probably not having been made or else was not aware of them. The committee could not so easily dismiss them.

[. . .]

(c) Oswald and anti-Castro Cubans

The committee recognized that an association by Oswald with anti-Castro Cubans would pose problems for its evaluation of the assassin and what might have motivated him. In reviewing Oswald's life, the committee found his actions and values to have been those of a self-proclaimed Marxist who would be bound to favor the Castro regime in Cuba, or at least not advocate its overthrow. For this reason, it did not seem likely to the committee that Oswald would have allied himself with an anti-Castro group or individual activist for the sole purpose of furthering the anti-Castro cause. The committee recognized the possibility that Oswald might have established contacts with such groups or persons to implicate the anti-Castro movement in the assassination. Such an implication might have protected the Castro regime and other left-wing suspects.

(1) Oswald in New Orleans.–Another contact by Lee Harvey Oswald with anti-Castro Cuban activists that was not only documented, but also publicized at the time in the news media, occurred when he was living in New Orleans in the summer of 1963, an especially puzzling period in Oswald's life. His actions were blatantly pro-Castro, as he carried a one-man Fair Play for Cuba Committee crusade into the streets of a city whose Cuban population was predominantly anti-Castro. Yet Oswald's known and alleged associations even at this time included Cubans who were of an anti-Castro persuasion and their anti-Communist American supporters.

New Orleans was Oswald's home town; he was born there on 18 October 1939. In April 1963, shortly after the Walker shooting, he moved back, having lived in Fort Worth and Dallas since his return from the Soviet Union the previous June. He spent the first 2 weeks job hunting, staying with the Murrets, Lillian and Charles, or "Dutz," as he was called, the sister and brother-in-law of Oswald's mother, Marguerite. After being hired by the Reily Coffee Co. as a maintenance man, he sent for his wife Marina and their baby daughter, who were still in Dallas, and they moved into an apartment on Magazine Street.

In May, Oswald wrote to Vincent T. Lee, national director of the Fair Play for Cuba Committee, expressing a desire to open an FPCC chapter in New Orleans and requesting literature to distribute. He also had handouts printed, some of which were stamped "L.H. Oswald, 4907 Magazine Street," others with the alias, "A.J. Hidell, P.O. Box 30016," still others listing the FPCC address as 544 Camp Street.

In letters written earlier that summer and spring to the FPCC headquarters in New York, Oswald had indicated that he intended to rent an office. In one letter he mentioned that he had acquired a space but had been told to vacate 3 days later because the building was to be remodeled. The Warren Commission failed to discover any record of

Oswald's having rented an office at 544 Camp and concluded he had fabricated the story.

In investigating Oswald after the assassination, the Secret Service learned that the New Orleans chapter of the Cuban Revolutionary Council (CRC), an anti-Castro organization, had occupied an office at 544 Camp Street for about 6 months during 1961–2. At that time, Sergio Arcacha Smith was the official CRC delegate for the New Orleans area. Since the CRC had vacated the building 15 months before Oswald arrived in New Orleans, the Warren Commission concluded that there was no connection with Oswald. Nevertheless, the riddle of 544 Camp Street persisted over the years.

Oswald lost his job at the Reily Coffee Co. in July, and his efforts to find another were futile. Through the rest of the summer, he filed claims at the unemployment office.

On 5 August, Oswald initiated contact with Carlos Bringuier, a delegate of the Directorio Revolucionario Estudiantil (DRE). According to his testimony before the Warren Commission, Bringuier was the only registered member of the group in New Orleans. Bringuier also said he had two friends at the time, Celso Hernandez and Miguel Cruz, who were also active in the anti-Castro cause. Oswald reportedly told Bringuier that he wished to join the DRE, offering money and assistance to train guerrillas. Bringuier, fearful of an infiltration attempt by Castro sympathizers or the FBI, told Oswald to deal directly with DRE headquarters in Miami. The next day, Oswald returned to Bringuier's store and left a copy of a Marine training manual with Rolando Pelaez, Bringuier's brother-in-law.

On 9 August, Bringuier learned that a man was carrying a pro-Castro sign and handing out literature on Canal Street. Carrying his own anti-Castro sign, Bringuier, along with Hernandez and Cruz, set out to demonstrate against the pro-Castro sympathizer. Bringuier recognized Oswald and began shouting that he was a traitor and a Communist. A scuffle ensued, and police arrested all participants. Oswald spent the night in jail. On 12 August, he pleaded guilty to disturbing the peace and was fined $10. The anti-Castro Cubans were not charged.

During the incident with Bringuier, Oswald also encountered Frank Bartes, the New Orleans delegate of the CRC from 1962–4. After Bringuier and Oswald were arrested in the street scuffle, Bartes appeared in court with Bringuier. According to Bartes, the news media surrounded Oswald for a statement after the hearing. Bartes then engaged in an argument with the media and Oswald because the Cubans were not being given an opportunity to present their anti-Castro views.

On 16 August, Oswald was again seen distributing pro-Castro literature. A friend of Bringuier, Carlos Quiroga, brought one of Oswald's leaflets to Bringuier and volunteered to visit Oswald and feign interest in the FPCC in order to determine Oswald's motives. Quiroga met with Oswald for about an hour. He learned that Oswald had a Russian wife and spoke Russian himself. Oswald gave Quiroga an application for membership in the FPCC chapter, but Quiroga noted he did not seem intent on actually enlisting members.

Oswald's campaign received newspaper, television, and radio coverage. William Stuckey, a reporter for radio station WDSU which had been following the FPCC, interviewed Oswald on 17 August and proposed a television debate between Oswald and Bringuier, to be held on 21 August. Bringuier issued a press release immediately after the debate, urging the citizens of New Orleans to write their Congressmen demanding a congressional investigation of Lee Harvey Oswald.

Oswald largely passed out of sight from 21 August until 17 September, the day he applied for a tourist card to Mexico. He is known to have written letters to left-wing political organizations, and he and Marina visited the Murrets on Labor Day. Marina said her husband spent his free time reading books and practicing with his rifle.

(2) Oswald in Clinton, La.–While reports of some Oswald contacts with anti-Castro Cubans were known at the time of the 1964 investigation, allegations of additional Cuba-related associations surfaced in subsequent years. As an example, Oswald reportedly appeared in August–September 1963 in Clinton, La., where a voting rights demonstration was in progress. The reports of Oswald in Clinton were not, as far as the committee could determine, available to the Warren Commission, although one witness said he notified the FBI when he recognized Oswald from news photographs right after the assassination. In fact, the Clinton sightings did not publicly surface until 1967, when they were introduced as evidence in the assassination investigation being conducted by New Orleans District Attorney Jim Garrison. In that investigation, one suspect, David W. Ferrie, a staunch anti-Castro partisan, died within days of having been named by Garrison; the other, Clay L. Shaw, was acquitted in 1969. Aware that Garrison had been fairly criticized for questionable tactics, the committee proceeded cautiously, making sure to determine on its own the credibility of information coming from his probe. The committee found that the Clinton witnesses were credible and significant. [. . .]
[. . .]

(3) David Ferrie.–The Clinton witnesses were not the only ones who linked Oswald to Ferrie. On 23 November, the day after the assassination, Jack S. Martin, a part-time private detective and police informant, told the office of the New Orleans District Attorney that a former Eastern Airlines pilot named David Ferrie might have aided Oswald in the assassination. Martin had known Ferrie for over 2 years, beginning when he and Ferrie had performed some investigative work on a case involving an illegitimate religious order in Louisville, Ky. Martin advised Assistant New Orleans District Attorney Herman Kohlman that he suspected Ferrie might have known Oswald for some time and that

Ferrie might have once been Oswald's superior officer in a New Orleans unit of the Civil Air Patrol. Martin made further allegations to the FBI on November 25. He indicated he thought he once saw a photograph of Oswald and other CAP members when he visited Ferrie's home and that Ferrie might have assisted Oswald in purchasing a foreign firearm. Martin also informed the FBI that Ferrie had a history of arrests and that Ferrie was an amateur hypnotist, possibly capable of hypnotizing Oswald.

The committee reviewed Ferrie's background. He had been fired by Eastern Airlines, and in litigation over the dismissal, which continued through August 1963, he was counseled by a New Orleans attorney named G. Wray Gill. Ferrie later stated that in March 1960, he and Gill made an agreement whereby Gill would represent Ferrie in his dismissal dispute in return for Ferrie's work as an investigator on other cases. One of these cases involved deportation proceedings against Carlos Marcello, the head of the organized crime network in Louisiana and a client of Gill. Ferrie also said he had entered into a similar agreement with Guy Banister, a former FBI agent (Special Agent-in-Charge in Chicago) who had opened a private detective agency in New Orleans.

(4) 544 Camp Street.–Banister's firm occupied an office in 1963 in the Newman Building at 531 Lafayette Street. Another entrance to the building was at 544 Camp Street, the address Oswald had stamped on his Fair Play for Cuba Committee handouts. During the summer of 1963, Ferrie frequented 544 Camp Street regularly as a result of his working relationship with Banister.

Another occupant of the Newman Building was the Cuban Revolutionary Council, whose chief New Orleans delegate until 1962 was Sergio Arcacha Smith. He was replaced by Luis Rabel who, in turn, was succeeded by Frank Bartes. The committee interviewed or deposed all three CRC New

Orleans delegates. Arcacha said he never encountered Oswald and that he left New Orleans when he was relieved of his CRC position in early 1962. Rabel said he held the post from January to October 1962, but that he likewise never knew or saw Oswald and that the only time he went to the Newman Building was to remove some office materials that Arcacha had left there. Bartes said the only time he was in contact with Oswald was in their courtroom confrontation, that he ran the CRC chapter from an office in his home and that he never visited an office at either 544 Camp Street or 531 Lafayette Street.

The committee, on the other hand, developed information that, in 1961, Banister, Ferrie, and Arcacha were working together in the anti-Castro cause. Banister, a fervent anti-Communist, was helping to establish Friends of Democratic Cuba as an adjunct to the New Orleans CRC chapter run by Arcacha in an office in the Newman Building. Banister was also conducting background investigations of CRC members for Arcacha. Ferrie, also strongly anti-Communist and anti-Castro, was associated with Arcacha (and probably Banister) in anti-Castro activism.

On 22 November 1963 Ferrie had been in a Federal courtroom in New Orleans in connection with legal proceedings against Carlos Marcello. That night he drove, with two young friends, to Houston, Tex. then to Galveston on Saturday 23 November and back to New Orleans on Sunday. Before reaching New Orleans, he learned from a telephone conversation with G. Wray Gill that Martin had implicated him in the assassination. Gill also told Ferrie about the rumors that he and Oswald had served together in the CAP and that Oswald supposedly had Ferrie's library card in his possession when he was arrested in Dallas. When he got to his residence, Ferrie did not go in, but sent in his place one of his companions on the trip, Alvin Beauboeuf. Beauboeuf and Ferrie's roommate, Layton Martens, were detained by officers from the district attorney's office. Ferrie drove to Hammond, La., and spent the night with a friend.

On Monday 25 November Ferrie turned himself in to the district attorney's office where he was arrested on suspicion of being involved in the assassination. In subsequent interviews with New Orleans authorities, the FBI and the Secret Service, Ferrie denied ever having known Oswald or having ever been involved in the assassination. He stated that in the days preceding 22 November he had been working intensively for Gill on the Marcello case. Ferrie said he was in New Orleans on the morning of 22 November, at which time Marcello was acquitted in Federal court of citizenship falsification. He stated that he took the weekend trip to Texas for relaxation. Ferrie acknowledged knowing Jack Martin, stating that Martin resented him for forcibly removing him from Gill's office earlier that year.

The FBI and Secret Service investigation into the possibility that Ferrie and Oswald had been associated ended a few days later. A Secret Service report concluded that the information provided by Jack Martin that Ferrie had been associated with Oswald and had trained him to fire a rifle was "without foundation." The Secret Service report went on to state that on 26 November 1963 the FBI had informed the Secret Service that Martin had admitted that his information was a "figment of his imagination." The investigation of Ferrie was subsequently closed for lack of evidence against him.

(5) A committee analysis of Oswald in New Orleans.–The Warren Commission had attempted to reconstruct a daily chronology of Oswald's activities in New Orleans during the summer of 1963, and the committee used it, as well as information arising from critics and the Garrison investigation, to select events and contacts that merited closer analysis. Among these were Oswald's confrontation with Carlos Bringuier and with Frank Bartes, his reported activities in

Clinton, La., and his ties, if any, to Guy Banister, David Ferrie, Sergio Arcacha Smith and others who frequented the office building at 544 Camp Street. The committee deposed Carlos Bringuier and interviewed or deposed several of his associates. It concluded that there had been no relationship between Oswald and Bringuier and the DRE with the exception of the confrontation over Oswald's distribution of pro-Castro literature. The committee was not able to determine why Oswald approached the anti-Castro Cubans, but it tended to concur with Bringuier and others in their belief that Oswald was seeking to infiltrate their ranks and obtain information about their activities.

As noted, the committee believed the Clinton witnesses to be telling the truth as they knew it. It was, therefore, inclined to believe that Oswald was in Clinton, La., in late August, early September 1963, and that he was in the company of David Ferrie, if not Clay Shaw. The committee was puzzled by Oswald's apparent association with Ferrie, a person whose anti-Castro sentiments were so distant from those of Oswald, the Fair Play for Cuba Committee campaigner. But the relationship with Ferrie may have been significant for more than its anti-Castro aspect, in light of Ferrie's connection with G. Wray Gill and Carlos Marcello.

The committee also found that there was at least possibility that Oswald and Guy Banister were acquainted. The following facts were considered:

- The 544 Camp Street address stamped on Oswald's FPCC handouts was that of the building where Banister had his office;
- Ross Banister told the committee that his brother had seen Oswald handing out FPCC literature during the summer of 1963; and
- Banister's secretary, Delphine Roberts, told the committee she saw Oswald in Banister's office on several occasions, the first being when he was interviewed for a job during the summer of 1963.

The committee learned that Banister left extensive files when he died in 1964. Later that year, they were purchased by the Louisiana State Police from Banister's widow. According to Joseph Cambre of the State police, Oswald's name was not the subject of any file, but it was included in a file for the Fair Play for Cuba Committee. Cambre said the FPCC file contained newspaper clippings and a transcript, of a radio program on which Oswald had appeared. The committee was not able to review Banister's files, since they had been destroyed pursuant to an order of the superintendent of Louisiana State Police that all files not part of the public record or pertinent to ongoing criminal investigations be burned.

Additional evidence that Oswald may have been associated or acquainted with Ferrie and Banister was provided by the testimony of Adrian Alba, proprietor of the Crescent City Garage which was next door to the Reily Coffee Co., where Oswald had worked for a couple of months in 1963. (The garage and the coffee company were both located less than a block from 544 Camp Street.) Although Alba's testimony on some points was questionable, he undoubtedly did know Oswald, who frequently visited his garage, and the committee found no reason to question his statement that he had often seen Oswald in Mancuso's Restaurant on the first floor of 544 Camp. Ferrie and Banister also were frequent customers at Mancuso's.

(6) Summary of the evidence. – In sum, the committee did not believe that an anti-Castro organization was involved in a conspiracy to assassinate President Kennedy. Even though the committee's investigation did reveal that in 1964 the FBI failed to pursue intelligence reports of possible anti-Castro involvement as vigorously as it might have, the committee found it significant that it discovered no information in US intelligence agency files that would implicate anti-Castroites. Contact between the intelligence community and the

anti-Castro movement was close, so it is logical to suppose that some trace of group involvement would have been detected had it existed.

The committee also thought it significant that it received no information from the Cuban Government that would implicate anti-Castroites. The Cubans had dependable information sources in the exile communities in Miami, New Orleans, Dallas and other US cities, so there is high probability that Cuban intelligence would have been aware of any group involvement by the exiles. Following the assassination, the Cuban Government would have had the highest incentive to report participation by anti-Castroites, had it existed to its knowledge, since it would have dispelled suspicions of pro-Castro Cuban involvement.

The committee was impressed with the cooperation it received from the Cuban Government, and while it acknowledged this cooperation might not have been forthcoming in 1964, it concluded that, had such information existed in 1978, it would have been supplied by Cuban officials.

On the other hand, the committee noted that it was unable to preclude from its investigation the possibility that individuals with anti-Castro leanings might have been involved in the assassination. The committee candidly acknowledged, for example, that it could not explain Oswald's associations – nor at this late date fully determine their extent – with anti-Castro Cubans. The committee remained convinced that since Oswald consistently demonstrated a left-wing Marxist ideology, he would not have supported the anti-Castro movement. At the same time, the committee noted that Oswald's possible association with Ferrie might be distinguishable, since it could not be simply termed an anti-Castro association. Ferrie and Oswald may have had a personal friendship unrelated to Cuban activities. Ferrie was not Cuban, and though he actively supported the anti-Castro cause, he had other interests. For one, he was employed by Carlos Marcello as an investigator. (It has been alleged that Ferrie operated a service station in 1964 the franchise for which was reportedly paid by Marcello.) The committee concluded, therefore, that Oswald's most significant apparent anti-Castro association, that with David Ferrie, might in fact not have been related to the Cuban issue.

In the end, the committee concluded that the evidence was sufficient to support the conclusion that anti-Castro Cuban groups, as groups, were not involved in the assassination, but it could not preclude the possibility that individual members may have been involved.

4.THE COMMITTEE BELIEVES, ON THE BASIS OF THE EVIDENCE AVAILABLE TO IT, THAT THE NATIONAL SYNDICATE OF ORGANIZED CRIME AS A GROUP, WAS NOT INVOLVED IN THE ASSASSINATION OF PRESIDENT KENNEDY, BUT THAT THE AVAILABLE EVIDENCE DOES NOT PRECLUDE THE POSSIBILITY THAT INDIVIDUAL MEMBERS MAY HAVE BEEN INVOLVED [. . .]

Lee Harvey Oswald was fatally shot by Jack Ruby at 11.21 a.m. on Sunday 24 November 1963, less than 48 hours after President Kennedy was assassinated. While many Americans were prepared to believe that Oswald had acted alone in shooting the President, they found their credulity strained when they were asked to accept a conclusion that Ruby, too, had not acted as part of a plot. As the Warren Commission observed,

> . . . almost immediately speculation arose that Ruby had acted on behalf of members of a conspiracy who had planned the killing of President Kennedy and wanted to silence Oswald.

The implications of the murder of Oswald are crucial to an understanding of the assassination itself. Several of the logical possibilities should be made explicit:

• Oswald was a member of a conspiracy, and he was killed by Ruby, also a conspirator, so that he would not reveal the plot.
• Oswald was a member of a conspiracy, yet Ruby acted alone, as he explained, for personal reasons.
• Oswald was not a member of a conspiracy as far as Ruby knew, but his murder was an act planned by Ruby and others to take justice into their own hands.
• Both Oswald and Ruby acted alone or with the assistance of only one or two confederates, but there was no wider conspiracy, one that extended beyond the immediate participants.

If it is determined that Ruby acted alone, it does not necessarily follow that there was no conspiracy to murder the President. But if Ruby was part of a sophisticated plot to murder Oswald, there would be troublesome implications with respect to the assassination of the President. While it is possible to develop an acceptable rationale of why a group might want to kill the President's accused assassin, even though its members were not in fact involved in the assassination, it is difficult to make the explanation sound convincing. There is a possibility, for example, that a Dallas citizen or groups of citizens planned the murder of Oswald by Ruby to revenge the murders of President Kennedy or Patrolman J.D. Tippit, or both. Nevertheless, the brief period of time between the two murders, during which the vengeful plotters would have had to formulate and execute Oswald's murder, would seem to indicate the improbability of such an explanation. A preexisting group might have taken action within 48 hours, but it is doubtful that a group could have planned and then carried out Oswald's murder in such a short period of time.

[. . .]

(4) Involvement of organized crime.–In contrast to the Warren Commission, the committee's investigation of the possible involvement of organized crime in the assassination was not limited to an examination of Jack Ruby. The committee also directed its attention to organized crime itself.

[. . .]

The committee found that the quality and scope of the investigation into the possibility of an organized crime conspiracy in the President's assassination by the Warren Commission and the FBI was not sufficient to uncover one, had it existed. The committee also found that it was possible, based on an analysis of motive, means and opportunity, that an individual organized crime leader, or a small combination of leaders, might have participated in a conspiracy to assassinate President Kennedy. The committee's extensive investigation led it to conclude that the most likely family bosses of organized crime to have participated in such a unilateral assassination plan were Carlos Marcello and Santos Trafficante. While other family bosses [. . .] were subjected to considerable coverage in the electronic surveillance program, such coverage was never applied to Marcello and almost never to Trafficante.

(6) Carlos Marcello.–The committee found that Marcello had the motive, means and opportunity to have President John F. Kennedy assassinated, though it was unable to establish direct evidence of Marcello's complicity.

In its investigation of Marcello, the committee identified the presence of one critical evidentiary element that was lacking with the other organized crime figures examined by the committee: credible associations relating both Lee Harvey Oswald and Jack Ruby to figures having a relationship, albeit tenuous, with Marcello's crime family or organization. At the same time, the committee explicitly cautioned: association is the first step in conspiracy; it is not identical to it, and while associations may legitimately give rise to suspicions, a careful distinction must always be drawn between suspicions suspected and facts found.

As the long-time La Cosa Nostra leader in an area that is based in New Orleans but extends throughout Louisiana and Texas, Marcello was one of the prime targets of Justice Department efforts during the Kennedy administration. He had, in fact, been temporarily removed from the country for a time in 1961 through deportation proceedings personally expedited by Attorney General Kennedy. In his appearance before the committee in executive session, Marcello exhibited an intense dislike for Robert Kennedy because of these actions, claiming that he had been illegally "kidnapped" by Government agents during the deportation.

While the Warren Commission devoted extensive attention to Oswald's background and activities, the committee uncovered significant details of his exposure to and contacts with figures associated with the underworld of New Orleans that apparently had escaped the Commission. One such relationship actually extended into Oswald's own family through his uncle, Charles "Dutz" Murret, a minor underworld gambling figure. The committee discovered that Murret, who served as a surrogate father of sorts throughout much of Oswald's life in New Orleans, was in the 1940s and 1950s (and possibly until his death in 1964) an associate of significant organized crime figures affiliated with the Marcello organization.

The committee established that Oswald was familiar with his uncle's underworld activities and had discussed them with his wife, Marina, in 1963. Additionally, the committee found that Oswald's mother, Marguerite Oswald, was acquainted with several men associated with lieutenants in the Marcello organization. One such acquaintance, who was also an associate of Dutz Murret, reportedly served as a personal aide or driver to Marcello at one time. In another instance, the committee found that an individual connected to Dutz Murret, the person who arranged bail for Oswald following his arrest in August 1963 for a street disturbance, was an associate of two of Marcello's syndicate deputies. (One of the two, Nofio Pecora, as noted, also received a telephone call from Ruby on 30 October 1963, according to the committee's computer analysis of Ruby's phone records.)

During the course of its investigation, the committee developed several areas of credible evidence and testimony indicating a possible association in New Orleans and elsewhere between Lee Harvey Oswald and David W. Ferrie, a private investigator and even, perhaps, a pilot for Marcello before and during 1963. From the evidence available to the committee, the nature of the Oswald–Ferrie association remained largely a mystery. The committee established that Oswald and Ferrie apparently first came into contact with each other during Oswald's participation as a teenager in a Civil Air Patrol unit for which Ferrie served as an instructor, although Ferrie, when he was interviewed by the FBI after his detainment as a suspect in the assassination, denied any past association with Oswald.

In interviews following the assassination, Ferrie stated that he may have spoken in an offhand manner of the desirability of having President Kennedy shot, but he denied wanting such a deed actually to be done. Ferrie also admitted his association with Marcello and stated that he had been in personal contact with the syndicate leader in the fall of 1963. He noted that on the morning of the day of the President's death he was present with Marcello at a courthouse in New Orleans. In his executive session testimony before the committee, Marcello acknowledged that Ferrie did work for his lawyer, G. Wray Gill, on his case, but Marcello denied that Ferrie worked for him or that their relationship was close. Ferrie died in 1967 of a ruptured blood vessel at the base of the brain, shortly after he was named in the assassination investigation of New Orleans District Attorney Jim Garrison.

The committee also confirmed that the address 544 Camp Street, that Oswald had printed on some Fair Play for Cuba Committee handouts in New Orleans, was the address of a small office building where Ferrie was working on at least a part-time basis in 1963. The Warren Commission stated in its report that, despite the Commission's probe into why Oswald used this return address on his literature, "investigation has indicated that neither the Fair Play for Cuba Committee nor Lee Oswald ever maintained an office at that address."

The committee also established associations between Jack Ruby and several individuals affiliated with the underworld activities of Carlos Marcello. Ruby was a personal acquaintance of Joseph Civello, the Marcello associate, who allegedly headed organized crime activities in Dallas; he also knew other individuals who have been linked with organized crime, including a New Orleans nightclub figure, Harold Tannenbaum, with whom Ruby was considering going into partnership in the fall of 1963.

The committee examined a widely circulated published account that Marcello made some kind of threat on the life of President Kennedy in September 1962 at a meeting at his Churchill Farms estate outside New Orleans. It was alleged that Marcello shouted an old Sicilian threat, *"Livarsi na petra di la scarpa!"* "Take the stone out of my shoe!" against the Kennedy brothers, stating that the President was going to be assassinated. He spoke of using a "nut" to carry out the murder.

The committee established the origin of the story and identified the informant who claimed to have been present at the meeting during which Marcello made the threat. The committee also learned that, even though the FBI was aware of the informant's allegations over a year and half before they were published in 1969 and possessed additional information indicating that the informant may in fact have met with Marcello in the fall of 1962, a substantive investigation of the information was never conducted. Director Hoover and other senior FBI officials were aware that FBI agents were initiating action to "discredit" the informant, without having conducted a significant investigation of his allegations. Further, the committee discovered that the originating office relied on derogatory information from a prominent underworld figure in the ongoing effort to discredit the informant. An internal memorandum to Hoover noted that another FBI source was taking action to discredit the informant, "in order that the Carlos Marcello incident would be deleted from the book that first recounted the information."

The committee determined that the informant who gave the account of the Marcello threat was in fact associated with various underworld figures, including at least one person well-acquainted with the Marcello organization. The committee noted, however, that as a consequence of his underworld involvement, the informant had a questionable reputation for honesty and may not be a credible source of information.

The committee noted further that it is unlikely that an organized crime leader personally involved in an assassination plot would discuss it with anyone other than his closest lieutenants, although he might be willing to discuss it more freely prior to a serious decision to undertake such an act. In his executive session appearance before the committee, Marcello categorically denied any involvement in organized crime or the assassination of President Kennedy. Marcello also denied ever making any kind of threat against the President's life.

As noted, Marcello was never the subject of electronic surveillance coverage by the FBI. The committee found that the Bureau did make two attempts to effect such surveillance during the early 1960s, but both attempts were unsuccessful. Marcello's sophisticated security system and close-knit organizational structure may have been a factor in preventing such surveillance. A former FBI official knowledgeable about the surveillance program told the committee, "That was our biggest gap . . . With Marcello, you've got the one big exception in our work back then. There was just no way of penetrating that area. He was too smart."

Any evaluation of Marcello's possible role in the assassination must take into consideration his unique stature within La Cosa Nostra. The FBI determined in the 1960s that because of Marcello's position as head of the New Orleans Mafia family (the oldest in the United States, having first entered the country in the 1880s), the Louisiana organized crime leader had been endowed with special powers and privileges not accorded to any other La Cosa Nostra members. As the leader of "the first family" of the Mafia in America, according to FBI information, Marcello has been the recipient of the extraordinary privilege of conducting syndicate operations without having to seek the approval of the national commission.

Finally, a caveat, Marcello's uniquely successful career in organized crime has been based to a large extent on a policy of prudence; he is not reckless. As with the case of the Soviet and Cuban Governments, a risk analysis indicated that he would be unlikely to undertake so dangerous a course of action as a Presidential assassination. Considering that record of prudence, and in the absence of direct evidence of involvement, it may be said that it is unlikely that Marcello was in fact involved in the assassination of the President. On the basis of the evidence available to it, and in the context of its duty to be cautious in its evaluation of the evidence, there is no other conclusion that the committee could reach. On the other hand, the evidence that he had the motive and the evidence of links through associates to both Oswald and Ruby, coupled with the failure of the 1963–4 investigation to explore adequately possible conspiratorial activity in the assassination, precluded a judgment by the committee that Marcello and his associates were not involved.

(7) Santos Trafficante.—The committee also concentrated its attention on Santos Trafficante, the La Cosa Nostra leader in Florida. The committee found that Trafficante, like Marcello, had the motive, means, and opportunity to assassinate President Kennedy.

Trafficante was a key subject of the Justice Department crackdown on organized crime during the Kennedy administration, with his name being added to a list of the top 10 syndicate leaders targeted for investigation. Ironically, Attorney General Kennedy's strong interest in having Trafficante prosecuted occurred during the same period in which CIA officials, unbeknownst to the Attorney General, were using Trafficante's services in assassination plots against the Cuban chief of state, Fidel Castro.

The committee found that Santos Trafficante's stature in the national syndicate of organized crime, notably the violent narcotics trade, and his role as the mob's chief liaison to criminal figures within the Cuban exile community, provided him with the capability of formulating an assassination conspiracy against President Kennedy. Trafficante had recruited Cuban nationals to help plan and execute the CIA's assignment to assassinate Castro. (The CIA gave the assignment to former FBI Agent Robert Maheu, who passed the contract along to Mafia figures Sam Giancana and John Roselli. They, in turn, enlisted Trafficante to have the intended assassination carried out.)

In his testimony before the committee, Trafficante admitted participating in the unsuccessful CIA conspiracy to assassináte Castro, an admission indicating his willingness to participate in political murder. Trafficante testified that he worked with the CIA out of a patriotic feeling for his country, an explanation the committee did not accept, at least not as his sole motivation.

As noted, the committee established a possible connection between Trafficante and Jack Ruby in Cuba in 1959. It determined there had been a close friendship between Ruby and Lewis McWillie, who, as a Havana gambler, worked in an area subject to the control of the Trafficante Mafia family. Further, it assembled documentary evidence that Ruby made at least two, if not three or more, trips to Havana in 1959 when McWillie was involved in underworld gambling operations there. Ruby may in fact have been serving as a courier for underworld gambling interests in Havana, probably for the purpose of transporting funds to a bank in Miami.

The committee also found that Ruby had been connected with other Trafficante associates – R.D. Matthews, Jack Todd, and James Dolan – all of Dallas.

Finally, the committee developed corroborating evidence that Ruby may have met with Trafficante at Trescornia prison in Cuba during one of his visits to Havana in 1959, as the CIA had learned but had discounted in 1964. While the committee was not able to determine the purpose of the meeting, there was considerable evidence that it did take place.

During the course of its investigation of Santos Trafficante, the committee examined an allegation that Trafficante had told a prominent Cuban exile, Jose Aleman, that President Kennedy was going to be assassinated. According to Aleman, Trafficante made the statement in a private conversation with him that took place sometime in September 1962. In an account of the alleged conversation published by the *Washington Post* in 1976, Aleman was quoted as stating that Trafficante had told him that President Kennedy was "going to be hit." Aleman further stated, however, that it was his impression that Trafficante was not the specific individual who was allegedly planning the murder. Aleman was quoted as having noted that Trafficante had spoken of Teamsters Union President James Hoffa during the same conversation, indicating that the President would "get what is coming to him" as a result of his administration's intense efforts to prosecute Hoffa.

During an interview with the committee in March 1977, Aleman provided further details of his alleged discussion with Trafficante in September 1962. Aleman stated that during the course of the discussion, Trafficante had made clear to him that he was not guessing that the President was going to be killed. Rather he did in fact know that such a crime was being planned. In his committee interview, Aleman further stated that Trafficante had given him the distinct impression that Hoffa was to be principally involved in planning the Presidential murder.

In September 1978, prior to his appearance before the committee in public session, Aleman reaffirmed his earlier account of the alleged September 1962 meeting with Trafficante. Nevertheless, shortly before his appearance in public session, Aleman informed the committee staff that he feared for his physical safety and was afraid of possible reprisal from Trafficante or his organization. In this testimony, Aleman changed his professed understanding of Trafficante's comments. Aleman repeated under oath that Trafficante had said Kennedy was "going to be hit," but he then stated it was his impression that Trafficante may have only meant the President was going to be hit by "a lot of Republican votes" in the 1964 election, not that he was going to be assassinated.

Appearing before the committee in public session on 28 September 1978, Trafficante categorically denied ever having discussed any plan to assassinate President Kennedy. Trafficante denied any foreknowledge of or participation in the President's murder. While stating that he did in fact know Aleman and that he had met with him on more than one occasion in 1962, Trafficante denied Aleman's account of their alleged conversation about President Kennedy, and he denied ever having made a threatening remark against the President.

The committee found it difficult to understand how Aleman could have misunderstood Trafficante during such a conversation, or why he would have fabricated such an account. Aleman appeared to be a reputable person, who did not seek to publicize his allegations, and he was well aware of the potential danger of making such allegations against a leader of La Costa Nostra. The committee noted, however, that Aleman's prior allegations and testimony before the committee had made him understandably fearful for his life.

The committee also did not fully understand why Aleman waited so many years before publicly disclosing the alleged incident. While he stated in 1976 that he had reported Trafficante's alleged remarks about the President to FBI agents in 1962 and 1963, the committee's review of Bureau reports on his contacts with FBI agents did not reveal a record of any such disclosure or comments at the time. Additionally, the FBI agent who served as Aleman's contact during that period denied ever being told such information by Aleman.

Further, the committee found it difficult to comprehend why Trafficante, if he was planning or had personal knowledge of an assassination plot, would have revealed or hinted at such a sensitive matter to Aleman. It is possible that Trafficante may have been expressing a personal opinion, "The President ought to be hit," but it is unlikely in the context of their relationship that Trafficante would have revealed to Aleman the existence of a current plot to kill the President. As previously noted with respect to Carlos Marcello, to have attained his stature as the recognized organized crime leader of Florida for a number of years, Trafficante necessarily had to operate in a characteristically calculating and discreet manner. The relationship between Trafficante and Aleman, a business acquaintance, does not seem to have been close enough for Trafficante to have mentioned or alluded to such a murder plot. The committee thus doubted that Trafficante would have inadvertently mentioned such a plot. In sum, the committee believed there were substantial factors that called into question the validity of Aleman's account.

Nonetheless, as the electronic surveillance transcripts of Angelo Bruno, Stefano Magaddino and other top organized crime leaders make clear, there were in fact various underworld conversations in which the desirability of having the President assassinated was discussed. There were private conversations in which assassination was mentioned, although not in a context that indicated such a crime had been specifically planned. With this in mind, and in the absence of additional evidence with which to evaluate the Aleman account of Trafficante's alleged 1962 remarks, the committee concluded that the conversation, if it did occur as Aleman testified, probably occurred in such a circumscribed context.

As noted earlier, the committee's examination of the FBI's electronic surveillance program of the early 1960's disclosed that Santos Trafficante was the subject of minimal, in fact almost nonexistent, surveillance coverage. During one conversation in 1963, overheard in a Miami restaurant, Trafficante had bitterly attacked the Kennedy administration's efforts against organized crime, making obscene comments about "Kennedy's right-hand man" who had recently coordinated various raids on Trafficante gambling establishments. In the conversation, Trafficante stated that he was under immense pressure from Federal investigators, commenting, "I know when I'm beat, you understand?" Nevertheless, it was not possible to draw conclusions about Trafficante actions based on the electronic surveillance program since the coverage was so limited. Finally, as with Marcello, the committee noted that Trafficante's cautious character is inconsistent with his taking the risk of being involved in an assassination plot against the President. The committee found, in the context of its duty to be cautious in its evaluation of the evidence, that it is unlikely that Trafficante plotted to kill the President, although it could not rule out the possibility of such participation on the basis of available evidence.

(c) Summary and analysis of the evidence

The committee also believed it appropriate to reflect on the general question of the possible complicity of organized crime members, such as Trafficante or Marcello, in the Kennedy assassination, and to try to put the evidence it had obtained in proper perspective.

The significance of the organized crime associations developed by the committee's investigation speaks for itself, but there are limitations that must be noted. That President Kennedy's assassin and the man who, in turn, murdered him can be tied to individuals connected to organized crime is important for one reason: for organized crime to have been involved in the assassination, it must have had access to Oswald or Ruby or both.

The evidence that has been presented by the committee demonstrates that Oswald did, in fact, have organized crime associations. Who he was and where he lived could have come to the attention of those in organized crime who had the motive and means to kill the President. Similarly, there is abundant evidence that Ruby was knowledgeable about and known to organized crime elements. Nevertheless, the committee felt compelled to stress that knowledge or availability through association falls considerably short of the sort of evidence that would be necessary to establish criminal responsibility for a conspiracy in the assassination. It is also considerably short of what a responsible congressional committee ought to have before it points a finger in a legislative context.

It must also be asked if it is likely that Oswald was, in fact, used by an individual such as Marcello or Trafficante in an organized crime plot. Here, Oswald's character comes into play. As the committee noted, it is not likely that Oswald was a hired killer; it is likely that his principal motivation in the assassination was political. Further, his politics have been shown to have been generally left-wing, as demonstrated by such aspects of his life as his avowed support of Fidel Castro. Yet the organized crime figures who had the motive and means to murder the President must be generally characterized as right-wing and anti-Castro. Knitting these two contradictory strands together posed a difficult problem. Either the assassination of President Kennedy was essentially an apolitical act undertaken by Oswald with full or partial knowledge of who he was working for – which would be hard to believe – or Oswald's organized crime contacts deceived him about their true identity and motivation, or else organized crime was not involved.

From an organized crime member's standpoint, the use of an assassin with political leanings inconsistent with his own would have enhanced his insulation from identification with the crime. Nevertheless, it would have made the conspiracy a more difficult undertaking, which raises questions about the likelihood that such a conspiracy occurred. The more complicated a plot becomes, the less likely it will work. Those who rationally set out to kill a king, it may be argued, first design a plot that will work. The Oswald plot did in fact work, at least for 15 years, but one must ask whether it would have looked workable 15 years ago. Oswald was an unstable individual. Shortly before the assassination, for example, he delivered a possibly threatening note to the Dallas FBI office. With his background, he would have been an immediate suspect in an assassination in Dallas, and those in contact with him would have known that. Conspirators could not have been assured that Oswald or his companion would be killed in Dealey Plaza; they could not be sure that they could silence them. The plot, because of Oswald's involvement, would hardly have seemed to be a low-risk undertaking.

The committee weighed other factors in its assessment of Oswald, his act and possible co-conspirators. It must be acknowledged that he did, in the end, exhibit a high degree of brutal proficiency in firing the shot that ended the President's life, and that, as an ex-marine, that proficiency may have been expected. In the final analysis, it must be admitted that he accomplished what he set out to do.

Further, while Oswald exhibited a leftist political stance for a number of years, his activities and associations were by no means exclusively left-wing. His close friendship with George de Mohrenschildt, an oilman in Dallas with right-wing connections, is a case in point. Additionally, questions have been raised about the specific nature of Oswald's pro-Castro activities. It has been established that, on at least one occasion in 1963, he offered his services for clandestine paramilitary actions against the Castro regime, though, as has been suggested, he may have merely been posing as an anti-Castro activist.

That the evidence points to the possibility that Oswald was also associated in 1963 with David Ferrie, the Marcello operative who was openly and actively anti-Castro, is troubling, too. Finally, the only Cuba-related activities that have ever been established at 544 Camp Street, New Orleans, the address of an office building that Oswald stamped on some of his Fair Play for Cuba Committee handouts, were virulently anti-Castro in nature.

Thus, the committee was unable to resolve its doubts about Lee Harvey Oswald. While the search for additional information in order to reach an understanding of Oswald's actions has continued for 15 years, and while the committee developed significant new details about his possible organized crime associations, particularly in New Orleans, the President's assassin himself remains not fully understood. The committee developed new information about Oswald and Ruby, thus altering previous perceptions, but the assassin and the man who murdered him still appear against a backdrop of unexplained, or at least not fully explained, occurrences, associations and motivations.

The scientific evidence available to the committee indicated that it is probable that more than one person was involved in the President's murder. That fact compels acceptance. And it demands re-examination of all that was thought to be true in the past. Further, the committee's investigation of Oswald and Ruby showed a variety of relationships that may have matured into an assassination conspiracy. Neither Oswald nor Ruby turned out to be "loners," as they had been painted in the 1964 investigation. Nevertheless, the committee frankly acknowledged that it was unable firmly to identify the other gunman or the nature and extent of the conspiracy.

ROBERT F. KENNEDY

The existence of a second gunman remains a possibility. Thus, I have never said that Sirhan Sirhan killed Robert Kennedy.

Thomas Noguchi, coroner

After the assassination of **John F. Kennedy** in 1963, the hopes of liberal America turned to his younger brother, Robert F. Kennedy. The third of Joe and Rose Kennedy's sons, Bobby Kennedy had much of JFK's white-toothed handsomeness and charisma and, if anything, was more of a political idealist. His favourite quote was: "Some men see things as they are and say, Why? I dream of things that never were and say, Why not?"

In the end it was politics that got Bobby Kennedy assassinated.

After education at Harvard and Virginia University Law School, Bobby Kennedy was called to the Massachusetts bar in 1951, but his powerful and ambitious father pulled strings that ensured he was lifted almost immediately to higher things. A stint in the Criminal Division of the Justice Department under Senator Joe McCarthy was followed by the very high-profile role of chief counsel to the Senate Select Committee on Improper Activities in the Labor or Management Field. Top of Kennedy's hit list was **Jimmy Hoffa**, head of the International Brotherhood of Teamsters, the truckers union, America's largest and richest labour organization. Hoffa was, Kennedy considered, the chief malefactor in a nationwide "conspiracy of evil"; he had tied the truckers in to the Mob and used the union's pension fund as his private bank account. Hoffa, the belligerent poor boy made good, and Kennedy, the Harvard-educated rich boy, hated each other. An obsessive rivalry ensued; when Hoffa was waiting at a federal court to be charged with bribery and conspiracy, he delighted in informing Kennedy that "I can do fifty one-handed push-ups. How many can you do?" RFK went home immediately and practised until he could do a hundred.

A lull in the Kennedy–Hoffa battle occurred when RFK became campaign manager for his brother John's successful run at the White House in 1960. RFK's reward was the post of Attorney General in the new administration, where he immediately made an enemy of FBI boss J. Edgar Hoover. Hoover wanted the FBI to focus exclusively on the old enemy, the Communists; Kennedy wanted to use the Bureau to smash gangland, and Hoffa in particular. Hoover and RFK developed a mutual detestation. "A psycho," said Kennedy of Hoover. "That sneaky little son of a bitch," said Hoover of Kennedy. Their opinions were well known to each other, because Hoover phone-tapped Kennedy, and vice versa. To get at RFK, Hoover at some point in the early 1960s gave Hoffa the files he had created on Kennedy's indiscriminate adulterous affairs. The stratagem did no good, and Hoffa went to the penitentiary anyway. In 1967 Hoffa told an informant that he had a contract out on RFK.

The Attorney General continued to make enemies. He energetically intervened in civil liberties, and supported desegregation in the South, thus alienating white Dixie (and the ultra-racist Hoover); he banished CIA officer William Harvey after Harvey sent illegal teams to Cuba to assassinate Castro; he unsuccessfully attempted to deport Mafia boss Carlos Marcello; he angered the military–industrial complex by proposing withdrawal from the Vietnam War; he dismayed Southern California ranchers by supporting the rights of migrant workers to the extent that the ranchers, according to the FBI, put a $500,000 contract on RFK's head.

After John F. Kennedy's assassination at Dallas, the younger Kennedy headed for the top spot in US politics. In 1968 RFK formally announced that he was standing as a Democratic presidential candidate in 1968. Just after midnight on 4 June that year, after victory in the California primary, Kennedy was shot as he walked through the kitchen area of the Ambassador Hotel in Los Angeles.

It seemed an open and shut case. Dozens of witnesses saw the assailant fire. Sirhan Sirhan was apprehended with the smoking gun in his hand. Evidence presented at Sirhan's trial showed him to be a misfit loner who had written in a notebook found by the LAPD: "My determination to eliminate RFK is becoming the more [sic] of an unshakable obsession." Of Jordanian descent, Sirhan had been enraged by pro-Israeli comments made by RFK. An open and shut case was followed by an open and shut trial. Sirhan admitted culpability: "I killed Robert Kennedy wilfully, premeditatedly, with twenty years of fore-thought." Convicted of first-degree murder, Sirhan was sentenced to the gas chamber; his sentence was later commuted to life imprisonment.

But there were holes – literally – in the prosecution case. In his exhaustive analysis of RFK's murder, *The Robert F. Kennedy Assassination* (1991), Professor Philip H. Melanson shows that at least 11 bullets were fired that night in the Ambassador kitchen. Sirhan's Iver–Johnson .22 revolver, the only weapon Sirhan had that evening, held *eight* bullets. Moreover, coroner Thomas Noguchi recorded that the bullet which actually killed Kennedy was fired from very close – inches at most – behind his head, leaving powder residue on his body. But every witness agreed Sirhan was to RFK's front, and no closer than a yard (1m) at most from him. Sirhan was thus not the only shooter on the scene, and likely was not the killer. Various eyewitnesses recalled a woman in a polka-dot dress running from the scene shouting, "We shot him!"

For almost 20 years the LAPD sat on its RFK assassination documents, and when Melanson and others were finally allowed to view the records many were found to have been lost, crudely censored or destroyed by the LAPD. Among the evidence destroyed were 2,400 photographs, including a roll of film taken of the actual shooting, 3,000 transcripts of interviews, and the door frame from the kitchen in which a number of bullets had lodged.

If there was another gun, who fired it? Aside from the mysterious woman in the polka-dot dress, the light of historical inquiry has begun to shine brighter and brighter on Thane Cesar, the Ace security guard who stood directly behind RFK in the Ambassador kitchen. Several bystanders testified that Cesar pulled a gun during the shooting. Don Schulman, an eyewitness and a journalist for KNXT-TV, reported live: "The security guard . . . hit Kennedy all three times." Despite being mortally wounded, RFK turned around and grabbed at Cesar and pulled his bow tie off. It can be seen clearly on the ground next to the stricken RFK in photographs. Was Kennedy's lunge at Cesar an attempt to get to grips with his assailant? Cesar, a vociferous right-winger, lied and contradicted himself in his testimonies to the police. He declared that he had sold his own .22 handgun before 4 June, but it was subsequently proved that he had sold it afterwards. Nevertheless, the LAPD refused to investigate Cesar.

Assuming a second gun killed RFK, the role of Sirhan Sirhan requires explanation – after all, Sirhan declared on oath that he was Kennedy's killer. William Turner and John Christian, in *The Assassination of Robert F. Kennedy* (1978) and Philip Melanson in *The Robert F. Kennedy Assassination* suggest the Manchurian Candidate theory – that Sirhan was programmed by hypnosis to kill RFK. The Manchurian Candidate theory is fantastic – but viable; in 1954 a CIA memo on the "Artichoke" project, undertaken as part of the notorious **MK-ULTRA** programme, proposed using a hypno-programmed assassin to assassinate "a prominent [deleted] politician or, if necessary, against an American official". One leading expert, Dr Herbert Spiegal, estimates that Sirhan is among the 10 per cent of the population most susceptible to hypnosis. The CIA had a possible motive as well as the means to kill Kennedy: on RFK's accession to the White House he would have discovered the Agency's complicity (if any) in the killing of his brother. Or maybe the CIA just wanted revenge for RFK's criticisms of its Bay of Pigs fiasco. On 20 November 2006 BBC's *Newsnight* presented research by Shane O'Sullivan alleging that several CIA agents were present in the Ambassador Hotel on the night of the assassination, even though the CIA had no reason to be there (it doesn't even have domestic jurisdiction). Three of those accused were ex-senior officers from JMWAVE, the CIA's main anti-Castro station based in Miami, and included David Morales, sometime Chief of Operations. Since Sirhan Sirhan was also revealed to be member of the **Rosicrucians**, it is believed by some conspiracists that the cult was behind Bobby Kennedy's offing.

The Manchurian Candidate theory also explains the enigmatic girl in the polka-dot dress. Under hypnosis by prosecution psychiatrist Dr Seymour Pollack, Sirhan answered the question, "Who was with you when you shot Kennedy?" as follows: "Girl the girl the girl . . ." A year later, when he was interviewed by NBC, Sirhan recalled having coffee with a girl immediately before the shooting. Of the shooting itself he could recall nothing; the incident was a complete blank. The temptation is to conclude that the polka-dot girl was Sirhan's handler. She has never been traced. But then the LAPD has never looked for her.

Today, Sirhan Sirhan protests his innocence. The official version remains that he alone killed RFK. Few believe it.

RFK was assassinated by a conspiracy which used Sirhan Sirhan as a patsy: ALERT LEVEL 9

Further Reading
Donald Freed, *The Killing of RFK*, 1975
Robert Blair Kaiser, *RFK Must Die!*, 1970
Gerald Kurlan, *The Assassination of Robert F. Kennedy*, 1973

Philip H. Melanson, *The Robert F. Kennedy Assassination: New Revelations on the Conspiracy and Cover Up*, 1991

Dan E. Moldea, *The Killing of Robert F. Kennedy*, 1995

William Turner and John G. Christian, *The Assassination of Robert F. Kennedy: A Searching Look at the Conspiracy and Cover-up 1968–1978*, 1978

MARTIN LUTHER KING

Dr Martin Luther King Jr had a dream, a dream of black and white Americans living in harmony. For some, however, King's dream was a nightmare.

King was only too aware of the forces arrayed against him. On 3 April 1968, while visiting Memphis to mediate in a strike, King told the euphoric congregation of the Mason Temple:

> It really doesn't matter what happens now . . . some began to . . . talk about the threats that were out – what would happen to me from some of our sick white brothers . . . Like anybody, I would like to live a long life. Longevity has its place, but I'm not concerned about that now. I just want to do God's will. And He's *allowed* me to go up to the mountain! And I've looked over, and I've seen the Promised Land. I may not get there with you. But I want you to know tonight, that we, as a people, will get to the Promised Land. And so I'm happy tonight. I'm not worried about anything. I'm not fearing any man. My eyes have seen the Glory of the coming of the Lord!

The next day at 6.01 p.m., as he lounged on the balcony of the Lorraine Motel in Memphis, King was fatally shot. Colleagues inside the motel room from King's civil rights organization, the Southern Christian Leadership Conference, on hearing shots ran out on to the balcony to find him severely wounded in the neck. The world's youngest recipient of the Nobel Peace Prize was pronounced dead at St Joseph's Hospital at 7.05 p.m. The murder led to riots in more than 60 American cities.

The shot which killed King was quickly traced to a flophouse opposite the motel, where police discovered a sniper's eyrie, complete with binoculars and rifle with telescopic sights. The fingerprints of one James Earl Ray were found on the rifle and other equipment. Two months later, after a massive manhunt, Ray was captured at London's Heathrow Airport while trying to leave Britain on a false Canadian passport in the name of Ramon George Sneyd. Ray was quickly extradited to Tennessee, where on 10 March 1969 he confessed to the assassination of King and was sentenced to a 99-year prison term.

Only days after his conviction, Ray began protesting his innocence, saying he had made a guilty plea on the advice of his attorney, Percy Foreman, to avoid a trial conviction and the possibility of execution. Ray declared he had been framed by a gun-smuggler called "Raul" or "Raoul".

Ray was not alone in protesting his innocence. For many observers, aspects of the King assassination simply didn't stack up. Ray was a two-bit petty criminal who somehow had found the financial wherewithal to fund an elaborate escape, complete with false passport, to Britain, whence he was intending to fly to South Africa. It beggared belief, too, that he could be so incompetent as to drop his private papers fleeing from the sniper den, not to mention leave his fingerprints behind. Ray was not a trained sniper, yet King's assailant pulled off a flawless single-shot kill. The drunk who supposedly identified Ray in the flophouse just after the shooting, Charles Stephens, repudiated his own identification when sober and shown a picture of Ray on camera in a CBS special report. (Stephen's uncooperative wife was put in a mental institution after disputing her husband's initial identification of Ray.) The bullet from King's body was never matched to the gun, despite a retesting of the rifle in 1997. Moreover, witnesses surrounding King at the moment of his death say the shot came from another location, from behind thick shrubbery near the flophouse, not from the flophouse itself.

In 1977 Ray testified to the House Select Committee on Assassinations that he did not shoot Martin Luther King Jr. The committee disbelieved him – although it allowed the "likelihood" that he did not act alone. Evidence was examined that the CIA supplied him with fake ID found on him at the time of his arrest. One alias belonged to a Canadian called Galt, who was known to be a trained rifleman.

The CIA was not the only party under suspicion for assisting the MLK assassination. In 1993 Loyd Jowers, the owner of the grill opposite the Lorraine Motel, informed ABC Television that he had hosted meetings between the Memphis police, the Mob and government agents at which King's killing had been planned. Ray's lawyer, William Pepper, in his book *Orders to Kill* (1995), pointed the finger of suspicion at the US 20th Special Forces Group. In another twist of the plot, an FBI agent called Donald Wilson announced in 1998 that he had seen papers in Ray's Mustang car with "Raul" and FBI phone numbers written on them. This evidence dovetailed with the FBI's known hostility to King; the Bureau had tried to discredit him with allegations of adultery and had even sent a letter urging him to commit suicide.

By now King's own family was convinced that Ray was not MLK's assassin, and in 1999 in Memphis won a wrongful death civil trial against Loyd Jowers and "other unknown co-conspirators". The jury of six whites and six blacks found Jowers guilty and that "governmental agencies were parties" to the assassination.

Such was the cascade of allegations against government agencies that Attorney General Janet Reno felt obliged to order a probe by the Department of Justice. This concluded in 2000:

> After original investigation and analysis of the historical record, we have concluded that neither the Jowers nor the Wilson allegations are substantiated or credible. We likewise have determined that the allegations relating to Raoul's participation in the assassination, which originated with James Earl Ray, have no merit. Finally, we find that there

is no reliable evidence to support the allegations presented in King *v.* Jowers of a government-directed conspiracy involving the Mafia and Dr King's associates. Accordingly, no further investigation is warranted.

MLK, like JFK and RFK, was killed by a "lone nut". America in the 1960s, it seems, was full of lone nuts who somehow managed to pull off the assassinations of great men.

Or maybe not. In 2004 Reverend Jesse Jackson, who was with King at the time of his murder, noted:

> . . . I will never believe that James Earl Ray had the motive, the money and the mobility to have done it himself. Our government was very involved in setting the stage for, and I think the escape route for, James Earl Ray.

Jackson voiced the beliefs of millions.

> MLK was murdered by an unidentified conspiracy in which James Earl Ray was patsy: ALERT LEVEL 8

Further Reading
William Pepper, *Orders to Kill: The Truth Behind the Murder of Martin Luther King*, 1995
David Garrow, *The FBI and Martin Luther King Jr*, 1981

DOCUMENT: THE SUIT OF THE KING FAMILY AGAINST LOYD JOWERS AND UNKNOWN CONSPIRATORS

IN THE CIRCUIT COURT OF TENNESSEE FOR THE THIRTIETH JUDICIAL DISTRICT AT MEMPHIS
PLAINTIFFS
   CORETTA SCOTT KING,
   MARTIN LUTHER KING III,
   BERNICE KING,
   DEXTER KING, &
   YOLANDA KING
vs.
DEFENDANTS
   LOYD JOWERS &
   OTHER UNKNOWN CO-CONSPIRATORS
DOCKET NO. 9724210
DIVISION 4

[. . .]

Preliminary Statement

1) Plaintiffs sue Defendant LOYD JOWERS and other unknown parties for having joined a conspiracy – both criminal and civil in origin in the year 1968 – to deprive the Hon. Dr Martin Luther King Jr of his life, Plaintiffs of the presence, companionship, love, benefits, both tangible and intangible, and available to them while he was alive.

2) Only recently have the Plaintiffs had the opportunity to identify Defendant JOWERS as one of the key players in this conspiracy. This, with precision, occurred within the last year, hereof, when confessed Defendant JOWERS confessed his role in the 1968 murder conspiracy and admitted to have been paid a large sum of money to participate in the conspiracy. Defendant JOWERS made these

admissions in the presence of his attorney and Plaintiff Dexter Scott King and Plaintiffs' counsel and on another occasion, also within the last year, in front of Plaintiff Dexter Scott King and former United States Ambassador to the United Nations, Andrew Young.

3) On those occasions, Defendant JOWERS said he had owed a "big favor" to the now deceased FRANK C. LIBERTO, a Memphis produce house operator, who was alive in 1968. LIBERTO advanced the money to further the conspiracy to kill Dr King to JOWERS as part of the plot to shoot Dr King from the back of JOWERS' cafe. This area was then heavily vegetated with large bushes and trees which could conceal a gunman with a clear view of the balcony of the Lorraine Motel.

4) Defendant JOWERS also admitted that the person accused of the crime, James Earl Ray, was not the gunman involved and that he, JOWERS, took the still smoking rifle from another person, carried it into the kitchen of his cafe, and concealed it until it was collected the next morning.

5) Defendant JOWERS confirmed the existence and the role of a man he knew as "Raul", who brought him the rifle to be used to kill Dr King. JOWERS, thereby, confirmed the existence of the person whom James Earl Ray had identified more than thirty years ago as the individual who lured him to Memphis on the pretext of participating in a gun-running scheme.

6) Plaintiffs sue Defendant JOWERS for the tortious actions that constitute: 1) outrage; 2) the deprivation of the life, companionship and benefits, tangible and intangible, material and spiritual, emotional and intellectual, all of which were available to the Plaintiffs in life and taken from them with the death of their husband and father which was the direct result of the Defendant's tortious actions. Such tortious actions grew out of an illegal conspiracy that had the common design, concert of action, and overt acts that included the killing of Dr King and the coverup of

that murder and the framing of another – James Earl Ray – for the murder of Dr King.

Jurisdiction

7) Memphis, Tennessee, in Shelby County, is the *Lex Loci Delictus* where the illegal conspiracy culminated and was consummated with the fatal shooting of Dr Martin Luther King Jr as he stood on the balcony of the Lorraine Motel at approximately 6.01 p.m., said motel being in the city limits of Memphis.

8) Memphis, Tennessee, in Shelby County, is also the *Lex Loc Contractus* where Defendant LOYD JOWERS admits he entered into the illegal conspiracy with FRANK C. LIBERTO and others, known and unknown, to kill Dr King.

9) Memphis, Tennessee, was the *Lex Loci Domicilii* of LOYD JOWERS at the time the illegal conspiracy was entered into. Defendant JOWERS today has sufficient contacts with the State of Tennessee as well as the City of Memphis and Shelby County, having owned and operated several businesses there and still having family in that city.

Parties

10) Plaintiffs are the widow and children of the victim of this illegal conspiracy and tortious actions of the Defendant.

11) Defendant LOYD JOWERS is a resident citizen of Tennessee with sufficient ties to Shelby County. In 1968, Defendant JOWERS was the owner of Jim's Grill, 422 1/2 South Main, Memphis, and Shelby County in which establishment amongst other places in Memphis and Shelby County. Defendant has admitted the conspiracy took place and the murder was planned. He has also confirmed that it was behind his establishment, Jim's Grill, where the murder was carried out.

Facts

12) In early 1968, Plaintiffs' husband and father the Rev. Dr Martin Luther King Jr decided to come to Memphis, Tennessee in order to support striking sanitation workers in that city.

13) In or around the middle of March, Defendant JOWERS was approached by one FRANK C. LIBERTO, a Memphis resident and produce dealer, and asked to participate in a conspiracy to kill Dr King. LIBERTO told JOWERS that a person – a "patsy" – was in place to take the blame and that no police would be around. Defendant agreed to participate in the conspiracy to kill Dr King and eventually was provided with a large sum of money, some or all of which he turned over as instructed to a man he knew only as Raul. Their money was delivered to Defendant JOWERS in a vegetable box from another Memphis produce house, and Defendant JOWERS believed that it came from New Orleans.

14) During this time between the middle of March and the date of the murder, Defendant JOWERS observed and participated in a number of acts in furtherance of the conspiracy. These included planning meetings attended by persons known to him which took place in his establishment – Jim's Grill.

15) In addition, in the morning of the day of the assassination, April 4, 1968, Defendant JOWERS received and concealed in Jim's Grill a rifle from the man he had come to know as Raul.

16) Late in the afternoon of that day – 4 April 1968 – Defendant JOWERS gave the rifle to a third party, now deceased and known to him, who took it away.

17) Sometime before 6 p.m. on that same day, 4 April 1968, Defendant JOWERS, as he had been instructed, went out the back door of Jim's Grill into the overgrown brush area at the rear of the building.

18) While waiting in that area sometime just after 6 p.m., he heard a shot and within seconds of that sound, the third party, to whom he had earlier given the gun, appeared and

gave him the still smoking rifle. The shot he heard was the firing of the single bullet which struck and ultimately killed the victim, Dr Martin Luther King Jr.

19) Defendant JOWERS then ran carrying the rifle back inside Jim's Grill entering through the rear kitchen door from which he had come out some time earlier.

20) He then proceeded to once again conceal the rifle, eventually placing it on the shelf under a counter in Jim's Grill.

21) The next morning Defendant JOWERS turned the rifle over to Raul or another person who took it away. He never saw it again.

22) Defendant JOWERS and other persons, in furtherance of the conspiracy and the concealment of the tortious actions herein alleged directly and indirectly for approximately 29 years, participated in covering up the said tortious acts to the detriment, harm, injury, and damage to the Plaintiffs.

Count One

23) Paragraphs One through 22 are restated and incorporated herein.

24) Defendant LOYD JOWERS and FRANK C. LIBERTO, along with other known and unknown parties living and dead, entered into a conspiracy with a common design and illegal purpose, to-wit, to murder Dr Martin Luther King Jr after his scheduled arrival in Memphis on 3 April 1968.

25) Defendant JOWERS, LIBERTO, and other unknown parties living and dead acted in concert by having a rifle with James Earl Ray's fingerprints on it placed on the sidewalk outside the rooming house adjacent to Jim's Grill shortly before or immediately after Dr King was shot.

26) Defendant JOWERS acted in concert and collusion with the said others by taking the rifle from another person in or near the bushes in the rear of the establishment immediately after the rifle was used to shoot Dr King, knowing that the rifle had been used to kill Dr King as he stood on the balcony of the Lorraine Motel across Mulberry Street.

27) By entering into the criminal conspiracy to murder Dr King, Defendant JOWERS had also entered into a civil conspiracy to deprive Plaintiffs of the life, presence, companionship, and all the benefits resulting therefrom, tangible and intangible, material and spiritual, emotional and intellectual, which were available to Plaintiffs while their loved one was alive and taken from them forever with the death of their husband and father, said loss being the direct result of the tortious actions of the Defendant and others.

Count Two

28) Paragraphs One through 27 are restated and incorporated herein.

29) Defendant JOWERS' actions, as described herein, constitute intentional and outrageous wanton, willful, and malicious conduct that reflect a common design, concert of action, participation in overt acts in furtherance of an illegal conspiracy. said conspiracy culminated with and resulted in injuries – both physical and mental – inflicted upon Plaintiffs for which they now seek redress.

WHEREFORE, PREMISES CONSIDERED, PLAINTIFFS PRAY THAT:

1) Proper process be issued requiring Defendant JOWERS to answer this complaint or be subject to a default judgment being entered against him.

2) Plaintiffs be entitled to recover from Defendant JOWERS or any other Defendant whose identity might be learned through the discovery process, who participated in the illegal conspiracy described herein, actual and compensatory damages as well as punitive damages, as a result of the tortious conduct of Defendant JOWERS and his co-conspirators.

3) Plaintiffs be awarded such other further relief to which this Honorable Court may deem them entitled.

4) Plaintiffs demand a jury trial to determine all issues of fact.

NORMAN KIRK

Norman Kirk, the leader of the New Zealand Labour Party, swept to power in 1972 on a radical platform. Two years later he was dead, and replaced by finance minister Wallace Rowling, a figure distinctly more friendly towards big business.

For some Down Under, Kirk's demise from a heart attack was regarded as altogether too convenient. The anonymous author of *The Opal File*, the antipodean equivalent of the **Gemstone File**, noted:

Mid-1974: Gough Whitlam and Norman Kirk begin a series of moves absolutely against the Mafia Trilateralists. Whitlam refuses to waive restrictions on overseas borrowings to finance Alwest Aluminium Consortium of Rupert Murdoch, BHP and R.J. Reynolds. Whitlam had also ended Vietnam War support, blocked uranium mining and wanted more control over US secret spy bases – e.g., Pine Gap.

Kirk had introduced a new, tough Anti-Monopoly Bill and had tried to redistribute income from big companies to the labour force through price regulation and a wages policy.

Kirk had also rejected plans to build a second aluminium smelter near Dunedin and was preparing the Petroleum Amendment Bill to give more control over New Zealand oil resources.

Kirk had found out that Hunt Petroleum, drilling in the Great South Basin, had discovered a huge resource of oil comparable in size to the North Sea or Alaskan North Slope. Gas reserves alone now estimated at 30 times bigger than Kapuni and oil reserves of at least 20 billion barrels – enough for New Zealand to be self-sufficient for years. Oil companies completely hushed up these facts. To have announced a vast new oil source would probably mean a decline in world oil prices, which would not have allowed OPEC and Onassis plans for the Arabs to eventuate. NZ could be exploited at a later date, particularly since the North Sea operations were about to come on stream – Kirk was the last to hold out.

September 1974: According to CIA sources, Kirk was killed by the Trilateralists using Sodium Morphate. Rowling's first act as NZ Prime Minister was to withdraw Kirk's Anti-Monopoly Bill and the Petroleum Amendment Bill.

Later, Rowling was to be rewarded with ambassadorship to Washington. Incidentally, the Shah of Iran was murdered the same way as Kirk on his arrival in the US.

Kirk, it might be added, had enemies other than "Trilateralists" and *über*-capitalists. He caused apoplexy within the French government when he protested against French nuclear tests in the Pacific (see *Rainbow Warrior*), and annoyed the apartheid regime in South Africa when he banned their rugby team from visiting NZ. The British-led conspiracy to oust Gough Whitlam, Kirk's Australian prime ministerial counterpart, is well documented. Outside of the self-referring evidence of antipodean conspiracy theorists, however, no one has tied any agency to Kirk's death, or forwarded convincing evidence that it was foul play.

Sodium morphate does not exist. Kirk had a history of heart trouble. The official cause of death was cardiac arrest. And there the Norman Kirk conspiracy rests.

NZ PM Norman Kirk was killed by Trilateralists: ALERT
LEVEL 3

Further Reading
www.mindcontrolforums.com/opalfile.htm

KNIGHTS TEMPLAR

Not so long ago, the medieval Christian warriors known as the Knights Templar were a subject fit only for tweed-jacketed scholars and archaeologists, but all that changed with the publication of *Holy Blood, Holy Grail* in 1982 by Michael Baigent, Richard Leigh and Henry Lincoln. Whereas orthodox scholarship determined that the Knights Templar had been dissolved by Pope Clement V in 1312, Baigent, Leigh and Lincoln proposed that the Templars were a front organization for a mysterious clique, the **Priory of Sion**, which survives to the present. Further, the three authors gave an answer to a puzzle which had long tantalized academic historians: how did the Knights Templar become so rich so quickly? The Templars had discovered the Holy Grail, said Baigent *et al.* It was, as many noted, the stuff of which thrillers were made . . . and years later Dan Brown duly obliged with *The Da Vinci Code*.

To begin at the beginning. In 1118, nine French crusaders asked Baldwin II of Jerusalem for permission to remain in the ruins of Solomon's Temple in order, they said, to protect passing pilgrims. Officially named by the Holy See "The Order of the Poor Knights of Christ and the Temple of Solomon", the Knights Templar eventually grew to over 20,000 strong, and they enjoyed extensive wealth.

To their detractors, the Templars became too numerous, too rich. On unlucky Friday 13 October 1307, all the Templars in France were arrested by King Philip IV "Le Bel" for crimes of

heresy. Within a handful of years Pope Clement had banned the
Knights Templar, and their Grand Master, Jacques de Molay,
was burning at the stake in Paris. Allegedly the dying de Molay
prophesied that Philip and Clement would die within the year.
They did.

The Templars were an easy mark for a cash-strapped mon-
arch like Philip IV. As one of the few organizations allowed to
lend money, the Templars figured in most medieval minds in
the same slot as the Jews. There were also widespread rumours
– many coming from the mouth of a disgruntled former Templar, de Flexian – that in their long sojourn in the Middle East
the Knights Templar had become corrupted by Mohammedan-
ism and esoteric local faiths. The Knights Templar were believed to worship a talking head called "Baphomet" and
undertake an initiation ceremony in which the Cross was spat
on, and buttocks and penises were kissed. Sodomy, indeed, was
said to be near mandatory within the Order. A "secret knowledge" guaranteed loyalty to the Order and silence over its
heretical practices.

With the Pope's bull of 1313 banning the Knights Templar,
the Order ceased to exist. Allegedly. According to the Sovereign
Military Order of the Temple of Jerusalem, one of the numerous modern claimants to the Templar title, a "Charter of
Transmission" traces their organization directly back in time
to de Molay. Other "alternative" theories have the Templars
fleeing to Scotland, where they founded the **Freemasons**, or
transmuting into the **Illuminati**.

Then there is the claim of *Holy Blood, Holy Grail*, repeated in
Brown's *Da Vinci Code*, that the clique behind the Templars,
the Priory of Sion, carried on regardless after the Pope's ban.
The Priory of Sion were the custodians of the Holy Grail – the
knowledge that Jesus had a child with Mary Magdalene, and
that the Holy bloodline moved to France, where their descendants still reside.

The Templars/Priory of Sion are said to have discovered the
Grail during their excavations of the Temple. It was this
knowledge of the Grail which was the true cause of the

Templars' fall to ruin. If Jesus's bloodline were still extant, the Papacy was illegitimate. To protect itself, the Papacy and its monarchical supporters ordered the extermination of those who knew the truth of the Grail – the Knights Templar.

The notion of still extant Knights Templar and documents proving the rewriting of Christianity by the Catholic Church is wildly popular – proof being the millions of copies of *The Da Vinci Code* which have been sold. Evidence to tie modern Templar claimants to the Knights Templar of yore is non-existent, however. If the Templars live on it is in placenames such as Temple Meads, in their round churches like Garway, and in their ruined castles like Crak des Chevaliers.

One mystery does survive the Templars. The Holy Grail as Christ's bloodline is, to quote historian Marina Warner, "hooey", but what *were* the Templars looking for in their nine years of excavations in the Temple of Jerusalem?

And did they find it?

The Knights Templar survived the cull of the 14th century and live on today as guardians of the Holy Grail: ALERT LEVEL 3

Further Reading

Michael Baigent, Richard Leigh and Henry Lincoln, *Holy Blood, Holy Grail*, 1982

Dan Brown, *The Da Vinci Code*, 2003 [novel]

Lynn Picknett and Clive Prince, *The Templar Revelations*, 1998

Piers Paul Read, *The Templars*, 1999

JOHN LENNON

Everyone knows who shot former Beatle John Lennon outside the Dakota Building, New York, at 10.50 p.m. on 8 December 1980. Mark David Chapman, far from fleeing the scene of the crime, walked up and down on the sidewalk and started to read J. D. Salinger's *The Catcher in the Rye*. "I just shot John Lennon," Chapman informed bewildered witnesses. He said the same to the judge months later at his court case, and was awarded 20 years to life in Attica State Prison as a result.

So that's that, then. Chapman was the classic deranged fan, a psycho loser who felt the need for some attention. His defence psychiatrist defined Chapman's condition as "paranoid schizophrenia".

For some observers, however, too much about the Chapman/Lennon case did not stand up. For a start Chapman, as a confirmed mental case, should not have been deemed fit to stand trial and certainly not sent to a standard prison to serve his time. On top of that, police detectives on the Chapman case noted that Chapman seemed "programmed" and, far from desiring attention, avoided it. In his one press interview Chapman said: "He [John Lennon] walked past me and then I heard in my head, 'do it, do it' . . . I don't remember aiming." But aim he did – using a classic "combat stance", according to eyewitnesses – and fired his Charter Arms .38 pistol five times. And, for someone who had spent years working as a children's counsellor in refugee camps for World Vision, then bumming around and imbibing drugs, Chapman had an awful lot of cash and credit cards to his name.

For the veteran Californian conspiracy theorist Mae Brussell, Chapman's strange mental state was clear evidence that he was a "Manchurian Candidate", an assassin programmed to kill. Brussell thought Chapman's masters were the Nazis, and that Lennon was killed as part of a long purge of rock stars from the US cultural scene. According to Brussell, only anodyne pop-sters like "Sonny and Cher, the Osmonds, John Denver, and Captain & Tennille make it", and hippie Lennon was a must-kill.

Fenton Bresler proposes a more sophisticated take on the Manchurian Candidate thesis in *Who Killed John Lennon?*, where he notes that World Vision, the religious charity for which Chapman worked, was purportedly a CIA front outfit linked to the sect which overdosed at **Jonestown**. Chapman, says Bresler, was hypnotized under the CIA's **MK-ULTRA** project to kill Lennon. Bresler hardly needs to look far for a motive. Lennon was a prominent critic of US foreign and domestic policy. His couplet "All we are saying is/Give peace a chance" seemed, from Vietnam to Central America, to be about the last thing on the minds of successive White House regimes. Lennon had also played a small part in the Watergate expose, when he financed the publication of Mae Brussell's prescient, insider-informed notes on the scandal (researched independently of Woodward and Bernstein at the *Washington Post*) in the underground magazine *The Realist*.

John Lennon was assassinated by a CIA-sponsored 'Man-churian Candidate': ALERT LEVEL 3

Further Reading
Fenton Bresler, *Who Killed John Lennon?*, 1989

ALEXANDER LITVINENKO

On 1 November 2006 London was full of Russians, there to watch Arsenal play CKSA Moscow in the Champions League. Mingling with the fans was a Russian killer, or killers, with a very different type of goal in mind.

That evening, in the London suburb of Muswell Hill, Russian dissident Alexander Litvinenko (born 1962) began vomiting. Within days he was in hospital; on 23 November he was dead, his internal organs destroyed by a radioactive isotope called polonium-210.

Polonium-210 is difficult to obtain in the UK, and in the amount used to poison Litvinenko – he received more than 100 times the lethal dose – must have come from either a commercial transaction abroad or a foreign nuclear reactor. Either way, it was imported into the country. Reconstructing the events of 1 November, police found that Litvinenko lunched with an Italian investigator, Mario Scaramella, at a sushi restaurant near Piccadilly; the Itsu restaurant later tested positive for alpha radiation. So did Scaramella himself. A security consultant and academic – though the university to which he was said to be attached had never heard of him – Scaramella had ostensibly met with Litvinenko to show the latter evidence of mounting death threats against him [Litvinenko]. After the lunch Litvinenko said Scaramella seemed "agitated".

Equipped with alpha detectors, British government scientists discovered a trail of polonium-210 around London, with 20 sites testing positive, some of which had been visited by Litvinenko after his lunch at the Itsu but others of which had not. The radioactive trail then led them to Heathrow, where two BA planes also showed the presence of polonium-210. To no one's great surprise, the planes had flown to and from Moscow. A former lieutenant colonel in the Russian FSB (the Foreign Intelligence Service, the successor to the KGB), Litvinenko had enemies galore in his former homeland.

Broadly, there are six possible solutions to the Litvinenko mystery.

First, he was killed on the official orders of Vladimir Putin. Litvinenko had noisily claimed, notably in his 2004 book *Blowing Up Russia*, co-written with Yuri Felshtinsky, that Putin and the FSB had conspired to perpetrate the **Chechen Bombings**. More recently Litvinenko had alleged that Putin was behind the murder of the investigative journalist Anna Politkovskaya and had links to organized crime in Russia. Putin would have had few regrets about Litvinenko being murdered, and the Russian parliament had passed legislation allowing the FSB to assassinate enemies of Russia abroad. The principal objection to this theory is that, if any tie between Putin and the assassination should ever be revealed, the diplomatic backlash would more than offset the gain of silencing a minor critic of his regime.

Second, while working for the FSB Litvinenko had targeted Russian mafiosi. Like elephants, they have long memories, but with much less sense of forgiveness. They would have enjoyed revenge, even if the dish was served very cold. Also, for all his assumed knight errantry, Litvinenko did work in murky waters as an envoy between Russian businesses, home and abroad, many of which had connections to organized crime. Yet it is unlikely that the Russian Mafia would have bothered with such an elaborate and potentially self-harming method of murder as radioactive poison.

Third, Litvinenko's murder was staged by Putin's enemies, knowing that suspicion would fall on the Russian president. Allies of Putin have put forward the name of Boris Berezovsky, the Russian tycoon living in London, as the perpetrator of the plot. However, Berezovsky was Litvinenko's friend and employer, and would be unlikely to do anything to endanger his political refugee status.

Fourth, the same Putin allies in the Kremlin have also floated the notion that Litvinenko staged his own murder, again with the notion of getting the blame to fall on Putin. The Putinites maintain Litvinenko was sliding towards madness, as evidenced by his ludicrous public claim that Putin was a paedophile. Against this is the problem Litvinenko would have had as an individual in sourcing polonium-210, not to mention the radioactive traces detected in London sites he had not visited.

The fifth solution is that Litvinenko was murdered by the FSB, but without Putin's direct say-so. Litvinenko was loathed within the FSB for betraying the service and for accusing it of corruption. Additionally, if the FSB was the perpetrator of the Chechen Bombings, it, like Putin, had every reason to silence Litvinenko. Assassinating him would also serve as a warning to others that defection would never be tolerated by the FSB.

The KGB, many of whose officers staffed the FSB in an archetypal case of old wine in a new bottle, had a track record of using radioactive poison to kill defected spies. In 1957 Nikolai Khokhlov, a KGB captain who went over to the West, addressed a conference of anti-Soviet activists in Germany where someone gave him an unsolicited cup of coffee. Although the coffee tasted normal, for some reason Khokhlov drank only half the cup. He later recorded:

I suddenly felt very tired. Things began to whirl about me in the hall, the electric bulbs were swaying, the rays of light were dancing doubled before my eyes. The world about me seemed to have retreated to nowhere, and my body was convulsed in a terrible struggle with some strange forces. Nobody suspected that a chemical agent of delayed action was working in my system like a time bomb. Friday night it broke loose in my system.

Khokhlov's eyes oozed a sticky white liquid, his hair fell out, and the blood in his veins turned to plasma. Only six weeks of blood transfusions and steroid injections saved him from what was later identified as poisoning by radioactive thallium.

The Russian authorities have laughed off suggestions that the FSB was involved in Litvinenko's murder, stating that "for us, Litvinenko was nothing" – a claim dealt a severe blow by an article in *The Times* in January 2007 which proved that Russian Spetnaz special forces used photographs of Litvinenko for target practice. Unlike the Mafia, the FSB as a government agency would have had little difficulty in obtaining polonium-210.

This leads to the sixth theory, that the FSB supplied the polonium-210 but subcontracted the actual hit to the Russian Mafia or, more likely, to a private Russian security agency. According to Scaramella, the documents he showed Litvinenko in the Itsu identified one such private outfit, Dignity & Honour, as the specific threat to Litvinenko's life. Headed by Colonel Valentin Velichko, a former KGB officer, Dignity & Honour is seen by many in Western intelligence as an official extension of the FSB.

In December 2006 investigators from Scotland Yard travelled to Russia to interview a suspect in the Litvinenko case, one Andrei Lugovoi, an ex-KGB officer turned owner of a security and consulting business, who admitted being contaminated with polonium-210. Lugovoi was known to have visited many of the sites in London where traces of the radioactive poison had been detected, as well as travelling on the contaminated BA London–Moscow airliners. He insisted, "I've been framed."

The veracity of Lugovoi's protestations, like much in the Litvinenko case, is unlikely to be proved one way or the other. In 2007 the British authorities requested his extradition from Russia to answer charges. The Russian constitution, maybe handily for Lugovoi and the Kremlin, bars the extradition of citizens to face trial abroad.

Alexander Litvinenko was assassinated by the Russian FSB or its sub-contractors: ALERT LEVEL 9

Further Reading
Tony Halpin *et al.*, "Russian Special Forces Used Image of Litvinenko for Target Practice", *The Times*, 30 January 2007
Alexander Litvinenko, "Why I Believe Putin Wanted Me Dead", *Mail on Sunday*, 25/11/06
Martin Sixsmith, *The Litvinenko File: The True Story of a Death Foretold*, 2007

DOCUMENT: ALEXANDER LITVINENKO –
WHY I BELIEVE PUTIN WANTED ME DEAD,
Mail on Sunday, 25 November 2006

In the summer of 1996, I returned to Moscow from Chechnya and was summoned to see my boss, General Vyacheslav Voloch, head of the Anti-Terrorist Directorate of the Federal Security Bureau (FSB).

"They are putting Khokholkov in charge of URPO," he said. "That man is a monster. We should do everything to stop him."

URPO was the acronym for a newly established top-secret unit at the FSB, and Evgeny Khokholkov was a colonel in the anti-terrorist directorate. More than that, he was General Voloch's subordinate-turned-rival.

The two men had fallen foul of each other ealier that year when Colonel Khokholkov masterminded the assassination of a Chechnyan separatist leader. An air-to-ground missile was used to home in on a satellite phone signal – there wasn't much left of him. It was a sophisticated and costly operation with a hefty budget that, as boss of the Anti-Terrorist Directorate, General Voloch was expected to sign off.

But when the dust had settled nearly a million dollars was missing and Voloch demanded a full account. He was never given one. His subordinate had powerful protectors within the bureau and the matter was papered over, much to General Voloch's embarrassment.

Now Colonel Khokholkov was being handed his own directorate to run – a special operations unit that would be allowed to break the law – and he was likely be promoted to full general.

In fact, the very idea of URPO came up as a result of the Chechen experience. In that undeclared war, secret services enjoyed generous operational freedom: they could detain, interrogate and kill without legal constraints. But while no one would think of "due process" before firing a missile in

Chechnya, back in Moscow the legal niceties had to be observed.

So the agency bosses decided that it would be handy to have an autonomous, secret unit to carry out occasional "special tasks", and thanks to his track record Colonel Khokholkov was the natural choice to lead it.

For General Voloch it was a devastating appointment – effectively placing his one-time subordinate in charge of a rival operational division with greater powers than his own. His response to the news of his rival's success and his reason for summoning me to FSB headquarters that day was to give me a secret assignment. I was to dig out all the dirt I could find on this Colonel Khokholkov.

So began a chain of events that would show just how deep the stain of corruption ran – and which would lead me to Vladimir Putin.

It was not the first time that Colonel Khokholkov had been brought to my attention. Three years earlier, as a young operativnik, I had helped unmask a group of corrupt FSB officers, most of them of Uzbek origin.

My report became known as the Uzbek file and Colonel Khokholkov's name surfaced in these investigations. But although several of his colleagues were transferred or fired, he remained untouched. I had found no direct evidence against him.

Shortly after I began digging again into his background, I was contacted by a source at the Ministry of Internal Affairs. The Organized Crime Unit of the Moscow City Police had some explosive material on Colonel Khokholkov, I was told.

He had been videotaped in the company of major crime figures as they gathered to carve up the Russian drugs market. This explained Khokholkov's wealth: he owned a posh restaurant on Moscow's Kutuzovsky Avenue and a country house worth hundreds of thousands of dollars. And one night, he lost some $120,000 gambling at Casino Leningrad.

It was no surprise to me that the police should have investigated an officer of the FSB. At the time, both the FSB and the police were so deeply involved in the city's protection rackets they were virtually at war. Some of their rivalry was over who would benefit from the supply of drugs pouring from Afghanistan into Europe.

I did not find the videotape, but I did find enough evidence against Khokholkov to charge him – if my superiors would agree.

General Voloch was reluctant to take the decision, so I took my file to the newly appointed FSB Director, Nikolai Kovaliov.

The meeting was brief and the Director defensive. He shrugged, "What can I do?" when told of the evidence against Khokholkov. I later learned that he had ordered an Internal Affairs file on Khokholkov to be closed the moment he was put in charge.

While the meeting at the Director's office failed to affect Colonel Khokholkov's career, it certainly changed mine. Before long, in the same office, the Director asked me to become his personal agent in his new department, the URPO.

I was speechless. Work for Colonel Khokholkov?

Reading my mind, the Director said: "Forget about Khokholkov. We checked him out. There is nothing there. But it would not harm if I had my own man keeping an eye on him. Agree? Call any time."

It was an order, not an offer.

So, for many months, I found myself working for the man I had been tasked to expose. But it was only a matter of time before the compromising videotape of Colonel Khokholkov's meeting to extort money from Moscow's drug barons surfaced once more.

The incident started with a simple enough case. A local shopowner had been visited by a man claiming to be a police officer and demanding protection money.

The demands went up and up from $5,000 a month to $9,000 then to $15,000 and more. Next the shopowner received a visit at his home – he was beaten up and threatened. He turned to the FSB.

We identified the vehicle used to visit the shopkeeper that night and it led us to a dingy den where we found a police officer, several men and two terrified girls, one under age. Both showed signs of abuse and had been raped.

We summoned the local police, who obtained a search warrant. The men were booked for rape and a local investigator began questioning them.

Then a remarkable thing happened. A lawyer for the policeman we had arrested showed up, but instead of dealing with his client's situation he told us that for the past three years the policeman had been forcing him to provide services to companies he had under protection, without any pay. But he wanted to take the opportunity to come clean.

I took the lawyer to the Lubyanka FSB headquarters and taped his testimony. He told us about the massive involvement of the Moscow City Police Organized Crime Unit in criminal activity. His evidence implicated the head of the unit and high officials at the Ministry of Internal Affairs. I was discovering that corruption was everywhere in this city – and I was to find out that it went right to the very top.

When the case was completed and everything was ready for the prosecutor, I felt a certain uneasiness about bringing it to Colonel Khokholkov for signature. Investigating such police corruption was a dangerous business when I knew that the tapes linking my own boss with similar protection rackets were still sitting in the vaults of the Moscow City Police.

As it was, Colonel Khokholkov was conveniently unwell, so his deputy signed off the case. And it was only a matter of time before the organization we were investigating revealed their own evidence about our boss. When it happened, it was calmly and deliberately done. Two police officers showed up at the FSB reception and left the tape of Colonel Khokholkov extorting protection money from drug barons. There was a clear message – forget the investigation or we'll bring down your boss.

I knew about it the next day when the irate Colonel barged into my office: "What have you been doing? Who authorized this? Why did you go to the prosecutors? Get the case back."

The case was recalled and I never saw the material again. Most of the criminals are still walking around. The policeman we had arrested was allowed to slip out to Turkey, with much of his money. As for me, I never felt more betrayed. But I was knee-deep in the dirty system in which men like Putin would flourish.

Shortly afterwards, I myself became the centre of a scandal when my unit was ordered to plan the assassination of Boris Berezovsky, the entrepreneur-turned-politician who was close to President Yeltsin. No one told us of the reason, but there was no need to: Berezovsky was the most visible of oligarchs, a billionaire tycoon whose Liberal Russia political party stood against the corruption that flowed through the heart of the FSB and our own unit. He was a threat.

I and five other officers refused to carry out the order. Instead, we went directly to Berezovsky and warned him about the plot. We also complained to the Prosecutor-General. The FSB pressured us to withdraw our complaints and suspended the whole group of officers.

Behind the scenes, Berezovsky was pulling levers in the Kremlin and persuaded Boris Yeltsin to turn on our department. Within a few weeks, our secret directorate was disbanded. Colonel Khokholkov was transferred, FSB Director Kovaliov fired. In his place, Yeltsin appointed Vladimir Putin, a little-known Colonel working inside the Kremlin.

Putin's appointment was a shock to everyone – and a disaster for me. I met him soon after his appointment. I was still technically suspended but one day Berezovsky called me. "Alexander, could you go to Putin and tell him everything that you have told me? And everything that you have not. He is new at the Service, you know, and would benefit from an insider's view."

Before our meeting, I spent all night drawing up a chart with names, places, links – everything.

I arrived with two colleagues, but Putin wanted to see me alone. It must be incredibly tough for him, I thought. We were of the same rank, and I imagined myself in his shoes – a mid-level operativnik suddenly put in charge of some hundred seasoned generals with all their vested interests, connections and dirty secrets.

I did not know how to salute him without causing embarrassment. Should I say "Comrade Colonel" as was required by the code? But he pre-empted me and got up from his desk and shook my hand. He seemed even shorter than on TV.

From that very first moment I felt that he was not sincere. He avoided eye contact and behaved as if he was not the Director, but an actor playing a role. He looked at my chart, appearing to study it, and asked a couple of random questions.

I knew he could not have grasped the details in the cursory glance he had given it. "Shall I leave the chart?" I asked.

"No, no, thank you. You keep it. It's your work."

I gave him another list I had compiled: "These officers are clean. I know for sure that you can rely on them in the war on corruption." Number one on the list was a colleague called General Trofimov. "There are honest people in the system," I said. "We could bring the situation under control." He nodded, acting as though in full agreement. He kept my files on Colonel Khokholkov and his links to the Uzbek drug barons and protection rackets. He said we would keep in touch and took my home number.

But he never called. Many months later, I got the chance to study my own file and I learned that he had ordered Internal Affairs to start a case against me right after that meeting. I regretted many of the names I had handed over. It seemed I had given them to the enemy as well as revealing just how much I knew.

Shortly afterwards, I was fired from the FSB. Before I left, a former boss at the Anti-Terrorist Centre went to Putin to put in a word on my behalf. Returning from the meeting, he looked at me, shook his head and said: "I do not envy you, Alexander. There is common money involved."

I did not understand then what he meant by "common money". Now I do. He was referring to Colonel Khokholkov and his dealings with the Uzbek drug barons. This under-standing came to me many months later. I discovered that Putin's connection with Colonel Khokholkov dated back to the time when Putin was a Deputy for Economic Affairs to the Mayor of St Petersburg.

I had an informer in St Petersburg's city hall. He kept an eye on the criminal connections of city officials. When the Mayor lost the elections, Putin lost his job. One day my informant had a beer with him. Putin was down and out and could not get hold of money he had stashed away. He was under surveillance by the new Mayor's people. My informant took pity on Putin and gave him $2,000 as an "open-ended" loan. When Putin became President, he repaid him by appointing him an economic adviser.

As for me, my years of service at the FSB were rewarded by being fired and thrown in jail. It was a year before I was released pending trial. My informant came to see me follow-ing my release: "Putin will squash you," he said, "and no one can help you. He has no choice because he was working with the Uzbek group. There is lots of common money there."

I could not believe that he was using the same phrase: common money. He was telling me that Putin had been directly linked with the mob that my investigations into Colonel Khokholkov had led me to. How close had I come to his name?

My informant smiled: "Remember the smuggling of rare metal in the early Nineties? Putin was in charge of export licensing. You worked on organized crime? Tell me, could anyone export a kilo of metal in those days without the mob? They would blow up the whole train. And he was right at the centre of it all. All his licensees were mob fronts."

The two of us were talking in a restaurant. "Vladimir fell for power very quickly," confided my informant. "Look, when Yeltsin drove to the Kremlin, only one traffic lane was cleared. But for Vladimir they close down the whole highway. He is not fit for power. He has no political skills and a certain weird way of thinking. He is dangerous."

My friend got drunk and I took him out to the lobby. "Are you crazy?" I said. "All of this will be at the FSB tomorrow morning. Don't you know that I am watched?"

But it was too late. Three weeks after that conversation, he was killed by a hit-man from a passing bicycle. A direct hit at close range. I learned about it from TV. A presidential aide has been shot. One of many during the past decade.

Concluding this story, I'm quite sure there will be an explosion of protests about my unsubstantiated allegations that President Putin is personally involved at least in a cover-up of organized criminal activities connected with drug traffic in Russia and Europe. People will demand hard proof. I am not going to try to prove anything. I am an operativnik, not a prosecutor. My job is to collect operational information and analyse it. This is my analysis:

First: two independent sources report that a suspect – call him Mr P. – has "common money" with Colonel Khokholkov at the FSB. One of the sources gets killed as soon as his connection to me is compromised.

Second: Colonel Khokholkov is tied to the Uzbek drug organization. He lives lavishly, well beyond his means.

Next: Mr P. protects Colonel Khokholkov. He neutralizes his internal opponents.

Further: Mr P. is fully aware that Colonel Khokholkov is involved with the Uzbeks.

Finally: when the crimes were committed, Mr P. held a key position in a northern metropolis, Russia's gateway to Europe. Much of the drug transit went through his city. This made him of tremendous value to the Uzbek friends of his friend Colonel Khokholkov.

As an operativnik, I have every reason to suspect Mr P. at least in criminal complicity. There is nothing unusual in that – in my time I have seen hundreds of similar situations. Sure, Mr P. happens to be the President of Russia. But the crimes were committed when he was a humble Deputy Mayor of St Petersburg.

Admittedly, the evidence against Mr P. is indirect and cannot be used in a court. And, of course, if Mr P. were not the President, I would not have publicized it, but would have opened a case and brought him in for questioning.

But he is the President, and there is no possibility of questioning him. He is accountable by a different standard. So he must respond to my questions before the public.

But first, I would like to see what will happen to the newspaper that prints this story.

Daily Mail 2007

LOCKERBIE BOMBING

On 21 December 1988, Pan Am Flight 103, bound from
Heathrow for New York's JFK International Airport, exploded
at an altitude of 31,000 feet (9,450m). All 259 passengers aboard
the Boeing 747-121 were killed, along with 11 residents of
Lockerbie, southern Scotland, hit by plane wreckage falling
from the sky.

In the ensuing crash investigation, forensic experts determined that 12–16 ounces (340–450g) of plastic explosive had
been detonated in the airplane's forward cargo hold. Since this
was a US plane with mostly US citizens aboard, the bombing
was widely regarded as an attack on the US. After a three-year
joint investigation by the Dumfries and Galloway Constabulary
and the FBI, indictments for murder in connection with the
Lockerbie bombing were issued on 13 November 1991 against
Abdelbasset Ali al-Megrahi, a Libyan intelligence officer and
the head of security for Libyan Arab Airlines (LAA), and
Khalifah Fhimahmen, the LAA manager at Malta's Luqa Airport.

Libya had a clear motive for the Lockerbie crime: revenge for
the 1986 Air Force raid on the Libyan cities of Tripoli and
Benghazi which killed, among others, the adopted daughter of
the Libyan president, Muammar al-Gaddafi. Neither was Libya
exactly a stranger to arranging terrorist attacks. Some forensic
evidence also seemed to link the bombing to Libya. Lord Boyd,
the Scottish advocate, noted:

In June 1990, with the assistance ultimately of the CIA and FBI, Alan Feraday of the Explosives Laboratory was able to identify the fragment as identical to circuitry from an MST-13 timer. It was already known to the CIA from an example seized in Togo in 1986 and photographed by them in Senegal in 1988. That took investigators to the firm of MEBO in Zurich. It was discovered that these timers had been manufactured to the order of two Libyans – Ezzadin Hinshin, at the time director of the Central Security Organization of the Libyan External Security Organization, and Said Rashid, then head of the Operations Administration of the ESO.

After ten years of United Nations sanctions Libya eventually handed over al-Megrahi and Fhimahmen in April 1999 to Scottish police at Camp Zeist, Netherlands, a neutral venue.

On 31 January 2001, a panel of three Scottish judges acquitted Fhimahmen but convicted al-Megrahi of murder and sentenced him to 27 years in prison. Al-Megrahi professed his innocence. He wasn't the only one. One observer of the trial, Dr Hans Koechler of the United Nations, called it a "spectacular miscarriage of justice"; as if to outdo Koechler, one professor of law at Edinburgh called al-Megrahi's conviction the "worst miscarriage of justice in Scotland for 100 years". Faith in the Camp Zeist judgment was severely shaken again when Libya's Prime Minister Shukri Ghanen told BBC Radio in 2004 that Libya had only paid US$2.7 billion compensation to the victims' families to get the sanctions against his country dropped. The money, said Ghanen, was "the price for peace".

All of which raised the question: were al-Megrahi and Libya framed?

In his book *Lockerbie: The Tragedy of Flight 103*, David Johnston asserts that, by the end of 1989, US and UK intelligence agents were near united in their agreement as to who was responsible for the 103 outrage – and it wasn't Libya. Their suspicion was confirmed in 2000 when one Ahmad Behbahani stepped forward to claim that the Iranian government had carried out the Lockerbie operation.

Behbahani was a former Iranian intelligence officer. His job: co-ordinating Iran's terrorist attacks on the West. According to him, he contracted out the bombing to Ahmed Jibril's Syrian-based Popular Front for the Liberation of Palestine-General Command (PFLP-GC). There was a deal of supporting evidence for this claim. The PFLP-GC ran a cell in Germany – where Pan Am 103 began its flight to the US – which built explosive devices hidden in Toshiba Bombeat radio cassette recorders. The source for this information is the bomb-maker himself, Marwan Khreesat, a Jordanian spy infiltrated into the PFLP-GC. According to most forensic evidence, the explosive device placed aboard Pan Am 103 was likewise hidden in a Toshiba Bombeat. So convinced were the Scottish police at one stage that Khreesat was the Lockerbie bomber that they drew up a warrant for his arrest. PFLP-GC watchers also remembered Jibril's 1985 warning: "There will be no safety for any traveller on an Israeli or US airliner." Pan Am 103 was, by this theory, an eye for an eye: an American warship had mistakenly shot down an Iranian civilian airbus in 1988.

Some journalists and observers account for the Lockerbie investigation switching track from Iran to Libya to a climate change in geopolitics. In the early 1990s the US and UK were enjoying a brief thaw with Syria and Iran, which had respectively supported and acquiesced in George H. W. Bush's Gulf War. Libya, on the other hand, had sided with Iraq, the enemy. Reputedly, Bush asked the British PM Margaret Thatcher for the Syria/Iran/PFLP-GC line of inquiry to be "toned down". (Thatcher's memoirs, interestingly, fail to blame Libya for the Pan Am tragedy.) Being nasty to Libya but nice to the Syrians and Iranians, who effectively controlled the Lebanese capital Beirut, had the added advantage that Western hostages held in the city received their freedom.

Oddly enough, the Beirut hostage crisis had another, more direct, connection to the Lockerbie bombing. On board the doomed flight were at least four US intelligence officers, one of whom was Matthew Gannon, the CIA's deputy station chief in Beirut. Sitting directly behind Gannon was Major Charles

McKee of the US Defense Intelligence Agency, who is believed to have been in Beirut searching for American hostages held by Hizbollah. According to Pan Am's own investigation, undertaken by former Mossad officer Juval Aviv, the CIA were couriering drugs in a protected suitcase aboard flight 103 on behalf of a Syrian arms dealer, who had the pull to get US hostages in Beirut released. It is widely reported that the crash area around Lockerbie was searched by scores of CIA officers, who removed cases of heroin and cannabis, together with $500,000. British soldiers found a map detailing the whereabouts of two US hostages.

That the CIA used flight 103 for drug couriering has caused some Lockerbie observers to wonder whether George Bush himself ordered the blowing up of 103 in order to eradicate evidence that the CIA was once again involved in dodgy drug operations. The **Iran–Contra Scandal** had almost brought down Reagan, and Bush would have been frantic to avoid a repeat performance.

The passenger list of flight 103 makes for fertile reading for conspiracy theory. Among the dead was Bernt Carlsson, the United Nations Commissioner for South West Africa (Namibia). Carlsson was due to fly to New York from Brussels to oversee the agreement by which the apartheid regime of South Africa relinquished control of Namibia as instructed by the UN Security Council; according to a report on 12 March 1990 in the Swedish daily *iDAG*, Carlsson was pressurized to abandon his plan to fly direct to NY and instead to stop over in London for a meeting with representatives of the De Beers mining group. Consequently, Carlsson ended up on fatal flight 103. The plot thickens: Pan Am witnesses at the Lockerbie Fatal Accident Inquiry confirmed that South African Airways was engaged in illegal baggage switching on 21 December. Was Carlsson's bag substituted while he was at the De Beers meeting? The plot congeals: booked on flight 103 was a South African delegation, headed by foreign minister Pik Botha, also flying to NY for the Namibia treaty signing. At the last moment the South African delegation cancelled their seats on flight 103 and made other arrangements for travel.

Carlsson's death came immediately before the planned Namibia independence signing, and it was impossible for the UN to find a replacement in time, with the result that the territory's South African administrator-general Louis Pienaar continued to administer South-West Africa in the run-up to the first election in November 1989. Free of Carlsson, the apartheid regime in South Africa foisted the constitution it wanted on Namibia.

It has also been suggested that the Lockerbie bomb was radio detonated, the explosive device being set off by simply coming into range of a certain aircraft navigational beacon (in the case of Flight 103, the Dean Cross beacon, south west of Carlisle, on 123.95MHZ). Only two years before the downing of flight 103, Soviet accident investigators had accused South Africa of using a false navigational radio beacon to lure the Tupolev Tu-134 of Mozambique president Samora Machel to its doom.

With so many allegations still swirling in the wake of the Lockerbie bombing, Dr Jim Swire of the bereaved families campaign group UK Families–Flight 103 (UKF103) has called for "a full review of the entire Lockerbie scenario through an appropriately empowered and independent inquiry". Before it came to power in the UK in 1997, the Labour Party supported an independent Lockerbie inquiry. When it reached Downing Street the Labour Party decided there was no need to "initiate any further form of review on Lockerbie".

Strange, that.

Libya was framed for the Lockerbie bombing: ALERT LEVEL 9

Further Reading
John Ashton and Ian Ferguson, *Cover-up of Convenience: The Hidden Scandal of Lockerbie*, 2002
David Johnston, *Lockerbie: The Tragedy of Flight 103*, 1989

MADRID TRAIN BOMBINGS

During rush-hour on the morning of 11 March 2004, ten bombs exploded more or less simultaneously around the Atocha railway station in Madrid, killing 192 commuters and injuring 1,800 others. Within hours, the conservative government of Jose Marisa Aznar was blaming ETA (Euskadi Ta Askatasuna), the terrorist Basque separatist organization, for the attack.

Three days after the train bombs, Spain went to the polls in the general election and voted Aznar's Popular Party out of office and the Socialists in. Henceforth the investigation into what Spaniards would call "11–M" concentrated not on ETA but on Islamic radicals attached to al-Qaeda. At this, Aznar, together with influential right-wing media such as the *El Mundo* newspaper, cried foul and accused the Socialists of a conspiracy to hide the identity of the true perpetrators: ETA.

It was widely known that ETA sought to attack targets in the capital and had previously tried to bomb trains, and only weeks before 11–M a vanload of ETA explosives had been seized approaching Madrid. Further, police in the northern region of Asturias had been tipped off that Basque separatists had sold dynamite for an imminent incident. The dynamite used in Madrid allegedly contained DNT, common in ETA blasts. Moreover, the Atocha attack was remarkably free of many of the hallmarks of an al-Qaeda attack, such as the suicide of the bomb carriers themselves.

The Socialists had a reason to shine the spotlight on al-Qaeda, not ETA. Before polling on 14 March they claimed, without any certain evidence, that al-Qaeda was responsible for the train attacks. Fearful of more al-Qaeda assaults on Spanish citizens, Spain voted to oust the party which had sent Spanish troops to Iraq – Aznar's Popular Party. In the three days between the bombings and the election, Aznar's Popular Party went from 5 per cent ahead in opinion polls to 7 per cent behind the Socialists. Once elected, the Socialists had to shore up their unfounded claims concerning Atocha.

On the other hand, Spain was indeed a prime target for al-Qaeda, as Aznar had been a high-profile supporter of the Bush-led ousting of Saddam Hussein in 2003. The Spanish police and judiciary continued on the al-Qaeda trail and within weeks surrounded Moroccan suspects in a hideout at Leganes. Rather than surrender, the suspects blew themselves up. Eventually, the Spanish police would arrest 29 more suspects in the Madrid train bombing investigation, and commit them to trial in 2007. The indictment ran to 96,000 pages, and failed to note any ETA connection with the Madrid bombings. It did find overwhelming evidence, however, of involvement in the crime by members of the Moroccan Islamic Combatant Group, which is loosely associated with al-Qaeda.

Despite the strength of the prosecution case, Aznar and the Popular Party refused to let go of their conspiracy theory, which fractured Spanish society almost exactly along right/left lines running back to the 1930s Civil War. Even the 11–M victims' groups were run on pro- and anti-conspiracy lines.

In truth, any conspiracy theorizing after 11–M was as likely to be directed by Aznar and the Popular Party as against them. According to the ESISC (European Strategic Intelligence and Security Centre), by late morning of the 11th the Spanish Intelligence Services had concluded the massacre was authored by an Islamist terrorist group, but were then ordered to deny the Islamic lead and insist that ETA was the sole suspect. The Popular Party government

followed up by sending messages to Spanish embassies ordering them to uphold the pro-ETA line. Aznar is further
reported to have phoned newspaper editors and personally
asked them to support his version.

Addendum: On 31 October 2007 the Spanish National Court
found 20 Islamists and Moroccan petty criminals guilty of
perpetrating the Madrid Train Bombings and/or belonging
to a terrorist organization. A Spanish miner was convicted of
supplying the explosives used in the bombing.

> It was ETA not al-Qaeda which committed the 11-M train
> bombings: ALERT LEVEL 4

Further Reading
www.realinstitutoeliano.org

MAJESTIC–12

Returning home on the evening of 11 December 1984, TV producer and UFO investigator Jaime Shandera found a bulky envelope stuffed into his mailbox. Inside was a roll of 35mm undeveloped black-and-white film. When Shandera and his colleague William Moore developed the film they found photographs of a "TOP SECRET – EYES ONLY" document from 1952 briefing the then president of the US, Dwight Eisenhower.

The document informed the newly installed Eisenhower on the crash of a UFO at **Roswell** in July 1947, from which the bodies of four aliens had been recovered. Attached was a 1947 memo from President Harry Truman authorizing the setting up of a 12-member panel of military officers, scientists and intelligence officers, under the codename "Majestic–12" (aka "Majic-12"), to study the aliens' technology.

After three years of research, Shandera and Moore became convinced that the Majestic–12 document was genuine, and released it on 29 May 1987 into the public domain. There were headlines around the world. A former CIA pilot called John Lear (son of the Learjet inventor) came forward to announce that he had discovered a paper trail of contacts between the Majestic–12 committee and alien visitors; the latter had, in order to heal genetic disorders, carried out experiments on cattle (resulting in the phenomenon which became known as "cattle mutilation") and humans. Sometimes the experiments were carried out aboard flying saucers (see **Alien Abductions**) but more usually in huge US subterranean cities, peopled by aliens and guarded by the US; afterwards abductees were returned to their lives with trackers installed in their bodies. In exchange for permitting the alien experiments, the White House received alien technological know-how. Alas, after a diplomatic spat the aliens withdrew from Earth and, fearful they might return with less-than-peaceful intentions, the US created the Strategic Defense Initiative ("Star Wars") to protect itself. According to the arch-UFOlogist William Cooper, the US government kept the lid on its long relationship with the aliens through a Mafia-like vow of silence. Any US subjects who blabbed were harassed into silence by **Men in Black**. Cooper claimed to have seen sheaves of UFO documents when he served in the navy, and even attempted the impeachment of George Bush Sr and Bill Clinton for complicity in Majestic–12. Cooper's investigations into Majestic–12 came to an abrupt end in November 2001 when he was shot dead in what the authorities said was an unrelated accident.

The original Majestic–12 document was proved beyond reasonable doubt to be a forgery in 1989, when conspiracy debunker Philip Klass showed that President Truman's signature on the document was an exact copy of his signature on an earlier letter. Nobody signs their name precisely the same way twice. Additionally, the 1947 memo was typed on a Smith Corona typewriter – a model not in production until 1963 – and CIA chief Admiral Hillenkoetter is referred to as "Adm. Roscoe H. Hillenkoetter" even though all known letters from the time refer to him as "Adm. R. H. Hillenkoetter".

Some suspect Bill Moore forged the original document himself. Moore is said to have written a novel in 1982 called *MAJIK-12*. That same year he suggested to ex-*National Enquirer* journalist Bob Pratt that they should publish phoney UFO documents to force the government to come up with the real ones. Moore himself has admitted informing on UFOlogists to the Air Force Office of Special Investigations (he says in order to win its trust so he could infiltrate it) and it has been mooted that he was willingly or unwillingly part of an AFOSI disinformation campaign.

Nevertheless, diehards continue to hold that a super-secret body called Majestic–12 exists and that William Cooper was permanently silenced by the Men in Black because he was about to expose the whole White House–UFO cosy relationship. Hundreds of other Majestic–12 documents of disputed authenticity have been discovered and published.

Majestic–12 aside, there are verifiable accounts of a UFO study group set up by the Pentagon in 1954 called NSC 5412/2 about which next to nothing is known. Perhaps the hoaxers who forged the original Majestic–12 documents had the right guys, just the wrong name.

US top-secret committee Majestic–12 treated with aliens:
ALERT LEVEL 2

Further Reading
William Cooper, *Behold a Pale Horse,* 1991
Stanton T. Friedman, *Top Secret/Magic: The Story of Operation Majestic–12 and the United States Government's UFO Cover-Up,* 1997
www.majesticdocuments.com

DOCUMENT: PURPORTED 18 NOVEMBER 1952 BRIEFING TO PRESIDENT-ELECT EISENHOWER ON MAJESTIC-12

WARNING: This is a TOP SECRET – EYES ONLY document containing compartmentalized information essential to the national security of the United States. EYES ONLY ACCESS to the material herein is strictly limited to those possessing Majestic–12 clearance level. Reproduction in any form or the taking of written or mechanically transcribed notes is strictly forbidden.

[. . .]

NOTE: This document has been prepared as a preliminary briefing only. It should be regarded as introductory to a full operations briefing intended to follow.

★ ★ ★ ★ ★

OPERATION MAJESTIC–12 is a TOP SECRET Research and Development/Intelligence operation responsible directly and only to the President of the United States. Operations of the project are carried out under control of the Majestic–12 (Majic-12) Group which was established by special classified executive order of President Truman on 24 September 1947, upon recommendation by Dr Vannevar Bush and Secretary James Forrestal. (See Attachment "A".) Members of the Majestic–12 Group were designated as follows:

    Adm. Roscoe H. Hillenkoetter
    Dr Vannevar Bush
    Secy James V. Forrestal
    Gen. Nathan F. Twining
    Gen. Hoyt S. Vandenberg

Dr Detlev Bronk
Dr Jerome Hunsaker
Mr Sidney W. Souers
Mr Gordon Gray
Dr Donald Menzel
Gen. Robert M. Montague
Dr Lloyd V. Berkner

The death of Secretary Forrestal on 22 May 1949 created a
vacancy which remained unfilled until 01 August 1950, upon
which date Gen. Walter B. Smith was designated as permanent replacement.

★ ★ ★ ★ ★

On 24 June, 1947, a civilian pilot, flying over the Cascade
Mountains in the State of Washington observed nine flying
disc-shaped aircraft travelling in formation at a high rate of
speed. Although this was not the first known sighting of such
objects, it was the first to gain widespread attention in the
public media. Hundreds of reports of sightings of similar
objects followed. Many of these came from highly credible
military and civilian sources. These reports resulted in
independent efforts by several different elements of the
military to ascertain the nature and purpose of these objects
in the interests of national defense. A number of witnesses
were interviewed and there were several unsuccessful attempts to utilize aircraft in efforts to pursue reported discs
in flight. Public reaction bordered on near hysteria at times.

In spite of these efforts, little of substance was learned
about the objects until a local rancher reported that one had
crashed in a remote region of New Mexico located approximately seventy-five miles northwest of Roswell Army Air
Base (now Walker Field).

On 07 July, 1947, a secret operation was begun to assure
recovery of the wreckage of this object for scientific study.

During the course of this operation, aerial reconnaissance discovered that four small human-like beings had apparently ejected from the craft at some point before it exploded. These had fallen to earth about two miles east of the wreckage site. All four were dead and badly decomposed due to action by predators and exposure to the elements during the approximately one week time period which had elapsed before their discovery. A special scientific team took charge of removing these bodies for study. (See Attachment "C".) The wreckage of the craft was also removed to several different locations. (See Attachment "B".) Civilian and military witnesses in the area were debriefed, and news reporters were given the effective cover story that the object had been a misguided weather research balloon.

A covert analytical effort organized by Gen. Twining and Dr Bush acting on the direct orders of the President, resulted in a preliminary consensus (19 September 1947) that the disc was most likely a short range reconnaissance craft. This conclusion was based for the most part on the craft's size and the apparent lack of any identifiable provisioning. (See Attachment "D".) A similar analysis of the four dead occupants was arranged by Dr Bronk. It was the tentative conclusion of this group (30 November 1947) that although these creatures are human-like in appearance, the biological and evolutionary processes responsible for their development has [sic] apparently been quite different from those observed or postulated in homo-sapiens. Dr Bronk's team has suggested the term "Extra-terrestrial Biological Entities", or "EBEs", be adopted as the standard term of reference for these creatures until such time as a more definitive designation can be agreed upon.

Since it is virtually certain that these craft do not originate in any country on earth, considerable speculation has centred around what their point of origin may be and how they get here. Mars was and remains a possibility, although some scientists, most notably Dr Menzel, consider it more likely that we are dealing with beings from another solar system entirely.

Numerous examples of what appear to be a form of writing were found in the wreckage. Efforts to decipher these have remained largely unsuccessful. (See Attachment "E".) Equally unsuccessful have been efforts to determine the methods of propulsion or the nature or method of transmission of the power source involved. Research along these lines has been complicated by the complete absence of identifiable wings, propellers, jets, or other conventional methods of propulsion and guidance, as well as a total lack of metallic wiring, vacuum tubes, or similar recognizable electronic components. (See Attachment "F".) It is assumed that the propulsion unit was completely destroyed by the explosion which caused the crash.

A need for as much additional information as possible about these craft, their performance characteristics and their purpose led to the undertaking known as US Air Force Project SIGN in December, 1947. In order to preserve security, liaison between SIGN and Majestic–12 was limited to two individuals within the Intelligence Division of Air Material Command whose role was to pass along certain types of information through channels. SIGN evolved into Project GRUDGE in December, 1948. The operation is currently being conducted under the code name BLUE BOOK, with liaison maintained through the Air Force officer who is head of the project.

On 06 December 1950, a second object, probably of similar origin, impacted the earth at high speed in the El Indio–Guerrero area of the Texas–Mexican border after following a long trajectory through the atmosphere. By the time a search team arrived, what remained of the object had been almost totally incinerated. Such material as could be recovered was transported to the A.E.C. facility at Sandia, New Mexico, for study.

Implications for the National Security are of continuing importance in that the motives and ultimate intentions of these visitors remain completely unknown. In addition, a significant upsurge in the surveillance activity of these craft beginning in May and continuing through the autumn of this year has caused considerable concern that new developments may be imminent. It is for these reasons, as well as the obvious international and technological considerations and the ultimate need to avoid a public panic at all costs, that the Majestic–12 Group remains of the unanimous opinion that imposition of the strictest security precautions should continue without interruption into the new administration. At the same time, contingency plan MJ-1949-04P/78 (Top Secret – Eyes Only) should be held in continued readiness should the need to make a public announcement present itself. (See Attachment "G".)

RENUMERATION OF ATTACHMENTS:

• ATTACHMENT "A"
Special Classified Executive
Order #092447. (TS/EO)

• ATTACHMENT "B"
Operation Majestic–12 Status
Report #1, Part A. 30 NOV '47.
(TS-MAJIC/EO)

• ATTACHMENT "C"
Operation Majestic–12 Status
Report #1, Part B. 30 NOV '47.
(TS-MAJIC/EO)

• ATTACHMENT "D"
Operation Majestic–12 Preliminary
Analytical Report. 19 SEP '47.
(TS-MAJIC/EO)

- ATTACHMENT "E"
  Operation Majestic–12 Blue Team
  Report #5. 30 JUN '52.
  (TS-MAJIC/EO)

- ATTACHMENT "F"
  Operation Majestic–12 Status
  Report #2. 31 JAN '48.
  (TS-MAJIC/EO)

- ATTACHMENT "G"
  Operation Majestic–12 Contingency
  Plan MJ-1949-04P/78: 31 JAN '49.
  (TS-MAJIC/EO)

- ATTACHMENT "H"
  Operation Majestic–12, Maps and
  Photographs Folio (Extractions).
  (TS-MAJIC/EO)

September 24, 1947.

MEMORANDUM FOR THE SECRETARY OF DEFENSE

Dear Secretary Forrestal:

As per our recent conversation on this matter, you are hereby authorized to proceed with all due speed and caution upon your undertaking. Hereafter this matter shall be referred to only as Operation Majestic Twelve.

   It continues to be my feeling that any future considerations relative to the ultimate disposition of this matter should rest solely with the Office of the President following appropriate discussions with yourself, Dr Bush and the Director of Central Intelligence.

   (SIGNED) Harry Truman

MARIJUANA

When Betsy Ross made the first "Old Glory" flag she fashioned it from hemp. When Jefferson wrote the draft of the Declaration of Independence he penned it on hemp paper. For more than a century, 90 per cent of US ships had their sails and ropes made from hemp ("canvas" being the Dutch for cannabis). Henry Ford made the bodywork of his first Model Ts from hemp, which he grew extensively. In 18th-century America, hemp was such a staple crop that in Virginia it was illegal *not* to grow it.

So why in 1937 was hemp production banned in the US? The answer lies in the soil. Billionaire industrialist and newspaper owner William Randolph Hearst (the model for Citizen Kane) owned extensive forests, the lumber from which was used for paper production. Hemp threatened Hearst's lumber profits, so he began a yellow journalistic campaign against the stuff, rebranding it with the Mexican slang name "marijuana" and portraying it as a dangerous drug which caused violence and immorality.

Hearst's disinformation campaign was supported by Andrew Mellon, President Hoover's Secretary of State, who also had a vested interest in halting hemp production: Mellon was a principal shareholder in Dupont, which patented the production of plastic from oil and coal, and also in the chemical used to break down wood pulp into paper. Since it was possible to make both plastic-like materials and paper from hemp, Dupont's

patents were potentially worthless if hemp production continued. Mellon appointed Henry Anslinger, his future son-in-law,
as head of the Federal Bureau of Narcotics and Dangerous
Drugs and the propaganda war against lax, immoral "marijuana" stepped up, reaching its climax in the film *Reefer
Madness*. On 14 April 1937, the Marijuana Tax Law, which
outlawed hemp, was directly brought to the House Ways and
Means Committee. This committee is the only one that can
introduce a bill to the House floor without it being debated by
other committees. The Chairman of the Ways and Means
Committee, Robert Doughton, was a Dupont supporter. The
bill became law.

The American Medical Association was dumbfounded, not
having realized that the "marijuana" of the propaganda campaign was the hemp from which many of their drugs derived.
(Hemp derivatives were the second most commonly prescribed
drugs in America in the early 20th century.) In 1941 hemp/
marijuana was dropped from the US *Pharmacopoeia* because the
1937 Marijuana Tax Act made it too difficult for physicians to
prescribe.

Save for a short period during the Second World War (when
the State Department urged farmers to plant "Hemp for Victory!"), hemp production has continued to be outlawed in the
US. No other major industrialized country has such legislation.
Despite hemp's potential as a bio-fuel – Henry Ford and
Rudolph Diesel both intended to run cars on the crop – there
is little likelihood of a change of heart by US government over
hemp production, since another loud voice has joined the
chorus of nay-sayers: the pharmaceutical industry. In an interview with Jana Ray of *Nexus* magazine, Professor Lester Grinspoon of Harvard Medical School was asked: "Do you think
pharmaceutical drug companies have anything to do with the
government's prohibitive stand against medicinal cannabis
use?" He replied:

Absolutely. The Partnership for a Drug Free America has a
budget of about a million dollars a day. A lot of that money

comes from drug companies and distilleries. You see, these companies and distilleries have something to lose – the distilleries for obvious reasons. The drug companies are not interested in marijuana as a medicine because the plant cannot be patented. If you can't patent it, you can't make money on it. Their only interest is a negative one. It will eventually displace some of their pharmaceutical products.

Imagine a patient who requires cancer chemotherapy. Now he can take the best of the anti-nausea drugs, which would be ondansetron. He would pay about US$35 or $40 per 8-milligram pill and would then take three or four of them for a treatment. Normally, he would take it orally, but people with that kind of nausea often can't, so he would take it intravenously. The cost of one treatment for that begins at US$600 because he will need a hospital bed, etc. Or he can smoke perhaps half of a marijuana cigarette and receive relief from the nausea.

Currently, marijuana on the streets is very expensive. One can pay from US$200 to $600 an ounce. This is what I call the prohibition tariff. When marijuana is available as a medicine, the cost would be significantly less than other medications; it would cost about US$20 to $30 an ounce. You can't tax it in the US because it is a medicine. So that would translate out to maybe about 30 cents for a marijuana cigarette.

So our chemotherapy patient could get, many people believe, better relief from the marijuana cigarette for 30 cents. This, in comparison to the ondansetron which would cost at the very least US$160 a day and, if he had to take it intravenously, more than US$600 per treatment.

Is your neighbourhood dopehead right, man, and a conspiracy exists against marijuana?: ALERT LEVEL 9

Further Reading
Lester Grinspoon and James B. Bakalar, *Marihuana: The Forbidden Medicine*, 1993
Jack Herer, *The Emperor Wears No Clothes: Hemp and the Marijuana Conspiracy*, 1998
Jana Ray, "Marijuana – A Medicinal Marvel", *Nexus*, vol. 3, No. 5, August–September 1996, http://nexusmagazine.com/

CHRISTOPHER MARLOWE

Elizabethan dramatist Christopher "Kit" Marlowe bequeathed the world a legacy of seven plays, sheaves of poems, a reputation for fast living . . . and mysteries galore. These begin where Marlowe's own life ended, on 30 May 1593, when he was killed in a brawl over the "recknynge" (bill) in Widow Bull's house in Deptford. Broadly, Marlowe is the centre of three conspiracy theories.

- Marlowe wasn't murdered, but faked his own death so as to escape the various charges hanging over his head. If he didn't die on 30 May 1593, what did he do next?
- Marlowe, an ex-spy, was killed to stop him talking.
- Marlowe survived 1593 and became Shakespeare. (Some people think he also became Miguel Cervantes, the author of *Don Quixote*, or at the very least translated that novel into English, and that he also found time to be all 47 translators of the King James Bible.)

Kit Marlowe, even by the louche standards of the Elizabethan theatre, was a rake and a radical. He was homosexual, atheistic and a member of the free-thinking "School of Night", patronized by Walter Raleigh. At the time of his death he was on bail from the Star Chamber, where a sometime colleague in espionage, Richard Baines, had testified that the playwright had once stated "that all they that loue not Tobacco & Boies were fooles". Marlowe looked set to have his tongue cut out. Or be hanged.

However, he had friends in high places – friends with the influence and the motive to make the playwright disappear before the Star Chamber hearing.

Ingram Frizer, Nicholas Skeres and Robert Poley, the men who shared Marlowe's last afternoon, were all linked to Sir Francis Walsingham, Elizabeth I's spy chief, for whom Marlowe had also worked in espionage. Walsingham appears to have saved Marlowe's head once before, when the playwright/spy was caught counterfeiting money in Holland, a capital offence. A charge of atheism and sodomy may have been too big for Walsingham to have removed from the charge sheet at the Star Chamber, but he certainly had the men and the know-how to fake a homicide. And a disappearance. Widow Bull's house was right on the Thames, ideal for a quick exit to the Continent. The matter of a corpse to substitute for Marlowe's was easy; there had been several recent executions in the Deptford area that could provide suitable candidates for the coroner's report. John Penry, a non-conformist Puritan preacher aged 30, one year older than Marlowe, is the favourite. Penry was executed a couple of miles from Deptford on the evening before Marlowe's death, and there is no known record of what happened to his body.

Arguably, the strongest evidence that Marlowe was "disappeared" rather than dispatched is the lenient treatment accorded the man who stabbed him in the eye, Ingram Frizer. He was pardoned by Queen Elizabeth a month after the allegedly fatal incident.

On the other hand, M. J. Trow in *Who Killed Kit Marlow?* (1992) suggests that the leniency extended to Frizer is proof that he *did* murder Marlowe – but on the orders of Lord Burghley, another of Elizabeth's spymasters, who feared that loose-cannon Marlowe might spill embarrassing beans at his trial. A similarly plausible argument, that the Earl of Essex arranged Marlowe's murder to clear the way to slandering Walter Raleigh, is deployed in Charles Nicholl's *The*

Reckoning. This turned Samuel Tannenbaum's 1926 classic *The Assassination of Christopher Marlowe* on its head, for Tannenbaum identified Raleigh as the organizer of the plot to kill Marlowe.

Those who hold that Marlowe survived his many enemies on 30 May 1593 generally propose that he then went into exile, first in France, later in Spain and maybe Italy. Naturally a writer as talented as Marlowe needed to carry on writing but, because of his new circumstances, he was obliged to adopt a *nom de plume*. It is at this juncture that the Marlowe conspiracy shades over into a Shakespearean one.

To those outside the ivory tower of Eng. Lit. academia, it may seem fantastic that the identity of the Bard, the world's greatest playwright, is in doubt. There is no question that a theatrical impresario called William Shakespeare lived and died in Strat-ford-upon-Avon, but a number of scholars find it impossible to believe that he authored the plays attributed to him. How could a man with only a provincial grammar school education have written plays and poems which were rich in Latin and Greek? Many of the Classics that "Shakespeare" referenced and plagi-arized were not even translated into English in the early 17th century, and would have been available only from the libraries of Oxford and Cambridge universities or rich collectors. Oddly enough, as "Marlovians" like to point out, Marlowe's studies at Cambridge, together with the contents of his patrons' libraries and his trips abroad as a spy, were exactly the training "Shakespeare" needed. Thus, the third Marlowe Conspiracy Theory suggests that Marlowe, living in exile and anonymity, continued to produce plays and poetry – but under the name William Shakespeare.

The strongest evidence that Marlowe was Shakespeare is timing. Shakespeare seems to have written nothing before 1593, the year of Marlowe's death. The first work attributed to Shakespeare was the epic poem *Venus and Adonis*, registered in the Stationers Register on 12 June 1593 (two weeks after the incident at Widow Bull's house). This was published with a dedication to Lord Burghley's ward, the Earl of Southampton, which included two lines from a verse by Ovid that Marlowe had translated some years earlier.

After the registration of *Venus and Adonis*, Shakespeare does not trouble the records again until he is paid for performances at Court in 1594; not until 1598 is there mention of him as a playwright. In that year he is cited as the author of 12 plays, emerging almost miraculously fully fledged as a great as well as a prolific dramatist. Since Marlowe's handwriting would have been familiar to London printers, it would have been necessary to have his scripts copied by someone else before sending them off to print; in this context, the unexplained bequest to a copyist from Marlowe's friend Thomas Walsingham becomes an interesting piece of circumstantial evidence in the "Marlowe is Shakespeare" debate.

There are those who suggest not only that Marlowe survived the Deptford incident to pen the plays of Shakespeare, but that during his European exile he translated the Spanish masterpiece *Don Quixote* into English.

Don Quixote was published in Madrid in 1604. By coincidence there is evidence from diplomatic records that an Englishman by the name of Christopher Marlowe was in Spain between 1599 and 1603. The first – and arguably the finest – English translation of the book was published in 1612, and attributed to one Thomas Shelton, who is reputed to have been the ever-present Thomas Walsingham's brother-in-law. Marlovians, however, speculate that the spectral Shelton, who seems to have authored nothing else in his life, was the *nom de plume* of Marlowe and used by him to disguise his brilliant translation of *Don Quixote* . . . or even his authorship of that novel!

In July 2002 the memorial plaque to Marlowe in Westminster Abbey's Poets' Corner was unveiled. Next to Marlowe's date of death is a question mark, setting in stone the mystery of Christopher Marlowe.

Christopher Marlowe was murdered by Elizabeth I's government to prevent him talking: ALERT LEVEL 4

Christopher Marlowe's death in 1593 was faked and he became Shakespeare: ALERT LEVEL 5

Further Reading
M. J. Trow, *Who Killed Kit Marlowe?*, 1992
Samuel Tannenbaum, *The Assassination of Christopher Marlowe*, 1926
Charles Nicholl, *The Reckoning: The Murder of Christopher Marlowe*, 1992

ROBERT MAXWELL

The corpse of British publishing magnate Robert Maxwell was found floating near his yacht *Lady Ghislaine* off the Canary Islands on 5 November 1991. An investigation by Spanish authorities concluded that the overweight Maxwell had died of a heart attack.

His family accepted the findings. Many did not. Maxwell had no history of heart disease. The interest of conspiracists became particularly engaged when a forensic scientist disclosed that a perforation behind Maxwell's left ear might have been caused by a needle. Speculation that Maxwell was murdered intensified when it became clear he had been evasive about his background: born in Czechoslovakia in 1923, he had escaped from the clutches of the Nazis in circumstances never adequately explained. From this conspiracists hypothesized that Maxwell was smuggled through Nazi-allied Croatia by Communist partisans and in return agreed to serve in the Russian NKVD (later KGB). The NKVD dispatched Maxwell to Britain as a refugee, where he exceeded all their hopes of infiltration by first serving in the Army, then setting up a publishing empire, and then securing election as a Labour MP. To ease Maxwell's climb up the greasy pole of the printing/publishing industry, the NKVD brokered deals between Maxwell's Pergamon Press and Eastern Bloc publishers.

Alas, the mighty fall. The Israeli secret service, Mossad, apparently discovered Maxwell's identity as a Soviet spy while interrogating a KGB archivist. This was a bitter blow to Mossad – they'd thought Maxwell was working for *them*. In revenge, Mossad dispatched an underwater assassination team to terminally spoil Maxwell's yachting holiday. Or so the story goes.

Mossad are the bugaboos of the conspiracy world. If the **Freemasons** didn't do it, Mossad did. They *are* effective, as ex-Nazi Adolf Eichmann found to his cost when they kidnapped him from South America and put him on trial for war crimes, but those who accuse them of every other conspiracy going often trail the odour of anti-Semitism.

A more plausible killer of Robert Maxwell is Maxwell himself. His vast business empire was starting to unravel. He had defrauded his own company pension fund, a happenstance about to come to public light. (Maxwell's sons were later convicted of the crime.) What simpler way to escape the tightening noose of scandal and justice than by slipping under the gentle waters of the Canaries?

A footnote: Maxwell's family had a financial interest in agreeing with the Spanish verdict on Robert Maxwell's death. He was insured for $35.8 million against accidental death. For suicide the payout would have been nil.

> Tycoon and Soviet agent Robert Maxwell was assassinated by Mossad: ALERT LEVEL 5

Further Reading
Tom Bower, *Maxwell: The Final Verdict,* 1996

MEN IN BLACK

Men in Black (MIBs) are mysterious figures who seek to conceal UFO evidence. Generally, they appear at a witness's home after a sighting or an abduction, remove any physical evidence, and threaten the witness into silence.

Early reports of MIBs suggested they were US government agents, but in 1952 Albert Bender, the Connecticut labourer who founded the grandiosely titled International Flying Saucer Bureau (an organization that consisted of little more than himself and a decrepit duplicating machine), was visited by some. "All of them were dressed in black clothes. They looked like clergymen, but wore hats similar to homburg style . . . Feelings of fear left me. The eyes of all three figures suddenly lit up like flashlight bulbs, and all these were focused on me . . . It was then I sensed that they were conveying a message to me by telepathy."

Bender was convinced the MIBs were aliens; certainly he heeded their message, and closed down his organization, telling only a few trusted confidants about the visit. One confidant, Gray Barker, went on to write a definitive book on the MIB phenomenon, *They Knew Too Much About Flying Saucers* (1956) as well as present an expanded version of Bender's own account, *Flying Saucers and the Three Men* (1962). In the latter book, Barker reported that Bender had been taken by aliens to a secret UFO base in Antarctica and that the MIBs sought to extract a special element from Earth's oceans. Many found Bender's claims unbelievable, but still the reports of encounters with alien MIBs proliferated.

Typically, the MIBs travel in threes, often in a black Lincoln or Cadillac car, display little or no facial expressions, and speak with a mechanical tone. A male MIB who in 1976 visited Dr Herbert Hopkins, a Maine hypnotherapist investigating alien abductions, wore lipstick and was hairless. At the end of the visit, the MIB slurred, "My energy is running low . . . must go now," and staggered to the door. Hopkins described himself as being in a trance-like state during the visit, as do others visited by MIBs, leading some observers to propose that MIBs are a figment of the imagination. Or that the visited have hysterically exaggerated an encounter with a real (human) government agent. According to UFOlogist William L. Moore, MIBs are, in the US at least, "really government people in disguise" and work for a branch of Air Intelligence known as Air Force Special Activities Center. In Britain MIBs have been traced to the Special Investigation Section of the RAF's Provost and Security Services, after documents relating to a UFO sighting by a 16-year-old schoolgirl, Anne Henson, surfaced in the Public Records Office in Kew. The documents, prepared by Sergeant S. W. Scott of the Special Investigation Section, detail visits made by officers of that department to Henson in 1962.

Government agents interview and intimidate UFO witnesses:
ALERT LEVEL 9

Further Reading

Gray Barker, *They Knew Too Much About Flying Saucers*, 1956

Albert K. Bender and Gray Barker, *Flying Saucers and the Three Men*, 1962

Peter Brookesmith, *UFO: The Complete Sightings Catalogue*, 1997

Nick Redfern and Andy Roberts, *Strange Secrets: Real Government Files on the Unknown*, 2003

MK-ULTRA

Long before the Beatles experimented with "Lucy in the Sky with Diamonds", an unlikely group of Americans got turned on to the possibilities of LSD: the CIA. Unlike the Beatles, Timothy Leary and the counter-cultural movements of the 1960s, the CIA had no interest in using LSD to open up "the doors of perception"; the Agency wanted a "truth drug" for use in interrogations or, even better, a drug that enabled mind control.

Set up by CIA head Allen Dulles in 1953, the CIA's mind-control and -alteration project was code-named MK-ULTRA, taking its name from the CIA's spy work behind Nazi lines in the Second World War. However, there was little noble about the MK-namesake.

Led by Dr Sidney Gottlieb, MK-ULTRA involved some 150 research programmes, many of them using unsuspecting or entrapped human subjects. The notorious "Operation Midnight Climax" recruited San Francisco prostitutes, who laced their unsuspecting clients' drinks with acid so that CIA operatives could film the ensuing shenanigans from behind a two-way mirror. Some sixties hippies – as Martin Lee and Bruce Shlain record in *Acid Dreams* (1985) – believe the CIA supplied them with LSD so they would go "tripping" instead of overthrowing the state, a claim given some currency by the exposure of LSD manufacturer Ronald Stark as a CIA operative.

If anything, volunteer guinea-pigs fared worse in MK-ULTRA experiments than unknowing Joe Public; one group of volunteers was subjected to large doses of LSD for 77 consecutive days, causing many of them irreversible brain damage.

Despite an obsession with LSD, the imagination of the CIA was not limited to it. Electronic brain implants, mescaline, alcohol, psilocybin, radiation, implanted electrodes, barbiturates and amphetamines were also subjected to scrutiny as mind-control agents. Some unfortunate volunteers were strapped to a chair and drip-fed amphetamines in one arm, barbiturates in the other. Dr Gottlieb, who was said to have been the inspiration for the mad scientist in the movie *Dr Strangelove*, also locked volunteers in sensory deprivation chambers. Later Gottlieb was revealed to have the use of files generated by Nazi medical researchers at Dachau.

Undoubtedly the most grotesque of the MK-ULTRA experiments was that subcontracted to Montreal-based psychiatrist D. Ewen Cameron. This involved the "breaking down of ongoing patterns of the patient's behaviour by means of particularly insensitive electroshocks" while LSD was given simultaneously. Cameron called this process "psychic driving" and held that the mind could be repatterned after being erased. Some of Cameron's subjects received electro-convulsive therapy at 30–40 times the normal rate, this followed by weeks of LSD-induced coma in which they were played an endless loop of noise or speech.

Mind control was the unholy grail of MK-ULTRA, which at one stage consumed 6 per cent of the CIA's entire budget. The impetus behind the programme, and its forebear Project Artichoke, was the alleged success of the Communist countries in "brainwashing" US prisoners during the Korean War. Returned home, these soldiers exhibited strange behaviour and were unable to recall their movements through Manchuria. The phenomenon gave novelist Richard Condon the inspiration for his twice-filmed novel *The Manchurian Candidate* (1959), in which an American GI is, through hypnosis, programmed by

Chinese and Korean Communists to assassinate a US presidential candidate.

Whether the CIA ever succeeded in programming its own Manchurian Candidate will probably never be publicly known, although hypnotized killers are alleged to have been used in the murders of **Robert F. Kennedy, Martin Luther Ling, John Lennon** and Israeli premier Yitzchak Rabin, while **Jonestown** is frequently cited as an MK-ULTRA brainwashing factory.

Sometime in 1972 CIA director Richard Helms ordered the destruction of the bulk of the MK-ULTRA files because of a "burgeoning paper problem". Despite Helms's timely action, there was enough of a paper trail left for the *New York Times* to blow the whistle on the project in 1974. Following the Congressional Church Committee (see below) and the Rockefeller Commission, President Ford prohibited similar projects by the CIA. Compensation was paid to a number of MK-ULTRA victims and their kin.

One stone, however, was left unturned. Among those paid compensation by the US government was the family of Dr Frank Olson, who committed suicide in 1953 by jumping from the tenth floor of New York's Hotel Statler after taking LSD at the behest of Gottlieb. Olson's son, Eric, was not so easily bought off, and decided to investigate his father's death. An examination of Olson's exhumed body found marks to the skull consistent with repeated attack from behind. At this New York assistant attorney Steve Saracco took up the case and subpoenaed CIA director William Colby as a witness. Colby was found shortly afterwards floating dead in a river. Olson Jr believes his father's death was murder, not suicide, the motive being the elimination of a researcher who had become opposed to Gottlieb's gruesome experiments. Again the definitive answer lies in Richard Helms's shredder.

> The CIA experimented on human subjects to develop methods of mind control: ALERT LEVEL 10

Further Reading
Martin Lee and Bruce Shlain, *Acid Dreams*, 1985
John Marks, *The Search for the Manchurian Candidate: The CIA and Mind Control*, 1989
Gordon Thomas, *Journey into Madness: The True Story of Secret CIA Mind Control and Medical Abuse*, 1989
http://www.frankolsonproject.org

DOCUMENT: FROM THE CHURCH COMMITTEE REPORT

94TH CONGRESS, 2D SESSION SENATE REPORT NO. 94-755
FOREIGN AND MILITARY INTELLIGENCE
BOOK I
FINAL REPORT OF THE SELECT COMMITTEE TO STUDY GOVERNMENTAL OPERATION WITH RESPECT TO INTELLIGENCE ACTIVITIES

XVII. Testing and Use of Chemical and Biological Agents by the Intelligence Community

Under its mandate, the Select Committee has studied the testing and use of chemical and biological agents by intelligence agencies. Detailed descriptions of the programs conducted by intelligence agencies involving chemical and biological agents will be included in a separately published appendix to the Senate Select Committee's report. This section of the report will discuss the rationale for the programs, their monitoring and control, and what the Committee's investigation has revealed [ab]out the relationships among the intelligence agencies and about their relations with other government agencies and private institutions and individuals.

Fears that countries hostile to the United States would use chemical and biological agents against Americans or America's allies led to the development of a defensive program designed to discover techniques for American intelligence agencies to detect and counteract chemical and biological agents. The defensive orientation soon became secondary as the possible use of these agents to obtain information from, or gain control over, enemy agents became apparent.

Research and development programs to find materials which could be used to alter human behavior were initiated in the late 1940s and early 1950s. These experimental programs originally included testing of drugs involving witting human subjects, and culminated in tests using unwitting, nonvolunteer human subjects. These tests were designed to determine the potential effects of chemical or biological agents when used operationally against individuals unaware that they had received a drug.

The testing programs were considered highly sensitive by the intelligence agencies administering them. Few people, even within the agencies, knew of the programs and there is no evidence that either the executive branch or Congress were ever informed of them. The highly compartmented nature of these programs may be explained in part by an observation made by the CIA Inspector General that, "the knowledge that the Agency is engaging in unethical and illicit activities would have serious repercussions in political and diplomatic circles and would be detrimental to the accomplishment of its missions."

The research and development program, and particularly the covert testing programs, resulted in massive abridgments of the rights of American citizens, sometimes with tragic consequences. The deaths of two Americans can be attributed to these programs; other participants in the testing programs may still suffer from the residual effects. While some controlled testing of these substances might be defended, the nature of the tests, their scale, and the fact that they were continued for years after the danger of surreptitious administration of LSD to unwitting individuals was known, demonstrate a fundamental disregard for the value of human life.

The Select Committee's investigation of the testing and use of chemical and biological agents also raises serious questions about the adequacy of command and control procedures within the Central Intelligence Agency and military intelligence, and about the relationships among the intelligence agencies, other governmental agencies, and private institutions and individuals. The CIA's normal administrative controls were waived for programs involving chemical and biological agents to protect their security. According to the head of the Audit Branch of the CIA, these waivers produced "gross administrative failures." They prevented the CIA's internal review mechanisms (the Office of General Counsel, the Inspector General, and the Audit Staff) from adequately supervising the programs. In general, the waivers had the paradoxical effect of providing less restrictive administrative controls and less effective internal review for controversial and highly sensitive projects than those governing normal Agency activities.

The security of the programs was protected not only by waivers of normal administrative controls, but also by a high degree of compartmentation within the CIA. This compartmentation excluded the CIA's Medical Staff from the principal research and testing program employing chemical and biological agents.

It also may have led to agency policymakers receiving differing and inconsistent responses when they posed questions to the CIA component involved.

Jurisdictional uncertainty within the CIA was matched by jurisdictional conflict among the various intelligence agencies. A spirit of cooperation and reciprocal exchanges of information which initially characterized the programs disappeared. Military testers withheld information from the CIA, ignoring suggestions for coordination from their superiors. The CIA similarly failed to provide information to the military on the CIA's testing program. This failure to cooperate was conspicuously manifested in an attempt by the Army to conceal their overseas testing program, which included surreptitious administration of LSD, from the CIA. Learning of the Army's program, the Agency surreptitiously attempted to obtain details of it.

The decision to institute one of the Army's LSD field testing projects had been based, at least in part, on the finding that no long-term residual effects had ever resulted from the drug's administration. The CIA's failure to inform the Army of a death which resulted from the surreptitious administration of LSD to unwitting Americans, may well have resulted in the institution of an unnecessary and potentially lethal program.

The development, testing, and use of chemical and biological agents by intelligence agencies raises serious questions about the relationship between the intelligence community and foreign governments, other agencies of the Federal Government, and other institutions and individuals. The questions raised range from the legitimacy of American complicity in actions abroad which violate American and foreign laws to the possible compromise of the integrity of public and private institutions used as cover by intelligence agencies.

[. . .]

4. MKULTRA

MKULTRA was the principal CIA program involving the research and development of chemical and biological agents. It was "concerned with the research and development of chemical, biological, and radiological materials capable of employment in clandestine operations to control human behavior."

In January 1973, MKULTRA records were destroyed by Technical Services Division personnel acting on the verbal orders of Dr Sidney Gottlieb, Chief of TSD. Dr Gottlieb has testified, and former Director Helms has confirmed, that in ordering the records destroyed, Dr Gottlieb was carrying out the verbal order of then DCI Helms.

MKULTRA began with a proposal from the Assistant Deputy Director for Plans, Richard Helms, to the DCI, outlining a special funding mechanism for highly sensitive CIA research and development projects that studied the use of biological and chemical materials in altering human behavior. The projects involved:

Research to develop a capability in the covert use of biological and chemical materials. This area involves production of various physiological conditions which could support present or future clandestine operations. Aside from the offensive potential, the development of a comprehensive ability in this field of covert chemical and biological warfare gives us a thorough knowledge of the enemy's theoretical potential, thus enabling us to defend ourselves against a foe who might not be as restrained in the use of these techniques as we are.

MKULTRA was approved by the DCI on 13 April 1953 along the lines proposed by ADDP Helms.

Part of the rationale for the establishment of this special funding mechanism was its extreme sensitivity. The Inspector General's survey of MKULTRA in 1963 noted the following reasons for this sensitivity:

a. Research in the manipulation of human behavior is considered by many authorities in medicine and related fields to be professionally unethical, therefore the reputations of professional participants in the MKULTRA program are on occasion in jeopardy.
b. Some MKULTRA activities raise questions of legality implicit in the original charter.
c. A final phase of the testing of MKULTRA products places the rights and interests of US citizens in jeopardy.
d. Public disclosure of some aspects of MKULTRA activity could induce serious adverse reaction in US public opinion, as well as stimulate offensive and defensive action in this field on the part of foreign intelligence services.

Over the ten-year life of the program, many "additional avenues to the control of human behavior" were designated as appropriate for investigation under the MKULTRA charter. These include radiation electroshock, various fields of psychology, psychiatry, sociology, and anthropology, graphology, harassment substances, and paramilitary devices and materials.

The research and development of materials to be used for altering human behavior consisted of three phases: first, the search for materials suitable for study; second, laboratory testing on voluntary human subjects in various types of institutions; third, the application of MKULTRA materials in normal life settings.

The search for suitable materials was conducted though standing arrangements with specialists in universities, pharmaceutical houses, hospitals, state and federal institutions, and private research organizations. The annual grants of funds to these specialists were made under ostensible research foundation auspices, thereby concealing the CIA's interest from the specialist's institution.

The next phase of the MKULTRA program involved physicians, toxicologists, and other specialists in mental, narcotics, and general hospitals, and in prisons. Utilizing the products and findings of the basic research phase, they conducted intensive tests on human subjects.

One of the first studies was conducted by the National Institute of Mental Health. This study was intended to test various drugs, including hallucinogenics, at the NIMH Addiction Research Center in Lexington, Kentucky. The "Lexington Rehabilitation Center," as it was then called, was a prison for drug addicts serving sentences for drug violations.

The test subjects were volunteer prisoners who, after taking a brief physical examination and signing a general consent form, were administered hallucinogenic drugs. As a reward for participation in the program, the addicts were provided with the drugs of their addiction.

LSD was one of the materials tested in the MKULTRA program. The final phase of LSD testing involved surreptitious administration to unwitting nonvolunteer subjects in normal life settings by undercover officers of the Bureau of Narcotics acting for the CIA.

The rationale for such testing was "that testing of materials under accepted scientific procedures fails to disclose the full pattern of reactions and attributions that may occur in operational situations."

According to the CIA, the advantage of the relationship with the Bureau was that

> test subjects could be sought and cultivated within the setting of narcotics control. Some subjects have been informers or members of suspect criminal elements from whom the [Bureau of Narcotics] has obtained results of operational value through the tests. On the other hand, the effectiveness of the substances on individuals at all social levels, high and low, native American and foreign, is of great significance and testing has been performed on a variety of individuals within these categories.

A special procedure, designated MKDELTA, was established to govern the use of MKULTRA materials abroad. Such materials were used on a number of occasions. Because MKULTRA records were destroyed, it is impossible to reconstruct the operational use of MKULTRA materials by the CIA overseas; it has been determined that the use of these materials abroad began in 1953, and possibly as early as 1950.

Drugs were used primarily as an aid to interrogations, but MKULTRA/MKDELTA materials were also used for harassment, discrediting or disabling purposes. According to an Inspector General Survey of the Technical Services Division of the CIA in 1957 – an inspection which did not discover the MKULTRA projects involving the surreptitious administration of LSD to unwitting, nonvolunteer subjects – the CIA had developed six drugs for operational use and they had been used in six different operations on a total of thirty-three subjects. By 1963 the number of operations and subjects had increased substantially.

In the spring of 1963, during a wide-ranging Inspector General survey of the Technical Services Division, a member of the Inspector General's staff, John Vance, learned about MKULTRA and about the project involving the surreptitious administration of LSD to unwitting, nonvoluntary human subjects. As a result of the discovery and the Inspector General's subsequent report, this testing was halted and much tighter administrative controls were imposed on the program. According to the CIA, the project was decreased significantly each budget year until its complete termination in the late 1960s.

MARILYN MONROE

By 1962 the career of screen goddess Marilyn Monroe was on a steep slide. *Gentlemen Prefer Blondes* and *Some Like It Hot* were behind her, while the filming of the so-so *Something's Got to Give* had been delayed and derailed by Monroe's own erratic behaviour. She had recently been divorced from her third husband, playwright Arthur Miller. She was going down into a vortex of depression, drink and barbiturates.

On 5 August 1962 Monroe was found dead by her housekeeper, Mrs Eunice Murray, from what appeared to be a massive overdose of Nembutal and chloral hydrate. The Los Angeles County Coroner's court, bearing in mind Monroe's mental health, returned a verdict of suicide.

The sad death of Marilyn Monroe might have remained lamented but uncontroversial had it not been for her fascinating choice of boyfriends in the last months of her life. One squeeze was **John F. Kennedy**, President of the United States of America. When "Jack" tired of Monroe he passed her on to his brother, **Robert F. Kennedy**, the Attorney General. Monroe also took as a bedtime companion Sam Giancana, the Mafia boss who ran Crime America Inc. while JFK ran the orthodox economy.

Giancana wiretapped her house. So did Teamsters boss **Jimmy Hoffa** and J. Edgar Hoover of the FBI. According to Hollywood private investigator Fred Otash, who carried out some of the wiretaps, the Monroe tapes "are probably the most interesting ever made – with the exception of **Watergate**". There are rumours that the tapes turned throughout the evening of Monroe's death and that what they reveal is a minute-by-minute record of Monroe's murder.

Nearly all the "Monroe was Murdered" conspiracy theories home in on JFK. According to these accounts, Monroe had fallen in love with the president and had been led to believe, or had persuaded herself, that JFK was going to leave Jackie for her. Monroe may even have become pregnant by him. When JFK dumped her she threatened to go public and "blow the lid off Washington". Any such eruption would have ended JFK's career. Needless to say, JFK needed Monroe silent. Permanently.

As did Bobby Kennedy. Sloughed off by JFK, Monroe fell into a passionate relationship with his brother, who likewise found Monroe emotionally demanding and indiscreet. Her constant calls to his office and home jeopardized both his professional and his personal life. Moreover, RFK, in some braggardly pillow talk, had illuminated Monroe about the CIA's attempts to kill Castro, leaving her in possession of state secrets which might end up being exposed in her proposed planned lid-lifting.

No one has seriously suggested that JFK took a literal hand in Monroe's demise, yet numerous witnesses place RFK at Monroe's bungalow on the eve of her death. According to James Hall, an ambulance driver, he [Hall] arrived at Monroe's house to find the star reviving from a drug coma; at this point bystanding RFK persuaded Monroe's psychiatrist, Dr Ralph Greenson, to inject the star with a lethal dose of Nembutal. This would explain one of the puzzles in Monroe's autopsy report: her stomach was devoid of tablet residue, despite the empty pill bottles around her corpse. In another version of Bobbydunnit, the Attorney General ordered the FBI to kill Monroe in order to save the Kennedys' careers; of course J. Edgar Hoover was only too pleased to do so because it gave him a stranglehold on the White House.

Joe DiMaggio, the baseball superstar who was Monroe's first husband, went to his deathbed convinced the Kennedys offed

the sex goddess with the help of the Mob, with whom they had
been in cahoots since old man Kennedy bootlegged alcohol
during Prohibition. Curiously, one of the Mob's most effective
and subtle methods of murder was a lethal enema of chloral
hydrate. Such an enema would explain the lack of pill residue in
Monroe's body; it would also explain the bruising on her body,
which was consistent with a violent struggle.

In *Double Cross* by Sam Giancana, godson of the same-
named Mafioso, a deadly enema is also the method by which
Monroe is dispatched, but here the motive was radically
different. According to Giancana, the Mob killed Monroe
to frame the Kennedys and bring about their downfall.
Listening to events in the bungalow on the evening of 4
August via Giancana's wiretaps, Mob goons heard Robert
Kennedy order that Monroe be sedated; when RFK left, the
Mob sneaked in and administered the chloral hydrate enema
to the stupefied star.

The known facts of Monroe's last evening are these. At
around 6.00 p.m. on 4 August 1962 Monroe's press agent
Pat Newcomb left the bungalow at 12,305 Fifth Helena Drive
in LA followed by Monroe's psychiatrist Greenson, who had
spent the afternoon with the movie star. At around 7.15 Monroe
took a call from DiMaggio's son Joe Jr, and half an hour later
rat-pack star Peter Lawford (who was JFK's and RFK's
brother-in-law) phoned to invite her to a party.

Thereafter, the many sources differ wildly over how and
when Monroe died. Not until 4.25 the next morning do un-
disputed facts re-enter the Monroe death story, when Sergeant
Jack Clemmons of the LAPD got a call he would never forget.
Dr Hyman Engelberg, Monroe's personal physician, informed
him she had committed suicide. When Clemmons arrived at
Helena Drive there were three people there: Greenson, Engelberg and the housekeeper, Murray. They led Clemmons into
the bedroom where Monroe's nude body was lying covered with
a sheet, and took care to point out bottles of sedatives. According to Clemmons, "She was lying face down in what I call the
soldier's position. Her face was in a pillow, her arms were by her

side, her right arm was slightly bent. Her legs were stretched out perfectly straight."

Clemmons immediately thought Monroe had been *arranged* in that "soldier's position", since an overdose of sleeping tablets usually causes victims to suffer convulsions, so their corpses are typically found in a contorted display.

The witness statements clanged with implausibility. Murray claimed that at about 3 a.m. she awoke and saw a light under Monroe's door. Finding the door locked, she contacted Greenson to alert him. In fact, the deep-pile carpeting in Monroe's bungalow would not have allowed light to seep under the bedroom door, on which there was no lock. Greenson allegedly forced entry into Monroe's bedroom at around 3.50 and pronounced her dead. The trio claimed they had waited until 4.00 before contacting police because they needed permission to do so. (This clearly contradicts Murray's statement that she had discovered Monroe's body at around 3.30.) Clemmons further noted there was no glass in the bedroom from which Monroe could have drunk to help down the pills she was supposed to have swallowed.

Despite Clemmons' observations, Coroner Curphey determined that Monroe had committed suicide – her corpse, after all, was surrounded by bottles of prescription sedatives and she did have a history of suicide attempts. Doubtless Curphey was influenced too by the opinion of Greenson. A number of major forensic experts have argued, however, that there were no traces of Nembutal in Monroe's intestinal tract or stomach and therefore she cannot have swallowed the barbiturates as tablets. Neither could she have injected herself with the overdose of barbiturates, since the injection of such a high dosage would have caused immediate death with evident bruising around the injection site – yet there were no needle marks or relevant bruises on her body. This leaves one possible explanation: that the OD was administered by an enema. Since a self-administered enema is a near-impossibility, Monroe did not commit suicide. She either died accidentally or was murdered.

So what did happen during the "missing hours" of Monroe's last day? According to the author Donald H. Wolfe, Murray's son-in-law Norman Jeffries was at Monroe's bungalow on the fatal night. At around 9.30 p.m., Robert Kennedy and two unknown men came to Monroe's door and ordered Murray and Jeffries to leave. (This timing dovetails with the recollection of Jose Bolanas that his phone call to Monroe at around 9.30 was broken off because of people arriving at the door. A neighbour of Monroe's, Elizabeth Pollard, confirmed that Bobby Kennedy arrived at the bungalow at around this time.) When Murray and Jeffries returned to the bungalow at 10.30, Jeffries says that he saw Monroe face down, naked, and holding a phone. Murray then called an ambulance and Dr Greenson. Jeffries's story is corroborated by the chief of the local ambulance company, who is on record as saying that Monroe's body was collected and taken to Santa Monica hospital, but then returned to Helena Drive. Sometime before midnight, Pat Newcomb and Peter Lawford turned up at the bungalow in high panic. They phoned Bobby Kennedy. Soon afterwards Monroe's personal journals and telephone records were apparently taken.

Did the Kennedy brothers have evidence of their affairs with Monroe removed? It would be astounding if they didn't. Did Bobby Kennedy murder Marilyn Monroe? It would be astounding if he did. Given Bobby Kennedy's personal moral compass, his position as Attorney General, his crusading against organized crime, he makes an unlikely hands-on killer.

In his re-creation of the evening of 4 August 1962, Monroe's biographer Donald Spoto makes a convincing case that the movie star's death was neither suicide nor murder but an accident. To aid Monroe sleep that night, Greenson arranged with Murray that the latter would give Monroe an enema of chloral hydrate; Greenson was, however, unaware that Monroe's physician Hyman Engelberg had supplied her with Nembutal. Monroe and Murray had no idea that Nembutal and chloral hydrate reacted adversely with each other. At around 9.30 Monroe began slipping into a coma. Bobby Kennedy arrived to find Monroe in a drugged stupor and called an ambulance, but when Monroe died en route to hospital he realized the public relations fallout of arriving at the hospital with an overdosed sex goddess could be lethal. He thus ordered the ambulance to return to Helena Drive, where Monroe's body was laid out and incriminating documents removed. Greenson, Engelberg and Murray all had a reason to acquiesce in the cover-up because they had killed – albeit unwittingly – Marilyn Monroe, movie star. Their careers, like those of the Kennedys, would have been ruined had the truth become known.

> Bobby Kennedy murdered Marilyn Monroe: ALERT LEVEL 4

Further Reading
Robert Slatzer, *The Marilyn Files*, 1991
Donald Spoto, *Marilyn Monroe: The Biography*, 1993
Anthony Summers, *Goddess: The Secret Lives of Marilyn Monroe*, 1986
Donald H. Wolfe, *The Last Days of Marilyn Monroe*, 1998

MONTAUK POINT

The conspiracy theories that surround Montauk Point, New York, call into doubt the whole existence of reality, truth and the universe as you have come to know it!

Montauk Point lies at the top end of Long Island, New York State, and is sometime home of Camp Hero, a USAF Radar Station. The camp was commissioned by the US Army in 1942 to defend New York in the event of an invasion. Designed to look vaguely like a fishing village, it consisted of a group of fairly innocent buildings flanked by two large concrete bunkers, half submerged beneath topsoil, which housed four 16-inch naval guns. As it turned out, the guns were never needed and, in the 1950s, the camp housed a joint Army and Air Force radar surveillance unit, the US Army leaving in 1957 and turning the base over entirely to the Air Force. Five years later a five-storey cubical tower was commissioned, housing a gigantic 75-foot (23m) radar dish, and the base operated as a coastal defence warning system until the end of the 1970s. It finally ceased operating in 1981.

That's the official story. The authors of *The Montauk Project: Experiments in Time* (1992), Preston Nichols and Peter Moon, have a very different version to tell. It all began, they claim, in 1943, when the US Navy and other government groups conducted experiments into possible secret weapons that could help the Allies win the Second World War. One of these experiments focused on achieving radar invisibility through the manipulation of electromagnetic waves (the forerunner of to-day's stealth technology). Small-scale tests were carried out on the destroyer USS *Eldridge*, first with animals aboard and then, reputedly, with the crew. Huge generators were installed in the forward turrets to create an electromagnetic bottle around the ship (see **Philadelphia Experiment**). The sailors returned from a four-hour period of invisibility exhibiting not only physical but also mental distress.

One particular group of scientists became interested in the latter effects, noting that the human mind, once in the hyper-space created by the electromagnetic field, no longer had any terms of reference in the "real" world and was easily broken. The group, allegedly affiliated to MIT and the Brookhaven National Laboratories, took its findings to Congress, seeking further funding, but was rejected – no doubt on ethical grounds.

Unwilling to give up what seemed like such a fascinating discovery, the group apparently approached the top brass of the US military claiming it had the means to make a potential enemy surrender without a shot being fired. Seduced by the thought of such a powerful weapon, the Army agreed to fund further research on a strictly hush-hush basis, and looked for somewhere suitably covert to carry out the work. Bingo! What better than a low-key coastal defence station near a sleepy little town, full of sleepy inhabitants?

Camp Hero had the SAGE Radar system installed, vital for the scientists' experiments. Psychically sensitive subjects were recruited and trained to focus their minds on particular objects; their powers were then hugely magnified by the radar system's emitting gigawatts of electromagnetic force at them, and their thoughts manipulated by their controllers to discover the effects.

One particularly able subject was a certain Duncan Cameron who, it was claimed, could make the distant objects upon which he focused his thoughts actually materialize at some location on the base. The scientists realized this materialization happened *after* his focusing, and concluded that not only matter but also time was being manipulated. Seeing the opportunity for more than just a little diverting mind control, the resident technicians got on the case and constructed a functioning portal through time using the power of the radar and the mental ability of the psychics.

Help came also from a rather unexpected source, in the shape of aliens from the Sirius star system whose ship was sucked into the time tunnel. Finding themselves at Montauk, the aliens supposedly helped develope the "Montauk Chair", in which Cameron sat during experiments, which helped hone his power and incorporated "orgone energy" (a concept dreamed up by Wilhelm Reich, onetime student of Sigmund Freud; Reich believed the power that fuelled the universe came from the sex drive).

As the complexity of operations increased, the base expanded beneath the ground, layer under layer, spreading as far as downtown Montauk itself. During the 1970s this labyrinth reputedly housed even more sinister and dubious experiments. Thousands of young boys were abducted, some say by aliens, and delivered to Montauk. Subjected to extreme physical and mental torture (an extension, it is claimed, of the CIA's **MK-ULTRA** project), their minds were broken and then reprogrammed. Some became willing participants in further experiments; others were designated as sleeper agents and returned to their communities, awaiting activation in the future. The Montauk Boys, as they became known, were supposed to exhibit typical Aryan characteristics – blue eyes, blond hair – and were selected for grooming as future leaders who would bring about the **New World Order**.

Where this particular conspiracy theory leaps from the level of merely bizarre into the realms of mindbogglingly weird is in August 1983. At this point the Montauk Project became horribly entangled, through means of the time portal, with the USS *Eldridge* at the moment of its disappearance in a hyperspatial impasse. Back in Camp Hero, a splinter group had already taken the decision to crash the project by some means or other. The plan they came up with (after far too many nights watching the

wrong kind of films, one imagines) was to subliminally introduce the idea of a monster to Cameron during his thought-into-
matter sessions. In a scene worthy of the best of *Star Trek*, a
Bigfoot-like creature ran amok on the base while other technicians battled to terminate the Rainbow Project, responsible for
the disappearance of the USS *Eldridge*, from 40 years away and
so disentangle the Montauk Project, presumably before the ship
itself materialized inside the base. Someone, somewhere must
have pressed the right switch, because eventually the time
tunnel collapsed, the USS *Eldridge* found itself back in the
Philadelphia Naval Yard, and the Bigfoot disappeared. The
whole Montauk Project was subsequently abandoned, its subjects brainwashed or sworn to oaths of silence and returned to
normality and the base closed.

Since then the US government has donated Camp Hero to
New York State as a public park, but the inner base containing
all the buildings remains off-limits. Unsurprisingly, the place
still holds a fascination for those intrigued by the stories of the
Montauk Project, and many people visit the area hoping for a
glimpse of the underground caverns. However, Jonathan Kostecky and Sean Rubinstein, in their article posted on www.geo-
cities.com, are quick to dispel the whole myth. Photographs of
their visit to the inner base reveal rotting and vandalized
buildings, with no evidence to suggest these buildings were
used for anything other than as a radar surveillance unit. Talk of
an underground city is impossible, they say, because geological
surveys show the area on which the camp is built to be made up
of unconsolidated sand and gravel with jointed limestone: any
tunnels would cave in or be flooded.

Of the continuing presence of State Park Police patrols on the
site, Kostecky and Rubinstein say the officers are required to
keep people from injuring themselves in buildings which are
nearing collapse. However, the two authors are at a loss to
explain why, in the building dubbed "The Acid House",
individual rooms are wallpapered in gold paisley patterns,
vertical black and white stripes, leopard print and aquamarine
psychedelic – surely out of the ordinary for a coastal defence

station? Neither can Kostecky and Rubinstein give a good reason why electricity still runs through the high-voltage power lines to an abandoned and derelict base.

The known survivors of the project who have been willing to speak of their experiences, including Preston Nichols and Al Bielek, have all stressed that their accounts relate merely what they understood happened to them, and have come up with no further evidence of a conspiracy to cover up goings-on at Montauk. There have been reports of local wildlife going berserk, a direct result some say of being bombarded by UHF/microwave mind-bending emissions from the radar, but again no firm evidence.

Strangely enough, it is other, less direct, occurrences which unsettle the obvious dismissal of the myth of Montauk. TWA Flight 800, SwissAir 111 and EgyptAir 990 all crashed inexplicably in the sea off Montauk Point. It is also close to the scene of the light airplane crash that killed John F. Kennedy Jr, his wife and a friend. Famous occultist Aleister Crowley, who purportedly used sexual "magick" to open holes in time, stayed at Montauk for some reason just after the First World War and complained of mysterious blisters he acquired while there that refused to heal for several years. The real owners of the site, the Montauk tribe, deemed to be extinct by the US government even though they have campaigned for their land to be returned to them, believe the place is sacred and hold a tribal memory of a stone pyramid that once existed there.

If stories of time travel, mind-control and Bigfoot seem too far-fetched for even the most hardened conspiracy theorist, it may be more plausible to consider that the secret to Montauk may lie not in what was done there but in the energy of the place itself which, perhaps, exerts a power over the people and objects which enter its sphere of influence.

No wonder conspiracy theorists themselves dub this one TBTB – "Too Big To be Believed".

> Montauk Project developed means of mind control and
> time travel: ALERT LEVEL 2

Further Reading
Preston Nichols and Peter Moon, *The Montauk Project:
Experiments in Time*, 1992

MOON LANDING HOAX

"That's one small step for man, one giant leap for mankind," said Neil Armstrong on 20 July 1969, as he stepped down from the lunar landing module on to the face of the moon and proudly planted a fluttering Stars and Stripes.

Except Armstrong wasn't really on the moon. He was in a lunar mock-up in the Nevada desert at **Area 51**. Despite being bunged $30 billion by **John F. Kennedy**, NASA had failed to achieve a viable moon landing project, so decided upon a hoax one. How could the flag flutter when there is no wind on the moon?

Rumours that *Apollo 11* didn't truly put a man on the moon were widespread by 1970, and are archly acknowledged in the 1971 Bond film *Diamonds are Forever* when 007 crashes through a staged lunar scene in the desert. However, the "*Apollo* Moon Landing Hoax" industry really hit its stride in 1976 with the publication of the book *We Never Went to the Moon: America's Thirty Billion Dollar Swindle!* by Bill Kaysing, an *Apollo* engineer and aeronautics writer. According to Kaysing, not only was the 1969 landing a fake but astronaut Gus Grissom was murdered to prevent him exposing the whole *Apollo* scam. There was more grist to the conspiracy mill with the release of the 1978 movie *Capricorn One*, which featured a faked mission to Mars. Kaysing himself repeated his claims in a 2001 TV programme called *Conspiracy Theory: Did We Land On The Moon?*, in which Gus Grissom's widow and son concurred that the launchpad fire which obliterated Grissom's *Apollo 1* mission had been deliberately staged. Bart Sibrel's 2001 movie *A Funny Thing Happened on the Way to the Moon* re-aired the hoax theory with the addendum that the faked landings were an intentional distraction from the disastrous Vietnam War.

Apollo 11, of course, did go to the moon. The billowing Stars and Stripes is explained by the simple fact that the flag was still swirling from being planted.

> The *Apollo* moon landings were an astronomical hoax:
> ALERT LEVEL 1

Further Reading
Bill Kaysing and Randy Reid, *We Never Went to the Moon: America's Thirty Billion Dollar Swindle*, 1999

WOLFGANG AMADEUS MOZART

On 14 October 1791, in his last surviving letter, the composer Mozart wrote to his wife Constanze that he had taken the Italian composer Antonio Salieri to a performance of *The Magic Flute*, and that Salieri had been laudatory: "From the overture to the last chorus there was not a single number that did not call forth from him a bravo! or bello!" Less than two months later, Mozart was dead.

Within a week of Mozart's death, there were rumours of poisoning based on the strangely swollen condition of his body. Suspicion soon focused on Salieri who, despite his loud enjoyment of *The Magic Flute*, had long been a rival of Mozart's on the Viennese music scene. Salieri was the mature Kappelmeister to the court of composers, Mozart the youthful upstart who threatened his position. Mozart had feared for some years before his death that his meteoric musical ascendancy would create a jealousy among his peers that might inspire one of them to murder him: in 1789 he had told Constanze "I am only too conscious [that] my end will not be long in coming; for sure, someone has poisoned me!" In summer 1791 Mozart claimed he had been given aqua toffana (an arsenic preparation); he also wrote to his father that "Salieri is poisoning me . . ." Only weeks before his death, Mozart tearfully told Constanze in the Prater Park, "I am sure I have been poisoned. I cannot rid myself of this idea." After Mozart's demise on 5 December 1791, Constanze regularly told anyone who would listen that

Salieri had conspired to murder her husband. And then, in his dotage, Salieri himself is said to have confessed to bringing down the baton on Mozart's life.

The rumours that Salieri assassinated Mozart were stoked by the Russian playwright Aleksandr Pushkin, who in 1830 wrote a short play called *Mozart and Salieri* in which envy drove the Kappelmeister to murder his rival. Rimksy-Korsakov turned the Pushkin piece into an opera, and the rivalrous Mozart–Salieri theme was later picked up by Peter Shaffer in his stage play *Amadeus*, which in 1984 became an award-winning movie of the same name, directed by by Milos Forman. According to Forman's twist, Salieri did not poison Mozart but caused his death by overwork, after provoking him to finish the *Requiem*.

Salieri, however, does not fit the bill of Mozart's murderer very neatly. The nurses who cared for Salieri in his dotage testified that they had never, contrary to gossip, heard Salieri confess to the deed. Salieri himself utterly refuted the suggestion, telling musician Ignaz Moscheles in 1823, "I can assure you on my word of honour that there is no truth in that absurd rumour: you know, that I was supposed to have poisoned Mozart." Neither did Salieri have a clear motive: in the 18th century it was *Salieri* who was the big noise – it was Salieri who was the Emperor Joseph II's chief musician, it was Salieri who had the wealth and reputation. Certainly, Salieri might have obstructed Mozart's career at court, but the reason was not personal resentment but professional estimation: Mozart's music was not in the Style Gallant that both Salieri and the Emperor favoured. When Mozart wrote that "Salieri is poisoning me" he meant it figuratively – that he would have to trim his style to the court taste if he wanted to get on.

Something of the close personal relations between Salieri and the Mozart family can be judged from the fact that Salieri was one of the small group of mourners who followed Mozart's coffin as it was carried from the funeral service at St Stephen's Cathedral to the cemetery. Salieri also became the teacher of Mozart's son Franz Xaver Wolfgang. Would Constanze Mozart really have entrusted her son to Salieri if she believed him her husband's murderer?

There are other candidates as Mozart's murderer. The composer was a serial womanizer and among his conquests was, allegedly, Magdalena Hofdemel, the 23-year-old wife of his Masonic brother Franz Hofdemel. On the day after Mozart's funeral, an altercation in the Hofdemel house ended with Franz brutally hacking Magdalena with a razor before slitting his own throat with the implement. Magdalena, five months pregnant, was revived and gave birth to a boy which she named Johann von Nepomuk Alexander Franz. Since she named the baby after both her husband and presumed lover (Johann was Mozart's given first name), many believed the child was Mozart's and that her cuckolded husband had poisoned the composer in revenge before committing suicide.

Inevitably, Mozart's and Hofdemel's membership of the **Freemasons** would eventually cause somebody to conjure up the theory that the composer was assassinated by the Brotherhood. The Mozart-Masonic murder theory originated in 1861 with Georg Friedrich Daumer, a researcher of antiquities and religious polemicist. His thesis was elaborated in the Third Reich period, chiefly by General Erich Ludendorff and his wife, the neuropsychiatrist Mathilde.

The case against the Freemasons takes two main lines. Daumer claimed Mozart had offended the Masons in *The Magic Flute* by his use of Christian religious music in the chorale of the Men of Armour. (For good measure, Daumer also believed the murder thwarted Mozart's desire to found his own secret lodge, "The Grotto".) Mathilde Ludendorff raised another anti-Masonic argument, suggesting the Masons were outraged at *The Magic Flute*'s covert counterplot, which depicted Mozart (as Tamino) attempting the release of Marie Antoinette (Pamina) from her Masonic jailers. Untroubled by historical reality, Frau Ludendorff suggested that Jews and Catholics – she was writing during the reign of Hitler after all – joined with the Freemasons in poisoning the Teutonic Mozart. Only marginally more sophisticated is *Mozarts Tod* ("Mozart's Death", 1971), by Drs Dalchow, Duda and Kerner, which found evidence of the Masonic conspiracy to murder Mozart in the eight allegories of Mercury on the frontispiece of the first libretto of *The Magic Flute*. Since mercury can be a poison as well as a winged messenger it is evident – to the learned doctors at least – that Mozart's life was brought to a premature end by ingestion of this toxin at the instigation of Freemasons. Why, if the Masons wanted to assassinate Mozart for his crimes against the Order, they simultaneously requested he compose a cantata for them and, after his death, published a fulsome eulogy to him is unclear.

The postulations that Mozart was assassinated, whether by Salieri or the Freemasons, fail finally on the forensic evidence. Although there was no official autopsy, Eduard Guldener von Lobes, the physician who examined the composer's corpse, found no evidence of foul play. In the numerous accounts of Mozart's symptoms pre-death, by those who attended and nursed him, there are no mentions of the conditions which would have occurred had he been poisoned by either mercury or arsenic. Mozart's handwriting on the final *Requiem* script evidenced no sign of the shakes, which commonly indicates mercury poisoning; and the tell-tale cyanosis of arsenic poisoning was absent from his body. All things considered, Mozart near certainly died of disease. Many diseases have been proposed, from rheumatic fever to uraemia, from syphilis to tuberculosis, although the deadly agent cannot have been communicable since Constanze, who crawled into her husband's bed hoping to catch his illness and perish too, would have succumbed.

In 2001 Dr Jan V. Hirschmann, an infectious disease specialist, posited an entirely new killer of Mozart – pork chops. Hirschmann noted that Mozart had written to Constanze on 7–8 October, 1791:

What do I smell? Why, here is Don Primus with the pork cutlets! *Che gusto*! Now I am eating to your health!

Improperly cooked tainted pork can harbour a parasitic burrowing worm called *Trichinella*. The typical incubation period for trichinosis is 50 days; the letter above was written 44 days before Mozart's death. The symptoms of Mozart's final illness – extreme swelling of the extremities, vomiting, fever, rashes and severe pain – are typical of trichinosis.

And no, General and Frau Ludendorff, the Jews didn't use pork chops to poison Mozart. They wouldn't have known to do so. Trichonisis was not clinically identified until 1860.

SALIERI MURDERED MOZART: ALERT LEVEL 4

Further Reading

Albert Borowitz, "Salieri and the 'Murder of Mozart' ", *Legal Studies Forum*, vol. 29, No. 2, 2001

Jan V. Hirschmann, MD, "What killed Mozart?", *Archives of Internal Medicine*, vol. 161, 2001

David Weiss, *The Assassination of Mozart*, 1970

HILDA MURRELL

In March 1984 an intruder broke into the Shropshire home of Hilda Murrell and abducted her. Her body was found three days later in a nearby wood, where she had died of hypothermia, although she had also been repeatedly stabbed. Because a little cash had been stolen from Murrell's home the police dismissed the case as a "bungled burglary". No fewer than seven books plus three police investigations and countless TV documentaries and newspaper articles have sought to show instead that Murrell was assassinated by the British state, namely MI5. For Hilda Murrell was not merely a harmless gardener; she was a prominent opponent of nuclear power and was scheduled to present her paper *An Ordinary Citizen's View of Radioactive Waste Management* at the Sizewell Inquiry. Murrell was also the aunt of Commander Robert Green RN, a staff naval intelligence officer during the 1982 Falklands War, who was suspected of having passed proof to her that Prime Minister Margaret Thatcher ordered the sinking of the Argentine ship *Belgrano* to provoke open war with Argentina.

Conspiracists are convinced that Murrell's anti-nuclear campaigning secured her state-sponsored death. Or perhaps MI5 raided her home to seize the top-secret *Belgrano* information but were discovered *in flagrante* by Murrell, necessitating her elimination (this was the favoured view of ex-Labour MP Tam Dalyell).

A two-year cold-case police reinvestigation of the Murrell case uncovered DNA evidence which linked labourer Andrew George to Murrell's killing, and in May 2005 George was found guilty of kidnapping, sexually assaulting and murdering the 78-year-old. A year later the Court of Appeal upheld the murder conviction.

Among those the police and judiciary have failed to convince is Commander Robert Green RN (Retd), who is on record as saying that George's conviction is "unsafe" and that "many unanswered questions" remain about Murrell's death.

> MI5 killed campaigner Hilda Murrell after botching robbery of her house: ALERT LEVEL 6

Further Reading
Judith Cook, *Unlawful Killing*, 1994
Graham Smith, *Death of a Rose Grower*, 1985

NAZI GOLD

In the dying days of the Second World War in Europe, there was a desperate scramble by Allied forces to fight their way into Germany. There were concentration camps to liberate, last-ditch SS fanatics to quell, regions to seize from rivals (US/UK versus the USSR), war criminals to apprehend, technological secrets to appropriate . . . and Nazi gold to grab.

Around $238 million of the Third Reich's gold reserves was sent from the Reichsbank to a mine at Merkers, 200 miles (320km) south-west of Berlin, after the Berlin Reichsbank was partially destroyed in a B-17 raid on 3 February 1945. With Berlin nearly encircled by the Red Army in early April, Reichsbank director Walter Funk removed the remaining gold reserves, together with large amounts of foreign currency, to Oberbayern in southern Bavaria, where the Nazis intended to create a redoubt. This gold was unloaded under cover of night by German Alpine troops commanded by Colonel Franz Pfeiffer, and hidden in the mountains above Lake Walchensee. Despite the last best hopes of the Nazis, neither the Merkers mine nor the Walchensee stash escaped seizure by the Allies. The mine was captured by Patton's Third Army and the Oberbayern occupied by the 10th Armoured Division. During April and May 1945 the Allies dug up the Nazi gold and placed it under military authority.

Or did they? Even by the estimates of the US Army, 2 per cent of the closing balance of the Reichsbank went missing, amounting to several million dollars (at 1945 values), and the true value of the disappeared gold was probably more. Additionally, jewellery and artworks hidden by the Nazis at Merkers were also "lost". Small wonder, then, that the *Guinness Book of Records* has called the disappearance of the Nazi gold from Merkers and Oberbayern "the largest robbery on record". Some conspiracy researchers suggest the missing gold was appropriated by the clandestine SS escape network ODESSA. Trenton Parker, an ex-Marine colonel with CIA connections, told Radio Free America on 29 July 1993 that the missing Nazi gold had been siphoned into Spain by ODESSA, where General Franco had kindly looked after it – with the help of the Third Reich's **Martin Bormann**. "I can assure you that Martin Bormann did *not* die in Berlin," Parker informed the audience. "He looked very much alive, in March of 1975, in a villa outside of Madrid, Spain, where I went to negotiate the liquidation of various tons of gold which were turned into perfect Krugerrands."

How does Parker know all this? Aside from his own meeting with Bormann, Franco's physician's sister passed the information on to *her* sister, who married one Ortega-Perez who served as a staff interpreter for General Eisenhower.

Ian Sayer, author of *Nazi Gold*, has a less convoluted explanation for the missing gold, the bulk of which was "lost" at Walchensee: it was heisted in bits by just about every GI and *soldat* who could get his hands on some of it. (Colonel Franz Pfeiffer, it is said, lived very well after the war in Argentina.) According to Sayer, the US government turned a blind eye to thefts by its own soldiers since it did not want to antagonize them or admit the crimes to the international public.

The Third Reich had a lot of gold aside from that stored in the vaults of the Berlin Reichsbank, however. The story of this further missing Nazi gold is yet more sordid still.

In 1997 the US Department of Commerce published "US and Allied Efforts to Recover and Restore Gold and other Assets Stolen or Hidden by Germany during WWII", a document more generally called the Eizenstat Report after its director, Undersecretary of Commerce Stuart E. Eizenstat. The report was harshly critical of Switzerland's wartime dealings with the Third Reich, saying that "in the unique circumstances of World War II neutrality collided with morality". Not to put too polite a point on it, the Swiss Bank for International Settlements and National Bank had laundered gold bullion from Nazi Germany, enabling the Third Reich to secure trade goods from other countries. Swiss banks, Eizenstat's report concluded, still clung obstinately to around $20 billion of Nazi gold deposits looted from the banks of occupied Europe and the victims of the Holocaust.

In response, the seven-page "Declaration of the Swiss Federal Council" asserted that the conclusions of the Eizenstat report were "unsupported" and its assessments "one-sided". The holier-than-thou demeanour of the "Gnomes of Zurich", however, was dented by the Swiss government's admission in 1998 that the national bank had not bothered to enquire until late in the war (that is, when the Allies were clearly winning) whether the gold paid in by the Nazis was from Holocaust victims – and much of it was, having been melted down from jewellery, gold coins and even dental fillings seized from Jewish victims. Faced with Eizenstat's report, class actions by US-based Holocaust survivors and the US government's threat to freeze Swiss assets, the Swiss government suddenly found $5 billion annually to compensate the victims of the Holocaust and other human tragedies.

Following the declassification of a 1946 US Army document, representatives of Holocaust victims also brought, in 2000, a civil action against the Vatican, alleging that it too held Nazi-era loot. The declassified document was an intelligence memo from treasury agent Emerson Bigelow asserting that, at the time of the collapse of Ustasha, the Nazi puppet state in Croatia, 200 million Swiss francs, together with gold looted from Serbs, gypsies and Jews, was lodged in the Vatican "for safekeeping", with the connivance of the Roman Catholic clergy and the Franciscan Order. Holocaust researchers further accused the Vatican of using this Nazi loot to set up "gold lines" to smuggle Nazi and SS officials to South America.

The Vatican strenuously denied handling the Nazis' stolen gold, and opened its Second World War archive to historians. There is no doubt that one pro-Nazi office of the Vatican, the German College of Santa Maria dell'Anima under Bishop Alois Hudal, was running a ratline for SS war criminals (including SS commando Otto Skorzeny), but whether this was funded by stolen gold held in the Vatican Bank is unclear.

The Vatican is a frequent target for conspiracy theories – not without cause, as the Roberto **Calvi** case proves – but during the Nazi era it tended to side with the angels. Any reckoning of the Vatican has to weigh in the 700,000 Jews Pope Pius XII saved from the Holocaust by providing them with sanctuary and false baptismal certificates.

US authorities turned a blind eye to $3 million stolen by its own troops in the "greatest robbery on record": ALERT LEVEL 9

Vatican Bank handled stolen Nazi gold: ALERT LEVEL 5

Further Reading
Kenneth Alford and T. P. Savas, *Nazi Millionaires: The Allied Search for Hidden SS Gold*, 2002
Ian Sayer and Douglas Botting, *Nazi Gold: The Story of the World's Greatest Robbery – and Its Aftermath*, 1984

NAZI MOON BASE

Towards the end of the Second World War, Allied airmen in Europe were astonished to encounter strange craft that flew at speeds far in advance of their propeller-driven planes. The high-speed craft turned out to be the Nazis' jet-engined Me262 fighter or, on rare occasions, the Me163 rocket plane. With the subsequent Allied takeover of Germany's military research facilities, the superiority of Nazi aeronautics and rocketry was confirmed. But was Nazi science sufficiently far advanced to have sent men to the moon?

Precisely where the idea came from that the Nazis had mounted a moon mission is unclear, but in 1993 the president of the American Academy of Dissident Sciences, Vladimir Terziski, published an article entitled "Half a Century of the German Moon Base". According to Terziski:

The Germans landed on the Moon as early as probably 1942, utilizing their larger exoatmospheric rocket saucers of the Miethe and Schriever type. The Miethe rocket craft was built in diameters of 15 and 50 meters [49ft and 164ft], and the Schriever Walter turbine-powered craft was designed as an interplanetary exploration vehicle. It had a diameter of 60 meters [197ft], had 10 stories of crew compartments, and stood 45 meters [148ft] high. Welcome to Alice in Saucerland. In my extensive research of dissident American theories about the physical conditions on the Moon I have proved beyond the shadow of a doubt that there is atmosphere, water and vegetation on the Moon, and that man does not need a space suit to walk on the Moon. A pair of jeans, a pullover and sneakers are just about enough.

According to Terziski, members of the occult pan-German Vril and Thule societies made contact with aliens during the inter-war period and were able to pass on alien technology to the Nazis, notably the SS Military Technical Branch E-IV. Aside from landing on the moon, the Nazis bored under the surface to create a lunar station, staffed by some 40,000 people, which in the 1950s was used by both the Russians and the Americans.

Oh, and the Nazis managed to reach Mars too. On earth, despite their defeat in the war, the Nazis continued space exploration from a secret underground base in New Swabia (Antarctica), where Hitler resided after his escape from the Berlin bunker.

There is no way of proving that aliens cooperated with the Third Reich in aviation design and technology, and the supersonic speeds of Luftwaffe aircraft can be explained in entirely mundane terms. By the Treaty of Versailles which ended the First World War, Germany was forbidden to build aircraft for military use. Frustrated aeronautical designers such as Reimar and Walter Horten turned instead to improving aerodynamics and wing-design in sporting gliders, perfecting both delta and disc wings. When Germany rearmed under Hitler, these gains in aviation technology were fed directly into the warplane industry. The apex of Nazi aeronautics, the Me163, was delta-winged.

The Nazis sent a successful mission to the moon: ALERT LEVEL 1

Further Reading
Vladimir Terziski, "Half a Century of the German Moon Base", http://greyfalcon.us/restored/ German%20Moon%20Base%20Alpha.htm

NEW WORLD ORDER

During the Persian Gulf War, US President George H. W. Bush sent right-wing conspiracists into paroxysms of excitement when, in a September 1990 speech to Congress, he announced: "Out of these troubled times . . . a new world order – can emerge."

Here finally the fears of the John Birch Society were confirmed: George Bush was bent on the introduction of a one-world government controlled by a small cabal of capitalists. To rub the noses of the Birch boys in the dirt, Poppy Bush just kept on repeating the NWO phrase at every public opportunity.

The John Birch Society based much of its analysis of the New World Order menace on a 1,300-page pioneering history of the 20th century by Professor Carroll Quigley of Georgetown University. In his *Tragedy and Hope* (1966), Quigley stated:

> There does exist, and has existed for a generation, an international Anglophile network . . . I have studied it for 20 years and was permitted . . . to examine its papers and secret records.

This was the Holy Grail for conspiracists, a certified top-drawer academic putting it on record that a worldwide conspiracy by a few truly existed. Quigley, warming to his hypothesis, explained that British diamond magnate Cecil Rhodes "left his fortune to form a secret society . . . [which] continues to exist to this day".

The "secret society" was the Round Table Group, later re-modelled as the **Royal Institute of International Affairs**. Quigley himself found the Round Table project to turn the world into a stable Anglophone society "largely commendable".

Others have not been so kindly disposed. The John Birch Society, founded in 1958 by Robert Welch and named for an American pastor killed by Mao's Reds, identified a Round Table Fifth Column in the US which sought nothing less than the wholesale abolition of the States. Funded by the Rock-efellers/the Morgans/the Carnegies, these Anglophile Eastern "Insiders" operated through front organizations such as the **Council on Foreign Relations**, the **Trilateral Commission** and the **Bilderberg Group**. The 100,000-strong John Birch Society also identified a distinctly Red tinge to the Round Table plan. According to Birch author Gary Allen in *None Dare Call It Conspiracy* (1971), the deal being done was for a "power-ful world socialist superstate", even if it was being paid for by billionaires like David Rockefeller. Communism, says Allen, is "an arm" of the bigger Round Table conspiracy. The Birchers also took the long view back on the Round Table plot, past Rhodes to the **Illuminati** of 18th-century Germany.

The Birchers were not alone in tracking those long roots. In *New World Order* (1990), William T. Still elucidated "the centuries-old plans of secret societies to wrench the Constitution from the citizens of the United States". The Christian conspiracy theorist Pat Robertson traces the Round Table one-world plot right back to before the Tower of Babel, when one language united the world. Since Revelations foretells global government, it follows that the New World Order must be the Devil's work. Literally.

Since the Second World War, the Round Table plotters have found the ideal vehicle for their global desires: the United Nations. The UN runs a *World* Bank and an *International* Monetary Fund and promulgates its decisions through the *World* Court. It even has its own blue-hatted army, the UN "Peace Keepers". The Gulf War, in the view of the anti-NWO brigades, was not about the freedom of Kuwait, it wasn't even about oil, it was a military exercise to keep the blue-hats on their toes. The late Jim Keith apparently exposed secret UN bases in the US, full of troops just waiting for the signal to take over the country, and Keith's keenest readers in the patriotic militias regularly spot **Black Helicopters**, using "back-engineered" alien technology, on surveillance missions against them.

Truth to tell, the New World Order conspiracy is an ideological Statue of Liberty: it welcomes in any poor and huddled idea. Britain's David Icke sees the shapeshifting reptiles of the **British Royal Family** as being behind the now. Lyndon LaRouche has the bad guys pegged as crypto-fascist synarchists influenced by . . . there's no real end to who's in on LaRouche's plot.

Time to row back towards the banks of reality. Quigley himself was seemingly embarrassed by the "Smoking Gun" he'd pointed at the Round Table Group and in private played it down. Do capitalists organize globally? Of course. Karl Marx noted the globalization of capitalism in the *Communist Manifesto* of 1848 – hence the need for "Workers of the *World* [to] Unite!" in response – and tracked the process minutely in the three volumes of *Das Kapital*. Fortunately cartels and forums, even the ones hosted by the **Bilderberg Group** or *Le Cercle*, are not equivalent to the secret back room where the Bushes and friends pull the strings of a puppet United Nations imagined by the NOW conspiracy believers.

Funnily enough, the greatest fear of the John Birch Society, the patriotic militias and all is that the UN is going to remove the sovereignty of the US. Outside the fevered club of predominantly US right-wing websites dedicated to exposing the NWO, the big concern of the rest of the world is that it's the *US* that's taking over the *UN*! The US's big-guy-on-the-block "cajoling" to secure a UN mandate for Bush Jr's invasion of Iraq is offered in evidence.

The Bushes say the "New World Order" is the replacement of the "Axis of Evil" by American-type democracies. They might mean it. After the debacle of Iraq, however, it is doubtful they can achieve it.

> A secret cabal is manipulating the UN to secure one-world government: ALERT LEVEL 4

Further Reading
Gary Allen, *None Dare Call It Conspiracy*, 1971
William Cooper, *Behold a Pale Horse*, 1989
Jim Marrs, *Rule by Secrecy*, 2001
Carroll Quigley, *Tragedy and Hope*, 1966
Pat Robertson, *The New World Order*, 1991
William T. Still, *New World Order: The Ancient Plan of Secret Societies*, 1990

DOCUMENT: A SPEECH BY GEORGE H. W. BUSH, PRESIDENT OF THE US, GIVEN TO A JOINT SESSION OF THE UNITED STATES CONGRESS, WASHINGTON DC ON 11 SEPTEMBER 1990

Mr President, Mr Speaker, members of the Congress, distinguished guests, fellow Americans, thank you very much for that warm welcome. We gather tonight, witness to events in the Persian Gulf as significant as they are tragic. In the early morning hours of 2 August, following negotiations and promises by Iraq's dictator Saddam Hussein not to use force, a powerful Iraqi Army invaded its trusting and much weaker neighbor, Kuwait. Within three days, 120,000 Iraqi troops with 850 tanks had poured into Kuwait and moved south to threaten Saudi Arabia. It was then that I decided to act to check that aggression.

[. . .]

[I]f ever there was a time to put country before self and patriotism before party, the time is now. And let me thank all Americans, especially those in this chamber tonight, for your support for our armed forces and for their mission.

That support will be even more important in the days to come.

So tonight, I want to talk to you about what's at stake – what we must do together to defend civilized values around the world and maintain our economic strength at home.

Our objectives in the Persian Gulf are clear, our goals defined and familiar:

Iraq must withdraw from Kuwait completely, immediately and without condition.

Kuwait's legitimate government must be restored.

The security and stability of the Persian Gulf must be assured.

And American citizens abroad must be protected.

These goals are not ours alone. They've been endorsed by

the UN Security Council five times in as many weeks. Most countries share our concern for principle, and many have a stake in the stability of the Persian Gulf. This is not, as Saddam Hussein would have it, the United States against Iraq. It is Iraq against the world.

As you know, I've just returned from a very productive meeting with Soviet President [Mikhail] Gorbachev, and I am pleased that we are working together to build a new relationship. In Helsinki, our joint statement affirmed to the world our shared resolve to counter Iraq's threat to peace. Let me quote: "We are united in the belief that Iraq's aggression must not be tolerated. No peaceful international order is possible if larger states can devour their smaller neighbors."

Clearly, no longer can a dictator count on East–West confrontation to stymie concerted United Nations action against aggression.

A new partnership of nations has begun, and we stand today at a unique and extraordinary moment. The crisis in the Persian Gulf, as grave as it is, also offers a rare opportunity to move toward an historic period of cooperation. Out of these troubled times, our fifth objective – a new world order – can emerge: a new era – freer from the threat of terror, stronger in the pursuit of justice and more secure in the quest for peace. An era in which the nations of the world, east and west, north and south, can prosper and live in harmony.

A hundred generations have searched for this elusive path to peace, while a thousand wars raged across the span of human endeavor, and today that new world is struggling to be born. A world quite different from the one we've known. A world where the rule of law supplants the rule of the jungle. A world in which nations recognize the shared responsibility for freedom and justice. A world where the strong respect the rights of the weak.

This is the vision that I shared with President Gorbachev in Helsinki. He and the other leaders from Europe, the Gulf and around the world understand that how we manage this crisis today could shape the future for generations to come.

The test we face is great and so are the stakes. This is the first assault on the new world that we seek, the first test of our mettle. Had we not responded to this first provocation with clarity of purpose, if we do not continue to demonstrate our determination, it would be a signal to actual and potential despots around the world.

America and the world must defend common vital interests. And we will.

America and the world must support the rule of law. And we will.

America and the world must stand up to aggression. And we will.

And one thing more: in the pursuit of these goals, America will not be intimidated.

Vital issues of principle are at stake. Saddam Hussein is literally trying to wipe a country off the face of the Earth.

We do not exaggerate. Nor do we exaggerate when we say: Saddam Hussein will fail.

Vital economic interests are at risk as well. Iraq itself controls some 10 per cent of the world's proven oil reserves. Iraq plus Kuwait controls twice that. An Iraq permitted to swallow Kuwait would have the economic and military power, as well as the arrogance, to intimidate and coerce its neighbors – neighbors who control the lion's share of the world's remaining oil reserves. We cannot permit a resource so vital to be dominated by one so ruthless. And we won't.

Recent events have surely proven that there is no substitute for American leadership. In the face of tyranny, let no one doubt American credibility and reliability. Let no one doubt our staying power. We will stand by our friends. One way or another, the leader of Iraq must learn this fundamental truth.

From the outset, acting hand-in-hand with others, we've sought to fashion the broadest possible international response to Iraq's aggression. The level of world cooperation and condemnation of Iraq is unprecedented.

Armed forces from countries spanning four continents are there at the request of King Fahd of Saudi Arabia to deter and, if need be, to defend against attack. Muslims and non-Muslims, Arabs and non-Arabs, soldiers from many nations, stand shoulder-to-shoulder, resolute against Saddam Hussein's ambitions.

And we can now point to five United Nations Security Council resolutions that condemn Iraq's aggression. They call for Iraq's immediate and unconditional withdrawal, the restoration of Kuwait's legitimate government and categorically reject Iraq's cynical and self-serving attempt to annex Kuwait.

Finally, the United Nations has demanded the release of all foreign nationals held hostage against their will and in contravention of international law. It's a mockery of human decency to call these people "guests". They are hostages, and the whole world knows it.

Prime Minister Margaret Thatcher, a dependable ally, said it all: "We do not bargain over hostages. We will not stoop to the level of using human beings as bargaining [chips]. Ever."

Of course, of course, our hearts go out to the hostages, to their families. But our policy cannot change. And it will not change. America and the world will not be blackmailed by this ruthless policy.

We're now in sight of a United Nations that performs as envisioned by its founders. We owe much to the outstanding leadership of Secretary General Javier Perez de Cuellar. The United Nations is backing up its words with action. The Security Council has imposed mandatory economic sanctions on Iraq, designed to force Iraq to relinquish the spoils of its illegal conquest. The Security Council has also taken the decisive step of authorizing the use of all means necessary to ensure compliance with these sanctions.

Together with our friends and allies, ships of the United

States Navy are today patrolling Mideast waters, and they've already intercepted more than 700 ships to enforce the sanctions. Three regional leaders I spoke with just yesterday told me that these sanctions are working. Iraq is feeling the heat.

We continue to hope that Iraq's leaders will recalculate just what their aggression has cost them. They are cut off from world trade, unable to sell their oil, and only a tiny fraction of goods gets through.

The communique with President Gorbachev made mention of what happens when the embargo is so effective that children of Iraq literally need milk, or the sick truly need medicine. Then, under strict international supervision that guarantees the proper destination, then – food will be permitted.

At home, the material cost of our leadership can be steep. And that's why Secretary of State [James A.] Baker and Treasury Secretary [Nicholas F.] Brady have met with many world leaders to underscore that the burden of this collective effort must be shared. We're prepared to do our share and more to help carry that load; we insist that others do their share as well.

The response of most of our friends and allies has been good. To help defray costs, the leaders of Saudi Arabia, Kuwait and the UAE [. . .] have pledged to provide our deployed troops with all the food and fuel they need. Generous assistance will also be provided to stalwart front-line nations, such as Turkey and Egypt.

And I'm also heartened to report that this international response extends to the neediest victims of this conflict – those refugees. For our part, we have contributed $28 million for relief efforts. This is but a portion of what is needed. I commend, in particular, Saudi Arabia, Japan and several European nations who have joined us in this purely humanitarian effort.

There's an energy-related cost to be borne as well. Oil-producing nations are already replacing lost Iraqi and

Kuwaiti output. More than half of what was lost has been made up, and we're getting superb cooperation. If producers, including the United States, continue steps to expand oil and gas production, we can stabilize prices and guarantee against hardship. Additionally, we and several of our allies always have the option to extract oil from our strategic petroleum reserves, if conditions warrant. As I've pointed out before, conservation efforts are essential to keep our energy needs as low as possible. We must then take advantage of our energy sources across the board: coal, natural gas, hydro and nuclear. Our failure to do these things has made us more dependent on foreign oil than ever before. And finally, let no one even contemplate profiteering from this crisis. We will not have it.

I cannot predict just how long it'll take to convince Iraq to withdraw from Kuwait. Sanctions will take time to have their full intended effect. We will continue to review all options with our allies, but let it be clear: We will not let this aggression stand.

Our interest, our involvement in the Gulf, is not transitory. It pre-dated Saddam Hussein's aggression and will survive it. Long after all our troops come home, and we all hope it's soon, very soon, there will be a lasting role for the United States in assisting the nations of the Persian Gulf. Our role then is to deter future aggression. Our role is to help our friends in their own self-defense. And something else: to curb the proliferation of chemical, biological, ballistic missile and, above all, nuclear technologies.

And let me also make clear that the United States has no quarrel with the Iraqi people. Our quarrel is with Iraq's dictator and with his aggression. Iraq will not be permitted to annex Kuwait. And that's not a threat. It's not a boast. That's just the way it's going to be.

Our ability to function effectively as a great power abroad depends on how we conduct ourselves at home. Our economy, our armed forces, our energy dependence and our cohesion all determine whether we can help our friends and stand up to our foes.

For America to lead, America must remain strong and vital. Our world leadership and domestic strength are mutual and reinforcing; a woven piece, as strongly bound as Old Glory.

[. . .]

Once again, Americans have stepped forward to share a tearful goodbye with their families before leaving for a strange and distant shore. At this very moment, they serve together with Arabs, Europeans, Asians and Africans in defense of principle and the dream of a new world order. That is why they sweat and toil in the sand and the heat and the sun.

If they can come together under such adversity; if old adversaries like the Soviet Union and the United States can work in common cause, then surely we who are so fortunate to be in this great chamber – Democrats, Republicans, liberals, conservatives – can come together to fulfil our responsibilities here.

Thank you. Good night. And God bless the United States of America.

9/11

At 8.35 on the humdrum morning of Tuesday 11 September 2001, a hijacked plane crashed into the north tower of New York City's World Trade Center. Thirty minutes later, a second plane hit the south tower. Over in Washington DC, a third crashed into the Pentagon.

Nearly 3,000 people died as a result of these attacks. The US had just suffered its worst terrorist incident in history. Kjalid Sheikh Mohammed, the head of the military committee of Islamic terrorist organization al-Qaeda, accepted responsibility: "Yes, we did it," he told al-Jazeera TV. According to intelligence received, the White House of George W. Bush agreed that al-Qaeda had committed the attack.

Case closed? Not quite.

9/11 was a tragedy for all except paranoid conspiracy theorists, to whom every cloud of explosive smoke has a silver lining. Within weeks of 9/11 the internet was humming with alternative versions of whodunnit and why? By mid-2007 the 9/11 internet conspiracy documentary *Loose Change* had been downloaded over 4 million times.

For all the multiplicity of post-9/11 conspiracy theories, they boil down to two main hypotheses: that George W. Bush either staged the 9/11 attacks or purposely allowed them to occur because the attacks would generate public support for an invasion of Afghanistan, Iraq and other fuel-rich countries. With American oil running out, such invasions were a strategic necessity.

Proponents of the theories – who include Hollywood luminaries Charlie Sheen and David Lynch – point accusingly at the Project for the New American Century, the right-wing think-tank that campaigns for increased American global leadership. Former PNAC members include 9/11-era Secretary of Defense Donald Rumsfeld and Vice-President Dick Cheney. An internal PNAC document, *Rebuilding America's Defenses*, allegedly claims that "some catastrophic and catalyzing event – like a new Pearl Harbor" would be needed to move public opinion in their favour. Proponents of this theory also note the **Bush–Bin Laden Connection**, the long ties between the two families, together with the administration's initial opposition to an investigation into the attacks. Could the US government willingly allow an attack on its own people?

Proponents answer "**Pearl Harbor**". Even commit a false-flag attack on its own people? Answer: Operation Northwoods. This latter plan, proposed by the Joint Chiefs of Staff in 1962, proposed a stage-managed "terrorist" attack on US soil; Castro would get the blame, thus providing the justification for an invasion of Cuba. Northwoods was rejected by the Kennedy administration.

So far as the false-flag case goes, theorists find quite a lot of evidence that the government put its rampant political desires into practice.

First there's the sheer amount of incriminating evidence the plotters left around. Oddly, amidst 1.6 million tons of debris, investigators found the intact passport of Mohammed Atta, the man alleged to be the ringleader of the 9/11 attacks. So fortuitous was this find, conspiracy researchers suggest, that it must have been a plant. In fact, a number of other laminated passports were found in the debris. Atta also left flight-simulation manuals behind in a car, and apparently a will. However, he cannot have minded their discovery since he was intent on suicide. In fact, he may have wished them to be discovered to let the world know his martyrdom.

Second, what befell the towers of the World Trade Center bears examination. To most observers what happened to the

WTC towers on 9/11 is straightforward: two planes hit the towers, then the towers fell down. This "reality" was soon challenged by conspiracy theorists, together with a covey of scientific experts.

Before 9/11 no steel-framed skyscraper had collapsed because of fire, yet WTC buildings 1, 2 and 7 collapsed like pancakes. Particularly unusual was the death of WTC 7, which was not hit by an aircraft. Additionally, according to at least one demolition expert, the billows of dust coming out of the towers were more indicative of explosion than fire. Steel wreckage recovered from the site shows that it became molten; fire is not usually able to effect this change in steel. But a bomb is.

The "controlled demolition hypothesis" is a central plank of 9/11 conspiracy theory, featuring heavily in David Ray Griffin's *The New Pearl Harbor* (2005), and most cogently argued by Steven Jones, a physicist at Brigham Young University. Jones asserts that without demolition charges a "gravity-driven collapse" of the sort that happened to the WTC buildings would defy the laws of physics.

By the laws of "controlled demolition hypothesis" the WTC was rigged with explosive devices, probably containing thermite. The strange comment by Larry Silverstein, owner of WTC 7, on a PBS documentary that he told the fire department to "pull it" makes sense in this scenario: "pull it" is demolition industry slang for setting off demolition charges. (Silverstein's spokesman said later that Silverstein meant "pull it" as in "pull outta there".) The bottom-to-top-style collapse of WTC buildings 1, 2 and 7 is said to be typical of controlled demolitions. Fuelling conspiracy theory is the fact that building 7 housed offices of the CIA and the FBI, plus New York City's emergency command bunker.

In counterpoint to the controlled-demolition hypothesis is the finding of the US Department of Commerce's National Institute of Standards and Technology (NIST) report into 9/11. According to this report the fireproofing on the Twin Towers' steel infrastructures was blown off by the impact of the planes, thus opening them to fire damage. Fires weakened the trusses supporting the floors, which made the floors sag. Sagging floors pulled on the exterior steel columns, making them bow inwards. Buckled columns could not support the building. Thus the buildings collapsed. NIST's finding are supported by a whole range of independent researchers.

What the controlled-demolition hypothesis fails to take into account is the aviation fuel carried by the planes. Skyscrapers were never made to withstand the effects of having thousands of gallons of ignited aviation fuel swilling around inside them.

Demolition experts have also weighed in on NIST's side. To place enough lethal charges around three skyscrapers would require weeks of work and tons of explosive. Security at the WTC was among the tightest in the US, following a terrorist attack there in 1993. Wouldn't *somebody* have noticed men carrying in bags of explosives for days on end or heard the drilling work needed to secure the devices to the steel frames?

Over to Washington DC. Like the WTC, the Pentagon was hit by a hijacked plane . . . or was it? Whereas in NY the dramatic extent of the damage done by the hijacked planes arouses suspicion, in Washington it is the *limited* extent of the damage done that incurs disbelief. In 2002 French writer Thierry Meyssan published *9/11: The Big Lie*, which noted that the hole in the outer wall of the west wing was too small to have been caused by an incoming Boeing 747 and that the interior of the Pentagon was suspiciously undamaged. According to Meyssan, the hole was caused by a cruise missile. (A more realistic weapon, some commentators feel, than the **HAARP**-like energy beam nominated by Assistant Professor Judy Woods as the doomslayer-of-the-day on 9/11.) To counter the growing controversy, the Pentagon released five frames of CCTV footage from the stock that it had, on security grounds, confiscated after 9/11.

But to release just five frames prompted an obvious question: what was being hidden that the remainder of the frames might reveal? The 9/11 conspiracy theory gained a new lease of life. The plane – most now agreed there *was* a plane – that crashed into the Pentagon had been able to fly towards Washington for

40 minutes, despite radar, despite missile batteries, despite the proximity of Andrews Air Force Base. The section of the Pentagon which the plane crashed into was nearly empty at the time. All this is taken by the 9/11 Truth Campaign as definite evidence that 9/11 was stage-managed or known about.

The clincher is the footage of George W. Bush's infamous response when his reading of a story to a Florida kindergarten was interrupted by an aide to tell him of the attacks. Bush continued reading. He could only have carried on being so calm, the theory goes, if he knew about the attacks in advance.

The fact is that the Pentagon was designed to withstand an air attack. The limestone layers shattered with the impact of the Boeing but the reinforced steel internal cage remained intact, hence the apparent lack of internal damage. Bush's response can be explained in a multitude of ways: he wanted to give the appearance of calm, he was shocked into immobility, he was too unintelligent to grasp what had occurred . . .

If the Pentagon didn't shoot down Flight 77 as it homed in on the Pentagon, the obvious question in the looking-glass world of paranoid conspiracy theory is: did the Pentagon shoot down Flight 93? Flight 93 was the fourth airliner hijacked by terrorists that morning. Unlike the others, it failed to find its target, instead plummeting into a Pennsylvania field. It is commonly considered that Flight 93 came down because its passengers heroically fought back against the hijackers and, in the melee, the plane went out of control or perhaps a terrorist aboard pulled the pin on a bomb.

The conspiracy theory is that Flight 93 was shot down on the orders of the White House before it could reach its target – which almost certainly was that selfsame White House. Here the evidence is unclear. By 8.52 the White House had ordered fighters into the air to seek out any hijacked airliners. Around 10 a.m. CBS TV reported that F-16 fighters were tailing Flight 93. Several witnesses to the Flight 93 crash report seeing a white plane nearby. The wide spread of debris from the plane, it is alleged, points to a midair crash. In 2004 Donald Rumsfeld seemed to say that Flight 93 had been shot down, though the White House later maintained he'd made a slip of the tongue.

Some cynics suggest that 9/11 was a poor false-flag operation if the White House had to then stage a cover-up of its shooting down of Flight 93. Whatever, shooting down a hijacked plane to stop its potential use as dive-bomber is not in the same moral league as a false-flag operation.

The weight of evidence is that al-Qaeda, and al-Qaeda alone, carried out the 9/11 attacks. Elements of the assault were planned and directed by al-Qaeda in Afghanistan, but the donkey work was done by a self-supporting al-Qaeda cell in Hamburg, led by Mohammed Atta. After receiving training in Afghanistan, the cell moved to the US by summer 2000; in Florida Atta opened an account at the SunTrust bank into which $109,000 was transferred from Dubai, seemingly to finance the upcoming operation. In the following year, al-Qaeda sent a number of Saudi volunteers to join Atta. On the morning of 9/11 a total of 19 terrorists hijacked four aircraft from East Coast airports . . .

The rest is history, not conspiracy theory.

Elements in the Pentagon conspired to stage or allow 9/11: ALERT LEVEL 3

Further Reading
David Ray Griffin, *The New Pearl Harbor*, 2005
Jim Marrs, *Inside Job: Unmasking the Conspiracies of 9/11*, 2005
National Commission on Terrorist Attacks, *The 9/11 Commission Report*, 2004
www.Loosechange911.com
www.911truth.org

OKLAHOMA CITY BOMBING

Just after 9 a.m. on 19 April 1995, a massive explosion ripped through the Alfred P. Murrah federal building in downtown Oklahoma City. When the clouds of dust settled, the face of the Murrah building had been shorn off and a crater created that was 30 feet (9m) wide. Sifting through the rubble and wreckage, emergency crews found 169 dead, including 19 children who had been attending a nursery for federal employees on the second floor. Another victim of that day was the American psyche; after Oklahoma it would be more fragmented and suspicious than ever before, with right and left both seeing the bloody hand of the other in the blast's perpetration. The Oklahoma blast, as federal investigators immediately announced, was no accident, but the result of a bomb.

The debris at the Murrah building offered up the evidence needed to identify one of the bomb-planters. Police found a truck axle which they traced to a Ryder truck rented in Junction City, Kansas. Eyewitnesses at the scene reported seeing a yellow Ryder truck stopped in the disabled parking area at the front of the building, from which two men had descended and hastily hopped into a Mercury car. It was then that the investigators got lucky; at 10.20 a.m., 60 miles (100km) north of Oklahoma, a traffic cop pulled over a 1977 Mercury Marquis for speeding. As officer Charles Hangar approached the car, he noticed it had no licence plates and that the driver appeared to have the tell-tale bulge of a handgun under his jacket. Hangar took out his own revolver and aimed it at the driver's head, at which the driver calmly handed over a .45 Glock pistol and a hunting knife.

The driver was one Timothy James McVeigh, a former army sergeant and the future star turn in conspiracy chat rooms. Initially 26-year-old McVeigh was charged with illegally transporting a loaded weapon and driving without licence plates. Two days after his arrest, the charges against him were added to; he was charged with perpetrating the worst terrorist bombing carried out on US soil to that date.

There was much to tie McVeigh to the Oklahoma City crime. He matched eyewitness descriptions of a man with a military haircut exiting the Ryder truck. He allegedly dropped a business card advertising Paulsen's Military Supply in Hangar's squad car; on the back of the card McVeigh had written, "More five-pound sticks of TNT by 1 May." He was found to be carrying a phone debit card issued by the anti-Semitic Liberty Group, and later investigations showed he had used the card to contact the suppliers of the plastic barrels and fertilizer used to make the home-made bomb placed at the Murrah building. Traces of explosive were found on his clothing and his fingerprints were discovered on a receipt for 2,000 lb (900kg) of fertilizer.

McVeigh's comedy of criminal errors continued. In the lock-up in Noble County he listed James Nichols as his next of kin; when Federal Bureau of Alcohol, Tobacco and Firearms officials visited the Nichols farm they turned up an array of bomb-making materials, including blasting caps, Primadet detonator cords, and ammonium nitrate. Nichols's brother Terry gave himself up and was charged with the Oklahoma City bombing alongside McVeigh.

The federal authorities had little trouble in finding the motive for the bombing. In the glove compartment of McVeigh's rented car the FBI found a letter written by him avowing revenge for the federal raid on the Branch Davidian compound at **Waco**; the attack on the Murrah building was staged exactly two years to the day after this raid. McVeigh and Nichols,

Michigan militiamen both, considered that the Branch Davidians had been murdered by the federal government. Quite possibly McVeigh was inspired to bomb the Murrah building by reading of a similar *coup de main* in the novel *The Turner Diaries* (1980) by the American Nazi William Pierce, aka Andrew Macdonald.

Initially McVeigh proclaimed his innocence, telling *Time* magazine, "I enjoy guns as a hobby . . . I follow the beliefs of the Founding Fathers. If that means I was involved in the bombing then . . . about a billion other Americans were involved in the bombing as well." Unfortunately for him, his own sister damned him in court, telling the jury he had bragged before the bombing that "something big is going to happen". He changed his tune after the federal court found him guilty on eight counts of murder, writing from prison that the bombing was "a retaliatory strike" for, as the police suspected, the federal attack on Waco.

Timothy McVeigh was killed by lethal injection at the federal penitentiary in Terre Haute, Indiana, on 11 June 2001. Terry Nichols was sentenced to life imprisonment.

The government then firmly closed the Oklahoma City bombing file. Others, though, have sought to keep it open, since disturbing questions about McVeigh's conviction have never been satisfactorily answered. Even the presiding judge, Richard P. Matsch, thought so.

In their investigation into the bombing of the Murrah building, the FBI rarely wavered from the track of McVeigh and Nichols. But were others involved? Eyewitnesses at the Murrah building on the morning of the blast spoke of McVeigh being accompanied by a dark-haired, possibly Middle Eastern man; the same man, John Doe 2, had been seen at the Kansas car rental office with him. Later the FBI stated that Nichols was John Doe 2, although Nichols looked nothing like the swarthy identikit picture they'd issued of that suspect. So who was he? According to deputy Kansas sheriff Jake Mauck, John Doe 2 was a local "Patriot", a claim that has strengthened over the years as reporters uncovered links between McVeigh and the far-right Aryan Republican Army. In 2004 Associated Press reported that the same type of blasting caps used in the Oklahoma City bombing had been used by the Aryan Republican Army in bank robberies across the Midwest.

More evidence that McVeigh and Nichols did not act alone is provided by explosive experts, who state that the duo could not, as the federal government claimed, have assembled a 4,800 lb (2,175kg) fertilizer bomb on the evening before the explosion. One prominent expert witness, Brigadier-General Benton Partin, claims the Murrah blast was caused by numerous bombs wired to the main supporting columns, not just the explosive device packed inside the Ryder truck. According to seismographic records held by the University of Oklahoma's Geological Survey, a second explosion occurred eight seconds after the first, although the Survey's director was at pains to point out that the second shock wave was probably caused by the same explosion and had merely travelled through denser earth to reach their seismograph.

For some, especially those on the American far right, the "evidence" of multiple explosions in the Murrah building leads us full-pelt to the conclusion that the federal government was involved in the bombing. Just as the Nazis, so the argument runs, set the Reichstag afire, so the Feds blew up the Murrah building in order to provide a pretext for a legal crackdown on the patriotic militias of America. After all, why was the BATF office in the Murrah building empty at the time of the explosion? Obviously, the staff had received an inside warning to stay away.

The theory that the FBI committed the Oklahoma City bombing founders on a moment's sanity. In order to secure a legal clampdown, the US establishment didn't need an excuse; civil liberties were being curtailed anyway. Furthermore, BATF staff *did* die in the explosion.

A more benevolent – and more likely – theory is that, yes, the FBI was indeed involved in a cover-up at Oklahoma City . . . but a cover-up designed to bolster its reputation as efficient lawmen. The FBI failed to track John Doe 2 because it wanted a quick, clean conviction of McVeigh and Nichols in order to reassure the US public that justice was being speedily done. Alas, by failing to investigate McVeigh's links with the Militias and by "accidentally" holding back 3,000 pages of documents from his defence team, the FBI acted in exactly the dubious manner its critics complained of. Which provided more grist to the mill of ultra-right-wing conspiracy theorists like ... Timothy McVeigh, Terry Nichols and their unknown co-bombers.

FBI. The Federal Bureau of Incompetence.

The FBI/BATF orchestrated the Oklahoma City bombing in order to create conditions necessary for crack-down on patriotic militias: ALERT LEVEL 3

Further Reading
Stephen Jones and Peter Israel, *Others Unknown: Timothy McVeigh and the Oklahoma City Bombing Conspiracy*, 1998
Gore Vidal, *Perpetual War for Perpetual Peace*, 2002
www.okcbombing.org

OMEGA AGENCY

Forget the **Bilderberg Group**, the **Council on Foreign Relations**, even the **Trilateral Commission**; according to www.totse.com "The Omega Agency is the one running the show . . . the whole ball of wax."

AboveTopSecret.com and a host of other websites agree: the 10–12 members of the ruling council of the OA are the supreme secret force behind the **New World Order**. George H. W. Bush, Colin Powell, Gerald Ford and Alexander C. Haig are among the present and past members of the OA council, which has its HQ at the FBI's Langley complex.

To instal the New World Order, the OA will use the troops of the United Nations who have practised large-scale manoeuvres under the pretence of fighting for freedom in Kuwait (the Gulf War), Bosnia and so on. However, sections of the existing ruling orders oppose the OA, being instead desirous of maintaining influence or having a different worldview; the CIA, for example, wants a "more Communistic-type government" than the OA, which will allow some individual freedom – except for those who are indolent and criminal. In the OA's New World Order there will be an "end of living off of society and not contributing your fair share . . . Crimes against another or against society will be met with the death penalty, if such crime is of a severe nature such as murder, rape or robbery."

There will be a forced reduction in population: "Population control will be accomplished by mandatory birth control by all people, men as well as women. Abortion will be freely available. There will be zero tolerance for child-bearing out of wedlock . . . There will be a limit of 2 children per couple allowed."

The Omega Agency also relies on the aid of extraterrestrials, who live under Kirtland Air Force Base, Albuquerque, New Mexico. "These ETs," says AboveTopSecret.com, "are helping the US with its space program and are working toward devising a plan to restore the planet's environment after the OA takes over". The aliens, however, are mainly resident on Earth because they wish to engineer away the innate violence of humans which potentially threatens, via the expanding space programme, the militaristic colonization of their pacific planets. The aliens working with the OA are both Greys and Greens; the Greys are mainly vegetarian, though they apparently "have been known to enjoy a steak now and then".

Outside self-referring internet websites, there is no evidence that the Omega Agency exists. Believers consider this lack of evidence merely proof of *how secret the OA really is*!

> The Omega Agency, together with aliens, is preparing the New World Order dictatorship: ALERT LEVEL 0

Further Reading
www.AboveTopSecret.com
www.totse.com

OPUS DEI

Opus Dei, meaning literally "God's Work" in Latin, is a Roman Catholic prelature founded in 1928 by Josemaria Escriva de Balaguer y Albas. According to its supporters, who include British politician Ruth Kelly, Opus Dei is an innocuous organization whose members seek simply to live the word of God in their professional lives. Which is not exactly how Dan Brown paints it in *The Da Vinci Code* (2003).

Balaguer created the order after seeing a vision of God in Madrid. Since then Opus Dei has garnered 85,000 members around the world. Pope John Paul II acknowledged the Order's influence by granting it the status of "personal prelature" in 1982. Twenty years later Balaguer (who died in 1975) was canonized. His elevation to sainthood was controversial. Few men had achieved such status so quickly – and few were as unpopular or as divisive a figure. Former members of Opus Dei led the appeals *against* Balaguer's canonization, citing his "arrogance and malevolent temper . . . his love of luxury and ostentation". Moreover, his political views were incontrovertibly fascistic, as any reading of his *The Way* (1934) confirms. A native Spaniard, he actively supported Franco's dictatorship and once claimed that Hitler would be the saving of Christianity from Communism. His views filtered right down through the Order: Opus Dei members in South America bankrolled the right-wing regime of Alberto Fujimori in Peru in the 1990s.

Then there is the Order's secretive, hierarchical nature. Membership is by invitation, although some members (priests) are more important than others (the laity). *The Way* argues the need for a ruling elite who should be followed blindly; lower-order members are required to reveal their souls to their spiritual leaders in a "weekly chat". Anti-Opus Dei websites, such as www.odan.org, list other cultish practices designed to keep membership tightly controlled, including the cutting off of family connections and self-flagellation. Lay members include "Numeraries", who are celibate and live in single-sex quasi-monasteries and give over all their money to Opus Dei, and "Supernumeraries", who can be married and who hand over only a percentage of their income – quite an earner when you have 85,000 members in the two categories. To see where $50 million of the money went, take a look at Opus Dei's imposing 17-storey US headquarters on NY's Lexington Avenue.

Critics commonly label Opus Dei a "Catholic Freemasonry" (Balaguer, incidentally, thought the activities of the real **Freemasons** to be "the work of the Devil"), and it does operate as a secret, self-contained society by virtue of its status as a "personal prelature" in the Church. Like other covert groups, it seeks influence beyond its closed circle: "Have you ever bothered to think," Balaguer once said, "how absurd it is to leave one's Catholicism aside on entering a university or a professional association or a scholarly meeting or Congress, as if you were checking your hat at the door?" Accusations that Opus Dei seeks to infiltrate the mass media were heated up in 1979 by the leaking of an Opus Dei document which showed that 604 of its members worked in journalism and 52 in radio/TV.

Opus Dei's message, at least, is clear enough. Like Hitler's *Mein Kampf*, Balaguer's *The Way* has the virtue of forthrightness. For Balaguer there is *only* the ultra-conservative Roman Catholic way and its end goal is a global theocracy.

All of which begs the question: if Opus Dei's only aims are charity and the "sanctifying of work", why *does* it need its secretive independent status as a personal prelature?

Opus Dei seeks to instal a right-wing Roman Catholic theocracy: ALERT LEVEL 8

Further Reading
John L. Allen Jr, *Opus Dei: An Objective Look Behind the Myths and Reality of the Most Controversial Force in the Catholic Church*, 2005
www.odan.org

PEARL HARBOR

Tora! Tora! Tora! As every good American boy and girl is brought up to believe, the Japanese made a sneaky unannounced attack on the US naval base at Pearl Harbor in Hawaii on 7 December 1941. After 350 Japanese fighter bombers unloaded their ordnance, 21 ships and 2,400 Americans lay dead in the water. President Franklin D. Roosevelt called 7 December 1941 "a date which will live in infamy" and promptly signed a declaration of war against Japan.

Sunday 7 December was certainly a day of infamy. Despite all his protestations of surprise and anger, Roosevelt knew a Japanese assault was imminent. More, the evidence suggests he provoked Japan into an attack so the US could appear the innocent party. Unlike 90 per cent of his countrymen, Roosevelt wanted to get involved in the Second World War. Letting the Japanese attack Pearl Harbor was his way of sea-changing US opinion.

Thanks to the US intelligence services, hundreds of Japanese "purple code" intercepts had been decrypted, showing Japan's build-up to a strike in the Pacific. On 27 November, the US Navy and War Departments warned: "Negotiations with Japan looking toward stabilization of conditions in the Pacific have ceased . . . an aggressive move by Japan is expected within the next few days." On the evening of 6 December the US Navy deciphered a message sent from Tokyo to the Japanese embassy in Washington. The intercept revealed that Japan was ending diplomatic relations with the US. On reading the translated message, Roosevelt announced, "This means war." The Australian and British intelligence services likewise informed Washington of Japan's intention.

According to Roosevelt's apologists, the warnings of war never reached Pearl Harbor, due to cock-up and bad weather. So on the morning of Sunday 7 December 1941 Pearl Harbor slept in instead of being up and ready behind the guns. No fewer than eight high-level investigations have investigated the reasons for the failure of the 27 November and 6 December intelligence to reach Pearl Harbor, beginning with the Roberts Commission of December 1941. This blamed the Pearl Harbor debacle on the local commanders, Admiral Kimmel and General Short, for not being sufficiently prepared. A 1944 Army Pearl Harbor Board blamed the disaster on the War Department for not sending out the 6 December communique. A 1945 Naval Court of Inquiry blamed the Navy Department head, Admiral Stark, for not forwarding the December communique. In other words, Pearl Harbor was everybody's fault except FDR's!

Little significance can be attached to the various commissions' findings. As one member of the Roberts Commission remarked, it was "crooked as a snake" and set up only to preserve FDR's reputation. (That member was no wild-eyed loony subversive but Admiral of the US Navy William Standley.) Much the same can be said for the subsequent inquiries. Not until the 1946 Joint Congressional Committee on Pearl Harbor did FDR receive even mild censure, but by then he was dead and the war won.

What of the charge that FDR intentionally provoked the war with Japan? The first such political shot came from a surprising source: Robert A. Theobald, the commander of destroyers at Pearl Harbor in 1941, in his 1954 book *The Final Secret of Pearl Harbor*. Another naval officer, Robert Stinnet, delivered a devastating broadside in *Day of Deceit* (2001), which quoted an eight-point plan drawn up for FDR in 1940 and much later found by Stinnet in the archives. The eight-point plan opened with the words "The United States desires that Japan commit the first overt act [of war]" and suggested inciting Japan by trade embargoes.

And, lo and behold, the US goaded Nippon throughout 1940–41 by restricting shipments of wheat, machinery and oil. On 26 November 1941 the US upped the ante by insisting Japan withdraw from Indochina and China and renounce its tripartite alliance with Germany and Italy. Tokyo cited this demand in its 6 December communique as the cause of the breakdown in diplomatic relations with the US.

Roosevelt thus engineered the war with Japan, just as he knew an attack on American forces was likely on 7 December 1941. (In fairness, he probably did not know the exact location of the assault – although the US Pacific Fleet at Pearl Harbor must have topped any list of likely targets.) Just after 7 December 1941 General George C. Marshall, supreme commander of the US Army, informed the handful of top brass involved in the Pear Harbor cover-up: "Gentlemen, this goes to the grave with us." The secret did; it has taken historians more than 50 years to recover the full story of the day of infamy.

Few, however, are keen to criticize FDR for his Pearl Harbor cover-up, even truth seekers like Standley and Stinnet. Pearl Harbor, it seems, is a case where the end really did justify the means: pushing the Japanese into attacking a naked Pearl Harbor allowed the US to enter the Second World War and join Britain and Russia in successfully defeating the twin menaces of German Nazism and Japanese militarism.

Usually, applications of Machiavelli's maxim go badly wrong. The Bay of Tonkin, anybody? But at Pearl Harbor, for once, things went right.

President Franklin D. Roosevelt conspired to cause attack on US Navy forces at Pearl Harbor: ALERT LEVEL 9

Further Reading
Robert Stinnet, *Day of Deceit*, 2001
Robert A. Theobald, *The Final Secret of Pearl Harbor*, 1954
John Toland, *Infamy: Pearl Harbor and Its Aftermath*, 1982

PHILADELPHIA EXPERIMENT

On 13 January 1955 Morris K. Jessup, author of *The Case for the UFO* (1955), received a letter from a man identifying himself as Carlos Allende. This informed Jessup of a top-secret naval project from the Second World War: the Philadelphia Experiment. According to Allende, the US Navy had attempted to render warships invisible, finally achieving success on 28 October 1943 when the escort destroyer USS *Eldridge* disappeared from its berth at the Philadelphia Navy Yard and was teleported 600 miles (1,000km) away to Virginia. Allende had apparently witnessed the invisibility experiment from a nearby merchant ship, the SS *Furuseth*. So horrific had been the effect on the *Eldridge*'s crew – some being lost for ever, some fused into bulkheads, some turned mad – that the Navy had hurriedly cancelled the project.

Jessup asked for more information from Allende. None came, and so Jessup dismissed Allende's claims as a hoax.

Others were more convinced by the story, among them Charles Berlitz and William L. Moore, who published the fullest account of the 1943 events as *The Philadelphia Experiment: The True Story Behind Project Invisibility* in 1978.

According to Berlitz and Moore, the US Navy achieved the disappearance of the *Eldridge* by application of the Unified Field Theory, essentially bending light around the vessel to make it "invisible". Berlitz and Moore noted that a major proponent and investigative theoretician of the theory, Albert

Einstein, was a US Navy consultant at the time of the Philadelphia Experiment. It was also suspicious that Jessup had
committed suicide (in 1959). Perhaps, rather, he had been killed
by the US government because he knew too much? In a bizarre
twist Al Bielek, who claimed to be a former seaman on the
Eldridge, came forward to say he had fallen from the ship's deck
while it was in "hyperspace" between Philadelphia and Norfolk
on 28 October 1943 and landed at the Air Force station **Montauk Point**, Long Island, in 1983, having undergone time
travel as well as teleportation.

The US Office of Naval Research (ONR) has consistently
denied the existence of the Philadelphia Experiment, or any
Second World War research into invisibility, denouncing the
Allende/Berlitz and Moore story as "science fiction". The ONR
has a point. The journalist Robert Goerman has claimed that
Allende (who changed his name to Carl Allen) had a history of
psychiatric illness and the Philadelphia story was a resultant
delusion. Allen certainly served on the SS *Furuseth*, but the
master of that vessel stated that neither he nor his crew saw
anything out of the ordinary in October 1943. The *Eldridge*,-
moreover, wasn't even in Philadelphia on 28 October of that
year: it was on duty in the Atlantic. A reunion of *Eldridge*
veterans told the *Philadelphia Inquirer* in 1999 that they "find
the story amusing – especially because the ship never docked in
Philadelphia".

UFO investigator Jacques Vallee has suggested the Philadelphia Experiment legend has a slender basis in reality. The US
Navy *was* experimenting with "invisibility" in the 1940s, but
not as Allen/Berlitz and Moore/Bielek understood it. Vallee
interviewed Edward Dudgeon, a seaman in the Philadelphia
yards in October 1943. The yards were seeking to make ships
"invisible to magnetic torpedoes by de-gaussing them". Dudgeon described the procedure:

> They sent the crew ashore and they wrapped the vessel in big
> cables, then they sent high voltages through these cables to
> scramble the ship's magnetic signature. This operation

involved contract workers, and of course there were also merchant ships around, so civilian sailors could well have heard Navy personnel saying something like, "they're going to make us invisible," meaning undetectable by magnetic torpedoes . . .

The US Navy covered up invisibility experiments which went horrifically wrong: ALERT LEVEL 2

Further Reading

Charles Berlitz and William L. Moore, *The Philadelphia Experiment: The True Story Behind Project Invisibility*, 1978

Goerman, Robert A., "Alias Carlos Allende: The Mystery Man Behind the Philadelphia Experiment", *Fate*, October 1980

Vallee, Jacques, "Anatomy of a Hoax: The Philadelphia Experiment 50 Years Later", *Journal of Scientific Exploration*, Vol. 8, No. 1, Spring 1994.

PORT CHICAGO EXPLOSION

In 1980 Paul Vogel was trawling through items at a rummage sale held by Christ Evangelical Lutheran Church, Santa Fe, New Mexico, when he found a photocopied document taken from Los Alamos Laboratories, birth place of the A-bomb: "History of 10,000 Ton Gadget". Reading on, Vogel found the document contained drawings for something resembling an A-bomb. The document might have been of no more than historical curiosity save for two things: it was dated September 1944, and it referred to "a ball of fire [which] mushroomed out at 18,000 feet in typical Port Chicago fashion".

Officially, the first A-bomb was tested on 16 July 1945 at Los Alamos. The explosion at Port Chicago, California, on 17 July 1944, in which 320 soldiers, seamen and dock workers were killed, was officially registered by the government as an accident involving ordinary ordnance. But a dark thought came into Vogel's head. Could the Port Chicago explosion have been a nuclear test that went wrong?

He decided to investigate. His first point of reference was Edward Teller, "Father of the Hydrogen Bomb", under whom Vogel had himself studied physics. Apparently, when asked about "History of 10,000 Ton Gadget", Teller ended the interview.

Next Vogel went to Port Chicago, now renamed Concord Naval Weapons Station, where the Navy informed him they held film of the 1944 blast. Vogel watched it and was convinced it showed an atomic explosion. After he'd alerted the USN to his opinion, the Navy recategorized the film as a Hollywood mock-up.

For two decades Vogel assembled evidence of a nuclear blast at Port Chicago. He noted that cancer rates around Port Chicago were among the highest in the US. He discovered that, contrary to government claims, the US possessed enough bomb-grade uranium in mid-1944 for a test A-bomb. He found that Los Alamos records relating to shipments to Port Chicago had been destroyed. He dug up the fact that one of the ships evaporated in the Port Chicago blast was destined for Tinian in the Mariana Islands, later the launchpad for the A-bombing of Hiroshima. From eyewitness descriptions of the blast, plus his own viewing of the Navy's film (and why *was* the Navy filming at Port Chicago that day? For that matter, why *was* an Army aircraft detailed to patrol above the site that day?), Vogel determined that the blast was greater than any possible from the official 1,780 tons of high explosive and that it produced a Wilson condensation cloud – a characteristic of nuclear detonations.

According to Vogel, the case for the nuclear nature of the Port Chicago explosion is proven; what needs to be investigated is whether or not the device was deliberately detonated by the military, using low-ranking (predominantly black) personnel as guinea pigs to test the effects.

It is not beyond the bounds of possibility that the US military authorities tested an atomic weapon on US citizens. The US government has a long, bad record of subjecting its citizens to experiments: in 1977 the Army admitted to having tested biological weapons in the open air 239 times between 1949 and 1969, including the dropping of *Bacillus niger*, a non-lethal (one hoped!) bacillus related to anthrax, on the Manhattan subway so that the Army could "monitor the spread of the agent through the tunnels"; from 1932 to 1972, medical experiments were conducted on syphilitic black farmers at Tuskegee, Alabama, allowing them to die in the interests of "Public Health Service" research; and so forth. According to its track record, then, the US government might indeed have happily sacrificed

320 mainly black workers in the interests of science. But it seems unlikely the military and the Manhattan Project would have tested an A-bomb in public view. All the known testings of the Manhattan Project were far away, out in the secret sands of the New Mexico desert.

Further, it is questionable whether the Port Chicago explosion could only have been caused by the discharge, intentional or accidental, of an atomic weapon. In the First World War detonations of ordnance more primitive than that handled at Port Chicago produced shock waves which could be felt up to 80 miles (130km) away.

> The 1944 Port Chicago blast was caused by the detonation of an A-bomb: ALERT LEVEL 6

Further Reading
Allen, Robert L., *The Port Chicago Mutiny*, 1989
www.portchicago.org

ELVIS PRESLEY

The clue lies in the name: "Elvis". Rearrange the letters and you get "lives".

From this slender thread has spun a conspiracy that Elvis Aaron Presley did not die an ignominious death on his lavatory at Gracclands in August 1977 but survived to sing another day. Although perhaps only in the shower, since one reason for the faked demise was so he could enjoy a banana fritter without the sound of screaming fans.

On tour Elvis used the pseudonym John Burrows. Apparently, in the weeks after the King's death a man with black hair called John Burrows bought an airline ticket for Buenos Aires. Since 1977, Elvis has been spotted everywhere from Alabama to Zambia, which makes for great news items in sensational magazines requiring increased circulation figures. Then someone called Sivle Nora (another anagram) released a record. Then fans spotted that his middle name was spelled on his gravestone as "Aaron", rather than "Aron", which was taken as another clue that he was alive. In fact, the middle name given on his birth certificate is "Aaron"; the "Aron" spelling seems to have been Elvis's own error.

Alternate theories are:

• 42-year-old Elvis staged his death so he could take his work as a "Federal Agent at Large" (no, really: Richard M. Nixon accorded him this status) undercover;

- he was "whacked" by the Mob because his pa, Vernon Presley, bodged some arcane deal over a jet with on-the-lam financier Robert Vesco;
- he was a victim of **Alien Abduction**.

His autopsy report is sometimes held up as a dodgy dossier. Shelby County Medical Examiner Dr Jerry Francisco gave the cause of Presley's death as "cardiac arrhythmia" (irregular heartbeat), which was not unreasonable in view of the fact that Presley was grossly overweight and suffering hypertension, but made no mention of the cocktail of (legal) drugs known to be coursing through Presley's bloodstream at the time of his death. No matter how hard conspiracy theorists try to make this omission suspicious, it isn't: Francisco has admitted that he deliberately left out mention of drugs because it was a possibility Elvis had overdosed, or had taken illegal drugs (a definite), and he, Francisco, did not want to upset the dead singer's friends, family and fans.

Ironically, Elvis fans inadvertently add to the Elvis Lives hysteria by dressing like him. Hence most of the many sightings of "the King".

Elvis lives: ALERT LEVEL 0

Further Reading
Gail Brewer-Giorgio, *Is Elvis Alive?*, 1988

PRIORY OF SION

Rennes-le-Chateau is a picture-postcard medieval town atop a hill in Languedoc, southern France – the sort of place where old men should sip pastis between rounds of *pétanque* in the village square. Instead, the cobbled streets of Rennes-le-Chateau are chock-a-block with 100,000 visitors a year and you can hardly swing an arm for *pétanque*.

Why the mass pilgrimage? Occultists head for the village because it's meant to have energy from ley lines; some UFO buffs regard it as a centre of alien-spaceship activity; but most of the pilgrims go armed with a copy of *Holy Blood, Holy Grail* by Michael Baigent, Richard Leigh and Henry Lincoln or *The Da Vinci Code* by Dan Brown. Rennes-le-Chateau is ostensibly where the 2,000-year-old proof that Christ survived the crucifixion was found, a secret held long and close by the French society known as the Prieure de Sion – the Priory of Sion.

The tale of Rennes-le-Chateau and the Priory of Sion begins in 1885 when the Catholic Church dispatched 33-year-old Berenger Sauniere to the village to serve as its priest. While renovating the Church of Mary Magadelene, Sauniere discovered in a hollow Visigothic pillar some parchment documents covered with codes. When he took the documents to his bishop in Carcasonne, the latter forwarded them to codebreaking priests in Paris, who translated one cipher as:

TO DAGOBERT II KING AND TO SION BELONGS
THIS TREASURE AND HE IS THERE DEAD

In Rennes-le-Chateau, meanwhile, Sauniere continued his restoration of the church, but with decorations unusual in the Catholic gallery of images. There was an image of the demon Asmodeus, a wall relief depicting Jesus on a hill at the base of which was a sack of money, and a picture of Jesus apparently being carried out of a tomb. Having revamped the church, Sauniere then forked out a small fortune for improvements in the village. He also began collecting rare and expensive antiques. Tongues wagged as to how he'd amassed his wealth. After his death in 1917, Sauniere's housekeeper mentioned that he'd possessed a secret that made him rich and powerful.

Most thought that his secret must be a stash of buried treasure, but the authors of *Holy Blood, Holy Grail* proposed Sauniere had discovered some form of hidden knowledge. With the help of French aristocrat Pierre Plantard de Saint-Clair, they uncovered secret dossiers in Paris's Bibliotheque Nationale that contained references to an ancient society called Prieure de Sion, whose members over the years had included Leonardo da Vinci, Sir Isaac Newton and Jean Cocteau. Checking with the French authorities, the authors found the Priory of Sion was still extant, and that the group's secretary-general was none other than Pierre Plantard de Saint-Clair. On the basis of the Bibliotheque Nationale documents and Hugh J. Schonfield's *The Passover Plot* (1965), Lincoln and his co-authors posited that Sauniere had found the Holy Grail but that, astonishingly, the Grail was not the chalice in which Christ's blood had been caught at the crucifixion but his *bloodline*.

Their reasoning was elaborate but went like this:

- According to the Cathar myths of Languedoc and other oral sources, Christ had two children by Mary Magdalene and these children fled from the Holy Land to France, where they married into the Frankish royal family to found the fabled Merovingian Dynasty.

- In medieval texts the Grail appeared as "Sangraal", which Baigent and his colleagues translated as "*sang réal*", meaning "royal blood" – the royal blood of Christ's line. *Ipso facto*, the descendants of Christ still walked the face of the earth (well, France at least).
- It had been the job of the Knights Templar and their inner circle, the Priory of Sion, to preserve the secret of Christ's bloodline from the Catholic Church. It was the paperwork to this secret, complete with genealogies, that Sauniere had discovered in the hollow pillar in Rennes-le-Chateau's parish church.

Christ's children. The Holy Grail. Secret societies . . . you couldn't make it all up.

Could you?

Rewind to Rennes-le-Chateau in the 1950s, when the village was a quintessential quiet French hamlet. *Too* quiet for Noel Corbu, owner of a local restaurant, who decided to drum up business by spreading a rumour that Sauniere had found treasure in his church and reburied it somewhere in the hamlet. After a newspaper published the rumour, hundreds descended on Rennes-le-Chateau, many armed with spades. Among the visitors was Pierre Plantard de Saint-Clair, a minor aristocrat who had delusions of regal grandeur and concocted a hoax which involved planting fabricated documents in the Bibliotheque Nationale which indicated him as the rightful king of France. The documents also mentioned the Priory of Sion organization, supposedly founded in the 11th century but in fact set up by Saint-Clair in 1956. To give his story credence, Saint-Clair persuaded a friend, Gerard de Sede, to write a history of the Priory of Sion. This was published in 1967 as *L'Or de Rennes* and presented a number of (forged) medieval documents allegedly discovered by Sauniere in the late 19th century. One avid reader of *L'Or de Rennes* was British science fiction writer Henry Lincoln, who declared that *he* could find in the documents hidden codes, including one which translated as TO DAGOBERT II KING AND TO SION BELONGS THIS TREASURE AND HE IS THERE DEAD. Lincoln parlayed his "discoveries" into a BBC2 documentary and then co-wrote *Holy Blood, Holy Grail* with Baigent and Leigh. *Holy Blood, Holy Grail* upgraded the Rennes-le-Chateau story to suggest Saint-Clair was actually a descendant of Jesus Christ. Then Dan Brown fictionalized the fiction as *The Da Vinci Code*. The rest is bestseller history.

Save perhaps for some proof of Saint-Clair's hoax. Two of Saint-Clair's accomplices, Gerard de Sede and Phillipe de Cherisey, admitted the documents placed in the Bibliotheque Nationale and *L'Or de Rennes* were forgeries (as any sensible examination of them anyway proved: they were written in modern, not medieval, Latin). Sauniere's wealth, as the records of the Carcassone Bishopric showed, came from a distinctly mundane source: he sold masses and solicited gifts from his flock. In 1910–11 Sauniere was tried in an ecumenical court for these frauds.

> French secret society the Priory of Sion protects the bloodline of Christ: ALERT LEVEL 2

Further Reading
Michael Baigent, Richard Leigh and Henry Lincoln, *Holy Blood, Holy Grail*, 1982
Dan Brown, *The Da Vinci Code*, 2003

PROJECT BLUE BOOK

During the great flying-saucer flap after the Second World War, there was just one group of people more interested in UFOs than UFOlogists: the US Air Force. No surprise there, since the boys in blue would be the front line against ETs or, if the saucers were proven to be a dastardly Commie invention, against the USSR.

At first the Air Force collected flying-saucer reports on an *ad hoc* basis, but soon began a series of official investigations. The first official UFO investigation was Project SIGN (1948), established by General Nathan Twining; it was followed by Project GRUDGE (1948–52), which was in turn superseded by Project Blue Book (1952–69).

In the early days of the USAF investigation, the military was split concerning the possible origins of the UFOs, with senior project officers writing a top-secret "Estimate of the Situation" in 1948 which identified them as interplanetary craft. A sceptical Pentagon destroyed the "Estimate", cancelled SIGN and replaced it with GRUDGE, which was duly more cautious about the UFO phenomenon – but was that because it was giving its master what the master wanted to hear?

During the early 1950s the Air Force's UFO investigation became further compromised by politics, when the CIA decided the panicky UFO flaps of the decade needed to be countered. Henceforth the Air Force investigation, now renamed Blue Book, did not just record UFO sightings but also propagandized against them having extraterrestrial causes. So charged, Blue Book backfired spectacularly: its secrecy and overly emphatic denials of extraterrestrial phenomena generated, not assuaged, public UFO paranoia. As a 1965 editorial from the *Richmond News Leader* opined, "Attempts to dismiss the reported sightings under the rationale as exhibited by Project Bluebook [*sic*] won't solve the mystery . . . and serve only to heighten the suspicion that there's something out there that the air force doesn't want us to know about." By the late 1960s, so discredited had Blue Book become that there were widespread calls for a Congressional investigation into its workings and into the whole UFO phenomenon. The subsequent Condon Committee concluded that UFOs were not of extraterrestrial origin, and that further research would be pointless. In response, the USAF closed Blue Book on 17 December 1969.

Since that date there has been, officially, no US government body actively investigating UFO sightings . . . although most UFOlogists believe this is a lie.

> USAF/CIA Project Blue Book covered up UFO sightings: ALERT LEVEL 10

Further Reading

Peter Brookesmith, *UFO: The Complete Sightings Catalogue*, 1995

J. Allen Hynek, *The UFO Experience: A Scientific Inquiry*, 1972

Jenny Randles and Peter Hough, *The Complete Book of UFOs*, 1994

DOCUMENT: EXTRACTS FROM THE US AIR FORCE'S "PROJECT BLUE BOOK" FACTSHEET

On 17 December 1969 the Secretary of the Air Force announced the termination of Project Blue Book, the Air Force program for the investigation of UFOs.

The decision to discontinue the UFO investigation was based on an evaluation of a report prepared by the University of Colorado entitled "Scientific Study of Unidentified Flying Objects"; a review of the University of Colorado's report by the National Academy of Sciences; and Air Force experience investigating UFO reports during the past two decades.

As a result of theses investigations and studies, and experience gained from investigating UFO reports since 1948, the conclusions of Project Blue Book are:

(1) no UFO reported, investigated, and evaluated by the Air Force has ever given any indication of threat to our national security;
(2) there has been no evidence submitted to or discovered by the Air Force that sightings categorized as "unidentified" represent technological developments or principles beyond the range of present day scientific knowledge; and
(3) there has been no evidence indicating that sightings categorized as "unidentified" are extraterrestrial vehicles.

With the termination of Project Blue Book, the Air Force regulation establishing and controlling the program for investigating and analysing UFOs was rescinded. All documentation regarding the former Blue Book investigation has been permanently transferred to the Modern Military Branch, National Archives and Records service, 8th and Pennsylvania Avenue, Washington, DC 20408, and is available for public review and analysis.

Attached for your information is the Project Blue Book sighting summary for the period 1947–69. Also included is a listing of UFO-related materials currently available.

Since the termination of the Project, no evidence has been presented to indicate that further investigation of UFOs by the Air Force is warranted. In view of the considerable Air Force commitment of resources in the past, and the extreme pressure on Air Force funds at this time, there is no likelihood of renewed Air Force involvement in this area.

TOTAL UFO SIGHTINGS, 1947–69

Year	Total Sightings	Unidentified
1947	122	12
1948	156	7
1949	186	22
1950	210	27
1951	169	22
1952	1,501	303
1953	509	42
1954	487	46
1955	545	24
1956	670	14
1957	1,006	14
1958	627	10
1959	390	12
1960	557	14
1961	591	13
1962	474	15
1963	399	14
1964	562	19
1965	887	16
1966	1,112	32
1967	937	19
1968	375	3
1969	146	1

PROMIS

In 1982 a Washington DC software firm, Inslaw, developed a programme called PROMIS (Prosecutors' Management Information System) for the US Justice Department. The unique feature of PROMIS was that it could collate information from different criminal databases without the information being re-entered. An unseemly dispute between Inslaw and the Justice Department soon occurred as to who controlled the rights to PROMIS. The Justice Department halted all payments and Inslaw went bankrupt.

After a tenacious campaign by Bill Hamilton, Inslaw's boss, a bankruptcy court concluded in 1987 that the Justice Department "took, converted and stole PROMIS software through trickery, fraud and deceit".

Why, people wondered, had the Justice Department been so desperate for the PROMIS software that it was prepared to steal it? According to some American conspiracy researchers, the men behind the theft of PROMIS software were the same Reagan stooges behind the alleged 1980 "October Surprise", whereby the Republicans did a deal with the Iranians not to release the 52 American Embassy hostages from Tehran until Reagan was ensconced in the White House. Afterwards, the software was touted to foreign intelligence agencies across the globe; not only did the exported PROMIS software garner revenue for secret CIA operations unauthorized by Congress, the software had been re-engineered to contain a "back door" that allowed the CIA to spy on its foreign users. Naturally, the Justice Department was keen to keep the lid on its creative improvement of PROMIS, and that was why it could not allow Inslaw to claim the rights.

Among the researchers on the PROMIS trail was Danny Casolaro, who believed the PROMIS theft was connected to the activities of a transnational cabal he called the Octopus. On 10 August 1990 Casolaro was found dead in room 517 of the Sheraton Hotel in Martinsburg, West Virginia. The official verdict was suicide, but former Attorney General Elliot Richardson, hired by Inslaw to investigate the case, said: "It's hard to come up with any reason for Casolaro's death other than he was deliberately murdered because he was so close to un-covering sinister elements in . . . the Octopus." However, Casalaro's notes on the Octopus, discovered after his death, turned out to be a far-fetched, fact-free, alternative history of post-war America *à la* the **Gemstone File**, in which the tentacles of the Octopus included the Mafia, Colonel Oliver D. North and the CIA.

It became tempting to dismiss Casolaro's allegations as more Walter Mitty imaginings – except that he was more likely "suicided" than a suicide. He had slashed both wrists 12 times (once so deeply that he cut a tendon, making it virtually impossible to continue holding the razorblade), his suicide note was implausible, his briefcase was missing, and he had warned his brother the previous week: "If anything happens to me, don't believe it was accidental." Casolaro's housekeeper con-firmed the journalist had been receiving threatening phone calls.

During his investigation into PROMIS/the Octopus, he had been meeting with a gallery of unsavoury people. The character who provided most of Casolaro's leads was Michael Riconos-cuito, a self-professed intelligence operative who doubled as a self-professed science genius (indeed, Riconoscuito claimed to be the inventor of the "back door" on the PROMIS software). Casolaro's other "Deep Throat" was Robert Booth Nichols. According to various sources, both Riconoscuito and Nichols worked for, or on behalf of, a private security firm called the Wackenhut Corporation, which used the semi-autonomous status of the Cabazon Indian Reservation in California to obviate laws on the manufacturing and selling of guns. The Wackenhut Corporation sometimes did "off-the-books" sales jobs for the CIA.

In his notebooks Casolaro christened Nichols "Extreme Danger Man". Accurately enough. In addition to whatever it was he was doing down in Cabazon, Nichols was a drug trafficker with ties to the Mafia and its Japanese counterpart, the Yakuza. And Casolaro, according to *Spy* journalist John Connolly, had coincidentally discovered that Nichols had once offered to be an informer for the FBI. In Connolly's words, "If John Gotti, for example, had ever found out what Danny Casolaro had found out, Nichols would be a dead man."

To paraphrase Elliot Richardson, it is hard to come up with any reason for Casolaro's death other than that he was deliberately murdered because he was so close to uncovering sinister elements in the PROMIS deception.

Or rogue arms sales.

Or he needed to be silenced by Nichols.

Casolaro, clearly, was on to something down in the badlands.

Conspiracy researcher Danny Casolaro was silenced to stop his investigation into the theft of PROMIS software: ALERT LEVEL 6

Further Reading

Jonathan Vankin and John Whalen, *The Giant Book of Conspiracies*, 1998

PROTOCOLS OF THE LEARNED ELDERS OF ZION

The Protocols of the Learned Elders of Zion, first published in its complete form as an appendix to *The Anti-Christ is Near at Hand* by Russian writer Sergei Nilus in 1897, is an instruction manual by which a cabal of anonymous but powerful Jews set out the secret means to rule the Christian world.

Among the chief points of the *Protocols* are:

- The Protocol mission "will remain invisible until the moment when it has gained such strength that no cunning can any longer undermine it". (Protocol I)
- "We shall create an intensified centralization of government." (Protocol V)
- "We shall saddle and bridle it [the press] with a tight curb." (Protocol XII)
- "In order that the *goyim* themselves may not guess what they are about, we further distract them with amusements, games, pastimes, passions . . ." (Protocol XIII)
- "It will be undesirable for us that there should exist any other religion than ours . . . We must therefore sweep away all other form of belief." (Protocol XIV)

The impact of the *Protocols* was immediate. They became a sensation in Russia, and after that the world. So taken was industrialist Henry Ford by the book that he printed sections in his *Dearborn Independent*, stating that the *Protocols* "have fitted the world situation up to this time". He also used them to influence the US Senate against joining the League of Nations. He might have done well to ponder his own maxim: History is Bunk. The *Protocols* were a massive hoax and forgery.

The first to debunk the *Protocols* was Lucien Wolf, whose *The Jewish Bogey and the Forged Protocols of the Learned Elders of Zion* (1920) proved that sections of the document had been lifted, with only cosmetic changes, from the 1855 satire *Dialogue aux Enfers entre Montesquieu et Machiavelli* ("Dialogue in Hell between Montesquieu and Machiavelli") by the French lawyer Maurice Joly, who in turn was heavily influenced by Eugene Sue's popular conspiracy novel *The Mysteries of Paris* (1843). Another important source for the *Protocols* was the 1868 novel *Biarritz* by Sir John Retcliffe (aka the German spy Hermann Goedsche), which included a chapter describing how a fictitious rabbinical cadre met in a cemetery at midnight every century to further the work of Jewish domination . . . oh, my.

So who was the forger who stitched the various sources together to make up the *Protocols*? Probably one Matvei Golovinski, an agent for the Russian Tsarist secret police, the Okhrana. By whipping up a scare about revolutionaries in the pay of Jews seeking to bring down the Tsar, the Okhrana intended to justify the regime's reactionary measures. The *Protocols* worked just fine: the 1905–06 pogroms against the Jews ensued. Just over a decade later, the "truth" of the Jewish plan outlined in the *Protocols* seemed confirmed by the 1917 Russian Revolution, some of whose leaders happened to be Jews.

In the febrile minds of far-right Europe, the *Protocols* now became indisputably real and revealing. When the Nazis seized power in Germany, Adolf Hitler made the *Protocols* mandatory reading in schools. He had written in his autobiography, *Mein Kampf*, "For once this book [i.e., the *Protocols*] has become the common property of a people, the Jewish danger is bound to be considered as broken."

Despite – or indeed, because of – the role of the *Protocols* in fanning the anti-Semitism that caused the Holocaust, they live on as "fact". In 2000 Egyptian TV made a series of programmes tracing the connection between the *Protocols*' message and the creation of Israel. In the US, Louis Farrakhan's Nation of Islam distributes the *Protocols*. They are popular, too, in al-Qaeda training camps. Hamas refers positively to them. In fact, wherever anti-Semites gather you'll find well-thumbed copies of the *Protocols*. That any of these organizations or their adherents could not discover within at most thirty seconds' worth of research that the *Protocols* are, as a Swiss court described them as long ago as 1935, "ridiculous nonsense", forgeries and plagiarisms, beggars belief.

The Protocols of the Learned Elders of Zion is the road-map for Jewish take-over of the world: ALERT LEVEL 0

Further Reading
Norman Cohn, *Warrant for Genocide: The Myth of the Jewish World Conspiracy and the Protocols of the Elders of Zion*, 1996
Daniel Pipes, *The Hidden Hand: Middle East Fears of Conspiracy*, 1998
Lucien Wolf, *The Jewish Bogey and the Forged Protocols of the Learned Elders of Zion*, 1920
http://www.radioislam.org

DOCUMENT: EXTRACTS FROM *THE PROTOCOLS OF THE LEARNED ELDERS OF ZION*

PROTOCOL No. 1

1. [. . .] Putting aside fine phrases we shall speak of the significance of each thought: by comparisons and deductions we shall throw light upon surrounding facts.

2. What I am about to set forth, then, is our system from the two points of view, that of ourselves and that of the goyim [i.e., non-Jews].

3. It must be noted that men with bad instincts are more in number than the good, and therefore the best results in governing them are attained by violence and terrorization, and not by academic discussions. Every man aims at power, everyone would like to become a dictator if only he could, and rare indeed are the men who would not be willing to sacrifice the welfare of all for the sake of securing their own welfare.

4. What has restrained the beasts of prey who are called men? What has served for their guidance hitherto?

5. In the beginnings of the structure of society, they were subjected to brutal and blind force; afterwards to Law, which is the same force, only disguised. I draw the conclusion that by the law of nature right lies in force.

6. Political freedom is an idea but not a fact. This idea one must know how to apply whenever it appears necessary with this bait of an idea to attract the masses of the people to one's party for the purpose of crushing another who is in authority. This task is rendered easier if the opponent has himself been infected with the idea of freedom, so-called liberalism, and, for the sake of an idea, is willing to yield some of his power. It is precisely here that the triumph of our theory appears; the slackened reins of government are immediately, by the law of life, caught up and gathered together by a new hand, because the blind might of the nation cannot for one

single day exist without guidance, and the new authority merely fits into the place of the old, already weakened by liberalism.

7. In our day the power which has replaced that of the rulers who were liberal is the power of Gold. Time was when Faith ruled. The idea of freedom is impossible of realization because no one knows how to use it with moderation. It is enough to hand over a people to self-government for a certain length of time for that people to be turned into a disorganized mob. From that moment on we get internecine strife which soon develops into battles between classes, in the midst of which States burn down and their importance is reduced to that of a heap of ashes.

8. Whether a State exhausts itself in its own convulsions, whether its internal discord brings it under the power of external foes – in any case it can be accounted irretrievably lost: it is in our power. The despotism of Capital, which is entirely in our hands, reaches out to it a straw that the State, willy-nilly, must take hold of: if not – it goes to the bottom.

9. Should anyone of a liberal mind say that such reflections as the above are immoral, I would put the following questions: – If every State has two foes and if in regard to the external foe it is allowed and not considered immoral to use every manner and art of conflict, as for example to keep the enemy in ignorance of plans of attack and defence, to attack him by night or in superior numbers, then in what way can the same means in regard to a worse foe, the destroyer of the structure of society and the commonweal, be called immoral and not permissible?

10. Is it possible for any sound logical mind to hope with any success to guide crowds by the aid of reasonable counsels and arguments, when any objection or contradiction, senseless though it may be, can be made and when such objection may find more favour with the people, whose powers of reasoning are superficial? Men in masses and the men of the

masses, being guided solely by petty passions, paltry beliefs, traditions and sentimental theorems, fall a prey to party dissension, which hinders any kind of agreement even on the basis of a perfectly reasonable argument. Every resolution of a crowd depends upon a chance or packed majority, which, in its ignorance of political secrets, puts forth some ridiculous resolution that lays in the administration a seed of anarchy.

11. The political has nothing in common with the moral. The ruler who is governed by the moral is not a skilled politician, and is therefore unstable on his throne. He who wishes to rule must have recourse both to cunning and to make-believe. Great national qualities, like frankness and honesty, are vices in politics, for they bring down rulers from their thrones more effectively and more certainly than the most powerful enemy. Such qualities must be the attributes of the kingdoms of the goyim, but we must in no wise be guided by them.

12. Our right lies in force. The word "right" is an abstract thought and proved by nothing. The word means no more than – Give me what I want in order that thereby I may have a proof that I am stronger than you.

13. Where does right begin? Where does it end?

14. In any State in which there is a bad organization of authority, an impersonality of laws and of the rulers who have lost their personality amid the flood of rights ever multiplying out of liberalism, I find a new right – to attack by the right of the strong, and to scatter to the winds all existing forces of order and regulation, to reconstruct all institutions and to become the sovereign lord of those who have left to us the rights of their power by laying them down voluntarily in their liberalism.

15. Our power in the present tottering condition of all forms of power will be more invincible than any other, because it will remain invisible until the moment when it has gained such strength that no cunning can any longer undermine it.

16. Out of the temporary evil we are now compelled to commit will emerge the good of an unshakable rule, which will restore the regular course of the machinery of the national life, brought to naught by liberalism. The result justifies the means. Let us, however, in our plans, direct our attention not so much to what is good and moral as to what is necessary and useful.

17. Before us is a plan in which is laid down strategically the line from which we cannot deviate without running the risk of seeing the labour of many centuries brought to naught.

18. In order to elaborate satisfactory forms of action it is necessary to have regard to the rascality, the slackness, the instability of the mob, its lack of capacity to understand and respect the conditions of its own life, or its own welfare. It must be understood that the might of a mob is blind, senseless and unreasoning force ever at the mercy of a suggestion from any side. The blind cannot lead the blind without bringing them into the abyss; consequently, members of the mob, upstarts from the people even though they should be as a genius for wisdom, yet having no understanding of the political, cannot come forward as leaders of the mob without bringing the whole nation to ruin.

19. Only one trained from childhood for independent rule can have understanding of the words that can be made up of the political alphabet.

20. A people left to itself, i.e., to upstarts from its midst, brings itself to ruin by party dissensions excited by the pursuit of power and honours and the disorders arising therefrom. Is it possible for the masses of the people calmly and without petty jealousies to form judgment, to deal with the affairs of the country, which cannot be mixed up with personal interest? Can they defend themselves from an external foe? It is unthinkable; for a plan broken up into as many parts as there are heads in the mob, loses all homogeneity, and thereby becomes unintelligible and impossible of execution.

21. It is only with a despotic ruler that plans can be elaborated extensively and clearly in such a way as to distribute the whole properly among the several parts of the machinery of the State: from this the conclusion is inevitable that a satisfactory form of government for any country is one that concentrates [rule] in the hands of one responsible person. Without an absolute despotism there can be no existence for civilization, which is carried on not by the masses but by their guide, whosoever that person may be. The mob is savage, and displays its savagery at every opportunity. The moment the mob seizes freedom in its hands it quickly turns to anarchy, which in itself is the highest degree of savagery.

22. Behold the alcoholic animals, bemused with drink, the right to an immoderate use of which comes along with freedom. It is not for us and ours to walk that road. The peoples of the goyim are bemused with alcoholic liquors; their youth has grown stupid on classicism and from early immorality, into which it has been inducted by our special agents – by tutors, lackeys, governesses in the houses of the wealthy, by clerks and others, by our women in the places of dissipation frequented by the goyim. In the number of these last I count also the so-called "society ladies", voluntary followers of the others in corruption and luxury.

23. Our countersign is – Force and Make-believe. Only force conquers in political affairs, especially if it be concealed in the talents essential to statesmen. Violence must be the principle, and cunning and make-believe the rule for governments which do not want to lay down their crowns at the feet of agents of some new power. This evil is the one and only means to attain the end, the good. Therefore we must not stop at bribery, deceit and treachery when they should serve towards the attainment of our end. In politics one must know how to seize the property of others without hesitation if by it we secure submission and sovereignty.

24. Our State, marching along the path of peaceful conquest, has the right to replace the horrors of war by less noticeable

and more satisfactory sentences of death, necessary to maintain the terror which tends to produce blind submission. Just but merciless severity is the greatest factor of strength in the State: not only for the sake of gain but also in the name of duty, for the sake of victory, we must keep to the programme of violence and make-believe. The doctrine of squaring accounts is precisely as strong as the means of which it makes use. Therefore it is not so much by the means themselves as by the doctrine of severity that we shall triumph and bring all governments into subjection to our super-government. It is enough for them to know that we are too merciless for all disobedience to cease.

25. Far back in ancient times we were the first to cry among the masses of the people the words "Liberty, Equality, Fraternity", words many times repeated since these days by stupid poll-parrots who, from all sides around, flew down upon these baits and with them carried away the well-being of the world, true freedom of the individual, formerly so well guarded against the pressure of the mob. The would-be wise men of the goyim, the intellectuals, could not make anything out of the uttered words in their abstractedness; did not see that in nature there is no equality, cannot be freedom: that Nature herself has established inequality of minds, of characters, and capacities, just as immutably as she has established subordination to her laws: never stopped to think that the mob is a blind thing, that upstarts elected from among it to bear rule are, in regard to the political, the same blind men as the mob itself, that the adept, though he be a fool, can yet rule, whereas the non-adept, even if he were a genius, understands nothing in the political – to all those things the goyim paid no regard; yet all the time it was based upon these things that dynastic rule rested: the father passed on to the son a knowledge of the course of political affairs in such wise that none should know it but members of the dynasty and none could betray it to the governed. As time went on, the meaning of the dynastic transference of

the true position of affairs in the political was lost, and this aided the success of our cause.

26. In all corners of the earth the words "Liberty, Equality, Fraternity" brought to our ranks, thanks to our blind agents, whole legions who bore our banners with enthusiasm. And all the time these words were canker-worms at work boring into the well-being of the goyim, putting an end everywhere to peace, quiet, solidarity and destroying all the foundations of the goyim states. As you will see later, this helped us to our triumph: it gave us the possibility, among other things, of getting into our hands the master card – the destruction of the privileges, or in other words of the very existence of the aristocracy of the goyim, that class which was the only defense peoples and countries had against us. On the ruins of the eternal and genealogical aristocracy of the goyim we have set up the aristocracy of our educated class headed by the aristocracy of money. The qualifications for this aristocracy we have established in wealth, which is dependent upon us, and in knowledge, for which our learned elders provide the motive force.

27. Our triumph has been rendered easier by the fact that in our relations with the men whom we wanted we have always worked upon the most sensitive chords of the human mind, upon the cash account, upon the cupidity, upon the insatiability for material needs of man: and each one of these human weaknesses, taken alone, is sufficient to paralyse initiative, for it hands over the will of men to the disposition of him who has bought their activities.

28. The abstraction of freedom has enabled us to persuade the mob in all countries that their government is nothing but the steward of the people who are the owners of the country, and that the steward may be replaced like a worn-out glove.

29. It is this possibility of replacing the representatives of the people which has placed them at our disposal, and, as it were, given us the power of appointment.

[. . .]

1. It is indispensable for our purpose that wars, so far as possible, should not result in territorial gains: war will thus be brought on to the economic ground, where the nations will not fail to perceive in the assistance we give the strength of our predominance, and this state of things will put both sides at the mercy of our international agentur; which possesses millions of eyes ever on the watch and unhampered by any limitations whatsoever. Our international rights will then wipe out national rights, in the proper sense of right, and will rule the nations precisely as the civil law of States rules the relations of their subjects among themselves.

2. The administrators, whom we shall choose from among the public, with strict regard to their capacities for servile obedience, will not be persons trained in the arts of government, and will therefore easily become pawns in our game in the hands of men of learning and genius who will be their advisers, specialists bred and reared from early childhood to rule the affairs of the whole world. As is well known to you, these specialists of ours have been drawing to fit them for rule the information they need from our political plans from the lessons of history, from observations made of the events of every moment as it passes. The goyim are not guided by practical use of unprejudiced historical observation, but by theoretical routine without any critical regard for consequent results. We need not, therefore, take any account of them – let them amuse themselves until the hour strikes, or live on hopes of new forms of enterprising pastime, or on the memories of all they have enjoyed. For them let that play the principal part which we have persuaded them to accept as the dictates of science (theory). It is with this object in view that we are constantly, by means of our press, arousing a blind confidence in these theories. The intellectuals of the goyim will puff themselves up with their knowledges and without any logical verification of them will put into effect

all the information available from science, which our agen-tur specialists have cunningly pieced together for the pur-pose of educating their minds in the direction we want.

3. Do not suppose for a moment that these statements are empty words: think carefully of the successes we arranged for Darwinism, Marxism, Nietzsche-ism. To us Jews, at any rate, it should be plain to see what a disintegrating impor-tance these directives have had upon the minds of the goyim.

4. It is indispensable for us to take account of the thoughts, characters, tendencies of the nations in order to avoid making slips in the political and in the direction of admin-istrative affairs. The triumph of our system, of which the component parts of the machinery may be variously dis-posed according to the temperament of the peoples met on our way, will fail of success if the practical application of it be not based upon a summing up of the lessons of the past in the light of the present.

5. In the hands of the States of today there is a great force that creates the movement of thought in the people, and that is the Press. The part played by the Press is to keep pointing out requirements supposed to be indispensable, to give voice to the complaints of the people, to express and to create discontent. It is in the Press that the triumph of freedom of speech finds its incarnation. But the goyim states have not known how to make use of this force; and it has fallen into our hands. Through the Press we have gained the power to influence while remaining ourselves in the shade; thanks to the Press we have got the gold in our hands, notwithstanding that we have had to gather it out of the oceans of blood and tears. But it has paid us, though we have sacrificed many of our people. Each victim on our side is worth in the sight of God a thousand goyim.

[. . .]

1. Today I may tell you that our goal is now only a few steps off. There remains a small space to cross and the whole long

path we have trodden is ready now to close its cycle of the Symbolic Snake, by which we symbolize our people. When this ring closes, all the States of Europe will be locked in its coil as in a powerful vice.

2. The constitution scales of these days will shortly break down, for we have established them with a certain lack of accurate balance in order that they may oscillate incessantly until they wear through the pivot on which they turn. The goyim are under the impression that they have welded them sufficiently strong and they have all along kept on expecting that the scales would come into equilibrium. But the pivots – the kings on their thrones – are hemmed in by their representatives, who play the fool, distraught with their own uncontrolled and irresponsible power. This power they owe to the terror which has been breathed into the palaces. As they have no means of getting at their people, into their very midst, the kings on their thrones are no longer able to come to terms with them and so strengthen themselves against seekers after power. We have made a gulf between the far-seeing Sovereign Power and the blind force of the people so that both have lost all meaning, for, like the blind man and his stick, both are powerless apart.

3. In order to incite seekers after power to a misuse of power, we have set all forces in opposition one to another, breaking up their liberal tendencies towards independence. To this end we have stirred up every form of enterprise, we have armed all parties, we have set up authority as a target for every ambition. Of States we have made gladiatorial arenas where a lot of confused issues contend. A little more, and disorders and bankruptcy will be universal.

4. Babblers inexhaustible have turned into oratorical contests the sittings of Parliament and Administrative Boards. Bold journalists and unscrupulous pamphleteers daily fall upon executive officials. Abuses of power will put the final touch in preparing all institutions for their overthrow and everything will fly skyward under the blows of the maddened mob.

5. All people are chained down to heavy toil by poverty more firmly than ever they were chained by slavery and serfdom; from these, one way and another, they might free themselves, these could be settled with, but from want they will never get away. We have included in the constitution such rights as to the masses appear fictitious and not actual rights. All these so-called "People's Rights" can exist only in idea, an idea which can never be realized in practical life. What is it to the proletariat labourer, bowed double over his heavy toil, crushed by his lot in life, if talkers get the right to babble, if journalists get the right to scribble any nonsense side-by-side with good stuff, once the proletariat has no other profit out of the constitution save only those pitiful crumbs which we fling them from our table in return for their voting in favour of what we dictate, in favour of the men we place in power, the servants of our agentur . . . Republican rights for a poor man are no more than a bitter piece of irony, for the necessity he is under of toiling almost all day gives him no present use of them, but the other hand robs him of all guarantee of regular and certain earnings by making him dependent on strikes by his comrades or lock-outs by his masters.

6. The people, under our guidance, have annihilated the aristocracy, who were their one and only defence and foster-mother for the sake of their own advantage, which is inseparably bound up with the well-being of the people. Nowadays, with the destruction of the aristocracy, the people have fallen into the grips of merciless money-grinding scoundrels who have laid a pitiless and cruel yoke upon the necks of the workers.

7. We appear on the scene as alleged saviours of the worker from this oppression when we propose to him to enter the ranks of our fighting forces – Socialists, Anarchists, Communists – to whom we always give support in accordance with an alleged brotherly rule (of the solidarity of all humanity) of our social masonry. The aristocracy, which

enjoyed by law the labour of the workers, was interested in seeing that the workers were well fed, healthy, and strong. We are interested in just the opposite – in the deminution [*sic*], the killing out of the goyim. Our power is in the chronic shortness of food and physical weakness of the worker because by all that this implies he is made the slave of our will, and he will not find in his own authorities either strength or energy to set against our will. Hunger creates the right of capital to rule the worker more surely than it was given to the aristocracy by the legal authority of kings.

8. By want and the envy and hatred which it engenders we shall move the mobs and with their hands we shall wipe out all those who hinder us on our way.

9. When the hour strikes for our sovereign lord of all the world to be crowned it is these same hands which will sweep away everything that might be a hindrance thereto.

10. The goyim have lost the habit of thinking unless prompted by the suggestions of our specialists. Therefore they do not see the urgent necessity of what we, when our kingdom comes, shall adopt at once, namely this, that it is essential to teach in national schools one simple, true piece of knowledge, the basis of all knowledge – the knowledge of the structure of human life, of social existence, which requires division of labour, and, consequently, the division of men into classes and conditions. It is essential for all to know that owing to difference in the objects of human activity there cannot be any equality, that he, who by any act of his compromises a whole class cannot be equally responsible before the law with him who affects no one but only his own honour. The true knowledge of the structure of society, into the secrets of which we do not admit the goyim, would demonstrate to all men that the positions and work must be kept within a certain circle, that they may not become a source of human suffering, arising from an education which does not correspond with the work which individuals are called upon to do. After a thorough study of this knowledge,

the peoples will voluntarily submit to authority and accept such position as is appointed them in the State. In the present state of knowledge and the direction we have given to its development the people – blindly believing things in print – cherishes, thanks to promptings intended to mislead and to its own ignorance, a blind hatred towards all conditions which it considers above itself, for it has no understanding of the meaning of class and condition.

11. This hatred will be still further magnified by the effects of an economic crisis, which will stop dealing on the exchanges and bring industry to a standstill. We shall create by all the secret subterranean methods open to us and with the aid of gold, which is all in our hands, a universal economic crisis whereby we shall throw upon the streets whole mobs of workers simultaneously in all the countries of Europe. These mobs will rush delightedly to shed the blood of those whom, in the simplicity of their ignorance, they have envied from their cradles, and whose property they will then be able to loot.

12. "Ours" they will not touch, because the moment of attack will be known to us and we shall take measures to protect our own.

13. We have demonstrated that progress will bring all the goyim to the sovereignty of reason. Our despotism will be precisely that; for it will know how, by wise severities, to pacificate all unrest, to cauterise liberalism out of all institutions.

14. When the populace has seen that all sorts of concessions and indulgences are yielded it in the name of freedom it has imagined itself to be sovereign lord and has stormed its way to power, but, naturally like every other blind man, it has come upon a host of stumbling blocks, it has rushed to find a guide, it has never had the sense to return to the former state and it has laid down its plenipotentiary powers at our feet. Remember the French Revolution, to which it was we who gave the name of "Great": the secrets of its preparations are well known to us for it was wholly the work of our hands.

15. Ever since that time we have been leading the peoples from one disenchantment to another, so that in the end they should turn also from us in favour of that King-Despot of the blood of Zion, whom we are preparing for the world.

16. At the present day we are, as an international force, invincible, because if attacked by some we are supported by other States. It is the bottomless rascality of the goyim peoples, who crawl on their bellies to force, but are merciless towards weakness, unsparing to faults and indulgent to crimes, unwilling to bear the contradictions of a free social system but patient unto martyrdom under the violence of a bold despotism – it is those qualities which are aiding us to independence. From the premier-dictators of the present day, the goyim peoples suffer patiently and bear such abuses as for the least of them they would have beheaded twenty kings.

17. What is the explanation of this phenomenon, this curious inconsequence of the masses of the people in their attitude towards what would appear to be events of the same order?

18. It is explained by the fact that these dictators whisper to the people through their agents that through these abuses they are inflicting injury on the States with the highest purpose – to secure the welfare of the people, the international brotherhood of them all, their solidarity and equality of rights. Naturally they do not tell the people that this unification must be accomplished only under our sovereign rule.

19. And thus the people condemn the upright and acquit the guilty, persuaded ever more and more that it can do whatsoever it wishes. Thanks to this state of things, the people are destroying every kind of stability and creating disorders at every step.

20. The word "freedom" brings out the communities of men to fight against every kind of force, against every kind of authority, even against God and the laws of nature. For

this reason we, when we come into our kingdom, shall have to erase this word from the lexicon of life as implying a principle of brute force which turns mobs into bloodthirsty beasts.

21. These beasts, it is true, fall asleep again every time when they have drunk their fill of blood, and at such times can easily be riveted into their chains. But if they be not given blood they will not sleep and [will] continue to struggle.

P2 (Propaganda Due)

In the course of their sniffing around the Vatican Bank scandal which claimed the life of Roberto **Calvi**, Italian magistrates repeatedly encountered the name of Licio Gelli, Grandmaster of the Italian Masonic Lodge Propaganda Due (P2). Eventually, in March 1981, enough proof of Gelli's role in the Vatican's money-laundering operation emerged for the police to raid his villa in Arezzo, where they found evidence that P2 was engaged in a crime far larger and more sinister than dealing dodgy money. It was plotting to take over Italy.

A list of 962 P2 conspirators found in Gelli's safe included three cabinet members, 40 MPs, the heads of the army and navy, police chiefs, intelligence officers, 14 judges, numerous industrialists (among them one Silvio Berlusconi) and Victor Emmanuel, Prince of Naples. Shortly afterwards, police found under the false bottom in Gelli's daughter's briefcase a copy of a document entitled *Piana di Rinascita Democratica* ("A Plan for the Rebirth of Democracy"). The title was a misnomer: the document set out a plan for a fascist coup in which unions would be banned and the media put under state control. Following the discovery of the P2 list and *Piana di Rinascita Democratica* the then prime minister Arnaldo Forlani was obliged to resign, causing the fall of the Italian government. Later a court indictment charged that P2's infiltration of the Italian state had "the incredible capacity to control a state's institutions to the point of virtually becoming a state-within-a-state".

Born in 1919, Gelli was a Mussolini-era fascist who had fought with the SS on the Eastern Front before fleeing to South America, where he was a financial backer of Argentinian dictator Juan Peron. Returning to Italy, he became a Mason in 1963 before taking over P2 in 1966. Under his tutelage P2 expanded nearly a hundredfold to 1,000 members, including branches in Argentina, Uruguay and Brazil. Funding P2 was the Mafia, whose role in the Lodge was so conspicuous that in 1976 the Italian Masonic authorities officially closed P2 down, after which it was obliged to meet in secret.

The Mafia wasn't P2's only provider. According to supergrass P2 member Mino Pecorelli, the Lodge was funded by the CIA and Gelli himself was a CIA officer. (Pecorelli was later found shot dead.) A 1990 article in the London *Observer* cited declassified US secret papers which linked Gelli to the CIA's Rome station and the continuance of the notorious Operation Gladio, the CIA-funded and -armed anti-Communist network set up in Italy in the wake of the Second World War. There have been frequent accusations of P2 complicity in the 1978 assassination of Italian Prime Minister Aldo Moro and the 1980 Bologna railway bombing, events which were part of the *"strategia della tensione"* intended to create the conditions for a P2 coup. (According to former CIA agent Richard Brenneke, Gelli and P2 were also entangled in everything "black" from the assassination of Swedish politician Olof Palme to the **Iran–Contra Scandal**.) In 1994 Gelli and other P2 members were acquitted of charges of "conspiracy against the state", though, as Gelli's detractors were quick to point out, the state which was judging him was still riddled with P2 members. Gelli was, however, convicted on charges relating to the Banco Ambrosiano crash and in 2005 was formally indicted for conspiring to murder Roberto Calvi.

P2 was formally banned by the Italian authorities in 1981. Gelli seemingly found some solace in his prison cell from the activities of Silvio Berlusconi's government outside, telling *La Repubblica*: "I look at the country, read the newspaper, and think: 'All [the *Piana di Rinascita Democratica*] is becoming a reality little by little, piece by piece.'"

The P2 lodge plotted a fascist coup in Italy: ALERT LEVEL 9

Further Reading
Philip Willan, *The Last Supper: The Mafia, the Masons and the Killing of Roberto Calvi*, 2007

RAINBOW WARRIOR

On 10 July 1985 the *Rainbow Warrior*, flagship of the conservation organization Greenpeace, was moored in Auckland, New Zealand, from where it was to lead a flotilla of yachts to protest against French nuclear testing on the Muroroa Atoll. Just before midnight, two high-explosive devices attached to the hull of the *Rainbow Warrior* detonated. So forceful were the explosions that a hole eight feet (2.44m) across was opened below the waterline next to the engine room. The vessel sank within minutes. Of the 12 people on board, 11 managed to make the safety of the wharf, but the ship's official photographer, 36-year-old Fernando Pereira, was drowned attempting to retrieve photographic equipment from his cabin.

The New Zealand police, who immediately treated the incident as a homicide enquiry, discovered an abandoned rubber Zodiac dinghy nearby. Within five days the police had arrested a French-speaking couple, initially identified as Alain Turenge and his wife Sophie Turenge. Subsequent inquiries revealed their true identities to be Major Alain Mafart, aged 35, and Captain Dominique Prieur, aged 36, French soldiers seconded to the French security service (Direction Generale de la Securite Exterieure, the DGSE). A number of other French agents were involved in the sinking of the *Rainbow Warrior* but managed to elude the NZ police.

Meanwhile, the Elysee in Paris denounced the sinking of the *Rainbow Warrior* as "criminal". President Mitterrand released a report on 27 August 1985 which completely exonerated the French secret services. This failed to satisfy the French media, who pressurized the Elysee Palace for the truth. After more official denials, Charles Hernu, the Defence Minister, resigned, and on 22 September Prime Minister Laurent Fabius admitted the DGSE had ordered the "neutralization" of the *Rainbow Warrior* in what had been termed, without conscious irony, "Operation Satanic".

On Monday 4 November 1985 Mafart and Prieur appeared in the Auckland District Court. They pleaded guilty to charges of arson and a reduced charge of manslaughter, and were sentenced to ten years' imprisonment on the charge of manslaughter and seven years' imprisonment on the charge of arson. Mitterrand responded by threatening to impose trade sanctions against New Zealand. Eventually, under UN brokerage, New Zealand accepted NZ$13 million compensation and Mafart and Prieur were released to France after serving fewer than four years of their sentences.

The commander of the operation, Louis-Pierre Dillais, later acknowledged his involvement to the New Zealand state broadcaster (TVNZ); despite this confessed connection to a terrorist offence he was allowed by the US government to settle in Virginia, working as an executive for arms dealer F. N. Herstal.

In 2005, the 20th anniversary of the *Rainbow Warrior* sinking, it was admitted by French authorities what many had suspected all along: the late President Francois Mitterrand had personally approved Operation Satanic.

> French DGSE spies sank Greenpeace ship *Rainbow Warrior* in waters of ally New Zealand: ALERT LEVEL 10

Further Reading
Michael King, *Death of the Rainbow Warrior*, 1986
David Robie, *Eyes of Fire*, 2005
Sunday Times Insight Team, *Rainbow Warrior: The French Attempt to Sink Greenpeace*, 1986

RONALD REAGAN

The Bush family, it has to be said, has a history of bad timing. On the morning of **9/11**, George H. W. Bush was meeting with Osama bin Laden's brother even as the jets crashed into the World Trade Center (see the **Bush–Bin Laden Connection**). On 30 March 1981 G. H. W. Bush's son Neil had a dinner date planned with Scott Hinckley for the following evening.

What was odd about that? Well, on 30 March 1981 George Bush was Vice-President of the United States of America, and the President, Ronald Reagan, had just been shot by Scott Hinckley's brother, John Hinckley Jr.

At 2.30 p.m. John Hinckley Jr stood on the sidewalk outside the Washington DC Hilton and popped off several .22 bullets at Reagan, one of which entered the President's lung. Rushed to George Washington University Hospital, the President underwent surgery and survived. If Hinckley's hand had been a little steadier, Reagan would have died.

Which is where the "Bushy knoll" conspiracy gets started up. With Reagan dead, George H. W. "Poppy" Bush would have been elevated to the Oval Office.

Fitting Bush into the frame for the Reagan shooting is not entirely impossible. By all accounts, Bush and Reagan hated each other's guts. Further, Bush had the sort of connections to pull off an assassination, having served as Director of the CIA. According to some intelligence analysts, Bush worked for the

CIA from the early 1960s, though Bush himself denies this. (Oddly, the former **Skull & Bones** boy had also been tied into the **John F. Kennedy** shooting by a 1963 FBI memorandum which briefed "Mr George Bush of the Central Intelligence Agency" on the event; Bush says the George Bush in the memo is someone else. Few agree. There's little dispute, however, that Lee Harvey Oswald's friend Baron De Mohrenschildt died with "Poppy" Bush's calling card in his jacket pocket.) In a sense it doesn't matter when Bush started his spook career, because it's where he ended up that matters: the head desk of the whole CIA shebang. George H. W. Bush became Director of the CIA. If he couldn't set up an assassination, who could?

Then there's John Hinckley Jr himself. According to reports, Hinckley was on valium and was obsessed with Sirhan Sirhan, the man allegedly hypnotically programmed to shoot **Robert F. Kennedy**.The natural follow-up question was: had Hinckley himself been brainwashed by an **MK-ULTRA**-like programme to terminate Reagan?

The widely accepted official story is that the disturbed Hinckley shot the President to get the attention of actress Jodie Foster. At Hinckley's trial he was found not guilty by reason of insanity, and was confined to St Elizabeth's Hospital in Washington DC. He is still there . . . conveniently, some say.

A steamroller could be driven through the Bushdunnit conspiracy by arguing that G.H.W.B., if he was planning a *coup d'état*, would never have let his son arrange dinner with the patsy's brother at such an inopportune time. Oh, and Hinckley did tell the media after the shooting that it was "the greatest love offering in the history of the world". And, of course, Hinckley was psychotic.

All of that said, the pall of a cover-up still lingers over the assassination attempt – the sort of pall, perhaps, that comes from a government conspiring to keep information from the public . . . information such as the decade-long connection between the Bush and Hinckley families, information such as the fact that the Hinckley-owned Vanderbilt Energy company was warned mere hours before the shooting that it likely faced a $2 million fine from the Department of Energy for overpricing oil.

Information like the full facts.

George H. W. Bush sought to assassinate Reagan in a *coup d'état*: ALERT LEVEL 5

Further Reading
James W. Clarke, *On Being Mad or Merely Angry: John W. Hinckley Jr and Other Dangerous People*, 1990

RENDLESHAM FOREST

Rendlesham Forest is the British **Roswell**. Early in the morning of 27 December 1980, radars at RAF Watton in Norfolk picked up an "unknown" flying towards the coast. Soon afterwards, security officers at RAF Woodbridge, a two-base complex run with the USAF in Suffolk, investigated a mystery fire in the bordering Rendlesham Forest. One of the security officers, Sergeant Jim Penniston, later reported: "The air was filled with electricity and we saw an object about the size of a tank. It was triangular, moulded of black glass and had symbols on it. Suddenly it shot off faster than any aircraft I have ever observed." When daylight came, security officers found indentations in the ground and scorchmarks on trees.

Two nights later, the object returned. Deputy Base Commander Lt.-Col. Charles Halt both taped and photographed the UFO. According to him, beams of light from the craft seemed to be aimed at the bunkers storing nuclear weapons. There were also reports of aliens dancing in beams of light. Halt's tape and film were confiscated by visiting US defence officials. Former British Chief of Defence Staff Lord Hill-Norton has said of the Rendlesham Forest incident: "Someone is sitting on information that should be in the public domain."

Under cross-examination, the Rendlesham Forest case collapses. Doubts were first raised when it was noted by investigators at the scene that the light from a nearby lighthouse shone through the trees of Rendlesham Forest; the timing and description of Halt's report showed he was looking in the direction of the lighthouse at the time of his observation. Contrary to fevered reports, radiation levels at the site were not significantly high. Sceptics have suggested other mundane explanations for the Rendlesham incident: on the night of the incident a meteor broke up brightly in the skies overhead and in 1980 the US Air Force was testing a prototype of the Stealth bomber, which has a black triangular shape and a strange radar print.

An alien space craft landed at Rendlesham Forest in 1980: ALERT LEVEL 2

Further Reading
Peter Brookesmith, *UFO: The Complete Sightings Catalogue,* 1995
www.ufoworld.co.uk/rendlshm.htm

ROSICRUCIANS

As for Rosycross Philosophers
Whom you will have to be but sorcerers,
What they pretend to is no more
Than Trismegistus did before
Pythagoras old Zoroastra,
And Apollonius their master

Butler: *Hudibras*, Pt II, *iii*

The mysterious sect known as the Rosicrucians may be a 3,000-year-old organization which holds the philosophical secrets of the Ancient Egyptian pharaohs, which begat the **Freemasons**, which was the humanistic force behind the Renaissance, which sponsored Sirhan Sirhan to assassinate **Robert F. Kennedy**, and which currently runs the **New World Order**.

Of course, the Rosicrucians might also be a gigantic con trick.

The Rosicrucians first announced their presence in 1614 with the publication of a tract entitled *Fama Fraternitatis Rosae Crucis*, which claimed that their fraternity was established in 1407 by Christian Rosencreutz (translated as "Rosy Cross"), a German nobleman-cum-monk who had travelled to the Holy Land, Egypt and Spain gathering esoteric knowledge, and who had erected a House of the Holy Spirit on his return. Two other tracts quickly followed, the *Confessio Fraternitatis Rosae Crucis Addressed to the Learned of Europe* (1615) and *The Chymical Marriage of Christian Rosencreutz* (1616). The tracts showed the

Rosicrucians as consummately skilled in the Hermetic arts – able to transmute metals and to render people invisible. The name "Rosicrucian", it is sometimes suggested, derives not from "Rosy Cross" or "Rosencreutz" but from "*ros crux*", meaning "dew cross". In alchemy the cross is the symbol of light or knowledge, while the "dew" is the medium for turning base metal to gold. Some Freemasons have also claimed that "*ros crux*" refers to the bloodstained cross of Christ, and that the Rosicrucians were actually the banned Knights Templar under a new label. The Catholic Church concurred, finding the symbolic references to the Knights Templar in *The Chymical Marriage* so frequent and objectionable that they condemned it.

The Catholic Church might have seen the Rosicrucians as heretics and Satanists, but the intelligentsia of Europe were madly attracted to the promise in the tracts of a "universal reformation of mankind". Strangely, though, the tracts gave no indication as to how "students of nature" might contact the Rosicrucians. This led some critics to dismiss the Rosicrucian tracts as a "ludibrium" or hoax. Here the plot congeals: among those who characterized the tracts thus was Johann Valentin Andreae, a German Lutheran cleric known to have authored *The Chymical Marriage* and suspected of having penned the other early papers. It can be guessed that Andreae intended the tracts to catalyse opposition to the Catholic Church, and, in order to make them more substantial, pretended they were the work of a fraternity, the "Rosicrucians".

Andreae caught the *Zeitgeist* like few before or after him. Such was the phenomenal impact of the tracts that the historian Frances Yates was minded to label the early 17th century "the Rosicrucian enlightenment". Groups of liberal-minded scholars began setting up Rosicrucian societies. Life imitated art. The first real Rosicrucian order appeared in Holland in the 1620s and was followed by the establishment of an order in London, which managed to recruit Elias Ashmole (founder of the Ashmolean Museum in Oxford) and the architect Christopher Wren. The first American group, the Chapter of Perfection, was set up in Pennsylvania in the 1690s. Needless to say a secret society required arcane rules and rituals; these were codified in the *Perfect and True Preparation of the Philosophical Stone, According to the Secret of the Brotherhoods of the Golden and Rosy Cross* (1710) and *Secret Symbols of the Rosicrucians of the Sixteenth and Seventeenth Centuries* (1785–88). In an admirable piece of recycling, the Freemasons of the 18th century borrowed terminology and practices from the Rosicrucians, including, it is alleged, the Rectified Scottish Rite and the Ancient and Accepted Scottish Rite (in which the 18th degree is called the Knight of the Rose Croix). According to the Masonic author J. M. Ragon, so interconnected did the Rosicrucians and Freemasons become in the 18th century that they eventually merged.

Today at least 20 Rosicrucian societies exist, most claiming a direct line back to Christian Rosencreutz, even to Pharaoh Thutmose III. Broadly, the contemporary Rosicrucians are either esoteric–Christian or para-Masonic, and never the twain shall meet. The Ancient Mystical Order Rosae Cruces (AMORC), the largest of the extant groups, offers open days which are "gentle and informal occasions where people can drop in and meet members of the local Affiliated Bodies. There will usually be a short presentation, called 'A Gentle Flame', followed by refreshments."

A cheese and wine party including mystical mumbo-jumbo from a guy with a beard and sandals. Is that any way to recruit for a secret society to implement the New World Order?

The Rosicrucians are an ancient esoteric order intent on global take-over: ALERT LEVEL 1

Further Reading
Frances Yates, *Rosicrucian Enlightenment,* 1971

ROSWELL

What *did* happen at Roswell, New Mexico, 60 years ago?

The world's most enduring UFO mystery began on 3 July 1947 when sheep farmer Mac Brazel was riding out over the isolated Foster ranch near Corona, New Mexico, and found some strange "metallic, foil-like debris" scattered around. A week later Brazel ventured into Corona, where he heard for the first time about the spate of "flying saucer" sightings in the US. Thinking the wreckage on his ranch might be associated, he informed Sheriff Wilcox, who in turn informed the Army Air Force base at Roswell, 75 miles (120km) to the south. Major Jesse Marcel, the base intelligence officer, duly travelled to Brazel's ranch to inspect the wreckage, and took much of it away. On the same day a civil engineer called Grady L. "Barney" Barnett found a "disc-shaped object" in the Socorro region some 150 miles (240km) west of the Foster spread, inside which were a number of small hairless humanoids. Before Barnett could investigate further, an army jeep rushed up and the occupants ordered him away.

Meanwhile, the base commander at Roswell authorized a press statement announcing the discovery of a flying disc in the locality. The headline in the *Roswell Daily Record* of 8 July blared: "RAAF [Roswell Army Air Field] Captures Flying Saucer on Ranch in Roswell Region." In the afternoon of 8 July, the army suddenly changed its story: the wreckage discovered in the Roswell region was from a high-altitude weather balloon, not an alien craft. The Army's steady insistence on its new line quenched public interest in the Roswell incident for 30 years.

In 1980 that interest was reignited by the publication of *The Roswell Incident* by Charles Berlitz and William Moore, with additional unaccredited material by Stanton Friedman. *The Roswell Incident* maintained categorically that an alien craft had crashed west of Roswell in July 1947, and that alien bodies had been recovered from the wreckage; the debris (like "nothing made on this earth", Marcel recalled) at Brazel's farm was break-up from this craft and that the Army's weather-balloon story was a cover-up to prevent hysteria over an alien invasion. Since *The Roswell Incident*, other UFO researchers have suggested that the US has back-engineered alien technology from the Roswell craft at **Area 51**, and many think – *à la* Nick Redfern in *Body Snatchers in the Desert* (2005) – that the Roswell craft was on a mission to experiment on human beings.

The Roswell Incident garnered an impressive array of new evidence. Among those interviewed by Friedman and Moore was a teletype operator called Lydia Sleppy, who in 1947 was typing out the story of the Roswell crash when she was interrupted by an incoming message: "Attention Albuquerque. Do not transmit. Repeat do not transmit this message. Stop communication immediately." Meanwhile, Roswell researchers Kevin Randle and Donald Schmitt found in the woodwork one Arthur Exon, a retired Air Force brigadier, who told of unusual debris brought into Wright Field in 1947 which was indestructible despite its extraordinarily light weight. Yet another retired USAF officer, Brigadier-General Thomas Dubose, stated in interviews that the White House had been involved in the cover-up and that the weather balloon story was a fabrication. Soon there was a positive rush of people and sources to back up the Roswell alien-crash story. New Mexico mortician Glenn Dennis recalled being asked to provide child-sized coffins for the Roswell base, documents from secret government committee **Majestic–12** confirmed the recovery of alien bodies at Roswell . . . and then in 1995 a film surfaced showing an autopsy on the recovered aliens.

Under scrutiny, however, most of the new information appeared riddled with holes. Sceptics proved conclusively that the Roswell autopsy film was a hoax, as were most if not all the Majestic–12 documents, while Lydia Sleppy's story became ever more fanciful. Declassified documents from 1948 included a secret memorandum by an Air Force intelligence officer reporting no "physical evidence of the existence [of extraterrestrial craft] has been obtained". Marcel contradicted himself on whether the debris he posed with in a 1947 photograph was the recovered debris or switched material.

In an attempt to pour oil on troubled waters, the US Air Force finally published two official reports on the Roswell incident, in 1994 and 1997. The second of these concluded: "But . . . witnesses are mistaken about when events they saw occurred, and they are also seriously mistaken about details of the events." This second report was entitled *The Roswell Report: Case Closed*.

Hardly. Counter-reports, books, films . . . all fly steadily into magazines, bookstores, websites, TV schedules . . . Such promiscuity is not aided by the fact that the UFO community itself is split on whether there was an alien crash at Roswell in 1947.

So, as we said at the beginning, what *did* happen at Roswell? According to the *Roswell Daily Record* of 8 July 1947, the debris Brazel found included "a paper fin . . . Scotch tape". Not exactly the kind of high tech you'd expect from interstellar-travelling Little Green Men, is it? In the absence of hard or convincing alien evidence, the high likelihood is that the debris found at Roswell was from a terrestrial craft. This craft could have been

• a prototype jetfighter which crashed (some researchers suggest the whole aliens-crash-at-Roswell story was actually concocted by an intelligence unit in the US military to cover up the embarrassing failure);

- a crashed missile from RAAF itself, which was home to the 509th Bomb Group, the world's only nuclear bomb squadron in 1947 (this would explain the armed guard used to move materials from Roswell);
- a fu-go incendiary balloon launched by Japan in 1945 but coming to earth two years later;
- or, as the Air Force contends in its 1990s reports, a high-altitude US balloon from the spying operation known as Operation Mogul against Russian nuclear facilities.

All these scenarios would require some minor (in Cold War terms) deceit, but the Air Force's explanation (see below) best fits the facts.

So overwhelming is the quality of the mundane cause for the Roswell incident that William Moore, co-author of the book which started the hullabaloo, has stated: "I am no longer of the opinion that the extraterrestrial explanation is the best explanation for the [Roswell] event."

> The US military/government covered up evidence of a UFO crash at Roswell: ALERT LEVEL 4

Further Reading
Charles Berlitz and William Moore, *The Roswell Incident*, 1980
Kevin D. Randle and Donald R. Schmitt, *UFO Crash at Roswell*, 1991

DOCUMENT: EXTRACTS FROM THE ROSWELL REPORT

FACT VS. FICTION IN THE NEW MEXICO DESERT PUBLISHED BY HEADQUARTERS, UNITED STATES AIR FORCE, 1995

EXECUTIVE SUMMARY

WHAT THE ROSWELL INCIDENT WAS NOT

Before discussing specific positive results that these efforts revealed, it is first appropriate to discuss those things, as indicated by information available to the Air Force, that the "Roswell Incident" was not:

An Airplane Crash
[. . .]
A Missile Crash
[. . .]
A Nuclear Accident
[. . .]
An Extraterrestrial Craft

The Air Force research found absolutely no indication that what happened near Roswell in 1947 involved any type of extraterrestrial spacecraft. This, of course, is the crux of this entire matter. "Pro-UFO" persons who obtain a copy of this report, at this point, most probably begin the "cover-up is still on" claims. Nevertheless, the research indicated absolutely no evidence of any kind that a spaceship crashed near Roswell or that any alien occupants were recovered therefrom, in some secret military operation or otherwise. This does not mean, however, that the early Air Force was not concerned about UFOs. However, in the early days, "UFO" meant Unidentified Flying Object, which literally translated as some object in the air that was not readily identifiable. It did not mean, as the term has evolved in today's language, to equate to alien spaceships. Records from the period reviewed by Air Force researchers as well as those cited by the authors mentioned before, do indicate that the USAF was seriously concerned about the inability to adequately identify unknown flying objects reported in American airspace. All the records, however, indicated that the focus of concern was not on aliens, hostile or otherwise, but on the Soviet Union. Many documents from that period speak to the possibility of developmental secret Soviet aircraft overflying US airspace. This, of course, was of major concern to the fledgling USAF, whose job it was to protect these same skies.

The research revealed only one official AAF document that indicated that there was any activity of any type that pertained to UFOs and Roswell in July 1947. This was a small section of the July Historical Report for the 509th Bomb Group and Roswell AAF that stated: "The Office of Public Information was quite busy during the month answering inquiries on the 'flying disk', which was reported to be in possession of the 509th Bomb Group. The object turned out to be a radar tracking balloon" [. . .] Additionally, this history showed that the 509th Commander, Colonel Blanchard, went on leave on 8 July 1947, which would be a somewhat unusual maneuver for a person involved in the supposed first ever recovery of extraterrestrial materials. (Detractors claim Blanchard did this as a ploy to elude the press and go to the scene to direct the recovery operations.) The history and the morning reports also showed that the subsequent activities at Roswell during the month were mostly mundane and not indicative of any unusual high-level activity, expenditure of manpower, resources or security.

Likewise, the researchers found no indication of heightened activity anywhere else in the military hierarchy in the July 1947 message traffic or orders (to include classified traffic). There were no indications and warnings, notice of alerts, or a higher tempo of operational activity reported that would be logically generated if an alien craft, whose intentions were unknown, entered US territory. To believe that such operational and high-level security activity could be conducted solely by relying on unsecured telecommunications or personal contact without creating any records of such activity certainly stretches the imagination of those who have served in the military who know that paperwork of some kind is necessary to accomplish even emergency, highly classified, or sensitive tasks.

An example of activity sometimes cited by pro-UFO writers to illustrate the point that something unusual was going on was the travel of Lt.-General Nathan Twining, Commander of the Air Materiel Command, to New Mexico in July 1947. Actually, records were located indicating that Twining went to the Bomb Commanders' Course on 8 July, along with a number of other general officers, and requested orders to do so a month before, on 5 June 1947 [. . .]

Similarly, it has also been alleged that General Hoyt Vandenberg, Deputy Chief of Staff at the time, had been involved in directing activity regarding events at Roswell. Activity reports [. . .] located in General Vandenberg's personal papers stored in the Library of Congress did indicate that on July 7 he was busy with a "flying disk" incident; however, this particular incident involved Ellington Field, Texas, and the Spokane (Washington) Depot. After much discussion and information-gathering on this incident, it was learned to be a hoax. There is no similar mention of his personal interest or involvement in Roswell events except in the newspapers.

The above are but two small examples that indicate that, if some event happened that was one of the "watershed happenings" in human history, the US military certainly reacted in an unconcerned and cavalier manner. In an actual case, the military would have had to order thousands of soldiers and airmen, not only at Roswell but throughout the US, to act nonchalantly, pretend to conduct and report business as usual, and generate absolutely no paperwork of a suspicious nature, while simultaneously anticipating that 20 years or more into the future people would have available a comprehensive Freedom of Information Act that would give them great leeway to review and explore government documents. The records indicate that none of this happened (or if it did, it was controlled by a security system so efficient and tight that no one, US or otherwise, has been able to duplicate it since. If such a system had been in effect at the time, it would have also been used to protect our atomic secrets from the Soviets, which history has showed obviously was not the case). The records reviewed confirmed that no such sophisticated and efficient security system existed.

WHAT THE "ROSWELL INCIDENT" WAS

As previously discussed, what was originally reported to have been recovered was a balloon of some sort, usually described as a "weather balloon," although the majority of the wreckage that was ultimately displayed by General Ramey and Major Marcel in the famous photos [. . .] in Ft Worth, was that of a radar target normally suspended from balloons. This radar target, discussed in more detail later, was certainly consistent with the description of a 9 July newspaper article which discussed "tinfoil, paper, tape, and sticks". Additionally, the description of the "flying disk" was consistent with a document routinely used by most pro-UFO writers to indicate a conspiracy in progress – the telegram from the Dallas FBI office of 8 July 1947. This document quoted in part states: ". . . The disk is hexagonal in shape and was suspended from a balloon by a cable, which balloon was approximately twenty feet [6m] in diameter . . . the object found resembles a high-altitude weather balloon with a radar reflector . . . disk and balloon being transported . . ."

Similarly, while conducting the popular-literature review, one of the documents reviewed was a paper entitled "The

Roswell Events" edited by Fred Whiting, and sponsored by the Fund for UFO Research (FUFOR). Although it was not the original intention to comment on what commercial authors interpreted or claimed that other persons supposedly said, this particular document was different because it contained actual copies of apparently authentic sworn affidavits received from a number of persons who claimed to have some knowledge of the Roswell event. Although many of the persons who provided these affidavits to the FUFOR researchers also expressed opinions that they thought there was something extraterrestrial about this incident, a number of them actually described materials that sounded suspiciously like wreckage from balloons. These included the following:

Jesse A. Marcel, NM (son of the late Major Jesse Marcel; 11 years old at the time of the incident). Affidavit dated 6 May 1991. ". . . There were three categories of debris: a thick, foil-like metallic-gray substance; a brittle, brownish-black plastic-like material, like Bakelite; and there were fragments of what appeared to be I-beams. On the inner surface of the I-beam, there appeared to be a type of writing. This writing was a purple-violet hue, and it had an embossed appearance. The figures were composed of curved, geometric shapes. It had no resemblance to Russian, Japanese or any other foreign language. It resembled hieroglyphics, but it had no animal-like characters . . ."

Loretta Proctor (former neighbor of rancher W.W. Brazel). Affidavit dated 5 May 1991. ". . . Brazel came to my ranch and showed my husband and me a piece of material he said came from a large pile of debris on the property he managed. The piece he brought was brown in color, similar to plastic . . . 'Mac' said the other material on the property looked like aluminum foil. It was very flexible and wouldn't crush or burn. There was also something he described as tape which had printing on it. The color of the printing was a kind of purple . . ."

Bessie Brazel Schreiber (daughter of W.W. Brazel; 14 years old at the time of the incident). Affidavit dated 22 September 1993. ". . . The debris looked like pieces of a large balloon which had burst. The pieces were small, the largest I remember measuring about the same as the diameter of a basketball. Most of it was a kind of double-sided material, foil-like on one side and rubber-like on the other. Both sides were grayish silver in color, the foil more silvery than the rubber. Sticks, like kite sticks, were attached to some of the pieces with a whitish tape. The tape was about two or three inches [5–8cm] wide and had flowerlike designs on it. The 'flowers' were faint, a variety of pastel colors, and reminded me of Japanese paintings in which the flowers are not all connected. I do not recall any other types of material or markings, nor do I remember seeing gouges in the ground or any other signs that anything may have hit the ground hard. The foil-rubber material could not be torn like ordinary aluminum foil can be torn . . ."

Sally Strickland Tadolini (neighbor of W.W. Brazel; nine years old in 1947). Affidavit dated 27 September 1993. ". . . What Bill showed us was a piece of what I still think as fabric. It was something like aluminum foil, something like satin, something like well-tanned leather in its toughness, yet was not precisely like any one of those materials . . . It was about the thickness of very fine kidskin glove leather and a dull metallic grayish silver, one side slightly darker than the other. I do not remember it having any design or embossing on it . . ."

Robert R. Porter (B-29 flight Engineer stationed at Roswell in 1947). Affidavit dated 7 June 1991. "On this occasion, I was a member of the crew which flew parts of what we were told was a flying saucer to Fort Worth. The people on board included [. . .] Maj. Jesse Marcel. Capt. William E. Anderson said it was from a flying saucer. After we arrived, the material was transferred to a B-25. I was told they were going to Wright Field in Dayton, Ohio. I was involved in loading the B-29 with the material, which was wrapped in packages with wrapping paper. One of the pieces was triangle-shaped, about 2½ feet [75cm] across the bottom. The rest were in small packages, about the size of a shoebox. The brown paper was held with tape. The material was extremely lightweight. When I picked it up, it was just like picking up an empty package. We loaded the triangle-shaped package and three shoebox-sized packages into the plane. All of the packages could have fit into the trunk of a car . . . When we came back from lunch, they told us they had transferred the material to a B-25. They told us the material was a weather balloon, but I'm certain it wasn't a weather balloon . . ."

In addition to those persons above still living who claim to have seen or examined the original material found on the Brazel Ranch, there is one additional person who was universally acknowledged to have been involved in its recovery, Sheridan Cavitt, Lt.-Col. USAF (Ret.). Cavitt is credited in all claims of having accompanied Major Marcel to the ranch to recover the debris, sometimes along with his Counter Intelligence Corps (CIC) subordinate, William Rickett, who, like Marcel, is deceased. Although there does not appear to be much dispute that Cavitt was involved in the material recovery, other claims about him prevail in the popular literature. He is sometimes portrayed as a closed-mouth (or sometimes even sinister) conspirator who was one of the early individuals who kept the "secret of Roswell" from getting out. Other things about him have been alleged, including the claim that he wrote a report of the incident at the time that has never surfaced.

Since Lt.-Col. Cavitt, who had first-hand knowledge, was still alive, a decision was made to interview him and get a signed sworn statement from him about his version of the events. Prior to the interview, the Secretary of the Air Force provided him with a written authorization and waiver to discuss classified information with the interviewer and release him from any security oath he may have taken.

Subsequently, Cavitt was interviewed on 24 May 1994, at his home. Cavitt provided a signed, sworn statement [. . .] of his recollections in this matter. He also consented to having the interview tape-recorded. [. . .] In this interview, Cavitt related that he had been contacted on numerous occasions by UFO researchers and had willingly talked with many of them; however, he felt that he had oftentimes been misrepresented or had his comments taken out of context so that their true meaning was changed. He stated unequivocally, however, that the material he recovered consisted of a reflective sort of material like aluminum foil, and some thin, bamboo-like sticks. He thought at the time, and continued to do so today, that what he found was a weather balloon, and has told other private researchers that. He also remembered finding a small "black box" type of instrument, which he thought at the time was probably a radiosonde. Lt.-Col. Cavitt also reviewed the famous Ramey/Marcel photographs [. . .] of the wreckage taken to Ft. Worth (often claimed by LITO researchers to have been switched and the remnants of a balloon substituted for it) and he identified the materials depicted in those photos as consistent with the materials that he recovered from the ranch. Lt.-Col. Cavitt also stated that he had never taken any oath or signed any agreement not to talk about this incident and had never been threatened by anyone in the government because of it. He did not even know the incident was claimed to be anything unusual until he was interviewed in the early 1980s.

Similarly, Irving Newton, Major, USAF (Ret.) was located and interviewed. Newton was a weather officer assigned to Fort Worth who was on duty when the Roswell debris was sent there in July 1947. He was told that he was to report to General Ramey's office to view the material. In a signed, sworn statement [. . .] Newton related that ". . . I walked into the General's office where this supposed flying saucer was lying all over the floor. As soon as I saw it, I giggled and asked if that was the flying saucer . . . I told them that this was a balloon and a RAWIN target . . ." Newton also stated that ". . . while I was examining the debris, Major Marcel was picking up pieces of the target sticks and trying to convince me that some notations on the sticks were alien writings. There were figures on the sticks, lavender or pink in color, appeared to be weather-faded markings, with no rhyme or reason [sic]. He did not convince me that these were alien writings." Newton concluded his statement by relating that ". . . During the ensuing years I have been interviewed by many authors, I have been quoted and misquoted. The facts remain as indicated above. I was not influenced during the original interview, nor today, to provide anything but what I know to be true, that is, the material I saw in General Ramey's office was the remains of a balloon and a RAWIN target."

Balloon Research
The original tasking from GAO noted that the search for information included "weather balloons." Comments about balloons and safety reports have already been made, however the SAF/AAZ research efforts also focused on reviewing historical records involving balloons, since, among other reasons, that was what was officially claimed by the AAF to have been found and recovered in 1947.

As early as 28 February 1994, the AAZD research team found references to balloon tests taking place at Alamogordo AAF (now Holloman AFB) and White Sands during June and July 1947, testing "constant level balloons" and a New York University (NYU)/Watson Labs effort that used ". . . meteorological devices . . . suspected for detecting shock waves generated by Soviet nuclear explosions" – a possible indication of a cover story associated with the NYU balloon project. Subsequently, a 1946 HQ AMC memorandum surfaced, describing the constant-altitude balloon project and specified that the scientific data be classified TOP SECRET Priority IA. Its name was Project Mogul [. . .]

Project Mogul was a then-sensitive classified project whose purpose was to determine the state of Soviet nuclear weapons research. This was the early Cold War period and there was serious concern within the US government about the Soviets developing a weaponized atomic device. Because the Soviet Union's borders were closed, the US Government sought to develop a long-range nuclear explosion detection capability. Long-range, balloon-borne, low-frequency acoustic detection was posed to General Spaatz in 1945 by Dr Maurice Ewing of Columbia University as a potential solution (atmospheric ducting of low-frequency pressure waves had been studied as early as 1900).

As part of the research into this matter, AAZD personnel located and obtained the original study papers and reports of the New York University project. Their efforts also revealed that some of the individuals involved in Project Mogul were still living. These persons included the NYU constant-altitude balloon Director of Research, Dr Athelstan F. Spilhaus; the Project Engineer, Professor Charles B. Moore; and the military Project Officer, Colonel Albert C. Trakowski.

All of these persons were subsequently interviewed and signed sworn statements about their activities. [. . .] These interviews confirmed that Project Mogul was a compartmented, sensitive effort. The NYU group was responsible for developing constant-level balloons and telemetering equipment that would remain at specified altitudes (within the acoustic duct) while a group from Columbia was to develop acoustic sensors. Doctor Spilhaus, Professor Moore, and certain others of the group were aware of the actual purpose of the project, but they did not know of the project nickname at the time. They handled casual inquiries and/or scientific inquiries/papers in terms of "unclassified meteorological or balloon research." Newly hired employees were not made aware that there was anything special or classified about their work; they were told only that their work dealt with meteorological equipment.

An advance ground team, led by Albert P. Crary, preceded the NYU group to Alamogordo AAF, New Mexico, setting up ground sensors and obtaining facilities for the NYU group. Upon their arrival, Professor Moore and his team experimented with various configurations of neoprene balloons; development of balloon "trains" [. . .]; automatic ballast systems, and use of Naval sonobuoys (as the Watson Lab acoustical sensors had not yet arrived). They also launched what they called "service flights." These "service flights" were not logged nor fully accounted for in the published Technical Reports generated as a result of the contract between NYU and Watson Labs. According to Professor Moore, the "service flights" were composed of balloons, radar reflectors and payloads specifically designed to test acoustic sensors (both early sonobuoys and the later Watson Labs devices). The "payload equipment" was expendable and some carried no "REWARD" or "RETURN TO . . ." tags because there was to be no association between these flights and the logged constant-altitude flights which were fully acknowledged. The NYU balloon flights were listed sequentially in their reports (i.e. A, B, 1, 5, 6, 7, 8, 10 . . .) yet gaps existed for Flights 2–4 and Flight 9. The interview with Professor Moore indicated that these gaps were the unlogged "service flights."

Professor Moore, the on-scene Project Engineer, gave detailed information concerning his team's efforts. He recalled that radar targets were used for tracking balloons because they did not have all the necessary equipment when they first arrived in New Mexico. Some of the early, developmental radar targets were manufactured by a toy or novelty company. These targets were made up of aluminum "foil" or foil-backed paper, balsa wood beams that were coated in an "Elmer's-type" glue to enhance their durability, acetate and/or cloth reinforcing tape, single strand and braided nylon twine, brass eyelets and swivels to form a multi-faced reflector somewhat similar in construction to a box kite [. . .] Some of these targets were also assembled with purplish-pink tape with symbols on it [. . .]

According to the log summary [. . .] of the NYU group, Flight A through Flight 7 (20 November 1946–2 July 1947) were made with neoprene meteorological balloons (as opposed to the later flights made with polyethylene balloons). Professor Moore stated that the neoprene balloons were susceptible to degradation in the sunlight, turning from a milky white to a dark brown. He described finding remains of balloon trains with reflectors and payloads that had landed in the desert: the ruptured and shredded neoprene would "almost look like dark gray or black flakes or ashes after exposure to the sun for only a few days. The plasticizers and antioxidants in the neoprene would emit a peculiar acrid odor and the balloon material and radar target material would be scattered after returning to earth, depending on the surface winds." Upon review of the local newspaper photographs from General Ramey's press conference in 1947 and descriptions in popular books by individuals who supposedly handled the debris recovered on the ranch, Professor Moore opined that the material was most likely the shredded remains of a multi-neoprene balloon train with multiple radar reflectors. The material and a "black box" described by Cavitt was, in Moore's scientific opinion, most probably from Flight 4, a "service flight" that included a cylindrical metal sonobuoy and portions of a weather instrument housed in a box, which was unlike typical weather radiosondes which were made of cardboard. Additionally, a copy of a professional journal maintained at the time by A.P. Crary, provided to the Air Force by his widow, showed that Flight 4 was launched on 4 June 1947 but was not recovered by the NYU group. It is very probable that this TOP SECRET project balloon train (Flight 4), made up of unclassified components, came to rest some miles northwest of Roswell, NM, became shredded in the surface winds and was ultimately found by the rancher, Brazel, ten days later. This possibility was supported by the observations of Lt.-Col. Cavitt [. . .], the only living eyewitness to the actual debris field and the material found. Lt.-Col. Cavitt described a small area of debris which appeared "to resemble bamboo type square sticks one quarter to one half inch square, that were very light, as well as some sort of metallic reflecting material that was also very light . . . I remember recognizing this material as being consistent with a weather balloon."

Concerning the initial announcement, "RAAF Captures Flying Disc," research failed to locate any documented evidence as to why that statement was made. However, on 10 July 1947, following the Ramey press conference, the *Alamogordo News* published an article with photographs demonstrating multiple balloons and targets at the same location as the NYU group operated from at Alamogordo AAF. Professor Moore expressed surprise at seeing this since his was the only balloon test group in the area. He stated, "It appears that there was some type of umbrella cover story to protect our work with Mogul." Although the Air Force did not find documented evidence that Gen. Ramey was directed to espouse a weather balloon in his press conference, he may have done so because either he was aware of Project Mogul and was trying to deflect interest from it, or he readily perceived the material to be a weather balloon based on the identification from his weather officer, Irving Newton. In either case, the materials recovered by the AAF in July 1947 were not readily recognizable as anything special (only the purpose was special) and the recovered debris itself was unclassified. Additionally, the press dropped its interest in the matter as quickly as they had jumped on it. Hence, there would be no particular reason to further document what quickly became a "non-event."

The interview with Colonel Trakowski [. . .] also provided valuable information. Trakowski provided specific details on Project Mogul and described how the security for the program was set up, as he was formerly the TOP SECRET

Control Officer for the program. He further related that many of the original radar targets that were produced around the end of World War II were fabricated by toy or novelty companies using a purplish-pink tape with flower and heart symbols on it. Trakowski also recounted a conversation that he had with his friend, and superior military officer in his chain of command, Colonel Marcellus Duffy, in July 1947. Duffy formerly had Trakowski's position on Mogul but had subsequently been transferred to Wright Field. He stated: ". . . Colonel Duffy called me on the telephone from Wright Field and gave me a story about a fellow that had come in from New Mexico, woke him up in the middle of the night or some such thing with a handful of debris, and wanted him, Colonel Duffy, to identify it. . . . He just said, 'It sure looks like some of the stuff you've been launching at Alamogordo,' and he described it, and I said, 'Yes, I think it is.' Certainly Colonel Duffy knew enough about radar targets, radio-sondes, balloon-borne weather devices. He was intimately familiar with all that apparatus."

Attempts were made to locate Colonel Duffy but it was ascertained that he had died. His widow explained that, although he had amassed a large amount of personal papers relating to his Air Force activities, she had recently disposed of these items. Likewise, it was learned that A.P. Crary was also deceased; however his surviving spouse had a number of his papers from his balloon-testing days, including his professional journal from the period in question. She provided the Air Force researchers with this material. [. . .] Overall, it helps fill in gaps of the Mogul story.

During the period the Air Force conducted this research, it was discovered that several others had also discovered the possibility that the "Roswell Incident" may have been generated by the recovery of a Project Mogul balloon device. These persons included Professor Charles B. Moore, Robert Todd, and coincidentally Karl Pflock, a researcher who is married to a staffer who works for Congressman Schiff.

Some of these persons provided suggestions as to where documentation might be located in various archives, histories and libraries. A review of the Freedom of Information Act (FOIA) requests revealed that Robert Todd, particularly, had become aware of Project Mogul several years ago and had doggedly obtained from the Air Force, through the FOIA, a large amount of material pertaining to it; long before the AAZD researchers independently seized on the same possibility.

Most interestingly, as this report was being written, Pflock published his own report of this matter under the auspices of FUFOR, entitled "Roswell in Perspective" (1994). Pflock concluded from his research that the Brazel Ranch debris originally reported as a "flying disc" was probably debris from a Mogul balloon; however, there was a simultaneous incident that occurred not far away that caused an alien craft to crash and that the AAF subsequently recovered three alien bodies therefrom. Air Force research did not locate any information to corroborate that this incredible coincidence occurred, however.

In order to provide a more detailed discussion of the specifics of Project Mogul and how it appeared to be directly responsible for the "Roswell Incident," a SAF/AAZD researcher prepared a more detailed discussion on the balloon project which is appended to this report [. . .]
[. . .]

Conclusion
The Air Force research did not locate or develop any information that the "Roswell Incident" was a UFO event. All available official materials, although they do not directly address Roswell *per se*, indicate that the most likely source of the wreckage recovered from the Brazel Ranch was from one of the Project Mogul balloon trains. Although that project was TOP SECRET at the time, there was also no specific indication found to indicate an official pre-planned cover

story was in place to explain an event such as that which ultimately happened. It appears that the identification of the wreckage as being part of a weather-balloon device, as reported in the newspapers at the time, was based on the fact that there was no physical difference in the radar targets and the neoprene balloons (other than the numbers and configuration) and between Mogul balloons and normal weather balloons. Additionally, it seems that there was over-reaction by Colonel Blanchard and Major Marcel, in originally reporting that a "flying disk" had been recovered when, at that time, nobody for sure knew what that term even meant since it had only been in use for a couple of weeks.

Likewise, there was no indication in official records from the period that there was heightened military operational or security activity which should have been generated if this was, in fact, the first recovery of materials and/or persons from another world. The post-War US Military (or today's for that matter) did not have the capability to rapidly identify, recover, coordinate, cover-up, and quickly minimize public scrutiny of such an event. The claim that they did so without leaving even a little bit of a suspicious paper trail for 47 years is incredible.

It should also be noted here that there was little mentioned in this report about the recovery of the so-called "alien bodies." This is for several reasons: First, the recovered wreckage was from a Project Mogul balloon. There were no "alien" passengers therein. Secondly, the pro-UFO groups who espouse the alien-bodies theories cannot even agree among themselves as to what, how many, and where, such bodies were supposedly recovered. Additionally, some of these claims have been shown to be hoaxes, even by other UFO researchers. Thirdly, when such claims are made, they are often attributed to people using pseudonyms or who otherwise do not want to be publicly identified, presumably so that some sort of retribution cannot be taken against them (notwithstanding that nobody has been shown to have died,

disappeared or otherwise suffered at the hands of the government during the last 47 years). Fourth, many of the
persons making the biggest claims of "alien bodies" make
their living from the "Roswell Incident." While having a
commercial interest in something does not automatically
make it suspect, it does raise interesting questions related
to authenticity. Such persons should be encouraged to present their evidence (not speculation) directly to the government and provide all pertinent details and evidence to
support their claims if honest fact-finding is what is wanted.
Lastly, persons who have come forward and provided their
names and made claims, may have, in good faith but in the
"fog of time," misinterpreted past events. The review of Air
Force records did not locate even one piece of evidence to
indicate that the Air Force has had any part in an "alien"
body recovery operation or continuing cover-up.

During the course of this effort, the Air Force has kept in
close touch with the GAO and responded to their various
queries and requests for assistance. This report was generated as an official response to the GAO, and to document the
considerable effort expended by the Air Force on their
behalf. It is anticipated that that they will request a copy
of this report to help formulate the formal report of their
efforts. It is recommended that this document serve as the
final Air Force report related to the Roswell matter, for the
GAO, or any other inquiries.

[. . .]

ROYAL INSTITUTE OF INTERNATIONAL AFFAIRS

The Royal Institute of International Affairs is the legal name for the British think-tank more popularly known as Chatham House. At first viewing everything about the RIIA seems open and above-board; it is a membership-based organization that hosts discussions any member can attend (providing he or she pays up an annual membership fee in excess of £300). Staff are listed on the RIIA website, and posts are advertised publicly.

Critics claim, however, that behind the elegant 18th-century facade of Chatham House there machinates a cabal of politicians which seeks to undemocratically influence world opinion. More darkly still, some internet websites argue that the RIIA and its sister US organization, the **Council on Foreign Relations** (CFR), are home to a secret society which actually runs the earth's affairs.

Few would disagree that Chatham House lies both literally and metaphorically in the heart of the British Establishment; founded in 1920, it provides a regular sounding board for senior statesmen, especially the incumbent of the head job at the Foreign Office. A *Guardian* report in December 2006 traced the ways in which the RIIA cosily spreads British government propaganda as news. What always sets conspiracy alarm bells ringing, however, is the famous Chatham House Rule, which, when invoked, ensures the confidentiality of all meeting participants. The rule currently reads as follows:

When a meeting, or part thereof, is held under the Chatham House Rule, participants are free to use the information received, but neither the identity nor the affiliation of the speaker(s), nor that of any other participant, may be revealed.

Inevitably, Chatham House maintains that the secrecy rule is necessary for free speech to occur at meetings; if there were no such rule, participants would not genuinely engage for fear of their comments being reported in the press.

As with the CFR, the origins of the RIIA lie in a dream of the British adventurer and diamond magnate Cecil Rhodes. In the late Victorian era, few men on Earth matched Rhodes's wealth and power; the country Rhodesia (now Zimbabwe) was named for him. In 1877, Rhodes wrote in *Confession of Faith*: "Why should we not form a secret society with but one object: the furtherance of the British Empire and the bringing of the whole civilized world under British rule, for the recovery of the United States, for making the Anglo-Saxon race but one Empire." Rhodes put his money where his mouth was and set up the Round Table organization, to be funded in perpetuity by a bequest in his will. (Rhodes also founded the Rhodes Scholarships at Oxford, of which Bill Clinton was a recipient . . . but that's another story.) Nearly 20 years later, at the Versailles Conference which ended the First World War, some men who shared Rhodes's Round Table ideals met with diplomats and statesmen from both Britain and the US. Out of their discussions both the RIIA and CFR were conceived. It follows, therefore, according to conspiracists, that both the CFR and RIIA are the present embodiments of Rhodes's secret society ideal.

RIIA undemocratically influences world agendas: ALERT LEVEL 8

RIIA is the cover for Round Table society of one-worlders: ALERT LEVEL 3

Further Reading
Robert Gaylon Ross, *Who's Who of the Elite*, 2002
http://www.riia.org/

SATANIC RITUAL ABUSE

In 1980 Canadian Michelle Smith and her psychiatrist Lawrence Pazder published *Michelle Remembers*, in which she told of the physical and sexual abuse she had suffered as a child in the hands of a Satanic cult. She had even witnessed human sacrifice. By 1983 the neighbouring US was in a state of near hysteria over "Satanic Ritual Abuse" (SRA) after a mother at the McMartin Pre-School in Manhattan, California, accused a social worker there of abusing her child; hundreds of children were interviewed by psychotherapists, and it was discovered that 360 children had been abused by McMartin teachers who belonged to a "Satanic Church" whose practices involved drinking the blood of ritually murdered babies.

In 1987 US talk-show host Geraldo Rivera presented a series of TV shows on the phenomenon, claiming: "There are over one million Satanists in this country . . . From small towns to large cities, they have attracted police and FBI attention to their ritual child abuse, child pornography and grisly Satanic murders. The odds are that this is happening in your town." It was estimated by Rivera and others in the media that thousands of children were disappearing every year into the hands of the cults.

Why was no one doing anything to stop it? Because in every city, every town, every settlement, the Satanists had co-opted local police officers and politicians into their conspiracy. Apocalyptic Christians proposed that the conspiracy ran to the top of the social pyramid, even unto the White House itself. Since in the end of times the Devil must establish himself everywhere, the SRA phenomenon spread abroad, notably to the UK; in 1993 children in the Orkney Islands were forcibly removed in dawn raids from their Satanic, abusive parents.

Sceptics claim that the only evidence for SRA comes from the victims themselves, usually through the technique of "recovered memory", in which psychotherapists aid the subject to "recall" the abuse suffered. The technique has been demonstrated since to be badly flawed, and many of the subjects (including Michelle Smith herself) were mentally ill. Her book has been proven a hoax by several independent investigators. A four-year study of SRA headed by University of California at Davis psychology professors Gail S. Goodman and Phillip R. Shaver assessed more than 12,000 accusations; the researchers could find no unequivocal evidence for SRA in the US.

Believers in SRA point to the testimony of ritually abused children, suggesting they are unlikely to have invented stories of macabre sexual practices. This is correct: research has demonstrated over and over that investigating social workers, police officers and adult authorities suggestively encourage or badger children to tell stories of abusive behaviour. John Stoll of Bakersfield, California, served a 20-year prison sentence for child abuse until a judge released him in 2004; it transpired that, in assembling the original "evidence" against Stoll, the county's Child Protective Services had informed child interviewees they could not go home until they admitted Stoll had abused them.

Typically of SRA cases, the evidence against John Stoll rested on testimony alone. The same was true of the McMartin trial, where the jury failed to make one conviction. Where medical evidence has been given in SRA cases of sodomy in Britain it has proven to be suspect.

The SRA panic has uncomfortable undertones of the medieval witch hunts.

Satanists ritually abuse and kill children: ALERT LEVEL 2

Further Reading
Elizabeth Loftus, *The Myth of Repressed Memory*, 1994
Debbie Nathan and Michael Snedeker, *Satan's Silence: Ritual Abuse and the Making of a Modern American Witch Hunt*, 2001

At the height of London's morning rush hour on 7 July 2005, a series of four coordinated bomb blasts hit the city's public transport system. Three of the bombs exploded within 50 seconds of each other on Underground trains (at King's Cross, Edgware Road and Liverpool Street/Aldgate); the fourth exploded nearly an hour later, at 9.47 a.m., on a Number 30 double-decker bus as it entered Tavistock Square. Altogether the explosions took 56 lives and injured 700 in what was the deadliest terror attack in Britain since the **Lockerbie Bombing** of 1988.

While ambulances were still rushing casualties to hospital, a flurry of conspiracy theories started on the internet concerning the attacks, but they boiled down to two main ideas:

- the British security services had advance warning of the terrorist attacks, yet failed to take action, either because of incompetence or because they wished the attacks to occur to justify the introduction of draconian laws
- the bombings were carried out by MI5 *themselves* as a false-flag operation to facilitate the implementation of those draconian laws

The evidence for the false-flag op centres on where the bombs were placed. According to the Metropolitan Police, which led the state's investigation, the bombs were carried into London in back-packs by four British-born supporters of al-Qaeda: Mohammad Sidique Khan, Shehzad Tanweer, Germain Lindsay and Hasib Hussain. Conspiracy blogger socialdemocracynow, however, asserts:

> The most damning piece of evidence against the government is the testimony of one of the victims, dancer Bruce Lait, who, along with his dance partner Crystal Main, was nearest to the bomb when it exploded. When he was being assisted out of the carriage, Lait recalls, "The policeman said, 'Mind that hole, that's where the bomb was.' The metal was pushed upwards as if the bomb was underneath the train."

MI5, in other words, laid explosive devices on the tracks. If the bombs were on the tracks it accounts for one of the peculiarities of the morning of 7 July: the shut-down of the electrically powered Underground system, since bombs placed in carriages could not have wrecked lines to the requisite extent. Some conspiracists favour a tweak to the MI5-bomb-plot scenario, alleging that the security service subcontracted the attacks to an outside agency. This is generally identified as London-based Visor Consultants, a security risk and assessment company. According to the company's website:

> Visor Consultants have been able to support many domestic and global organizations to prevent chaos in a crisis and increase their overall resilience. Our clients include one of the top seven companies in the US and key Departments of the UK Government. Making any crisis an "abrupt audit" rather than a presumed catastrophe has helped many organizations grow as a result.

Visor Consultants, by their own admission, were engaged in a city-wide operation on the morning of 7 July. The company's managing director, Peter Power, told a BBC Radio 5 interviewer that evening: "At half past nine this morning we were actually running an exercise for a company of over a thousand people in London based on simultaneous bombs going off precisely at the railway stations where it happened this morning, so I still have the hairs on the back of my neck standing up right now." He dismissed the similarity between the Visor Consultants' exercise and the actual bombings as coincidence.

Some conspiracists speculate that Visor Consultants were not MI5 proxy bombers but genuine casualty/crisis experts put on alert by "key Departments of the UK Government" to assist in the aftermath of the attacks, of which the government had prior knowledge. In this version, Visor were responsible for the medical supplies said by several witnesses to be on site at Edgware Road before the bombs detonated. The Israeli intelligence agency Mossad is frequently reported as having tipped off the British government about a planned al-Qaeda attack on London; as early as December 2004 FBI operatives in London, *Newsweek* reported, were avoiding the underground because of the impending al-Qaeda attack upon it. The British government has consistently maintained that it had no advance warning of the 7/7 bombs.

The difficulty for all false-flag explanations for 7/7 is the video testament by bomber Mohammad Sidique Khan, aired by Arab TV network al-Jazeera on 1 September 2005, in which he said:

> I and thousands like me are forsaking everything for what we believe. Our drive and motivation doesn't come from tangible commodities that this world has to offer. Our religion is Islam, obedience to the one true God and following the footsteps of the final prophet messenger.
>
> Your democratically elected governments continuously perpetrate atrocities against my people all over the world. And your support of them makes you directly responsible, just as I am directly responsible for protecting and avenging my Muslim brothers and sisters.
>
> Until we feel security you will be our targets and until you stop the bombing, gassing, imprisonment and torture of my people we will not stop this fight. We are at war and I am a soldier. Now you too will taste the reality of this situation.

To most observers Sidique Khan's taped message sounded like a suicide mission note, not the sign-off of an MI5 stooge. As for the witness evidence suggesting bomb blasts beneath the trains, this is unreliable: it consists of one or two traumatized people who are unlikely to have been able to recall events accurately. The power went down on the Underground network because a Code Amber Alert (emergency suspension of service) was declared at 09.19 a.m., and not because of collateral blast damage.

A number of pressure groups such as J7: The July 7th Truth Campaign have demanded that "the government RELEASE THE EVIDENCE which conclusively proves, beyond reasonable doubt, the official Home Office narrative". A public inquiry has been several times denied on the grounds that it would both undermine the work of the security services and affect the legality of any forthcoming trial of suspected plot accessories. If the government is sitting on evidence it is likely to be of the most mundane sort: that MI5 and Scotland Yard bungled. Far from being the super-efficient machines of paranoid conspiracy, MI5 and Scotland Yard are large tankers which, having been ordered to change course from spying on Communists and the IRA, are taking years to get on to the new anti-Islamic terrorism bearing. It is clear from the House of Commons Intelligence and Security Committee Report into The London Terrorists on 7 July 2005 that Khan and Tanweer were identified by intelligence officers months before the attack and had even been interviewed by Scotland Yard.

Prior to the 7 July attacks, the Security Service had come across Sidique Khan and Shehzad Tanweer on the peripheries of other surveillance and investigative operations. At that time their identities were unknown to the Security Service and there was no appreciation of their subsequent significance. As there were more pressing priorities at the time, including the need to disrupt known plans to attack the UK, it was decided not to investigate them further or seek to identify them. When resources became available, attempts were made to find out more about these two and other peripheral contacts, but these resources were soon diverted back to what were considered to be higher investigative priorities. The chances of identifying the planners and preventing the 7 July attacks might have been greater had different investigative decisions been taken by the Security Service in 2003–05. However, someone, somewhere made the decision that Khan and Tanweer were fry not worth bothering with . . . and 7 July was the tragic result. A terrorist outrage committed by home-grown Islamic fanatics inspired by, but not in the control of, al-Qaeda.

7/7 was a state terror operation orchestrated by MI5: ALERT LEVEL 3

The government is covering up evidence of intelligence service bungling before 7/7: ALERT LEVEL 8

Further Reading
The Intelligence and Security Committee Report into the London Terrorist Attacks on 7 July 2005, 2006
http://www.julyseventh.co.uk/

SHAG HARBOUR

Before 1967 only a handful of people in the world would have been able to find the small Nova Scotia fishing village of Shag Harbour on a map. All that changed on the late evening of 4 October 1967, with one of the best documented UFO sightings of all time.

At around 11.20 p.m. local teenager Laurie Wickens and four of his friends, driving through Shag Harbour on Highway 3, spotted a large object with flashing amber lights descend into the waters of the harbour, where it floated about 1,000 feet (300m) out from shore. Believing an aircraft had crashed, Wickens alerted the RCMP; other residents had seen the object descend, and they too contacted the police. Within quarter of an hour, three RCMP officers arrived at Shag Harbour, where they witnessed the object floating on the water; one of the Mounties, Ron Pound, later recalled the craft as being around 60 feet (18m) long. Concerned that the crashed craft might have survivors aboard, the RCMP contacted the Rescue Coordination Centre in Halifax, who dispatched Coast Guard boat 101 to the scene. Before this boat arrived the object sank, leaving only a wide trail of yellow foam behind it.

On checking with the NORAD radar station at Baccaro the RMCP discovered there were no reports of missing aircraft in the region. At 3.00 a.m. the next day the Coast Guard called off its hunt for survivors. However, Rescue Coordination Centre ordered a team of Navy divers from HMCS *Granby* to comb the harbour bottom for the object. One local fisherman reported he saw the naval divers retrieve aluminium-coloured debris. The final report from the Canadian authorities stated that not a trace of the crashed object had been found.

For 30 years the Shag Harbour mystery went cold, until one of the original witnesses, Chris Styles, decided to reinvestigate the case. He interviewed two of the navy divers from HMCS *Granby*, who informed him that the crashed craft was a UFO which had then gone 25 miles (40km) underwater to Government Point, near the Shelburne submarine detection base. There it waited for a week, when it was met by another UFO and together they sped off into the skies. There were indeed, Styles discovered, reports of strange lights in the sky on 11 October, the night the UFOs allegedly vamoosed.

The verdict? Something clearly occurred in the Shag Harbour region in late October 1967, as archived Navy records show an unusually high amount of patrolling at the time. One diver claims that the Shag Harbour object was "not of this world", although a number of terrestrial explanations have been put forward. Noting the mention in naval witness interviews of a Russian submarine in the Shelburne area, it is speculated the Shag Harbour UFO was a crashed Russian "sputnik" and that Moscow dispatched the subs to retrieve the object; or that the craft and lights witnessed by Shag Harbour residents belonged to RCN antisubmarine units, their earthly presence distorted by moonlight on water.

Canadian/US authorities covered up truth of alien UFO crash at Shag Harbour: ALERT LEVEL 4

Further Reading
Don Ledger, Chris Styles and Whitley Strieber, *Dark Object: The World's Only Government-Documented UFO Crash*, 2001

TUPAC SHAKUR

On 7 September 1996 rap superstar Tupac Shakur was mortally hit four times in a drive-by shooting in Las Vegas, after coming out of the prizefight between Mike Tyson and Bruce Seldon. What **Elvis Presley** was to white-boy rock'n'roll in the 50s, what John Lennon was to the freaks of the 60s, Tupac was to the hip-hop scene of the 90s. Now rap found its icon removed in suspicious circumstances. To this day nobody has ever been charged with Tupac's homicide. But, then, is "2pac" really dead?

Tupac Shakur was born in the Bronx, New York, in 1971. His given name was Lesane Parish Crooks but it was later changed by his mother, Afeni Shakur, a Black Panther, to Tupac Amaru Shakur. During his teens he studied dance and theatre at Baltimore School for the Arts, and in 1991 he won a lead part in the gangster film *Juice*. That same year, Tupac made his first rap album – and had his first big, violent run-in with police, when he was beaten up by Oakland's finest. Turning the tables in Atlanta, he shot two policemen. Charges against him were dropped because the police were intoxicated, but in 1993 he was sentenced to the penitentiary for sexually assaulting a woman in his hotel room. The vortex of violence and crime in which he found himself gripped ever tighter: while on remand he was shot five times in a New York recording studio, surviving despite a bullet hole in his head. He said he believed his assailants were connected to the Notorious BIG (aka Biggie Smalls,

Christopher Wallace), the rap star who had once been Tupac's friend and was now his rival. The Notorious BIG was signed to Sean "Puffy" Combs's Bad Boy Records; Tupac was signed to Marion "Suge" Knight's Death Row Records.

After serving eight months in prison, Tupac was released when "Suge" Knight put up $1.4 million bail. Knight then hustled Tupac into the recording studio, from which emerged the 9-million-selling album *All Eyez on Me*, with its disturbing video for the single "I Ain't Mad at Cha" showing Tupac dying in a gundown. Even more weirdly prophetic was the next album, *The Don Killuminati: The 7 Day Theory*, released under the pseudonym Makaveli, which overflowed with death imagery. Then, on 7 – note that – on 7 September 1996 Tupac was murdered.

The LAPD suspected the killers were members of LA's infamous Southside gang the Crips, one of whom, Orlando "Baby Lane" Anderson, had been arguing in a hotel lobby with Tupac earlier in the day. Although Anderson was interviewed by the police he was never charged, apparently due to the lack of witnesses willing to come forward. He then inconveniently got himself shot in an unrelated gang killing. The Anderson–Tupac argument took place against a background of historical animosity between the Crips and the Bloods, who provided security for Tupac's label, Death Row Records. The LAPD Compton Gang Unit privately maintains that Anderson was the shooter in what was essentially a private affair.

In rapland, however, suspicion fell on Tupac's rival, the Notorious BIG, and his label manager, "Puffy" Combs. Rumours flew that "Biggie" and Combs had paid the Crips to assassinate Tupac, and the *Los Angeles Times* offered evidence that "Biggie" had sold the Crips the fatal gun and been in town to oversee the hit. Few were surprised when, on 9 March 1997, "Biggie" was shot dead leaving a *Vibe* magazine party in LA.

Most assumed "Biggie" had been assassinated by a Tupac fan out for revenge, but some began to see the hand of the FBI and government in the Tupac–"Biggie" fallout. Why, they asked, did the authorities fail to protect Yafeu "Kadafi" Fula? Fula, a

witness willing to identify Tupac's killer, was shot down dead
shortly afterwards. Could it be because the killer was a government agent? In this scenario, Tupac's death was an indirect
blow against his mother, hated by the FBI for her prominent
role in the revolutionary Black Panther Party. An FBI fink in
Tupac's entourage, so the theory goes, persuaded him to leave
off his usual bullet-proof vest on the fateful night.

There is also a widespread theory that Tupac faked his death,
the main clue being the image of Tupac being crucified *à la*
Jesus on the cover of *The Don Killuminati: The 7 Day Theory*
and the use of the pseudonym "Makaveli". Machiavelli, the
Renaissance philosopher, had written that a staged suicide is a
useful way to fool the enemy. If you rearrange the letters of the
album name you get: "OK on tha 7th u think I'm dead yet I'm
really alive". Makaveli itself is an anagram for "mak(e) alive".
Adherents of the "7 Theory" also point out that Tupac was shot
on the 7th, 7 months after *All Eyez on Me* was released; and that
he lived for 7 days after the shooting. Tupac was to come back to
rapland 7 years on (in 2003: he didn't), but perhaps it was 77
years on.

Why would Tupac fake his own death?

"Ms D" on the *ThugLifeArmy* website has the most convincing answer. Tired of being shot at by gangstas, Tupac wanted
out, and so he entered Witness Protection, where he received
plastic surgery. His mom had, after all, lived underground for
years, so it was in the family, so to speak. As for leaked
photographs of Tupac on the autopsy table, Ms D details
peculiarities – such as the absence of the "50 niggas" tattoo –
which suggest that the body belonged to some other stiff. Of
course, the photography might have been a con by some wise
guy seeking to sell some John Doe's autopsy snaps as the real
Tupac article.

Biggie and Tupac, a documentary by British film-maker Nick
Broomfield released in 2002, firmly puts the blame for Tupac's
death on his own record boss, "Suge" Knight. According to
Broomfield, Shakur had discovered that Knight was cheating
him out of royalties and intended to leave the appropriately

named Death Row Records. Figuring Tupac was worth more dead than alive and certainly of no value to him on another label, Knight contracted the hit on Tupac. He then killed "Biggie". Broomfield's theory is given substance by Knight's history of using violence for business ends and by an alleged prison confession. If it was Knight who orchestrated Tupac's death, he must have had nerves of steel: he was in the car with Shakur at the time and took a (presumably deflected) bullet. Many people have called "Suge" Knight many things, yet none of them has ever said he was a brave soldier.

2pac, RIP? The rapstar *may* be alive and well and in Witness Protection.

The Notorious BIG contracted the hit on rival Tupac Shakur: ALERT LEVEL 6

Tupac Shakur faked his own death: ALERT LEVEL 6

Further Reading
http://www.thuglifearmy.com/

KAREN SILKWOOD

Shortly after six o'clock on the evening of 13 November 1974, labour activist Karen Silkwood left a union meeting at the Hub Cafe in the city of Crescent, Oklahoma, to drive to Oklahoma City. There she was scheduled to meet *New York Times* journalist David Burnham to provide him with evidence of safety violations at the Kerr–McGee Cimarron nuclear plant where she was a representative for the Oil, Chemical & Atomic Workers Union (OCAW). Silkwood had a bundle of documentation with her in the car.

She never made her Oklahoma City meeting. Her white Honda Civic car left Highway 74, ran along a ditch and hit the side of a concrete culvert. Silkwood was killed outright. Did she fall asleep at the wheel in a tragic accident? Or was her car shunted off the road by someone desperate to stop her whistle-blowing? The controversy eventually reached Hollywood, with Meryl Streep playing the title role in the 1983 movie *Silkwood*.

Karen Gay Silkwood began working in the laboratory at the Kerr–McGee Cimarron facility, which manufactured plutonium for nuclear reactors, in the fall of 1972 after her six-year marriage had broken up. She was 26. At the plant, Silkwood joined OCAW, and in the spring of 1974 she was elected to the union's steering committee. Throughout the summer she noticed a steep decline in safety standards after a production speed-up caused a rapid worker turnover; new employees were being appointed to positions for which they had inadequate training. Silkwood herself became contaminated by airborne radioactive particles. Invited to the OCAW national office in Washington DC, she informed officials of the Cimarron plant's unsafe procedures, which included improper storage and handling of the fuel rods themselves, some of which were defective. She also alleged that the company falsified inspection records. These OCAW headquarters officials were the first to tell Silkwood that plutonium radiation was carcinogenic and potentially lethal. The OCAW Washington officials asked her to covertly gather information, including company documents, to corroborate Kerr–McGee's violations of safety legislation.

On 5 November 1974, Silkwood performed a routine radiation self-check and found herself at almost 40 times the legal limit for plutonium contamination. She was decontaminated at the plant and sent home with a testing kit to collect faeces and urine and for further analysis. The next day, despite performing only paperwork duties at Cimarron, she again tested positive for plutonium and was decontaminated. On the following day, 7 November, she was found to be so contaminated she was expelling plutonium particles from her lungs – and this was before she had even entered the plant. She was given a more aggressive decontamination. Health inspectors sent to her home found it to be "hot", with plutonium traces in, among other places, the bathroom and the refrigerator. The house, too, was decontaminated, and Silkwood and her two housemates were sent to Los Alamos National Laboratory for in-depth testing.

Since plutonium has to be kept under the strictest security, the question arose as to how the plutonium entered the house. According to Kerr–McGee, Silkwood herself must have carried it back to her apartment in order to paint the company in a bad light. On decontaminating Silkwood's home, Kerr–McGee employees found pieces of lab equipment from the plant. Furthermore, Silkwood had previously inquired about the health effects of swallowing plutonium pellets.

Silkwood herself alleged that the testing jars she had been given were intentionally laced with plutonium and that Kerr–McGee was responsible, their intention being to scare her off whistle-blowing. The fact that the samples taken in new jars at Los Alamos showed much lower contamination rates than those used by Silkwood at home supports the notion of malicious planting of plutonium. Richard Raske's 2000 book *The Killing of Karen Silkwood* also asserts that the soluble plutonium found in Silkwood's body came from pellets stored in the facility's vault, to which she had not had access for six months.

When doctors informed Silkwood that she was infected with "less than one-half of the maximum permissible body burden" of plutonium, her worries were assuaged a little and she returned to work at the lab. She also decided to go through with her plan to meet David Burnham and OCAW official Steve Wodka on the night of 13 November.

According to the Oklahoma State Highway Patrol, Silkwood's death was a one-car accident. She fell asleep at the wheel and her Honda Civic drifted off the left side of the road. The patrol also cites an autopsy report showing that methaqualone, a sleep-inducing drug prescribed for Silkwood to combat stress, was present in her body. If Silkwood fell asleep at the wheel, this explains why she made no attempt to veer away from the concrete culvert. A dent discovered in the Honda's rear bumper was determined to have been caused by the recovery vehicle that had pulled the Honda out of the culvert. Subsequent investigations by the Justice Department and FBI agreed there was no foul play, and two congressional subcommittees dropped their investigations.

The unofficial version is a little different. The OCAW accident investigator found the Honda's tyre tracks showed the car had skidded violently off the left side of the highway, then straightened out and driven along the shoulder. He believed this was evidence that Silkwood was prevented from returning to the highway by another car, and that a "drifting car" would anyway have veered into a field before reaching the culvert. Another OCAW-hired expert found the dent in the Honda's rear bumper resulted from "contact between two metal surfaces". Scratch marks in the dent were from rear to front, indicating the car had been hit from behind. No fewer than eight independent toxicologists agreed that Silkwood had built up such a tolerance to methaqualone (Quaalude) that the 0.35 milligrams of the drug found in her body would not have caused her to fall asleep at the wheel.

In March 1979 the Silkwood case finally reached the courts, with a suit brought by her father and children. The presiding judge allowed only one issue to be decided: Kerr–McGee's negligence or not in Silkwood's contamination. Other counts, which might have uncovered liability for her death, were barred. Lawyers for Silkwood's estate theorized that she had been under surveillance by Kerr–McGee, who knew she was about to blow the whistle on the company. The lawyers were not allowed to present testimony that documents with the Kerr–McGee insignia had been found in Silkwood's wrecked car and that – according to the owner of the garage where the car was taken – only government, police and Kerr–McGee officials visited the wreck during the night after the accident.

On 18 May 1979 the jury awarded $10 million in punitive damages to the Silkwood estate. On appeal, the judgment was reduced to US $5,000. In 1986, the Supreme Court restored the original verdict. The case was headed for retrial when Kerr–McGee settled out of court for $1.38 million, admitting no liability.

There is still no legal closure, however, on the question of whether Silkwood was murdered, and, if so, by whom. It is a heck of a coincidence, though, that she died en route to the very meeting where she was due to hand over the proof of Kerr–McGee's negligence.

Kerr–McGee, incidentally, closed its nuclear plants in 1975.

> Union activist Karen Silkwood was murdered to prevent her whistle-blowing on the Kerr–McGee nuclear company: ALERT LEVEL 8

Further Reading
Richard Raske, *The Killing of Karen Silkwood*, 2000

SKULL & BONES

It's so secret that we can't talk about it.

President George W. Bush on membership
of Skull & Bones, NBC's *Meet the Press*, 2004

Win some, win some. When Democrat John Kerry took on
Republican George W. Bush for the US presidency in 2004, one
group of Americans was assured of victory whichever way the
result went. For Kerry and Bush were both members of the
secretive Yale University society known as Skull & Bones.

Skull & Bones was founded in 1832 by Yale University
student William H. Russell. He had spent some time in Germany, and based Skull & Bones on the secret societies then
popular in that country; some even hold that Russell was
introduced in Germany to the **Illuminati**, and that Skull &
Bones was set up as that organization's US branch. (The skull-
and-bones emblem is the official crest of the Illuminati.) What
is certain is that Skull & Bones flourished; by 1856 it built its
own headquarters, a windowless campus building known to
"Bonesmen" as "The Tomb". Membership was, and remains,
highly exclusive. Total living membership stands at around 600;
each year just 15 Yale students are "tapped" (literally) and
invited to join Skull & Bones. A majority of those so tapped
come from private school, the establishments of preference
being the Anglophile Phillips Academies and Groton. It helps
of course to come from one of America's blue-blood dynasties;

aside from George W. Bush, his father, George H. W. Bush, and his grandfather, Senator Prescott Bush, all featured on the membership roll. Alphonso Taft, a founder member, was the father of Bonesman and US president Howard Taft. Other prominent members of the Skull & Bones – which is also known as "Chapter 322", "The Brotherhood of Death" and "The Order" – have included Howard Stanley (founder of Morgan Stanley), political pundit William F. Buckley, magazine baron Henry Luce and War Secretary Henry Stimson.

According to the numerous conspiracy websites devoted to detailing the shenanigans of the Skull & Bones fraternity, initiation takes place in the Tomb's inner sanctum, entered through a door which bears the legend (in German): "Who was the fool, who was the wise man, beggar or king? Whether poor or rich, all's the same in death." Initiation involves bizarre quasi-Masonic rituals, said to include nude confessions of sexual histories, and masturbation while lying in a coffin. A skull stolen from the grave of Geronimo by Prescott Bush is a frequent prop in ceremonies. (In fact, a DNA test undertaken at the behest of the Apache nation revealed that the skull did not actually belong to the old warrior.) Presumably, the rituals are designed to bind by shame: no Bonesman can denounce the society or another member, because he/she would then be open to blackmail. Or ridicule.

Certainly, Skull & Bones has proved one of the most impenetrable of secret organizations. Ron Rosenbaum, chief Skull & Bones expert, once noted, "I think Skull & Bones has had slightly more success than the Mafia in the sense that the leaders of the five Mafia families are all doing 100 years in jail, while the leaders of the Skull & Bones families are doing four and eight years in the White House."

According to conspiracy author Anthony C. Sutton, the influence of Skull & Bones is by no means limited to the Oval Office, and the fraternity "more or less controls the CFR" (**Council on Foreign Relations**) and has "either set up or penetrated just about every significant research policy and opinion-making organization in the United States". The

Order's relationship with the CIA is particularly close, and George H. W. Bush, William Bundy, Hugh Cunningham and Archibald MacLeish are just a few of the Bonesmen to take prominent office in the CIA.

While Skull & Bones is indisputably the foremost secret student club, it is by no means the only one. Yale also has the Scroll & Key and the Wolf's Head, while Harvard boasts the Porcelain Club and Princeton has the Ivy & Cottage Club. As Rosenbaum states, anyone who is anyone in the Eastern establishment attended one of those clubs if not Skull & Bones itself. Such clubs have played a long game of nepotism and matchmaking for Eastern families, but in truth they are in decline. Accusations of homophobia and racism have required Skull & Bones and its WASP fellows to admit the sorts it was founded to protect society from: gays, Asians, Chinese, Hispanics and blacks. In consequence, says Rosenbaum, Skull & Bones has become "a more lackadaisical, hedonistic, comfortable, even, said some, decadent group".

> The Skull & Bones fraternity covertly controls the US:
> ALERT LEVEL 3

Further Reading

Alexandra Robbins, *Secrets of the Tomb: Skull & Bones, the Ivy League, and the Hidden Paths of Power*, 2003

Ron Rosenbaum, "The Last Secrets of Skull & Bones", *Esquire*, September, 1977

Anthony C. Sutton and Patrick M. Wood, *Trilaterals Over Washington*, 1979

Kris Mulligan (ed.), *Fleshing Out Skull & Bones*, 2003

www.freemasonrywatch.org/bones.html

SOVEREIGN MILITARY
ORDER OF MALTA

Originally known as the Knights Hospitaller, the Sovereign
Military Order of Malta was founded in the 11th century in
Jerusalem, where it protected Christian pilgrims visiting the
Holy Sepulchre. When the Holy Land was lost to the Saracens
in 1291, the Hospitallers moved to Cyprus and then Rhodes.
Much of the property of the banned **Knights Templar** seems
to have accrued to the Hospitallers in the meantime. In 1523 the
Turkish siege of Cyprus put the Knights Hospitaller on the
move again, and they found refuge in Malta, given to them by
the Holy Roman Emperor Charles V, where they became
known as the Knights of Malta or the Sovereign Military Order
of Malta.

Napoleon's invasion of Malta in 1798 forced the Sovereign
Military Order into a diaspora, and today it exists as scattered
branches throughout the world. There is a headquarters in
Rome. In line with its founding principle, the Order continues
its charitable work of defending the sick and the poor.

But is that all it does? For a charity, the Sovereign Military
Order wields unusual power. It has Permanent Observer Status
at the UN General Assembly and diplomatic relations with 40
countries. The authors of *Holy Blood, Holy Grail* spotlight the
Catholic anti-Communist Knights of Malta as "one of the
primary channels of communication between the Vatican and
the CIA". Evidence of the connection comes primarily from the
alleged membership in the Order of CIA chiefs William "Wild

Bill" Donovan, Allen Dulles, John McCone and William Casey. James Angleton was awarded the Croci Al Merito Seconda Classe from the Knights, while George H. W. Bush was reputed to be an honorary initiate. Equally, the Order is closely connected to the Vatican; one of its leading members in the 20th century was the American Cardinal Francis Spellman. Among those awarded the Order's Grand Cross of Merit has been Reinhard Gehlen, the former Nazi chief of intelligence on the Soviet front. Gehlen was subsequently installed by the CIA as the first chief of West Germany's equivalent of the CIA, the BND.

Gehlen is not the only fascist to have been welcomed into the arms of the Order. So was Franco. According to conspiracy reporter Francoise Hervet, Count Umberto Ortolani, the Order's Ambassador to Uruguay, was the "brains behind" the crypto-fascist **P2** Masonic Lodge.

Somehow, the Sovereign Order finds the time, according to some paranoid conspiracy theorists, to also hold Satanic rituals and help run the **New World Order**.

The Sovereign Military Order of Malta moonlights as an intelligence broker: ALERT LEVEL 8

Further Reading
Michael Baigent, Richard Leigh and Henry Lincoln, *Holy Blood, Holy Grail*, 1982
Francoise Hervet, "The Sovereign Military Order of Malta", *Covert Action*, Winter 1986

STAR GATE

Star Gate was one of a number of psi-ops "remote viewing programs" conducted by the CIA from 1972 onwards. Developed in response to reported Soviet investigations of psychic phenomena (funded, the CIA estimated, to the tune of 60 million roubles a year), Star Gate was based at the Stanford Research Institute in Menlo Park, CA. Many of the first remote viewers, among them New York artist Ingo Swann, were from the Church of Scientology. By 1983 Swann and Star Gate's director Harold Puthoff were developing instructions which theoretically allowed anyone to be trained to produce accurate visualizations of targets. Allegedly. A 1995 analysis of the Star Gate project by the American Institutes for Research (AIR) found that even "gifted" subjects only scored 5–15 per cent above chance and advised that Star Gate be closed down. In not one single case, the CIA concluded, had ESP remote viewing provided data able to guide intelligence operations. For decades whispers of a CIA psychic viewing programme had bounced around conspiracy circles. The AIR report confirmed its existence, even if it was at the very end of the project's life.

Over $20 million was spent on Star Gate – ill-advisedly, according to the Agency. However, according to Star Gate psychic Joe McMoneagle (who left Star Gate in 1984, reportedly with a Legion of Merit Award for his services) the project had a string of "eight martini" results, so-called because the remote viewing data was so accurate that programme workers needed eight martinis to recover. These included:

- Locating kidnapped Brigadier General James L. Dozier, who had been kidnapped by the Red Brigades in Italy in 1981
- Disclosing that chemicals (for a weapons programme) would be transported from Tripoli to a port in the east of Libya aboard a ship named either *Patua* or *Potua* (in fact, a ship named *Batato* made such a journey)

The Star Gate project is not to be confused with *The Stargate Conspiracy* (2000) by Lynn Picknett and Clive Prince, which uncovers a group of "respected, powerful individuals who believe that the ancient Egyptian gods are real extraterrestrials who will soon return to earth". Now that *would* be something best viewed remotely.

CIA developed secret psi-war programme on remote viewing: ALERT LEVEL 10

Further Reading
Joseph McMoneagle, *The Stargate Chronicles: Memoirs of a Psychic Spy*, 2002
Jon Ronson, *The Men Who Stare at Goats*, 2004

TEMPLE MOUNT PLOT

Christian fundamentalist preacher Texe Marrs is a very worried man. He's uncovered the Big One, a conspiracy by the **Illuminati**, the **Freemasons** and the same Jews who brought you the **Protocols of the Learned Elders of Zion** – to take over the world. On his website (www.texemarrs.com) Marrs writes:

> Now the lid is blown off the forbidden, secret powderkeg of the Masonic Jews who run Israel and, by extension, the United States and the world. Unbeknownst to either the Israeli elite or to America's pro-Israel cabal in Washington, DC, for over six years I have conducted an intensive investigation of Jewish Masonic influence. Finally, I have released three bombshell videos unmasking my grotesque discoveries in this area.
>
> *Masonic Lodge Over Jerusalem* (Available in *VHS* or *DVD*), *Thunder Over Zion* (Available in *VHS* or *DVD*), and *Cauldron of Abaddon* (Available in *VHS* or *DVD*).

Illuministic Communism the Goal

The goal of the Jewish Masonic elite is to establish dictatorial Illuministic Communism and to enslave all of mankind under the thumb of a Jewish master race led by a world messiah who is to rule from Jerusalem.

An essential element in this grandiose plan is the Masonic plot to blow up and destroy Islam's golden-domed monument now sitting ' on the Temple Mount in Jerusalem, despised by Orthodox Jewish rabbis and the secularist Masonic Illuminists alike.

In fact, Marrs suggests, the plot is not limited to the destruction of the Dome of the Rock but will also raze another Islamic holy site on the mount, the Mosque of Omar. The edifices will be brought down by the Israeli Defence Forces in the midst of a war and the "disaster will be scandalously blamed" on an errant Arab missile or bomb. After the bulldozers have cleared the Temple Mount of its Islamic relics, the Freemasons/Illuminati/Jews will "build a Jewish Masonic temple where they and their satanically energized messiah shall worship and pay homage to the Egyptian double-headed eagle deity, Mammon-Ra, the god of money and prosperity".

Marrs might be one of the most energetic denouncers of the "Temple Mount Plot" – he has videos and DVDs to sell, after all – but he is not the first.

The Temple Mount in Jerusalem is a holy place for all branches of the Abrahamic religions – Christianity, Islam and Judaism. In June 1967 the Israelis won the Six Day War and the Mount came under Jewish control for the first time in 2,000 years; shortly afterwards, archaeological expeditions began work on the site, one being headed by Dr Asher Kaufman, a member of the Quatuor Coronati Lodge of the British Freemasons. Some Freemason-watchers feared Kaufman's dig was a cover for a Freemason takeover of the site.

Nearly 20 years later, in September 1995, the Freemason-connected "Land of Israel Faithful Movement" and a group of Orthodox Jews attempted to enter the Dome of the Rock to lay the cornerstone of a Third Temple (which would hasten the return of the Messiah). This action – portrayed by Marrs and others as evidence of the Jewish–Masonic conspiracy – was turned back by the Israeli Army. Also in 1995, a Jerusalem branch of Freemasons was founded next to the Mount; its leader was Giuliano di Bernardo, author of *The Reconstruction of the Temple* (1996).

The actions of the Freemasons in Jerusalem seem provocative, but then the Temple Mount is the most contested religious site in the world, where damage to feelings and holy shrines is spark enough to light a war. There is no plausible evidence of a Masonic–Jewish plot to take over the Mount. The 1995 joint invasion was a marriage of opportunistic convenience and has not been repeated. If the Jews collectively were intent on taking over the Islamic sites on the Mount, why did the Israeli Army turn back the Orthodox protesters? (A number of Israeli rabbis, incidentally, forbid adherents to enter any part of the Mount.) The published accounts of Quatuor Coronati Lodge show that it granted the Temple Mount dig of Kaufman a mere £100, hardly enough to finance an appropriation of the site.

> Freemasons and Jews in plot to destroy Islamic holy sites on Jerusalem's Temple Mount: ALERT LEVEL 3

Further Reading

Thom Burnett, *Conspiracy Encyclopedia: The Encyclopedia of Conspiracy Theories*, 2005

Texe Marrs, "Masonic Jews Plot to Control World", www.exemarrs.com/042003/masonic_jews_plot_world_control.htm

TITANIC

On 10 April, 1912, RMS *Titanic* left Southampton for New York under the command of Captain Edward J. Smith. Aboard the ship, then the largest in the world at 852 feet (260m) long, were 2,224 passengers and crew. Four days later, just before midnight on 14 April, the *Titanic* hit an iceberg 400 miles (650km) south of Newfoundland, which ruptured five bulkheads on the starboard side. At 2.20 a.m. the ship slipped below the surface of the black Atlantic with the loss of 1,503 lives.

For over 70 years people agreed the *Titanic* disaster was a concantenation of fate (the iceberg) and folly (she was governed by maritime legislation which required her to carry lifeboats for only 1,178 people), but then Oxford plasterer Robin Gardiner published *"Titanic": The Ship that Never Sank?* (1998). Gardiner's thesis – elucidated also in his books *The Riddle of the Titanic* (1997) and *The Titanic Conspiracy* (1998; with Dan Van der Vat) – is that the *Titanic* disaster was, well, a titanic insurance fraud. According to Gardiner it was not the *Titanic* which left Southampton on 10 April but her older sister ship, the *Olympic*. This had been damaged by a Royal Navy ship, rendering her worthless. The cash-strapped White Star Line, owner of both ships, faced bankruptcy . . . until someone hit on the idea of switching the *Olympic* for the *Titanic*, then sinking the *"Titanic"* in mid-Atlantic and claiming oodles of insurance money. To pass off the *Olympic* as the *Titanic* was easy, since they were near-identical. All that was required was a week in a Belfast dry dock for a paint job that included a change of name.

The fraudsters, however, weren't heartless: they arranged for the SS *Californian* and other rescue ships to be nearby in the middle of the Atlantic when the sea cocks of the false *Titanic* were opened . . . but the plan went awry when the *Titanic* hit a rescue vessel placed on station by White Star and sank sooner than expected, with the loss of many lives.

Gardiner picks up some oddities in the official *Titanic* saga, chiefly the suspicious behaviour of the *Californian*, which lurked 20 miles (32km) from the *Titanic*'s death-site on the fatal night. Owned by financier J.P. Morgan, the *Californian* was carrying an unusual cargo: 3,000 woollen blankets and jumpers. Morgan was a co-owner of White Star. He had been booked to travel on the *Titanic* but had cried off at the last minute.

In *Olympic and Titanic* Steve Hall and Bruce Beveridge sought to sink Gardiner's insurance-con theory by referencing the *Titanic* debris found on the Atlantic seabed by Professor Robert Ballard. A propeller numbered 401 (the *Titanic*'s number) and the straight-faced wheelhouse both definitely identify the debris as belonging to the *Titanic*.

Unless the propeller and wheelhouse were among the cosmetic changes made to the *Olympia* in dry dock . . .

RMS *Titanic* was replaced by sister ship in insurance fraud: ALERT LEVEL 3

Further Reading
Robin Gardiner, *"Titanic": The Ship That Never Sank?*, 1998
Steve Hall and Bruce Beveridge, *Olympic and Titanic: The Truth Behind the Conspiracy*, 2004

TRILATERAL COMMISSION

The Trilateral Commission was founded in 1973 by banking titan David Rockefeller as an invitation-only think-tank. Rockefeller had the bucks, the organizational skills and the contacts, but the Trilateral Commission's philosophy was provided by Columbia university professor, Zbigniew Brzezinski, author of *Between Two Ages: America's Role in the Technetronic Era* (1970). This was a prophetic look at a future "shaped culturally, psychologically, socially, and economically by the impact of technology and electronics – particularly in the area of computers and communication". Explaining that "National sovereignty is no longer a viable concept", Brzezinski foresaw "movement toward a larger community by the developing nations" funded by "a global taxation system". However, since this end-goal of "world government" was some way off, an initial "attainable" step should be closer trilateral co-operation between the nations of America, Europe and Asia, in the latter instance specifically Japan.

Membership of the Trilateral Commission was limited to 300 (later expanded to 450), and early participants included *Time, Inc.* editor-in-chief Hedley Donovan, British politician Reginald Maudling, FIAT president Giovanni Agnelli, and former French premier Raymond Barre. Among the more recent members are Alan Greenspan of the American Federal Reserve, Dick Cheney, Enron's Ken Lay, Paul Wolfowitz and George H. W. Bush . . . in other words, the Trilateral Commission is stuffed full of exactly the same sort of mondo politicians and businessmen who sit on the plush chairs at the **Bilderberg Group** and **Council for Foreign Relations**. Naturally, then, the Trilateral Commission comes in for the same critical fire as those two – that is, it's attempting to covertly instal a shadow global government run by its members. They must be busy boys and girls, these Trilateralists, because they've also been accused by *über*-conservative Lyndon LaRouche of running the drugs trade, been denounced by black rappers Public Enemy for organizing Zionist plots, fingered as agents of the **Illuminati** by fundamentalist–conspiracist Texe Marrs, and marked by evangelist Pat Robertson for promoting Satanism.

For a supposed "secret society", the Trilateral Commission is disappointingly open: its membership can be viewed at its website, www.trilateral.org/. Meetings are held *in camera*, but it would be a wonder if globalism weren't a frequent fixture on the agenda – after all, world order was the *raison d'être* for the creation of the Commission. Many Trilateralists represent big business – the likes of Exxon, Mobil, Goldman Sachs – which finds the nation state inimical to its interests and consequently seeks to extend the remit of transnational institutions such as the International Monetary Fund and the World Bank.

So is the Trilateral Commission, as feared by the American far right, the executive board of the New World Order? The Commission does not have its hands on the surreptitious levers of global power for a simple reason: there aren't any. International politics and economics are more complex than the instrumentalist philosophy of far-right conspiracists realize.

Indeed, focusing on the Trilateral Commission's international agenda-setting carries the risk of blindness to its interesting role in the US. One early member of the Commission was a down-home Southern Democrat by the name of Jimmy Carter. According to former Republican Senator Barry Goldwater, the Trilateral Commission eased Carter into the White House in 1973 by mobilizing "the money power of the Wall Street bankers, the intellectual influence of the academic community . . . and the media controllers". With Mr Carter to Washington went fellow Trilateralists Walter Mondale as V.P. and old Zbigniew Brzezinski as National Security Advisor. Anthony C. Sutton and Patrick M. Wood, authors of *Trilaterals Over Washington* (1979), commented: "If you are trying to calculate the odds of three unknown men [Carter, Mondale and Brzezinski], out of 60 [Trilateral] Commissioners from the US, capturing the three most powerful positions in the land, don't bother. Your calculations will be meaningless."

Carter, Mondale and Brzezinski weren't the only Trilateralists to get their feet in the door of the Carter administration: Secretary of State Cyrus R. Vance, Deputy Secretary of State Warren Christopher, Director Paul Warnke of the Arms Control and Disarmament Agency, Undersecretary of the Treasury Anthony Solomon, Undersecretary of Economic Affairs Richard Cooper and Assistant Secretary of State Richard Holbrooke were among nearly 20 Trilateralists to hold prominent positions in the government. Then Carter selected banker Paul Volcker to head the American Federal Reserve; Volcker was the chair of the North American branch of the Trilateral Commission. So dominating were the Trilateralists that even the normally supine Beltway press took notice, with the *Washington Post* calling the Trilateralist influence "unsettling".

Being in power enabled pet projects of the Commission to come to pass. One will serve in evidence. A 1975 Commission task-force paper, *The Crisis of Democracy*, by Harvard academic Samuel P. Huntington, proposed that democracy was inadequate in the face of national emergencies; appointed to Carter's National Security Council, Huntington prepared the Presidential Review Memorandum which created the Federal Emergency Management Agency (FEMA).

Of course, the Trilateral Commission can't be all-powerful, since it was unable to stop Jimmy Carter from being electorally ejected from the White House. As consolation, the Commission found another good ol' Southern Democrat to join their ranks. Few Americans then knew his name, but they would later.

Bill Clinton.

> The Trilateral Commission is the board of directors of New World Order Inc.: ALERT LEVEL 4
>
> The Trilateral Commission is the executive committee of the US: ALERT LEVEL 8

Further Reading
Jim Marrs, *Rule by Secrecy*, 2000
James Perloff, *The Shadows of Power*, 1988
Anthony C. Sutton and Patrick M. Wood, *Trilaterals Over Washington*, 1979

TWA FLIGHT 800

At 8.31 on 17 July 1996, 12 minutes after take-off from New York's JFK airport, a catastrophic explosion caused TWA Flight 800 to disintegrate over the Atlantic. All 212 passengers and 18 crew aboard the Boeing 747-131 were killed.

After 90 per cent of the plane's remains were dredged from the Atlantic, an investigation by the National Transportation Safety Board concluded that the explosion had been caused by an electrical short circuit near the centre wing fuel tank. The NTSB issued 15 safety recommendations, mostly covering fuel tank and wiring-related issues, notably the development and installation of fuel inerting systems. "The 230 men, women and children on board TWA800," said the NTSB, "lost their lives not as result of a bomb or missile or some other nefarious act but the result of a tragic accident."

Note the word "missile". No fewer than 38 witnesses had come forward to say they'd seen missile(s) streaking towards the plane just before it exploded. (Another 220 had seen a "streak of light", variously characterized as a shooting star, a flare, or something similar near the TWA800.) The witnesses even formed themselves into an action group, running full-page ads in national US newspapers: "We the eyewitnesses know that missiles were involved . . . for some reason our government has lied and tried to discredit us."

If it was a missile, who fired it and why? In *The Downing of TWA Flight 800* (1997), journalist James Sanders proposed that the Boeing was shot down by a Stinger missile from a US Navy cruiser on a training exercise nearby; instead of locking on to a Navy drone, the missile mistakenly locked on to the Boeing. Sanders further claimed that the FBI suppressed Federal Aviation Administration radar records which showed "an unexplained blip" near TWA800. Sanders's book has photographs of reddish residue, supposedly of missile fuel, on retrieved seats. When the NTSB began its public hearings into the TWA800 disaster, FBI deputy director James Kallstrom requested that the residue not be discussed.

Led by William Donaldson, a retired naval officer, a number of conspiracy theorists have proposed that TWA Flight 800 was downed by terrorist action. In the "Interim Report on the Crash of TWA Flight 800 and the Actions of the NTSB and the FBI" (1998) Donaldson stated that TWA800 was struck by two missiles, and subsequently the FBI, NTSB and Justice Department covered up the fact to save the Clinton administration embarrassment. Donaldson noted: "In the history of aviation, there has never been an in-flight explosion in any Boeing airliner of a Jet-A Kerosene fuel vapor/air mixture in any tank, caused by mechanical failure." Another former US military man, Colonel Robert Patterson, speculated in *Dereliction of Duty* (2003) that TWA800 had been downed by a US Navy Stinger – but that the Stinger had been launched to intercept a terrorist (read Iraqi) missile heading towards the plane. In yet another variant of the terrorist-attack theory, Peter Lance concluded in *Cover Up: What the Government is Still Hiding About the War on Terror* (2004), that TWA800 was blown up by a bomb with the intention of disrupting the trial of terrorist Ramzi Yousef for conspiring to blow up US airliners.

As of 2007, the NTSB, the Senate and the FAA all maintain that TWA Flight 800 crashed due to some form of mechanical or electrical failure. But can 38 independent witnesses all be wrong? Witnesses that even the FBI calls "credible"?

TWA Flight 800 crashed due to "friendly fire": ALERT
LEVEL 7

TWA Flight 800 crashed due to terrorist attack: ALERT
LEVEL 5

Further Reading
Peter Lance, *Cover Up*, 2004
Robert Patterson, *Dereliction of Duty*, 2003
James Sanders, *The Downing of Flight 800*, 1997

WACO

If the results had not been so tragic, the story of the Siege of Waco could be rewritten as a routine for circus clowns.

On 28 February 1993 the Bureau of Alcohol, Tobacco and Firearms raided the ranch compound of the Branch Davidians at Mount Carmel, near Waco, Texas. Led by self-appointed Messiah David Koresh, the Branch Davidians were an offshoot of the Seventh Day Adventists and had been based at Mount Carmel since the 1950s. More recently, Texan newspapers had rumoured that Koresh was a polygamist and even a child-abuser; the BATF had become interested in him and his sect for firearms violations, including the converting of semi-automatics to full automatics and the manufacture of grenades. Since the Branch Davidians were legal dealers of weaponry (indeed, gun-dealing was one of the sect's most significant money-making activities), the violations were relatively minor infractions.

Koresh could easily have been arrested on one of his weekly visits to Waco, but the BATF chose instead to launch a full-scale raid on the sect's compound. On the morning of Sunday 28 February 1993, BATF agents moseyed up to the compound, hiding in cattle trailers. Unfortunately, the element of surprise was lost thanks to a large black BATF helicopter circling overhead, not to mention the accidental discharge of a gun by a BATF agent which killed a fellow BATF besieger. Believing themselves under fire, the Branch Davidians returned fire.

In the ensuing gun battle, five Branch Davidians died, as did four BATF agents – all of the latter probably victims of "friendly fire" – before the government agency beat a hasty retreat. To the embarrassment of the BATF and the White House, the whole fiasco had been caught by news cameras.

Pride dictated that the falling low of the US government be made good. The Waco operation was handed over to the FBI, who settled down to besiege the Branch Davidian compound with the methods of psych-warfare. Bradley fighting vehicles and helicopters endlessly encircled the compound, while taped loops – which included the sound of rabbits dying, Tibetan chants, bagpipes and Nancy Sinatra singing "These Boots are Made for Walking" – were broadcast at deafening volume. Noise torture had worked to flush out Panamanian leader General Noriega some years before, but the Koresh sect were made of tougher stuff. For 51 days the Branch Davidians withstood the governmental goliath, until Attorney General Janet Reno approved a final, all-out assault after being told of child abuse in the compound.

On the morning of Monday 19 April the Feds smashed into the compound with Bradley fighting vehicles and M-60 tanks. Still Koresh and his followers refused to surrender. Suddenly, at around noon, the compound erupted into flames. Nine occupants emerged alive. The body of David Koresh and 79 other Branch Davidians, including 23 children, were found in the smouldering ashes. Koresh and many of the others had been shot in the head.

Much of the subsequent controversy over Waco hinges on responsibility for the fatal fire at high noon. In October 1993 the Justice Department determined from its investigation that Koresh had ordered the fire in order to facilitate a mass suicide à la Jonestown; bugging devices planted by the FBI in the compound recorded cult members spreading fuel around. According to the Justice Department, Koresh was a brainwashing, sex-addicted guru who wanted martyrdom. The Wacko from Waco.

To this day, the FBI continues to blame Koresh for the conflagration. It's not a claim that has stood the test of time unscathed. As the Academy Award-nominated *Waco: The Rules of Engagement* (1997) by maverick film-maker William Gazecki forced the FBI to admit, they fired and sprayed CS tear-gas into the compound for six hours. CS gas is highly flammable, frequently containing kerosene or methyl chloride. A bullet is sufficient to ignite dense CS vapour in a confined space, and the FBI's own aerial infrared recordings seemingly confirm that the Bureau fired weapons into the compound after the CS barrage. The FBI also fired pyrotechnic grenades at Waco, though the Bureau adds that the grenades were launched "in a direction far away from the compound" – which has caused critics to wonder why they were fired at all. Some of the dead children at Waco were found in postures strongly suggestive of cyanide poisoning caused by ignited CS gas. Even if the Bureau did not deliberately set Waco alight, it may have caused the fire by accident; according to surviving Branch Davidians, the FBI's tanks knocked over the kerosene lamps the sect was using for lighting after the G-men had cut off their electricity supply.

Then there is the mystery of why the Waco blaze, however it started, was not extinguished by the waiting firefighters. Initially, Branch Davidian snipers were blamed for keeping the fire department at bay; later the FBI agreed that it had ordered the fire department to hold back from the compound because of the danger of exploding ammunition. This claim does not square easily with the Bureau's own order to bulldoze the Waco remains – while the debris was still flaming. As in the Oklahoma City Bombing, the FBI's proclivity to order in the bulldozers destroyed potentially vital evidence.

For many right-wing conspiracy theorists, the siege of Waco was stage one in the plan for the **New World Order**, in the guise of the United Nations, to take over the US. Waco, according to this perspective, was provoked by the Feds in order to justify a clampdown on gun ownership, leaving Joe Public unable to bear arms when the guys in the blue hats came. One of those who blamed the FBI for the bloodshed at Waco was an ex-soldier called Timothy McVeigh who, on the second anniversary of Waco, expressed his rage by carrying out the

Oklahoma City Bombing. McVeigh wasn't the only one to blame the Feds: a poll taken in 1999 found that 66 per cent of Americans believed the Waco fire was deliberately caused by the FBI.

A Texas civil jury, Congress and a Special Counsel have all cleared the FBI of intentional wrongdoing at Waco. Maybe correctly. Yet, at the very least, the FBI acted with criminal recklessness at Waco. Aside from using teargas against children, the FBI deployed a Bradley fighting vehicle to ram-raid the room where the Branch Davidian children were holed up. Autopsies showed that a number of the children died from crush injuries.

After Waco, America became a more suspicious place. The FBI bears a share of the guilt for that.

> The FBI incinerated the Branch Davidians at Waco: ALERT LEVEL 8

Further Reading
William Gazecki (director), *Waco: The Rules of Engagement*, 1997 [movie]
Dick J. Reavis, *The Ashes of Waco: An Investigation*, 1998

WATERGATE

Everybody knows about the Watergate conspiracy. President Richard Milhous Nixon organized cronies to burglarize the Democratic offices in the Watergate Hotel, Washington DC; when the break-in was investigated by *Washington Post* reporters Bob Woodward and Carl Bernstein, who traced the plot back to the White House, Nixon tried to cover up his role. With evidence mounting against him, he resigned on 9 August 1974.

In the accepted Watergate story, James McCord and his fellow-Plumbers, as Nixon's private burglars were known, illegally entered the Democratic National Committee to place bugs. Nixon's supporters, however, allege there was *another* Watergate conspiracy – one in which Nixon was the victim. McCord and the four other men who burgled Watergate were CIA pros. Consequently, they could easily have effected the break-in without leaving traces. The obvious conclusion is that they bungled the break-in in order to implicate and sabotage Nixon.

Then there are the sources for the Woodward and Bernstein stories. The anonymous Deep Throat was long assumed to be Robert Bennett, manager of the Mullen Company (a CIA cover outfit). Why was the CIA briefing against Nixon? A fit of scruples because they didn't like a President who ordered burglaries of opponents? Hardly. The obvious conclusion, again, is that the CIA was sabotaging Nixon.

In 1984 Jim Hougan published *Secret Agenda*. This revealed that, when the FBI examined the Democratic offices at

Watergate, they found no evidence of it ever having been bugged. "It doesn't take a genius," former CIA agent Frank Sturgis informed the *San Francisco Chronicle* in 1977, "to figure out that Watergate was a CIA set-up." Nixon agreed, writing in his memoirs: "The whole thing was so senseless and bungled that it almost looked like some kind of a set-up."

The reason the CIA wanted Nixon out of the Oval Office is explained by Len Colodny and Robert Gettlin in *Silent Coup* (1991), the Magnum .45 of pro-Nixon literature. Nixon wanted out of the Vietnam War.

There was, of course, another plausible reason for removing Nixon, not one to be breathed by pro-Nixonites like Colodny and Gettlin. He was paranoid and going off the rails.

Against the "Nixon was smeared by the CIA" theory there have to be weighed the White House Tapes. These record Nixon's conversations in the Oval Office and clearly capture him plotting with regard to Watergate. Also the "Nixon was smeared" case was weakened in 2005 when it was revealed that Woodward's and Bernstein's snitch Deep Throat was not Bennett but the deputy director of the FBI, Mark Felt.

On the 20th anniversary of the Watergate break-in, investigative reporter Jim Hougan commented, "If one tries to understand Watergate in terms of a single monolithic operation by a team of spooks with a unified goal, it will defy understanding." The burglars themselves have given differing reasons as to why they were in the Watergate building on 17 June 1972.

Although Nixon was guilty of all the crimes that caused him to resign, it is by no means impossible that he was edged on his way by the CIA and elements in the White House who used Watergate to smear him.

Watergate was a CIA trap to smear Nixon and cause his downfall: ALERT LEVEL 7

Further Reading

Carl Bernstein and Bob Woodward, *All the President's Men,* 1974

Len Colodny and Robert Gettlin, *Silent Coup: The Removal of a President,* 1991

Jim Hougan, *Secret Agenda: Watergate, Deep Throat and the CIA,* 1984

HAROLD WILSON

During the 1930s the KGB targeted bright young things at British universities for recruitment as spies, men and women who might quietly worm their way up the fabric of the British state while really working for the USSR. Kim Philby, Anthony Blunt, Donald MacLean, Guy Burgess – all were testament to the KGB's success. Philby even made it to the head desk at MI6's anti-Soviet IX Section. All these men were eventually unmasked, but there remained the nagging doubt that somewhere deep in the British state there were other spies as yet uncovered. The nightmare scenario, of course, was that one such plant would become the Prime Minister of Great Britain.

In 1963 Hugh Gaitskell suddenly resigned as leader of the Labour Party; he died shortly afterwards of lupus disseminata. So unusual was the disease in the UK that Gaitskell's doctor is said to have reported the matter to MI5. Gaitskell had recently visited the USSR and, according to Soviet defector Anatoli Golitsin, the KGB Assassinations Department 13 was seeking to assassinate a European politician and put their man in his place. At this point, MI5 agent Peter Wright revealed in his memoir *Spycatcher* (1987), the security service became seriously interested in Gaitskell's replacement as Labour leader: Harold Wilson.

Wilson had been a minor blip on MI5's radar for a long while. He had flirted with Communists at Oxford in the 1930s, and in 1947 he'd made several trips to Russia as the government's

Secretary for Overseas Trade. If not already a Soviet agent, Wilson, MI5 believed, was recruited on these trips by the old means of a "honey trap" – a sexual liaison with a female KGB member. Filmed or photographed, the liaison opened up Wilson to perpetual blackmail. Proof that Wilson was "turned" ostensibly came during the Korean War, when the Labour MP was less than red-blooded in seeking North Korea's eradication. James Angleton of the CIA is said to have confirmed to MI5 Wilson's role as a Soviet stooge.

By any measure, though, MI5's evidence against Wilson was meagre. This did not stop the spooks from running a major smear campaign against him, which was steadily stepped up over the course of Wilson's four tenures as Prime Minister. Termed "Clockwork Orange", the MI5 smear campaign dripped media stories that Wilson was having an affair with his aide Marcia Williams, and falsely alleged links between Wilson's Labour Party and the KGB. According to Peter Wright, at least 30 MI5 officers were involved in the mid-1970s plot to destabilize Wilson, an accusation supported by MI6 chief Sir Maurice Oldfield and Captain Colin Wallace of Army intelligence. (Wallace was later framed for manslaughter because of his refusal to aid the Wilson plot; in 1996 a court quashed his conviction.)

With no prior warning, on 15 March 1976, Wilson announced his resignation as Prime Minister. The official explanation was that at 60 he was too tired to go on. Soon afterwards, however, he began briefing journalists about an MI5 plot against him, adding that in 1968 and 1978 "dark forces" had planned a military coup against him. So far-fetched did these claims seem that they met with all-round amusement, forcing Wilson to deny his own words.

In 1993 an official government investigation, *MI5: The Security Service*, asserts "no such [MI5] plot [against Wilson] existed". Peter Wright's *Spycatcher* has been proven to be exaggerated, and Wilson's own cabinet colleague Dennis Healey (now Lord Healey) says Wilson "made Walter Mitty look unimaginative".

Even so, there is enough evidence from Colin Wallace to

incriminate sections of MI5 in the destabilization of Wilson's 1970s governments. Wilson's retirement is thus explained by the fatigue and depression caused by having his own security force turned against him.

Of Wilson's alleged covert Communism, though, there is not a jot of proof.

British PM Harold Wilson was a KGB stooge: ALERT LEVEL 3

Elements in MI5 plotted downfall of Wilson's Labour governments in 1970s: ALERT LEVEL 9

Further Reading

Paul Foot, *Who Framed Colin Wallace?*, 1990

Robin Ramsay and Steven Dorril, *Smear! Wilson and the Secret State*, 1991

Peter Wright, *Spycatcher: The Candid Autobiography of a Senior Intelligence Officer*, 1987

WINGDINGS

In the aftermath of **9/11** there resurfaced a popular early-1990s conspiracy that within Microsoft's Wingdings font were secreted hidden messages. One such message was to be found if "NYC" [New York City] was typed in Wingdings. Up came:

☠✡👍

Some conspiracists read the symbols as Microsoft's approval for the killing of New York's Jews, and eventually the brouhaha reached the *New York Post*, which excitedly reported "ANTI-JEWISH CODE LURKS IN POPULAR SOFTWARE". Microsoft dismissed the charge, saying that the skull, Star of David and thumbs-up sequence was pure coincidence – a claim somewhat undermined by the admission of Microsoft spokesperson Kimberley Kuresman that the symbols for "NYC" in the somewhat similar Webdings font were intentionally designed to be associated with happiness. They were: an eye, a heart and a skyline. That is, I LOVE NEW YORK.

Then came 9/11, and someone on the internet decided Microsoft's Wingdings had forecast – even signalled – the terror attack on the World Trade Center. As one email posted on AboveTopSecret.com put it:

> *The "Wingdings" Conspiracy*. Has anyone heard of this? I'm shocked! Go to notepad, set the font to highest, select Wingd-

ings font, and type in caps Q33 NY. This is the flight number of the first plane to hit the World Trade Center . . . Coincidence? I doubt it . . .

Q33NY in Wingdings is:

✈▤▤☠✿

An airplane attacks two buildings and kills the Jews . . .

The conspiracy is undone by significant faults. Most notably, Q33NY was not the number of any of the aircraft involved in 9/11. Further, the 3-3 symbols are not "buildings" but lined documents. If you want a secret message from Wingdings, try this:

♈︎🖐♋︎🖐♋︎♋︎♌ ◐🏵♋︎❀🖐🖐♋︎♌ ♐🖐♉♉♐♋ 🌢♉♌♌♌♋♌♐

┌───┐
│ Microsoft's Wingdings font is designed to convey secret │
│ anti-Semitic messages: ALERT LEVEL 1   │
└───┘

Further Reading
http://www.snopes.com/rumors/wingdings.asp

DOCUMENT: "ANTI-JEWISH CODE LURKS IN POPULAR SOFTWARE", *NEW YORK POST*, 1992

One of the world's bestselling computer programs contains a secret anti-Semitic message apparently urging death to Jews in New York City.

A computer consultant discovered the diabolic message while installing Microsoft's new Windows 3.1 software for a client yesterday.

The consultant was testing a mailing-address use of the program when he noticed the letters "NYC" had been replaced by a hateful message – a skull and crossbones, the Star of David and an approving thumbs-up symbol.

Microsoft strongly denies any hidden message. Others disagree.

"There's no way it could be a random coincidence," said Brian Young, a friend of the consultant, who does not wish to be named.

"It's pretty scary. I was pretty shocked by the whole thing."

Computer owners who use Microsoft Excel, Microsoft Word or any other Microsoft program containing a print font named "Wingdings" can duplicate the anti-Semitic message by typing the letters "NYC" on their screen.

Microsoft said "Wingdings" was designed by Bigelow and Holmes, an outside vendor, and denied that Microsoft intentionally designed the secret message.

Prof. Charles Bigelow confirmed that his company provided the symbols, but insisted that Microsoft made the final "mapping" decisions assigning his symbols to specific keys on the keyboard.

But a senior Microsoft spokesman said the charge that the fonts contain a hidden message is "outrageous".

"It's like saying that if you randomly type out characters on a keyboard to spell 'Satan', you can do that, but it's incredible to say that there's anti-Semitism in Microsoft or one of its vendors," said Charles Hemingway.

But Young, who discussed the matter with other computer consultants, isn't so sure it's just a coincidence.

The "Wingdings" font contains no letters – just 255 symbols.

Young calculated the odds of three letters of the alphabet being combined with 255 symbols, and said he found that the odds of obtaining the message were less than one in a trillion.

"It's mind-blowing," said Young. "Somebody's responsible for this. This is very offensive.

"I found it hard to believe some of the stories about the resurgence of Nazi sympathizers – but this puts things back into perspective."

MALCOLM X

The Audubon Ballroom in Harlem, 3.05 p.m., 21 February 1965: someone in the crowd of 400 shouts out, "Get your hand outta my pocket! Don't be messin' with my pockets!" A smoke bomb goes off at the back of the auditorium. Chaos ensues. Out of the agitated mass of people a black man moves to the stage with a sawn-off shotgun and fires point blank at the speaker. Behind him two other men charge forward with handguns, and they likewise fire at the figure on the stage.

Hit by what the autopsy report later called "multiple wounds in the chest, heart and aorta", the speaker died almost instantaneously, despite the efforts of his bodyguard Gene Roberts to resuscitate him.

The speaker was Malcolm X, the leading black politician of post-war America aside from the also-assassinated **Martin Luther King**.

As Malcolm X lay with his life racing away, his assassins tried to escape, but one of the shooters, Talmadge Hayer, was caught by the crowd. Almost a year later Hayer and two other men, Norman "3X" Butler and Thomas "15X" Johnson, were convicted of the first-degree murder of Malcolm X. The case was closed, tied up with ribbon and put away in the vault. Hayer had admitted the crime and the motive was plain: internecine war between black radicals. Hayer, Butler and Johnson belonged to the Nation of Islam, from which Malcolm X had been expelled after accusing founder Elijah

Muhammad of the distinctly non-Koranic behaviour of fathering illegitimate children. Malcolm X had afterwards founded his own Organization of Afro-American Unity (OAAU). A running war between the two outfits ensued. Louis Farrakhan of the Nation of Islam was reported as saying only weeks before the killing that Malcolm X was "worthy of death". Malcolm X's daughter Qubilah certainly considered Farrakhan the architect of her father's death; she contracted a (failed) hit on Farrakhan in 1994.

The assassination of Malcolm X, however, presented some discrepancies which suggested that it was not an "inside job" by black radicals:

- Hayer might have been guilty, but there was plenty of evidence to suggest that "3X" Butler and "15X" Johnson were not even in the Audubon Ballroom on the fateful day.
- Malcolm X's meetings were usually overflowing with police, yet almost none were present on 21 February 1965.
- One of the few NYPD cops who was on duty that day (Gene Roberts) turned out to be working undercover – as Malcolm X's bodyguard.
- Four days after Malcolm X's assassination, one of the principal officers at OAAU, Leon "4X" Ameer, announced that he had important information on the case but feared his life was in danger. Just under three weeks later he was dead, apparently from an overdose of sleeping pills.
- Talmadge Hayer stated that, although he pulled the trigger, he was not a member of the Nation of Islam. Moreover, the man who hired him was "not a Muslim".

The scuttlebutt, which grew louder and louder, was that Malcolm X's assassination had been ordered by FBI director J. Edgar Hoover. Malcolm X had attributes which failed to endear him to the FBI director: just for a start, he wanted the overthrow of the racially tainted American capitalist system "by any means necessary". He kept bad company, too; he met with the likes of Fidel Castro and Che Guevara.

Hoover did not balk at assassinating those he deemed Public Enemies, as the gundown of John Dillinger outside the Biograph Theater in Chicago at the outset of Hoover's career attested. Malcolm X would certainly have qualified in Hoover's head as a Public Enemy, although calling for revolution was not actually a crime in the "land of the free". Some strong circumstantial evidence of FBI involvement in Malcolm X's assassination came with the uncovering of an FBI Counter-Intelligence Program (COINTELPRO) memo which takes credit for the shooting. The same memo also states that Gene Roberts worked for the Bureau as well as the NYPD.

COINTELPRO was Hoover's personal covert agency, its stock-in-trade being the infiltration of radical groups with the intention of fomenting discord, or setting up members of radical groups for assassination. In 1968 Black Panther Fred Hampton was shot dead as he slept by Chicago police (who fired a generous 89 bullets around his apartment) after an FBI tipoff.

Could FBI *agents provocateurs* have manoeuvred the Nation of Islam into killing Malcolm X? Yes.

The FBI set up Malcolm X for assassination by black radicals: ALERT LEVEL 7

Further Reading
Michael Friedly, *Malcolm X: The Assassination*, 1992